Social Policy and Social Programs
A Method for the Practical Public Policy Analyst

SECOND EDITION

Donald E. Chambers
University of Kansas

ALLYN AND BACON
Boston London Toronto Sydney Tokyo Singapore

Editor: Linda James Scharp MSW
Production Editor: Stephen C. Robb
Art Coordinator: Peter A. Robison
Artist: Jane Lopez
Text Designer: Jill E. Bonar
Cover Designer: Robert Vega
Production Buyer: Pamela D. Bennett
Electronic Text Management: Ben Ko, Marilyn Wilson Phelps

This book was set in Classical Garamond and Swiss 721 by Macmillan Publishing
Company and was printed and bound by Arcata Graphics/Martinsburg. The cover was
printed by New England Book Components.

ISBN 0-02-320582-2

Printed in the United States of America

10 9 8 7 6 5   01 00 99 98

Preface

THE GENERAL DESIGN OF THE BOOK

This book is about public social welfare policy, social welfare program designs, and the instruments through which they are expressed: governmental organizations, public departments, and welfare bureaus. The book is intended for use in courses that prepare students for practice in social work or in one of the many other human service fields. It is written with the young student-practitioner in mind, assuming little or no experience with social programs and nothing more than an ordinary citizen's exposure to social problems. No doubt there will be many readers who do not fit this description, readers with years of rich experience as paraprofessional human service workers. Instructors know that such students bring additional depth and flavor to the material; the text is written with a view toward facilitating that kind of enrichment.

Of course, writing a social policy text is a special challenge precisely because of the wide variability in the age, experience, and preparation of the potential student group. Although social policy texts have multiplied in the last decade, no single text has been totally successful. It is quite clear why success has been so long in coming: the task is simply too demanding. The text must be written with the simplicity and clarity appropriate for beginning-level practitioners, yet still deal with the extraordinary complexity of the world of public social policy and social programs. In a text for frontline practitioners, it is not appropriate to linger over the fine details of social policy abstractions or the finer, more technical points at the heart of current academic debate. In addition, there is the distressing fact that the basic concepts in this field (by whatever name it is called— public policy, social welfare policy, social administration, policy analysis or public administration) are fundamentally vague and incomplete. Given all this, it would not be unreasonable to conclude that a textbook on this topic might be premature. That will be left to the tender mercies of those who can judge it best:

the readers and instructors who use this book. The solution I have chosen is to present a general orientation to the topic and its major elements, to focus on its most basic structure, and to bring into sharp focus only the most central issues: social problems, programs, and policies. My criterion was to focus on social problems, social policies, and programs that are the main concern of organizations in whose employ the students who use this textbook are likely to find themselves. The following social problems and program areas are representative in that way: child welfare, health, poverty, and mental illness. There are other good candidates for inclusion—corrections, special education, aging, and physical disablement, for example—that are referred to in the exercises and special projects suggested at the end of chapters. Instructors will find source material listed and annotated at the end of chapters.

The general approach of this text is designed for social work and human service practitioners (including their immediate supervisors) functioning as "street-level bureaucrats"—staff members of an organization whose task it is to enact social policy in direct encounters with citizens.[1] Such a practitioner selects and packages services and benefits, certifies eligibility, makes referrals, and is understanding and supportive, among other things. It pays to keep in mind that direct-service practitioners also take benefits and services away and deliver negative sanctions and other sometimes punitive measures that society deems appropriate under given circumstances. Of course, social practitioners do not deal in abstractions but with living, breathing people. For the conscientious and service-oriented practitioner, the consequence of a mistaken social policy or program design is not just an overstressed budget to be set right with an adroit accounting maneuver or a condition that can be dismissed with some statement like, "Well, we'll have to get that right in next year's legislature." The consequence is a hungry mother or child; a wronged, irate, and morally indignant citizen; a neighborhood terrorized by a violent psychotic; or a hospitalized child bruised, battered, and broken by an out-of-control parent. What street-level social practitioners need most to know about social policy and program design are those things that will increase their ability to extract resources and capacities from social programs that are necessary to alleviate or prevent any or all of the catalog of modern social horrors listed above. There are three general aspects here, and the major share of this book will be devoted to them.

First, orchestrating the resources and assets of a community so that they effectively serve needs requires a practitioner's clear-eyed grasp of the way a particular social problem is viewed by the program staff who control the money, goods, or services that clients need. The sophisticated street-level practitioner knows that it is not necessary to agree with that viewpoint, but whether a client gets benefits they need may well depend on the practitioner's ability to present client needs in ways that are compatible with the viewpoints of program staff or administrators. For example, the practitioner must understand what the staff member or administrator takes to be the concrete indicators of a problem—its causes and its consequences—that it is *really* important to relieve. The practitioner who understands and can use the method of analyzing social problems presented in Chapter 1 will be prepared to do that.

Second, working practitioners need to know some of the more important structural elements of particular social program designs: social program goals and objectives, service-delivery administrative-system characteristics, entitlement rules, and so on. For example, an understanding of eligibility rules permits an advance estimate of the extent to which staff members are allowed to use their own discretion in awarding benefits or services of various kinds. Alternatively, understanding eligibility rules can yield important predictions as to what administrative level must be contacted before discretion is possible. The chapter on entitlement rules and other chapters on various other structural features of social programs are intended to prepare practitioners with a method of analyzing social program features so that they can anticipate such things.

Third, practitioners need to understand the legal constraints on both policy makers who control program resources and upon clients' use of them. Increasingly, an activist judiciary at all levels from the U.S. Supreme Court to state district courts make and break social policies and both create and withdraw important social services and benefits. Chapter 3 on the judiciary is intended to prepare students to be alert to and understand the practice constraints and freedoms created by the judiciary.

This approach helps the student-practitioner develop an understanding of how others view social problems and how their views affect the administration of social policies and social programs. This book does not take a detailed look at the legislative and political factors (policy as "process") that account for the formation of policy and social programs—no doubt a very important aspect, of course, and worthy of a textbook all its own. This choice results from my view of the typical social practitioner to whom this book is addressed as not primarily responsible for nor active in the legislative and political process. While that might not conform to professional ideals, a good case can be made that it is an accurate description of the facts of the matter. My conclusion is that nothing is served by adding complexities to a book already over-burdened with the same.

Instructors who take exception to that choice, or who view it in a different way, will want to add material. This approach applauds the effort and involvement of practitioners in the political process and supports the notion that such efforts are an important professional obligation. Although neither this textbook nor the course for which it is intended adequately addresses those functions, students will be better informed on the subject for having read it and will be better able thereby to participate in such efforts when the occasion arises.

The main features of the approach taken by this book are matters of direct, practical importance to frontline practitioners. However, even though the chapter on social policy history serves practicality indirectly, this book will give it unbegrudged attention, welcoming it for its irreplaceable contribution to understanding. The historical development of social welfare programs and policies is part and parcel of a professional rather than a purely technical approach to this subject matter. That is the reason for Chapter 2, "Historical Context," which addresses the broad-scale historical changes that occurred coincidentally with and following the Great Depression of the 1930s, and the civil rights struggle and the War on Poverty in the Johnson Administration in the 1960s. The proximate roots of so much of today's social policy innovation are to be found in those decades. Note, however, that the full attention historical background merits cannot be given in a single volume or in a single course.

Finally, my particular objective in writing this book is to put together a method of analysis that ensures that students are taught how to come to judgment about whether a social policy or program could be good or bad for their clients—and to provide them with particular and explicit criteria by which to generate those judgments. Of course, this method in this book can only generate conclusions about *potential* merit since it is not a book about that very specialized kind of research ordinarily called "program evaluation," which generates data for judgments about actual program outcomes. But there is plenty of ground to cover here. Most of my twenty years of experience in conducting research to evaluate local social program and policy outcomes for personal social service programs has produced findings of "little effect" or "no effect"— the most common program evaluation findings in fact, no matter who conducts the evaluation.

As I changed my way of conducting program evaluations from close examination of outcomes to close examination of program designs and their implementation, it became clear that programs were alternatively vague, unspecified, unclear, and administered in quite different ways by different departments, regions, and practitioners (not to mention implemented toward highly variable objectives). Little wonder that only small or no-effect findings were the rule! Clearly, most social program evaluation is wasted effort simply because what is implemented does not ordinarily have enough overall coherence and cohesiveness to generate noticeable overall outcomes. That does not create pessimism about the utility of personal social services because I have directly observed so much really good work being done out there by personal social service workers helping people. In fact, it is my experience that many really good program and policy designs have been discarded not because they are inherently invalid or useless but because they have not (a) been made clear with respect to outcomes expected or (b) have not been implemented with sufficient care and thoroughness so that they had a fair chance to demonstrate their possibilities. Of course, it does not take much "bad" work to obscure the good. My net conclusion is that the social work and human services professions must become much more clear, directed, and even single-minded, about what they do and why. This book is intended to help practitioners do just that by presenting a method of policy analysis that requires a close description of policy and program intentions and features.

But, a method of policy and program analysis that only describes and cannot draw conclusions about whether the policy or program is *potentially* good for clients and consumers can be practical or useful in nearly any sense. Many program designs and features can be judged *in advance* to have such serious design faults and side effects that they cannot possibly achieve their goals. In order to draw that kind of conclusion, a method of policy and program analysis must include criteria that will generate the relevant information. Here I have called those standards *criteria for evaluation,* and there are evaluative criteria included in each chapter for each program or policy operating feature. Many, if not most, books on social policy lack them entirely or rely on the traditional concepts of adequacy, equity, and efficiency taken from the field of economics. These refer to quite abstract concepts of justice and cost benefit/cost-effectiveness to give them substance. The term "adequacy" does not immediately imply "adequacy-for-what-purpose" for example; rather, it must be given some kind of concrete definition. This book will take some pains to illustrate how the social problem analysis underlying the social policy/program conception provides a much more concrete context for defining those abstractions and applying them to the pressing realities that programs, policies, and practitioners deal with in everyday life.

THE ORGANIZATION OF THE BOOK

This book is intended for frontline practitioners and has two major aspects: social problem analysis and social policy and program analysis. The book opens with a presentation of the central importance of social policy in the professional practice of social work and other human services. Because social policies both create and constrain the possibilities in any social practice, students must grasp the fact that understanding social policies is not a matter of choice. The major task of Part I of this book is to show students how social problems can be analyzed using four interrelated but different aspects: problem definition, ideology, causal explanation, and identification of gainers and losers. The second chapter in Part I shows the reader the importance of historical context in the analysis of social problems (and social policies and programs as well) and demonstrates some methods for gathering the historical context into an analysis.

This style of policy analysis asks the reader to back off from a purely practical perspective at one point in the analysis and to view social policies and programs from a historical perspective. This perspective describes how social policies and programs have changed over time; how competing political processes, agendas, and compromise form operating programs and policy; and how different the actual operating characteristics can be from the legislative, political, or even judicial intention. The objective here is to sensitize students to the importance of history in policy and program development and analysis. Analysis at this level is at some remove from the fundamental concerns of the practitioner, but it is essential in enabling intelligent participation in the public forum and the legislative process.

The third chapter in Part I demonstrates how judicial decisions create social policies and provide many constraints and freedoms for social programs and social practitioners. It also teaches students a short method of analyzing judicial decisions for their practice and local policy implications. This last chapter is also intended to sensitize readers to the legal rights of clients to public social services and benefits, a topic that is further elaborated in chapter 8 on administrative and service delivery systems.

Part II introduces the reader to a straightforward method of analyzing a social policy or social program. The intention is to help the student quickly grasp the minimum fundamental elements (or operating characteristics) involved in a program or policy. More complex or sophisticated policy and program issues can follow in later courses.[2] The following elements (later called operating characteristics) are used in this policy and program analytic scheme:

1. Policy and program *goals and objectives*.
2. *Forms of public benefits*.
3. Eligibility or *entitlement rules* for receiving benefits or services.
4. *Administrative or organizational structure or service-delivery system* (including program design(s)) through which benefits or services are delivered to consumers.
5. The method of *financing* the program benefits or services delivered.
6. Identifying important *interactions* within and between the preceding elements.

Chapters 4 through 10 present a set of basic concepts useful for analyzing each of those program operating characteristics. Sometimes classification schemes are developed to help the reader to cope with the occasionally confusing variations within some of the operating characteristics; for example, classifications are developed for types of entitlement rules and for types of benefits. In each chapter, evaluative criteria are presented for the operating characteristics discussed. With one exception, each operating characteristic has a unique set of criteria by which its merit should be evaluated; for example, clarity and measurability are of particular importance to evaluating goals and objectives, whereas consumer sovereignty and potential for stigma are of significance to entitlement rules and accountability, and response time and integration are of particular importance to service-delivery systems. These criteria are presented so that the reader can draw conclusions about the merit of particular operating characteristics of specific social programs and policies.

Having shown the student a general method for analysis and having provided a set of standards by which policies and program operating characteristics can be judged, the book demonstrates in Part III the use of the method of analysis in regard to the social problem of chronic mental illness. The chapter opens with an analysis of the social problem viewpoints to which the social policy and programs embodied in the various Community Mental Health acts are committed. Some leading alternative viewpoints are reviewed and a concise description of the historical issues, former program and policy efforts, competing political agendas, and various judicial decisions that have shaped present policy and program design follow. Next an analysis of a particular program or policy effort using the analytic method of this book is presented. Each chapter concludes with a discussion of how the criteria for evaluating the merit of the effort are to be applied to each operating characteristic.

ACKNOWLEDGMENTS

Because I neither was taught by nor even conversed with the three people who have had the greatest influence on forming my ideas of what should be in this book, this is probably the only occasion there will ever be for acknowledging their influence and delivering my thanks for their contribution. They have been my teachers, and I am hopeful that this volume will advance their work in some way. The intellectual ground from which this book is taken uses concepts that Richard Titmuss first set to paper during his years at the London School of Economics and uses an analytic approach that Evelyn Burns, an LSE product herself, used in her 1948 classic, *The American Social Security System.* If this book succeeds in its aim, it is simply because it applies some of their ideas to the contemporary American social policy context, a very different world from that of Titmuss in the 1950s and 1960s and from that of Burns in the late 1940s. Finally, this book is indebted to Martin Rein whose marvelously clear essays on value-critical policy analysis enabled me to think in a quite different way about how to teach students to make clear, practical, and unashamed value-based judgements about whether social policies and social programs are good for the clients they are intended to serve. I can only regret I did not come across them earlier. I have hopes that their inclusion here might promote the wider diffusion in the profession that they deserve. And, of course, I have been solely responsible for their application here, so any responsibility for departure from Rein's original intentions remains mine.

Whatever other ideas there are that framed this book are likely to have come from that extraordinary group of teachers with whom I have been blessed and who have been (under)paid to teach me at various times over the course of almost forty years and two careers. For the most part they have been gifts to me out of the abundance of the universe: they are not those whom I have sought as a response to their reputation nor who have sought me out. They are an oddly assorted lot with almost nothing in common except that they are the objects of my most sincere gratitude.

There is Professor Claude Henry, Ph.D., who taught me the wonder of ideas in the great literary classics; Professor Maude Merrill; Professor Garnet Larsen, Ph.D., who introduced, with great patience and forbearance, the subject of social policy to a very young, impertinent graduate student; Elizabeth Ossorio, Ph.D., who taught me about perseverance and wisdom in the research process; and William E. Gordon, Ph.D., a biologist teaching research methods to social workers, and Richard Rudner, Ph.D., a philosopher, both of whom taught me what science was about after years of courses in chemistry, physics, and biological science had failed to do that.

More immediately, I would also like to acknowledge the help of those who read the manuscript in one or another of its four drafts. Their fair and generous criticism is sincerely appreciated: Bradford Sheafor, Ph.D., Colorado State University; Anne Weick, Ph.D., University of Kansas; Arthur J. Katz, Ph.D.,

Council on Social Work Education; Forrest Swall, M.S.W., University of
Kansas; Winifred Bell, D.S.W., Cleveland State University; Mary Ellen Elwell,
Western Maryland College; John M. Herrick, Ph.D., Michigan State University;
Milton S. Rosner, Ph.D., The Ohio State University; Mitchell A. Greene, Ph.D.,
University of Northern Iowa; Kenneth R. Wedel, Ph.D., University of
Oklahoma; Arthur J. Cox, D.S.W., East Tennessee State University; Joseph
Kuttler, Tabor College; Gary L. Shaffer, Ph.D., University of Illinois at Urbana-
Champaign; Jane F.R.C. Bonk, M.S.S.A., Juvenile Protective Association,
Chicago, Ill.; Charles Rapp, Ph.D., University of Kansas; Richard Wintersteen,
Ph.D., University of Minnesota-Mankato; Rebecca Lopez, California State
University-Long Beach; Murray Gruber, Loyola University-Chicago; Sharon
Eisen, Mott Community College; David Iacono-Harris, University of Texas-El
Paso. I want to extend very special thanks to my (former) doctoral student, now
colleague and coauthor, Mary Katherine Rodwell, Virginia Commonwealth
University, for her careful reading and intellectual contributions to many of the
chapters. In the same way I am indebted to John Pierpont, M.S.W., teaching colleague at the University of Kansas, whose ideas about policy matters and his
experience in using this method of policy analysis shaped the second edition in
quite important ways.

I would also like to thank my editors at Macmillan Publishing Company for
their efforts in the making of this book, particularly Linda James Scharp,
M.S.W., editor; Steve Robb, production editor; and Loretta Faber, copy editor.

Special thanks go to my late wife, Mary Anne, who taught me so much about
life and law and to whom much of Chapter 3 is indebted. Also special thanks to
James Bonk, M.A., without whose helpful assistance while I was in Central
America I could not have managed. And, finally, I would like to thank Marylee
Brochmann, M.S.W., University of Kansas, for her patient reading, support, and
judicious suggestions (and helpful argument) during the second edition revi-
sions.

D. E. C.

NOTES

1. Michael Lipsky, Street Level Bureaucracy: The Dilemma of the Individual in Public Services (New York: Russell Sage Foundation, 1980), pp. 4–10.
2. Notice that no great attention is paid here to the distinction between *policy* and *program*. Although that distinction can deserve much attention in some contexts, it is not taken to be crucial here in this book for street-level, frontline practitioners—other than to note that policies are taken to be general rules or guides for action, whereas programs are taken to be the general human and organizational apparatus, or the instruments, through which policies are implemented.

Contents

CHAPTER 7
Analysis of Types of Entitlement Rules (Who Gets What, How Much, and Under What Conditions)   151

PART ONE

Creating the Context for Social Policy Analysis: The Social Problem and Historical Context

A man said to the universe:
"Sir, I exist!"
"However," replied the universe,
"That fact has not created in me
a sense of obligation."

Stephen Crane, *War is Kind*

INTRODUCTION: THE PROBLEM OF POLICY FOR PRACTITIONERS

The objective of this book is to help readers develop skill in the critical analysis of modern social welfare policies and programs. That objective is directed toward preserving the sanity and dedication of social practitioners who, on behalf of clients, must daily interpret, enforce, advocate, circumvent, or challenge those policies and programs. Much of the working life of professional practitioners is spent in the context of those policies and programs. If practitioners are not employed on the staff of an agency administering such programs, they serve clients whose lives are affected vitally and daily by those programs: the client whose child is detained in a local juvenile detention center, the client whose Social Security disability benefit is suspended because a judgment of work capacity has been changed, or the client whose daughter must drop out of college to help support her family because the state legislature no longer will include children over sixteen in its Aid to Families with Dependent Children (AFDC) budget. Without being concerned about such policies or being prepared to analyze the nature of their strengths and shortcomings, no social worker can aspire to a professional calling.

Social work is unique for its simultaneous focus on the client *and* the social environment. Like family, community, psychological, and work factors, social policies and programs are a critical feature of the clients' surroundings, and demand every bit as much care and attention from the working professional. For

1

better or worse, the lives of all private citizens are subject to serious and widespread invasions by governmental social policy. For clients it poses a special stress, because it affects lives already burdened with fearsome and demoralizing social problems: hunger, illness, physical or mental disablement, violence, or disease.

Stephen Crane's lines at the head of this chapter are a moving rendition of the idea that immense forces are at work in the world, forces that have no concern for their effect on the fates of particular individuals. Crane means to call our attention to the idea that an earthquake or a volcano does not consider the suffering it causes to individuals in the cataclysmic changes it wreaks—changes begun long before those individuals were born, changes whose effects will outlive human memory.

Crane's point can be extended to modern social welfare policies and programs. Public policies generally are not designed with the needs of *individuals* in mind; social welfare policies and programs certainly are not exceptions, for they are designed for *groups of people* who share a common social problem. It is of utmost importance for social work practitioners to understand that precisely because of this feature, *social policies and programs will fail some individuals on some occasions*. This fact of life is a pervasive problem and a prominent part of the work of most program administrators. It also identifies an important area of social work practice for those who work with individual clients: finding ways to meet clients' urgent and unique needs that cannot, at first glance, be met through existing programs. Examples are not difficult to find:

> John Samuelson is a construction worker. Every year for the past five years he has received notice from the county attorney's office that Mildred Singer has filed suit against him for nonsupport of a child she claims is theirs. Each time suit is filed, John loses about five working days' pay because of the time it takes to talk to his Legal Aid attorney, give depositions, and appear in court. Each year he and his wife spend hours patching up the hard feelings recalled by his former relationship with Mildred. Each year thus far, the local judge has dismissed the case for lack of evidence because John has denied paternity on the basis that the baby was born ten and one-half months after he left Mildred. Mildred has admitted that she lived with other men during the time her child could have been conceived but nevertheless has identified John as the father. John once received a letter from Mildred admitting that, contrary to her allegation, she believed another man to be the baby's father, but John's wife destroyed the letter in a fit of jealousy. John agreed to take a blood test that, with 97 percent accuracy, tells whether a specific man can be *excluded* as a child's father.[1] The test declared that John could very well be the father. The prevailing judicial policy is to consider the test accurate, despite a 3 percent margin of error. John now must pay $200 per month in child support until the child is eighteen. In fact, Mildred, (now the mother of three) does not wish to press nonsupport charges against John (now the father of four), but federal policy requires applicants for AFDC (like Mildred) to press nonsupport charges as a condition for continuing to receive financial assistance.

Note that in this case it would be a peculiar moral position to argue that it is somehow wrong to enforce a public policy that makes fathers financially responsible for their children, pursues fathers across state lines to do so, and makes an accurate paternity test available on a voluntary basis. The reason, in this instance, that these public policies come to grief is that they did not anticipate the incredible complexity that characterizes the lives of individual ordinary citizens. Legal procedures assume—reasonably in most instances—that people will present *all* evidence where clearly it is in their self-interest to do so. A test that is 97 percent accurate makes very few mistakes indeed; the fact that it made a mistake in this instance must be viewed in the context of ninety-seven other cases. Most people would be willing to let stand the injustice done to John. Here is another example:

> Nancy Willard's arms were burned off below the elbow when she caught them in the corner of a plastic injection mold. (Hot plastic disintegrates flesh and bone instantly.) Nancy was a dependable and efficient worker who earned $9 per hour. The law in her state requires all employers of more than six people to carry Workers Compensation insurance to provide for just such accidents. Nancy is twenty-eight years old and the mother of two children. The plant she works in spends a lot of money to keep it accident free and has a 99 percent success rate—only two other serious accidents in its ten-year history. State law specifies that Nancy must agree to a lump-sum settlement of $25,000 in compensation for the loss of both arms below the elbow. Nancy's average annual earnings were $18,600 over the past four years—$15,000 net after taxes. She also had $1,000 worth of fringe benefits per year (medical and life insurance, uniforms, and bonuses).

There is nothing intrinsically wrong with the idea of worker-injury compensation or with public policy that requires lump-sum settlements. The problems here are with equity and adequacy that flow from the individual attributes of Nancy Willard. Were she working at minimum wage ($8,840 per year), or were she sixty-four with one year to go before retirement, a $25,000 settlement would be handsome compensation for loss of one year's work. At the age of twenty-eight, however, she has lost thirty-seven years of wages earned at full working capacity because with prostheses to replace her arms she probably will work at only minimum wage. Furthermore, she will lose all her earnings for a one-year period—the time it will take for surgery, prosthetic fitting, and training. This period alone will cost her $15,000, or one year of net income. (Her employer's insurance company is required to pay her medical bills.) The $25,000 lump-sum settlement will replace only a small fraction of her long-term economic loss, *and that settlement assumes that rehabilitation will be successful and that she can return to work.*

It is clear from these examples that, despite a practitioner's best efforts and the best policy and program design and administration, some clients' needs will go unmet. That knowledge will be the cause of much hard feeling, bad public relations, and personal distress on the part of the social worker. If a client goes hungry for a week, loses a child, or loses a job that required months of effort to obtain, simply because public policy could not deal with the unique circumstances of his or her life, it cannot be easily forgotten or suffered willingly—nor should it be.

Neither are clients' lives measurably improved by drawing sweeping conclusions that such instances are the result of inadequacy or corruptness of the welfare system or its personnel. Although some features of some welfare systems can be shown (on certain moral assumptions) to be corrupt—and surely there is evidence that some personnel are corrupt—it is neither useful nor accurate to generalize along those lines. What is intended to be shown by the preceding illustrations is that there are natural limits to the effectiveness of social policies and programs. The more unique a citizen's situation is, the less likely it is that policies and programs will meet his or her need.

Therefore, the question might arise, "If so much deprivation continues because social welfare programs and policies cannot take individual circumstances into account, then might it be better if all programs intended for groups of people were replaced with programs intended for, and consciously designed to meet, *individual* needs?" This solution might entail a social welfare system where persons in need applied for any kind of assistance to one—and only one—social worker who had access to the resources of *all* available programs. If the client needed financial assistance, the social worker would decide not only whether but how much to give. If the client needed medical care, the social worker would tell the client where to get it and would pay the bill. In fact, this vision might be sufficiently detailed to suggest that all monies from all current programs be put into one big pot and allocated to each social worker in proportion to the number of clients he or she served. The key constraint on largesse would be that the social worker must ensure that the pot last long enough. The vision might even anticipate that because each package of services and benefits would be individually tailored, no general standards of need would be necessary. Further, no paperwork would be necessary because the social worker would be accountable only to the client (and to the fiscal officer, to ensure that all monies went to clients). The issue here is that this is a legitimate, even plausible, style for the delivery of social benefits. In fact, a widely used strategy called purchase-of-service contracting (POSC) bears some resemblance to the system envisioned.

Although it is intrinsically appealing, this extremely custom-tailored approach to social policy is not without its own problems. For example, every social worker will likely have different standards for determining how much money, medical care, housing, and so on, is needed. That would result in noticeable differences in benefits among people similarly situated. That would be a natural enough effect, for treating people individually was the basic idea behind this way of doing things. Consequently, we have a dilemma here: Even if we construct our social welfare system so that it is equitable for all citizens, its programs won't be adequate in the sense that they take unique circumstances into account; the system inevitably will fail to meet the needs of some individuals. If we construct our social welfare system to be adequate, that is, to have maximum capacity to meet individual needs, the system and its programs will be unjust to some people because in straining to meet individual needs, it will create inequitable benefits among clients. Equity and adequacy, as will be discussed at greater length later, are two major criteria by which modern social welfare programs are evaluated. A third criterion is efficiency.

No doubt there are ways in which these inherent conflicts among equity, adequacy, and efficiency could be overcome and still keep social programs sufficiently flexible to take unique client need into account. I would encourage the reader to think along those lines because that is the way better policy solutions are developed.

However, the search for better solutions also reveals the limits of social welfare program design and demonstrates an important principle about social policies and programs: every policy or program that solves the social needs of one client or client group will create additional problems for another needy client or client group. Social policy and program solutions are inherently imperfect to some degree and are constantly in need of revision. Far from being the occasion for disillusionment, it is this very fact that creates the opportunity for service by dedicated professional practitioners to people in need. Social policies and programs left to their own devices are unguided missiles, guaranteed to harm the unwitting and unwary. That danger can be tempered only by frontline practitioners devoted to seeking humane and rational interpretations of social policies directed toward human needs. It is the practitioner's responsibility to know the policy system well enough to do that, and it is to that end that the following chapters are directed.

NOTE

1. Harry D. Krause, *Child Support in America: The Legal Perspective* (Charlottesville, Va.: The Mitchie Co., 1981), pp. 213–22.

CHAPTER 1

Analyzing the Social Problem Background of Social Policies and Social Programs

THE NATURE OF SOCIAL PROBLEMS

Earlier the point was made that social welfare programs are solutions to social problems. Social problems that spawn social welfare programs are inevitably those that affect a large number of people. In fact, for a problem to be a social problem at all, it must affect more than one person. If it does not, it is not a social, but a personal, problem. Notice also that social problems are not all equally important. Some argue that the "importance" of a social problem depends on two things: (1) the power and social status of those who are defining the problem and urging the expenditure of resources toward a solution and (2) the sheer number of people affected. Thus, the more people affected and the greater the social power and status of those urging a solution, the more important the social problem.

Examples of "big" and "little" social problems abound. Social problems often arise as a consequence of rare diseases with strong social effects—retinitis pigmentosa, for example. A relatively rare congenital defect that prevents those afflicted from seeing in the dark, retinitis pigmentosa is a medical problem surely, but it is also a social problem because it creates serious social consequences: For all practical purposes the sufferer is blind during more than half the hours in a day. The disease is a small problem to most people because very few of us even know anyone with such a medical problem—the number affected is comparatively small. To those so afflicted, however, it is a very big problem indeed, and they can cite persons of great social stature who have the defect. To date no one with widespread credibility (power and status) has presented the problem to the public as a matter of concern, so that to the world at large it will remain a minor problem until it either affects more people or is redefined as socially important by a public opinion maker.

Less exotic examples of major social problems include unemployment, because it affects so many people; health, because potentially it affects everyone; mental retardation, because after Rose Kennedy (mother of a U.S. president) became a public advocate of the issue, federal appropriations for the needs of the mentally retarded increased.

7

Whereas not all problems are social problems, of course, many do have important social consequences: When someone loses a job, it is a *personal* problem only for that individual and his or her immediate family; when a machine operator loses a job because of modern standards of worker safety or product quality, it is a *technological* problem; when there is a declining market for the things the machine produced, it is a *business* problem; when consumers no longer have money to buy what the machine produces, it is an *economic* problem. When, as a result of any or all of the foregoing problems, many people lose jobs and are unemployed, or when people of power, wealth, and social status become concerned about the effects of these problems, such concern becomes a *social* problem. Usually, an existing policy or program solution to the problem will remain in place at least until the personal, technological, business, or economic problem that created the social problem is solved. The social program may continue past that time; for example, social programs such as unemployment compensation were created to meet human social problems that are created by first-order economic, business, or technological problems. It may be the case that all of what we commonly call social problems are always the aftereffects of first-order economic, business, technological, and/or environmental problems.

In summary, social problems are those concerns about the quality of life for large groups of people where the concern is held as a consensus populationwide, and/or the concern is voiced by the socially powerful or the economically privileged. In general, it is these types of problems that spawn social policies and programs as corrective measures. Although this account of social problems is certainly not the only one, it is arguably the one most relevant to those who must understand social problems as a prerequisite of understanding social programs operated by the social welfare institution.

The purpose of this book is to help readers understand social programs and policies, and that understanding cannot be complete without ability to analyze the social problem for which the program or policy is intended to correct. In turning to the issue of how social problems should be analyzed, this next section demonstrates how attention to four specific aspects of social problem viewpoints or statements will yield a basic understanding.

SOCIAL PROBLEM ANALYSIS

Understanding a social problem is not quite the same thing as understanding the truth of "how things really are." It is not quite the same thing as understanding how highways are built or trees grow. *To understand a social problem is to understand how and what another person (or group) thinks and believes about the social events being defined as a problem.* When you do that, you are doing an *analysis* of a social problem. A central aspect of social problems is that, although the events that identify or define them may be the same no matter who views them, the way in which those events are interpreted is likely to vary considerably. That a family of four has, say, $6,000 annual (gross) income is, on the face of it, an unambiguous fact but one bound to be interpreted differently by different observers. Whether the fact is a social problem depends on the value bias and ideology used to render that judgment. For example, a person might believe (with some modern U.S. nutritionists and home economics specialists agreeing) that consuming six ounces of red meat per day is vital to maintaining health, or that no more than two persons should share a bedroom. In that case, then, $12,000 per year is unlikely to provide for those minimum standards for four people, and the straightforward conclusion is that a $12,000 annual income is an indicator of the presence of a social problem called poverty. However, notice that these standards clearly are value biased; they are founded on cultural preferences because most people outside North America survive on less.[1]

Note also how the reason for the existence of the social problem can vary with the viewer. Based on one kind of idea about how the economy and labor markets work, one person might say that this low income was the result of the skill this worker offered to an employer, the employer's need for it (how good business was), how good a worker the person was (productivity), and how many other people offered the same skill and effort (competition). Another person might say that the low income that creates this social problem is caused by the tradition among employers to pay workers according to the social status and prestige of the work they do and the families from which they come. The point in the initial stage of social problem analysis is not to decide whether the viewpoint presented is right, but to sort out what is being offered by way of explanation.

It should be clear from the preceding examples that the way social problems are understood is highly variable and depends on the viewer. On that account there is no such thing as the "right" or the "only true" social problem viewpoint. Social problem viewpoints may be factual or not, clear or muddled, complete or incomplete, logical or illogical, or even useful or useless, but they are not right or wrong in some absolute sense. An unemployed person who has seen savings wither to nothing, while debts mount and children go hungry, will view the general problem of unemployment as excruciating, whereas those who believe they are paying high taxes so that the unemployed can loaf will not view it that way. Those who are outraged at a society that permits unemployment will view the problem differently from those for whom unemployment is merely a newspaper item. Unemployed persons stress food for children, whereas taxpayers stress the cost of that food and current events followers stress the difference between this year's and last year's unemployment figures. No one is wrong in any absolute sense here, and the basic issue for the person who wishes to understand social policies and programs is that a particular social problem viewpoint underlies every social policy and program.

The social problem analysis does *not* begin by judging whether something is right or wrong. Before that task can be done accurately, it must await a clear understanding of the social problem viewpoint itself. The last thing to do in a social problem analysis is to make moral judgments about the substance of the argument; the first thing to do is to specify what the viewpoint is and how it differs from others. The reason for bearing down so hard on this idea is twofold:

(1) Social problem analysis is a demanding task and, (2) at the end of the chapter you will do analyses of the social problem viewpoints of other persons. In doing the exercises, another caution for the beginner is *to be sure to hold your own views very much apart while doing each social problem analysis.* Your own views are very important, but you will find that initially it takes some discipline to avoid letting them get in the way of the viewpoints of the writers whose materials you will analyze.

The remainder of this chapter is taken up with a discussion of the four dimensions to consider in doing a social problem analysis:

1. Identify the way the problem is defined.
2. Identify the cause(s) to which the problem is attributed (its antecedents) and its most serious consequences.
3. Identify the ideology—the values, that is—that makes the events of concern come to be defined as a problem.
4. Identify who benefits (gains) and who suffers (loses) from the existence of the problem.[2]

There are other aspects of social problems, of course (history and legal status, for example); and although it is important to understand them, they are, arguably, not as important to a basic understanding of a current social problem as are these four dimensions, discussed in the following sections.

Problem Definition

It is essential to begin a social problem analysis by determining its distinguishing marks or identifiers, that is, to state the *concrete observable signs by which the existence of the problem can be known.* A social problem can be identified in a wide variety of ways. For example, one way to identify the problem of drug abuse is by noting the use, intentional exposure to, or ingestion of *any illegal chemical substances* in a nonmedical way (not prescribed by a physician). Thus, the non–medically prescribed use of an illegal substance identifies this social problem. Another way is by defining drug abuse as an addiction; for example, defining drug abuse as occurring when most daily life affairs and social encounters are organized around the problems and pleasures of obtaining and using a chemical substance. Here the indicator of the existence of a social problem is determined not by the use or the legality of the chemical but by its preeminence and the amount of time devoted to it in the user's life. The indicator here is an observer's judgment of the prominence of drug use in daily life.

Obviously it makes an enormous difference whether the former or latter definition of the problem is chosen. For example, the first definition includes the occasional marijuana smoker and the long-haul trucker's use of amphetamines. The latter definition does not include such instances but *does* include all alcoholics and many tobacco smokers. Not only would conclusions about the qualitative nature and the number of people affected differ in each case, but conclusions about what kinds of people comprise the social problem group would differ radically. Clearly, it can be seen how different social programs would be depending on which view of the social problem is adopted. Table 1–1 presents examples of how two social problems may be defined differently. Each definition in the table was chosen precisely because it was used recently as a basis for distributing sizable cash and material benefits to real people. Each definition is said to define poverty or physical disablement, yet each definition refers to different kinds of people, different circumstances, and, certainly, different group sizes.

Even though social programs and policies are usually designed to solve social problems, sometimes (as noted earlier) *the social program creates social problems of its own*. This fact immediately creates interesting complications for the analysis of social problems. For example, in the material that follows, the U.S. minimum wage law (considered here as an example of a social policy and program) is said to *create* unemployment because, it is argued, the law reduces the incomes of those very citizens whose income it is intended to raise.[3]

Table 1–1   Alternative Definitions for Social Problems.

Social Problem Name	Alternative Definitions
Poverty	1. 1982 standard of need for AFDC eligibility. Texas: cash income less than $221 per month. Kansas: cash income less than $468 per month. New York: cash income less than $638 per month.
	2. Adjusted gross annual income of less than $21,000 (1991 National Student Direct Loan (NSDL) eligibility qualification).
	3. Cash income less than $1300 per month for a family of four (1991 food stamp qualification).
Physical Disablement	1. Unable to work at any occupation for which the person is qualified by experience or education (commonly used by health insurance companies for determining disability).
	2. Unable to earn more than $9,720 per year because of physical impairment (1991 definition used by Social Security Division).
	3. Restricted choice among options open to the nondisabled because of impairment (used by Independence, Inc., 1983).

MINIMUM WAGE—MAXIMUM FOLLY*

Federal minimum wage laws represent a tragic irony. In the name of "preventing worker exploitation," "providing a living wage," and "reducing poverty," these measures in fact impede the upward mobility and increase the dependence of the most disadvantaged among us. National leaders, including black leaders, fail to recognize that many economic problems faced by a large segment of the black population are the result of *government-imposed restrictions on voluntary exchange*.

The Strange History of Unemployment for Black Youth

Today's youth joblessness is unprecedented: nearly 40 percent among blacks and 16 percent among whites, nationally. Black youth unemployment in some major cities is estimated to be 70 percent. In dramatic contrast, black youth unemployment in 1948 was 9.4 percent and white youth unemployment was 10.2 percent. In further contrast to today, until 1954 blacks in every age group were *at least* as active in the labor market as whites were.

These facts demand that we challenge the official and popular explanations of current black youth joblessness. Employers have not become more discriminatory. Black youth of earlier times were not better skilled or educated than their white counterparts. Neither can we attribute the problem to slow economic growth. Even during the relative prosperity of the sixties and seventies, black youth unemployment rose—both absolutely and in relation to white youth unemployment. The real explanation lies in the limitations of law itself. By increasing the minimum wage, Congress has caused a significant loss of job opportunities for young blacks. When employers are required to pay a minimum labor *price* of $2.90 an hour, they have no economic incentive to hire workers whose labor *value,* in the production of goods or delivery of services, may be only $2.00 an hour. Congress can legislate a higher wage, but it cannot legislate that workers be more productive. Because Congress has not yet seized complete control of personnel operations in private firms, the minimum wage law thus discriminates against the low-skilled.

Basic Economics and Practical Politics

A law that reduces opportunity for some almost always increases it for others. To see how the minimum wage law accomplishes this, recognize, as economists do, that low-skilled labor and high-skilled labor can often be substituted for each other.

Imagine an employer can build a particular fence by using three low-skilled workers each earning $14 a day ($42 total labor cost per day), or by using one high-skilled worker who earns $38 a day. To minimize labor costs, the employer hires the high-skilled worker.

But suppose the high-skilled worker suddenly demands $55 a day. The fence firm then hires the three low-skilled workers, and the high-skilled worker loses his job.

On the other hand, the high-skilled worker may understand politics and economics. He may now join with others like himself and lobby for a minimum wage law of $20 a day (claiming noble motivations like "prevention of worker exploitation" and "provision of a living wage"??).

---

*From Walter E. Williams, *The SmithKline Forum for a Healthier America,* 1:6 (Sept. 1979), pp. 1–6. Reprinted by permission of the author and VanSant Dugdale Advertising, Baltimore, Md.

Once the $20 minimum wage is law, the high-skilled worker can demand and get his $55 a day—because it now costs $60 to build the fence using low-skilled labor. By law, the high-skilled worker's competition is priced out of the market.

An Incentive to Discriminate

Aside from causing unemployment for some, the minimum wage law encourages racial discrimination. If an employer must pay a minimum of $2.90 an hour no matter whom he hires, he may as well hire someone whose color he likes. Economists would explain this by saying that the minimum wage law prevents the worker from offering a "compensating difference" for less-preferred characteristics.

The same principle applies to groceries. Less-preferred chuck steak can compete with more-preferred filet mignon only by offering a compensating difference—a lower price. If we had a minimum price law for steak of, say $4 a pound, sales of chuck would fall relative to sales of filet. Because it is *perceived* as less valuable, chuck steak would be "unemployed."

The minimum wage law's powerful incentive for racial discrimination is clearly illustrated in South Africa. There, the white unions are the strongest supporters of minimum wage laws and their counterpart, "equal-pay-for-equal-work" *for blacks*! There, unions advocate these laws with the *stated* purpose of protecting white jobs against black competition.

The Burden on the Young

Young people suffer most from any law that discourages employment of low-skilled workers, simply because the young normally have the lowest skills.

If joblessness merely deprived young people of pocket money, we might shrug it off as another minor consequence of foolish government intervention. But early work experience produces more than money. It teaches job-search skills, effective work habits, and respect for supervisors. It produces pride and self-respect. It lets a worker make mistakes when they are not terribly costly—when there are probably no dependents counting on the worker for continuous income. These labor market lessons are critical, particularly for minority youths who attend grossly inferior schools, where these lessons are not learned.

Moreover, an absence of job opportunity may account for much of the crime and other antisocial behavior among many of today's youth.

Government Privileges: Granted to Some, Denied to Others

Many other restrictive laws grant monopoly power to the few at the expense of the many. This not only makes us a poorer nation, but also heightens conflict between classes of Americans.

These laws handicap minorities, even though racial discrimination is not their intent. Occupational licensure and business regulation laws deserve special mention. Taxi licensure laws in most cities are among the most flagrant forms of monopoly and collusion.

In the 1920s, a poor, industrious immigrant in New York City could buy a used car, paint *taxi* on it, and be in business. Today's poor New Yorker must have not only a car, but also $60,000 for a taxi license. In Boston it's $45,000. In Philadelphia, $35,000. In Chicago, $40,000.

There is no social justification for such entry costs. They serve only to protect the incomes of incumbent taxi owners and to deny people the opportunity to enter a business whose skill and capital requirements are low. Washington, D.C., is unusual.

There, fees to own and operate a taxi are under $100. As a result, there are more minority owner-operators (as a percentage of minority population); the ratio of taxis to population is higher (8,400 taxis in Washington, 11,700 in New York, 600 in Philadelphia, 4,600 in Chicago); and taxi fares are lower than they are in most cities.

Note in this example how the focus is on the *effects* of the minimum wage law. The problem is the minimum wage law itself because the law is said to be the *cause* of undesirable effects, in this case *unemployment*. What is central for Williams in the material quoted here is that the minimum wage law "impedes upward mobility and increases the dependency of the most disadvantaged. . . ." Employment is important for Williams because it is the key element in upward mobility and economic independence. Thus, the central social problem defined here is unemployment, the immediate cause of which are certain features of the minimum wage law; the central values that are thought to be threatened here are upward mobility and economic independence. Note that Williams does not tell us exactly what he means by unemployment. It is clear that he is not as concerned about the level of pay as the *number* of *available low-paying* jobs. He believes that this is the major problem among black youth.[4]

Social problem analysis should state clearly the concrete measures and indicators of the social problem of concern. Definitions that are specific, concrete, and measurable are useful in these respects:

1. Everyone then knows precisely to what they refer.
2. It is possible to construct comparable estimates of incidence and prevalence so that quantification, importance, and change over time can be judged.
3. It makes it possible to discuss causation. Unless the problem is clearly defined, it is fruitless to discuss causes: What is it that is being caused? It is also fruitless to speculate about "cures" under these conditions.

Note that a definition is not "good" or "bad" because you either agree or disagree with it. It is common to have serious disagreement about how a given social problem should be defined. For example, many people have disagreed violently with a definition of racism (a serious social problem, surely) that refers to differential access to institutional resources on the basis of color. That definition implies that if dark-skinned people have lower-quality education (for whatever stated reason), it is first-order evidence of white racism. Such definition is one of the central issues around which the whole school-busing-to-achieve-integration argument has revolved. Are blacks and Latinos the victims of white racism because, for example, their school districts have less taxable property yielding less tax revenue, which results in fewer resources for education in that district? Based on the preceding definition of racism, the example unequivocally constitutes racism. Following some other definitions of racism, particularly those that define racism as overt and intentional discrimination based on color, this would not be an example of racism because no "intentional" discrimination can be distinguished.

The point is that both definitions are "good" insofar as definitions go, irrespective of which you think is the better. The criteria for definitions revolve around clarity, not "truth"; therefore, both definitions are satisfactorily clear. On ideological or value grounds I would argue that the first definition is preferable to the second, but that is a different issue than whether it is a clear definition.

Earlier the statement was made that the importance of social problems—in fact their rise to public consciousness—depends not only on the social status of those who speak publicly about them, but on the sheer number of those who are affected as well. Because of the latter factor, you should expect the problem-definition section of careful social problem analysis to give attention to a presentation of the quantitative dimensions—the sheer size—of the problem: estimates of the number of persons (or families), estimates of the percentage or proportion of the total population affected; estimates of the demographics of the problem (for example, the numbers and percentages of the different ages, sexes, and geographic localities affected). In looking again at the Williams presentation of the social problem of minimum wage, you will see how carefully he has quantified the problem for us. He notes that in 1979 youth joblessness was nearly 40 percent for blacks and 16 percent among whites nationally. These figures are even higher now. He adds demographic data showing that unemployment for black youths in particular cities is as high as 70 percent. He could have carried this kind of analysis even further (and did in other places where his work is published), as you might imagine. Quantifications such as these are often very important in judging the adequacy of social programs and policies to solve the social problem. Without such data it is impossible to determine whether, for example, the eligibility rules or other features of the program are directing program benefits and services to the people who have the problem or are directing the most benefit or service to those who are affected the most by it. Furthermore, adequacy of funding for the program cannot be assessed without some idea of how many people are affected. Do not be misled by thinking that quantification is important only in regard to this example concerning minimum wage and youth unemployment; quantification is crucial in the analysis of any social problem. Child abuse, for example, cannot be properly understood without some idea of how widespread it is or the types of people and families in which it appears the most frequently.

Another way in which to deepen the understanding of social problems is to present common variations within the problem category itself. The author of a social problem presentation is very likely to refer to several subtypes of a given social problem and expend some effort at distinguishing among them. For example, in discussions about the social problem of crime, distinction is made among the legal subtypes of crime: premeditated homicide, felony murder, manslaughter, and assault. These are legal categories, but they also may serve the social problem presenter well in giving the opportunity to speak of different causes for different subcategories, to speak of different ideological issues, to speak of different prevalence data for each, and so on. In fact, it is not uncommon for the discussion to direct itself mainly to a single subtype of a particular social problem, particularly where the broader problem is not well understood or is particularly complex. For example, you are most likely to read about sexual abuse apart from a discussion of child abuse in general, and you may read about the social problem of the commercial sexual exploitation of children (pornography or prostitution) apart from the more general topic of the sexual abuse of children (incest or kidnapping). The task of social problem analysis is to track the subclassifications being used, and how they relate to larger social problems and their major focus—that is, how much and in what regard a narrowing of focus has occurred. One reason for this careful tracking is to avoid being misled by later data that are presented about the problem. Sometimes, for example, social problem presentations will focus only on a subtopic but will present data on the *whole* social problem. Sometimes this is intentional; other times presenters themselves are unaware of the error.

Causes and Consequences

Another factor to consider in doing a social problem analysis is what causal explanations are offered as to why a social problem has come to exist. Sometimes the focus is more on predicting *consequences* that will accompany the present social problem. Sorting out this pattern of attributed causes and consequences is at the core of analyzing a social problem viewpoint for causation. A primary goal of the analysis is to discover whether it is the causes (antecedents), the consequences (effects), or both that are of utmost importance to the particular social problem presentation being analyzed. One way to separate antecedents from consequences is to try to diagram, to capture what is being said by setting down on paper what appears to be the causal pattern the author is asserting.

Causal patterns can be described in many ways; one simple method is to describe what will be called causal chains. A *causal chain* consists of a set of events (or variables or factors) arranged in a time sequence that shows the social problem event that is to be explained—what comes before the event and therefore is said to "cause" it and what comes after the event and is said to be a consequence. Causal chains are to be read from left to right so that the "event-to-be-explained" is always some variable to the right of the center of the chain. If only antecedents are of concern, the social problem event-to-be-explained will always appear on the *far* right of the causal chain. Let us now focus only on such causal chains as these, for simplicity. Figure 1–1 presents a simple causal chain "explaining" high unemployment rates (follow the arrows).

It should be clear that this is neither the only, nor even a complete, explanation for unemployment, only one plausible explanation. Remember, the object here is to find the expressed *belief* about the causes of the social problem. This causal chain could also be used to explain poverty and economic deprivation because poverty can be a result of the fact that people are just not working and earning wages. However, another author concerned with poverty and economic deprivation might explain it on the basis of high prices rather than low wages. That causal chain might look something like the one in Figure 1–2.

Some causal chains or "explanations" can be very complicated. We can put both these diagrammed causal chains together and add some other features to

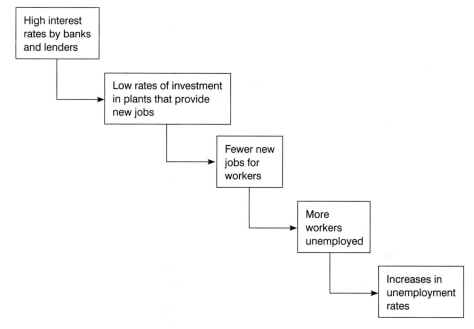

Figure 1–1   A simple causal chain "explaining" high unemployment.
(*Source:* Based on Walter Williams, "Minimum Wage—Maximum Folly," in *The SmithKline Forum for a Healthier America*, 1:6 [Sept. 1979], pp. 1–6.)

generate a broader and more complex explanation of poverty. Thus, Figure 1–3 shows how *both* high prices and low earnings produce poverty; it also shows some of the reasons for high prices and low earnings.

Let us now return to Williams's analysis of the minimum wage law and its relation to unemployment. Could we express Williams's argument in the form of a causal chain? I would suggest the example in Figure 1–4 as appropriate to Williams's line of reasoning.

Note that although Williams has not spoken explicitly of an employer's profit motive, it is crucial to understanding his argument. Discussions of social problems do not always make explicit all the assumptions they make in presenting their explanations for the cause of a social problem. One of the reasons for making a special effort to understand an author's explanation for a social problem is to uncover "hidden" assumptions.

Ideology and Values

Another crucial aspect of a social problem analysis is the identification of major ideological positions and value biases embedded in a description of a social problem. For our purposes here, by a *value* we mean simply a conception of what is preferred. Values express a vision of how things "ought" to be. Note that value statements can be simple or complex, but in the end they need no justification because they are personal or social preferences. For example, if poverty as a social problem is identified by a lack of minimum nutritional standards, a

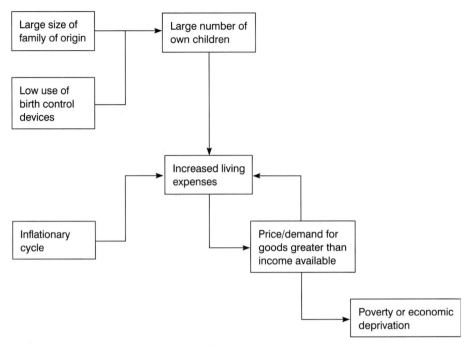

Figure 1–2   A simple causal chain explaining poverty and economic deprivation.
(*Source:* Based on Walter Williams, "Minimum Wage—Maximum Folly," in *The SmithKline Forum for a Healthier America*, 1:6 [Sept. 1979], pp. 1–6.)

value stance is implied that prefers that no one be hungry. However, if poverty as a social problem is identified by some large difference between annual incomes of certain types of citizens, a value stance is implied that prefers that income be more *equally distributed*, without respect to the differing needs of individuals or any concept of how social merit should be rewarded.

Value statements are usually expressed in phrases using the words *should, ought,* or *must.* For example, the statements, "No one should be hungry" or "Employers should not refuse a job because of an applicant's racial background" are value statements using *should* terms. Value statements are usually more numerous and more complex than can be stated in single sentences. On that account, and for our particular purposes, let us use the term *ideology* to refer to sets of value statements.

Sometimes it is difficult to disentangle value and knowledge statements. Ideology is built from value statements, and explanations and causal chains are built from sentences that describe what *is* the case about one thing or another. These latter sentences are "factual" statements, statements asserting what exists or characterizes what is said to exist. Recall that value statements are sentences about what is to be preferred. So, it is one thing to say, "No human being *should* be hungry" (a value statement, a statement of preference), but it is another thing to say, "From 12 to 15 percent of the U.S. population lives in conditions of poverty where they *are* hungry some part of each week" (a statement of fact).

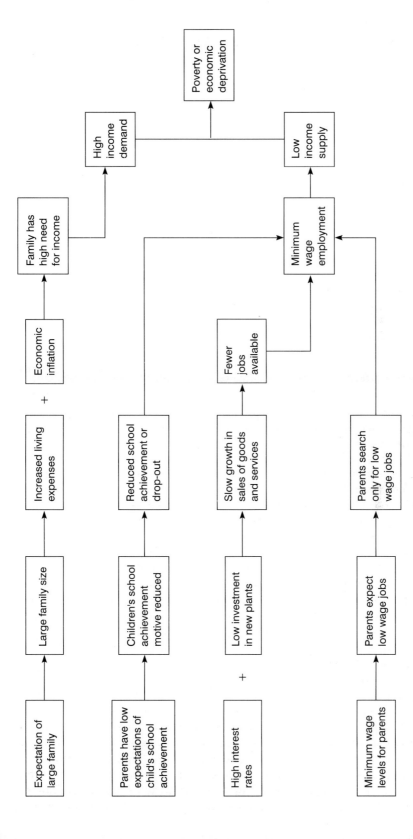

Figure 1–3   A complex causal chain explaining poverty and economic deprivation.
(*Source*: Based on Walter Williams, "Minimum Wage—Maximum Folly," in *The SmithKline Forum for a Healthier America*, 1:6 [Sept. 1979], pp. 1–6.)

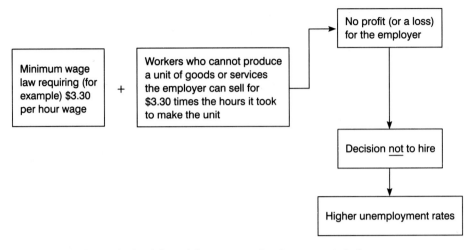

Figure 1–4   An analysis of the minimum wage law in a causal chain.
(*Source:* Based on Walter Williams, "Minimum Wage—Maximum Folly," in *The SmithKline Forum for a Healthier America,* 1:6 [Sept. 1979], pp. 1–6.)

The operating terms are italicized. Again, value and ideological statements feature verbs such as *should, ought,* or *must*; knowledge and factual statements feature verbs such as *are* and *is.* The reason it is sometimes difficult to disentangle value and knowledge statements is that they concern the same event; it is important to distinguish between the two statements because they are intended to deliver two very different messages. The correct reading of the message of the value statement gives the reader of a social problem description advance information about *outcomes* that the author will advocate. The correct reading of the message in the factual statements of the causation analysis will give the reader advance information about the kind of program interventions or policy or legislative changes the author will seek.

Let us now return to the Williams material on minimum wage just to search for examples of the difference between value and knowledge statements. Our conclusion was that Williams's causal argument necessarily entailed a statement about employers' profits. That is a factual statement as it stands—that is, we are saying that Williams implies that employers *do* consider the effect on their profit in making hiring decisions. Note that it would be a value statement if it involved some term such as *should* or *ought*: "Employers *should* consider profit . . ., etc., in their hiring decisions." The point is that his argument does not say that; all it says is that employers *do* consider that issue.

Unfortunately for us, the value statements in the Williams excerpt are not distinguished by the presence of the revealing verbs *should* and *ought.* Therefore, to identify his ideology we must search for statements whose meaning is not substantially altered by transforming them into statements containing *should* and *ought* terms. For example, we *cannot* take such a statement as "Black youth unemployment in some major cities is estimated to be 70 percent," and transform it into the statement, "Black youth unemployment in some major cities should be 70 percent" and contend that we have not changed the meaning radically. However, we can take a sentence from the first paragraph of the excerpt and transform it into a value statement without altering its meaning. Thus: "Federal minimum wage laws represent a tragic irony. . . . [T]hese measures in fact impede the upward mobility and increase the dependence of the most disadvantaged among us." We can restate this sentence as a value statement as follows: "Impeding upward mobility and increasing the dependence of the most disadvantaged among us are effects of the minimum wage law that we should not allow." What we have done is to take a cue from the phrase "tragic irony" and interpret it to be equivalent to saying that there are effects of the minimum wage law that *should* not occur.

Gainers and Losers

The focus of this aspect of social problem analysis is on three things: (1) *who* loses and gains, (2) *what kind* of gains and losses are involved, and (3) *how much* value is entailed. The reason to examine this angle is that it is not always obvious what losses and costs are of concern; different groups value different kinds of losses and costs. We do not trouble to take a stand about a social problem unless we are concerned about a loss of some kind, so in almost any social problem description some attention is paid to the issue of losses and costs.

The first principle here is that social problem costs (losses) are seldom, if ever, shared equally among citizens. The first question is, "Who loses most?" In some ultimate sense there is probably no citizen who is not affected in an indirect way by all social problems. The issue here is to identify those who pay the biggest costs. For example, it is quite clear that the group that pays the biggest cost of the very high rates of crime in inner cities is made up of the local inner-city residents themselves. It is they who are robbed, raped, mugged, and murdered. On the other hand, by any measure, the most prominent victims of the "white-collar crime" of tax evasion are the middle-income classes, who pay the biggest share of the taxes collected by the U.S. Treasury. They bear most of the cost of the social problem because they must pay most of the extra tax needed to make up for the evaded taxes.

One of the important costs of the social problem of maintaining the health of the population is the dollar costs of medical care for the aged. Those costs are paid largely through Medicare, a Social Security subprogram financed by the Social Security withholding tax paid by those now in the work force. The amount withheld from the preretirement wages of those now receiving medical care was always far less than present average costs, so current recipients cannot be said to have paid for the Medicare benefits they now receive. That is not necessarily because of their unwillingness to do so but simply because (1) many people retired before Medicare was enacted, (2) the costs of medical care have risen enormously in recent years, (3) wages were less inflated in earlier years and, therefore, (4) contributions for Medicare were less. In addition, no one foresaw the incredible advances in medical care now available—for example the expensive medical technology developed mainly for the older population: (e.g., bone and joint transplants and heart bypass procedures). The unpredicted costs here are paid from the contributions to Social Security by those who now work and pay withholding taxes. Note carefully that what has been said has not *yet* judged the way these charges are distributed; such judgment will evolve from the *shoulds* and *oughts* of the value and ideology analysis. A judgment of desirability will not be made at this point because it would divert too much from our main purpose here, which is simply to illustrate what a social problem analysis should contain.

Sometimes very small details designed into public programs make an important difference in who ends up paying the biggest share of the costs. Consider again the example of wage losses for workers permanently and totally work-injured who receive Workers Compensation benefits. Lost wages are the amount a person could be expected to earn (at present wage levels) from the date of injury to the date of retirement. It is a cost to the *worker* when not all of the loss is repaid by the Workers Compensation program. It is a cost to *taxpayers* when the Workers Compensation benefit is not paid at all or is so insufficient that some other public welfare benefits must be paid to keep the disabled worker and his or her family afloat. However, it is a different case when a company buys Workers Compensation insurance coverage that is sufficient to pay the worker's full lost wages but *increases the price of its product or service to pay for the insurance*. Thus, it turns out that the *consumer* is actually paying for the worker's injury. These examples show why it is important to take careful notice of who pays social problem costs; existing social program details can and often do make substantial alterations in what would appear to be the obvious pattern of cost bearing for social problems.

After considering who loses from a social problem, the next issue to consider is the type of loss involved. In the preceding examples, money (or income) was the prominent kind of loss of immediate concern. Other concerns—pain, discomfort, inconvenience, time, and geographic dislocation—are examples of other types of losses that sometimes are discussed in presenting social problems. One obvious example is found in discussions of the social problem of abortion. For some, the concern is the loss and costs of the extinction of human life; for others, the concern is each woman's loss of autonomy over her body and its products. Much of the argument here turns on precisely what type of loss is viewed as important. Similarly, the social cost of a brutal beating might be said to be pain, disablement, discomfort, injustice, shame, and terror—which could be said of most violent crimes, including rape. Although some of these social costs can be said to be subjective in some sense, none would argue that they are unimportant, incalculable, or uncompensable.[5]

Sometimes social problems incur costs that revolve around the loss of *potential gains* rather than immediate losses, monetary or otherwise. For example, one of the costs for the parents of a severely retarded child may be in what those parents are prevented from doing by way of their own future employment, further education, or professional advancement. They may have to choose among spending their future caring for such a child at home, working, or obtaining further business or professional credentials that would advance their incomes. To the extent that increased income and enhanced employment can increase social standing, the consequence of the social problem of child retardation can certainly incur cost in status. Other social problems also can incur heavy status costs; for example, cost of crime or mental illness to the families of those involved can be negative social labeling that results in losses in both social status and personal esteem.

Finally, consideration must be made of the magnitude of costs—*how much* (whether money or some other measurement). It is convenient to express social costs in dollar terms because that measurement is easily interpreted by a wide audience. There are widely accepted ways of translating almost any kind of loss into dollar terms. The value of life is translated daily into dollar terms when civil courts hand down judicial decisions—for example, whether a physician was guilty of malpractice in a patient's disablement or death or whether a certain dollar value relieved "pain and suffering." We will not discuss further exactly how these more subjective losses are translated into money losses, except to say that economists do it by imagining (or gathering data on) how much most people would be willing to pay either to get rid of the effects of particular pain or suffering or status loss, or how much someone else would demand to take on the problem intentionally. One simple test is to ask yourself, for instance, how many dollars it would take to get *you* to take on the care of a severely intellectually disabled child in your own home or to have it generally known that a close family member is mentally ill or imprisoned for a serious crime. Estimating the *magnitude of social costs of a social problem* is an important process in understanding a social problem because doing so provides at least one standard by which a problem's "importance" can be measured both absolutely and relatively to other social problems.

If the first principle is that social problem costs are seldom shared equally among citizens, then the second principle is that *some people and some social groups actually benefit from others' social problems.* It is quite possible that some social problems are not solvable in any important and immediate sense simply because they create benefits that others are reluctant to give up. The general—albeit unsavory—idea here is that indeed some people do profit from others' misery. The extent to which this idea is true is debatable, but it does not seem wise to assume that such is never (or only seldom) the case. The most obvious evidence of this truth is the documented fact that a small number of people profit handsomely from others' addictions (liquor, tobacco, pharmaceuticals, illegal narcotics, and such). Less obvious is how this principle operates in relation to other more controversial social problems like unemployment, physical disablement, and aging. For example, it is not merely cynical to observe that the lower the general level of employment, the more welfare recipients will be forced into the work force and, therefore, the larger is the pool from which employers can draw low-wage employees. Employers of unskilled labor would certainly seem to profit from reduced welfare benefit levels. (It is Williams's point that if minimum wages drop, unskilled teenagers will profit as well.)

It would be unfortunate to conclude that only employers benefit from the existence of social problems. One rather well-known line of social analysis views racial prejudice and discrimination as one means of establishing an "underclass," a scapegoated "bottom-of-the-social ladder" group, against whom all other classes and types can be measured and positively valued. Theoretically then, wherever racial discrimination reduces competition from persons of color, whites must gain in terms of money and status. Some believe that the big gainers form the social unrest and racial tensions of the sixties and seventies were not working-class blacks but the black middle class, who achieved gains in income and increased their entrance at educational institutions and their starts up career ladders. Another commonly discussed example is the ability of the medical profession to profit from disease. Although no one doubts that physicians work hard for their pay, it is a fact that the *average* U.S. physician's income now approaches $200,000 per year.[6] This can lead one to conclude that the medical profession thrives on the misery of others and to overlook health care's conquests—for example, Tay-Sachs disease or open-heart surgical and organ-transplant techniques. Physicians are not the only professionals who profit from social problems; if there were no social problems there would be no need for social workers or human service personnel.

Understanding who profits from the existence of a social problem can reveal the forces that act against its elimination. It is very likely that where a shortage of good housing exists and large profits are being made from existing stock, associations of rental property owners, in serving their own interests, will oppose the building of public housing. Similarly, it is unlikely that physicians will support either serious limitation on their own fees or creation of a large number of medical schools—despite clear evidence that all citizens would get better medical care at reduced cost if the patient-physician ratio were decreased. It is equally unlikely that traditional craft unions (plumbing, carpentry, toolmakers) will admit minorities for fear they will become job and career competitors—especially in a stagnant economy where the threat of any competition willing to work for less wages is more keenly felt. The point is that the social problems of unemployment, housing, health, and racism all have some built-in resistance to solution simply because they generate strong economic and status rewards for other citizen groups.

The next section shows how conclusions from a social problem analysis are used to shape the basic features of a social policy or program.

USING THE CONCLUSIONS OF SOCIAL PROBLEM ANALYSIS TO JUDGE SOCIAL POLICIES AND PROGRAMS

When political scientists, students of government, or sociologists study a social policy or program, their interest traditionally is centered on explaining it as a fact of social life; that is, how the policy or program came to be, what broad social function it serves, why it appeared in one form and not another, or (perhaps) what the personal and role relations are among those who implement the policy. The social practitioners for whom this book is intended have different questions in mind because their interest lies in how social policies and programs can be instrumental in solving, or helping to solve, social problems for their clients. How much difference does this program or policy make to those who suffer from the effects of the social problem the program or policy is intended to solve?[7] *Qualitative judgments about the merit of a social program or policy cannot be made without reference to the original understanding of the problem; that is, they cannot be made without reference to the conclusions of the social problem analysis.* The idea here is that social policies and programs should be judged against the needs and causal analysis implied in the conclusions of the study of the social problem. Social policies should not be designed in the abstract or in relation to more or less random ideas about the nature of the social problem toward which they are directed as a solution.

Table 1–2 contrasts the components of social problem analysis with the operating characteristics of social policies and programs. What is the relationship between the two?

Table 1–2   Each Social Problem Analysis Component Specifies an Aspect of a Social Policy and Program Operating Characteristic.

Problem Analysis Component	Policy and Program Operating Characteristic
1. Problem definition (terms)	Specifies the terms that must be used in the *entitlement rules* determining who is/is not entitled to benefits or services and specifies the general *goals* to be achieved.
• (Subtypes)	Specifies the specific *target populations*.
• (Quantifications)	Can specify the priorities on the basis of which one *goal* rather than another is chosen where size of the problem is believed to be the determining issue.
2. Causal analysis	Specifies the particular *types of benefits and/or services* that must be delivered to address the problem.
	Specifies the *type of personnel* required to deliver the services or benefits where causation implicates cultural factors or implies a particular expertise and/or training or experience of the helper.
3. Ideology and values	Can determine choice of type of *entitlement rule* (e.g., means test rather than insurance principle).
	Can determine *goals* by establishing priorities to serve preferred subcategories of the problem.
	Determines *amount of financing* made available.
4. Gainer and loser analysis	Can specify method of *financing* where dollar loss is clear, ability to pay is obvious, and responsibility for loss can be assigned (e.g., worker's compensation).

Perhaps the most obvious relationship in Table 1–2 is between "problem definition (terms)" and "entitlement rules." Consider entitlement rules, in their most elementary sense, as policies that tell who should and should not get benefits or services. Then ask the question, "Does a problem definition influence how such a rule could be constructed?" The most straightforward answer is that ideally an entitlement rule should make services and benefits of the program available *only* to those who have the problem, a determination based on who meets the terms of the problem definition. Conversely, the rule should make it *impossible* for those who do not meet the terms of that definition to receive benefits and services. For example, if the social problem of concern is long-term hospitalization of the chronic psychotic, then an entitlement rule is appropriately derived from the definition for that condition used in the social problem analysis underlying the original general conception of the program or policy. If, for example, the definition used was the one found in the current *American Psychiatric Association Diagnostic and Statistical Manual (DSM-III)*, the entitlement rule should restrict benefits and services to individuals with these characteristics: "Delusions, hallucinations, or . . . disturbances in the form of thought."[8]

The "fit" with which we are so concerned here is not just a matter of its being logically "neat," because the lack of fit has serious consequences. For example, the program either overlooks needful citizens (underinclusion) or is more expensive than it should be (produces overwhelming cost) because program benefits or services are wasted on those who do not have the problem and do not need the benefits. Furthermore, without a clear entitlement rule in place, it is impossible to determine whether a program or policy had an impact on the problem and thus whether the causal explanations in the analysis were right. Data on the results of the program are useless if contaminated by (1) inclusion of those whose problems the program was never intended to solve or (2) data from an ill-formed entitlement rule that excludes either too many or the wrong people. In the example of long-term hospitalization of psychotics, no one would be able to tell whether people with a chronic psychosis and a history of long hospitalization could be helped by a programmed intervention that involved their living outside an institution independently if, for example, nonpsychotic chronically delinquent youngsters and the senile elderly were accepted into the program by an ill-fitting or misapplied entitlement rule. Not only might important resources be misdirected and therefore unavailable to those for whom they were originally intended, but the chance to learn something about the validity of the ideas in the social problem analysis would be lost.

Almost any citizen could tell you from personal experience that entitlement rules are not always constructed out of their relationship to the social problem; that same citizen will be able to cite actual contrary examples. Consider that any honorably discharged veteran is entitled to free hospitalization in any Veterans Administration hospital is clearly a welfare benefit according to the generally accepted definition (a material gain resulting from the direct or indirect redistribution of someone else's income).[9] This is not to say that the benefit is undeserved, but only to make the point that the entitlement rule for the benefit is *not* based on the conclusions from a social problem analysis. Rather, the basis for this entitlement rule is society's desire to *reward* those who in serving their country risked their own lives.

The problem-definition aspect of social problem analysis also prescribes the terms in which the program goals and objectives must be stated. Where policy and program goals fully destroy the "fit" between understanding the social problem and designing a solution is when goals and objectives become so general and so diffuse that the particular social problem that generated the policy and program in the first place is lost from sight. For example, a city's summer recreation program that was originally intended simply to provide adult supervision for out-of-school children transforms its goal into a grand statement about "providing for the child's total well-being during the summer period." There is nothing wrong with concern about children's "total well-being" (even if only "during the summer period"), but in this instance the goal is misguided because it is unfaithful to the original conception of the problem.

Before leaving our consideration of how qualitative standards for policy and program design can be derived from problem definitions, recall that there is a subsection of the problem-identification aspect called *subtypes*, which allows for variability within the social problem to be noted and reviewed; for example, key differences among sexual abuse, neglect, and physical abuse within the larger social problem category of child abuse. Once a subclass is "declared," there should also be some awareness of its numerical—that is, its *quantitative*—importance. These issues from social problem analysis should guide judgments about whether the goals of the policy or program are directed toward the *whole* social problem or only one of its parts; if the concern is with a subtype, analysis should help determine whether its size is warranted relative to other subtypes. Size is not the only determiner of priorities, but it is important to understand that magnitude provides the basis for a claim on public resources.

Now let us pay some attention to the relationship between causal explanation and the operating characteristic "types of services or benefits delivered." In an earlier section we showed how the most powerful kind of causal analysis proceeds by identifying the factors (variables) believed to be the crucial determiners of the problem. Where that is the case, it should be obvious that the types of benefits or services should be those that are influential in reducing the influence of those determiners. For example, if the social problem of concern is the physical abuse of children and the causal analysis identifies severe economic stress as the major determinant of abuse, then among the benefits provided by the policy and program must be money, goods, or their equivalent to relieve economic stress. If the causal analysis identifies as the key cause of maternal child abuse the presence of a nonnurturing, abusive mother who never shows her daughters how to rear children without physical abuse, then the program or policy design simply must provide the substitute parent model that abusing mothers did not get in their own homes.

Even though it would seem that no rational policy or program designer would violate this simple, straightforward, and obvious idea, that is just not the case. Some programs, despite their objective to alleviate child abuse based on an understanding of the problem as described in the preceding theory, in fact only provide education about child-development stages. As uplifting (even useful) as that education might be, such a program must be judged to be a bad "fit" and an irrational policy. Even the casual observer of social policy and programs does not have to look hard to find bad examples along this line: One program design is based on a causal analysis that identifies the major factor in poor social adjustment of some developmentally disabled children as their isolation from children in ordinary classrooms. However, this same program develops a policy to scatter special-education classrooms for these children throughout ordinary neighborhood schools—but it staggers and limits the daily schedule of the special-education classrooms so that these disabled pupils have no chance to be with mainstream schoolchildren. The fit between the causal analysis and the policy solution is lost because the type of benefit intended as a solution consistent with (even suggested by) the causal analysis turns out not to be the one implemented.[10]

Another possibility is that the causal analysis may direct the program or policy to employ only certain types of personnel to deliver benefits or services; that is, the causal analysis creates certain standards for the administrative service-delivery system. As will be discussed in Chapter 6 on administrative service-delivery systems, personnel specifications are an important feature in benefits and services. A common example is found in the causal analysis that explains the fact that some subgroups of certain ethnic or racial minorities do not apply for important health or school-based services because of the cultural and language barriers created by nonethnic or nonminority personnel. Where that causal view is taken, a heavy obligation is laid on the personnel policies of the delivery system: sufficient ethnic or minority personnel must be on-line if the services are to be delivered effectively. Here the issue is not an affirmative-action agenda or a concern with elimination of racially or ethnically biased hiring practices. After all, causal analysis can dictate personnel criteria other than cultural or ethnic features; for example, special expertise, education, or experience.

The analysis of major gainers and losers as a result of social problems is also a source of rational expectations for social policies and programs. These conclusions are particularly relevant for specifying methods of financing. Where the loss involved is a tangible material or financial loss, one obvious method of financing is implied: The gainers should repay the losers. In fact, that is exactly what is behind the "victim restitution" programs operated in relation to the social problem of crimes against property (theft, larceny, and misdemeanors, for example). The causal explanation usually invoked by these programs is that offenders repeat such crimes because (1) doing so costs the offenders nothing out of their own pockets and (2) offenders never have to encounter their victims face to face in terms of being held accountable for their criminal acts. Victim restitution programs, both the direct program cost and the cost arising from the adverse effect(s) of the crime, ideally should be paid for by the offenders themselves. This financing feature is entirely consistent with the causal analysis. Another example is the Workers Compensation program, the goal of which is to compensate workers injured on their jobs so that their income will not suffer irremediable damage. Workers Compensation legislation characteristically assumes that the cause of the income loss is the workplace incident (even though the personal blame for that accident is not assigned and its determination is not made a part of the program or policy—a "no-fault" system). Because the workplace "caused" an income loss, the policy pursued in legislation is to place responsibility on the employer to provide insurance payments to pay the cost of replacing the injured employee's lost income. Table 1–2 shows examples of these expectations.

SUMMARY

Chapter 1 discussed the central importance of social policy in the professional practice of social work and other human services. Social policies both create and constrain the possibilities of any social practice. Central to that understanding is an ability to ferret out the view of the social problem taken by legislative bodies, policy and program designers, political critics, and program and policy administrators. An analytic framework—that is, a set of concepts by which the fundamental dimensions of *any* view of a social problem can be understood—was presented. This framework takes into consideration four activities:

1. Identify the way the problem is defined.
2. Identify the cause(s) to which the problem is attributed and its most serious consequences.
3. Identify the ideology and the values that make the events of concern come to be defined as a problem.
4. Identify major gainers and losers with respect to the problem.

These activities were discussed and examples were given so that readers can learn to analyze social problems. The chapter closed with a discussion of how to use the results of the problem analysis to make judgments of the merit of the program.

EXERCISES

1. Do an analysis of the social problem viewpoints about child support as expressed in the following excerpt. Use the four social problem analysis categories discussed in the chapter.

Adequacy, Equity, and Responsibility in Child Support*

. . . [W]e have seen that the present child support enforcement system has the result of imposing most of the costs, both real and personal, of family dissolution on the female-headed family. . . . [M]ost child support payments are so low, if they exist at all, as to require supplementation from some other source. Indeed, *supplementation*

---

*From Judith Cassetty, *Child Support and Public Policy,* Chapter 8 (Toronto: Lexington Books, 1978), pp. 135–138. Reprinted with permission of the author.

is hardly the correct term. Child support payments are seldom found to be the primary source of income for the recipient family. Our own data suggest that, in the aggregate, mothers' earnings are the primary source of income, followed by public transfer payments as the secondary source, with child support ranking a poor third place. Had our subsample from the Michigan Survey on Income Dynamics been more representative of the population as a whole, we would probably have had a larger proportion of poor, female-headed families. Then, the ranking of source of support for these families more likely would have been public transfers, earnings of the female head, and finally child support payments. Together with the fact that the custodial parent—usually the mother—must provide the children with the bulk of nurturance, supervision, care taking, transportation, recreation, and so forth during sickness and health of all parties, it is clear which parent carries the disproportionate share of the cost of family dissolution in most cases. That this solitary burden extends for an average of five or six years, until remarriage or the youngest child reaches the age of majority, only compounds the inequities.

The present system offers few incentives for and imposes enormous costs upon a parent who is granted custody of the children when a union fails or when a marriage fails to eventuate. On the other hand, the personal and economic costs to the absent parent of that failure are too often minimal. In fact, to the extent that his responsibility can be shifted to the mother and/or the public, there may be a positive incentive for him to leave his spouse and children, even if, and perhaps because, he cares very much for their economic well-being. Although the exact shape of welfare reform is unknown at this time, it does appear that features which encourage family dissolution and parental irresponsibility are unavoidable without the disincentives afforded by vigorous child support enforcement. All other things being equal, a family should not benefit economically from dissolution. Under the proposed system, which provides fewer transfers to the intact family than to family members maintaining separate households, and a great many cash and benefits in kind to the fatherless family, a vigorously and successfully pursued system of child support enforcement may contribute to family dissolution in that it adds to total well-being. The magnitude of this effect would be contingent upon the extent to which females could be induced to dissolve unions by a social guarantee of child support, which would increase their net incomes. This effect might be modified, however, if child support payments offset the transfer payment at a high rate. The present welfare reform proposal before Congress calls for a reduction of eighty cents in transfer benefits for every dollar received in child support payments.

On the other hand, increasing the benefits of dissolution to the custodial parent by guaranteeing the payment of equitable levels of child support increases the costs of dissolution from the absent parent's point of view. If these costs are greater than the costs of maintaining an intact family (or getting married if the pregnancy is illegitimate), a reduction in family dissolution and an increase in family formation could be expected to the extent that men are the initiators of such. This effect would cut across income classes and is the one which the author believes would be most likely to dominate. This opinion is based on the recognition that sexual bias pervades society, resulting in women being awarded custody and conservatorship with far greater frequency than men; greater educational, occupational, and financial opportunities for men than for women. Because of these cumulative economic inequities, it is difficult to believe that in general women are the primary initiators of marital dissolution, in spite of the frequency with which they initiate divorce litigation.

The actual net effect of child support enforcement on dissolution rates, produced by the positive effect when women are the initiators of dissolution and the negative effect when men are the initiators, is unpredictable because we have no way of knowing the extent to which anticipated child support presently enters into a decision about marital dissolution. Assuming only that most of the present inequities are known, as would be their removal by substantial reform, the above effects for men and women can be anticipated. Though the net effect and its magnitude cannot be predicted with certainty, it is in keeping with our general goals of promoting equity and responsibility after marital dissolution that we have proposed a reevaluation of both the child support enforcement system as we know it today and the traditional minimizing approach to setting child support payment levels.

The issue of promotion of responsible behavior in relation to reproduction, or natality, is a more complex issue and more difficult to predict. It is likely that the present child support enforcement system has an antireproductive effect only upon those men who are not very mobile, who are attached to jobs and social groups that discourage neglect of one's responsibilities, and who regard very seriously their duty to provide the most amenities possible for their children, regardless of the quality of their relationship with the former spouse. For all others, however, the present system has little, if any, antinatal effect. As a sense of responsibility entails economic and personal costs, a decision to have another child should not be made lightly. This is precisely the foresight one would hope to encourage with a mandatory child support program. It is unlikely that the present system, which allows 79 percent of the absent fathers in our sample to avoid the child support obligation altogether, encourages much thought as to the consequences of reproduction. With each additional child a greater proportion of the responsibility for former children can be shifted to the mother and/or the state. This is not only inequitable, as mothers cannot shift the costs of their further reproduction to fathers of earlier children, but such irresponsible behavior can impose costs on the rest of society as well.

Policymakers who wish to arrest this effective shift in responsibility and also discourage the further reproduction of absent fathers can fix child support at a given level or percentage of income, as we have earlier suggested. However, to the extent that reproduction is not economically rational, they must be prepared to subsidize the subsequent children of an absent father whose net income after child support payments is insufficient to meet the needs of his new family. This is perhaps one of the most difficult inequities with which policymakers must deal, for it appears to be tantamount to choosing which children are to be given preference over which others when enforcing a claim to the father's income. At the very least, policymakers must decide which family the public should be prepared to subsidize. Consistent with the value made explicit at the beginning of the previous chapter, we feel priority should be given to earlier families in regard to the father's income, and society should subsidize subsequent families, if necessary.

The third issue—that of the family relationships—flows naturally out of the above discussion. It is quite possible that, as we interpreted some of our results . . . an absent father might view the payment of child support as entitlement to the right of meaningful involvement in his child's life. Therefore, the larger the child support, the greater his efforts to exercise his paternal rights and responsibilities. Also, we would expect that a father making a larger contribution to his child's life would be anxious to remain in fairly close proximity to the child and thus more easily collect the rewards (for example, the child's love and affection) of his investment.

There are of course opposing views. The traditional social casework view is that social workers should not encourage a woman to take legal action against a father for support of their child, on the grounds that it discourages reconciliation. Rapidly rising separation, divorce, and illegitimacy rates, coupled with appallingly low child support payments (when they exist at all) and little evidence of reconciliation, have cast doubts on this traditional view. We are now forced to reassess this implicitly male-centered perspective and look toward policies that foster, rather than ignore, parental responsibility. A federal program of child support enforcement and collection would be designed in such a way as to minimize adversary aspects of this function.

There remain a number of questions for which we still need answers. Most of these surround the measurement of the absent father's ability to pay support vis-à-vis the need of the dependent family. In particular, what is the maximum reasonable amount of support that we could demand from the absent father before collection would become virtually impossible? And should actual earned income or some other measure, such as wealth or estimates of earnings capacity, be used as the basic measure of ability to pay? The answers to these and other questions are necessary in order that we might develop an equitable and enforceable child support payment standard and the appropriate machinery for payment collection.

In the final analysis, the justification for expanding federal involvement in support enforcement efforts must be made in terms of securing the right of children to enjoy the fullest possible benefits to be derived from the resources of *both* parents. Maximum exploitation of the real and personal resources of custodial parents has in most cases already been realized. That fostering a more equitable sharing of this personal responsibility is within the purview of government is most certainly true, as is the encouragement of behavior consistent with a notion of social responsibility.

2. Do an analysis of the social problem viewpoint expressed in the following historical document. Use the four social problem analysis categories discussed in this chapter.

Dangers in Half-Dime Novels and Story Papers, 1883*

Satan stirred up certain of his willing tools on earth by the promise of a few paltry dollars to improve greatly on the death-dealing quality of the weekly death traps, and forthwith came a series of new snares of fascinating construction, small and tempting in price, and baited with high-sounding names. These sure-ruin traps comprise a large variety of half-dime novels, five- and ten-cent story papers, and low-priced pamphlets for boys and girls.

Again, these stories breed vulgarity, profanity, loose ideas of life, impurity of thought and deed. They render the imagination unclean, destroy domestic peace, desolate homes, cheapen woman's virtue, and make foul-mouthed bullies, cheats, vagabonds, thieves, desperadoes, and libertines. They disparage honest toil and make real life a drudge and burden. What young man will serve an apprenticeship, working early and late, if his mind is filled with the idea that sudden wealth may be acquired by following the hero of the story? In real life, to begin at the foot of the ladder and work up, step by step, is the rule; but in these stories, inexperienced youth, with no moral character, take the foremost positions, and by trick and device, knife and revolver, bribery and corruption, carry everything before them, lifting themselves in a few short weeks to positions of ease and affluence. Moral courage with such is a thing to be sneered at and despised in many of these stories. If one is

*From Anthony Comstock, "Dangers in Half-Dime Novels and Story Papers," in Robert H. Bremner (ed.), *Traps for the Young* (Cambridge, Mass.: Belknap Press of Harvard University Press, 1967), pp. 21–28, 238–242, first published in 1883.

asked to drink and refuses, he is set up and twitted till he yields or is compelled to by force. The idea of doing anything from principle is ridiculous in the extreme. As well fill a kerosene-oil lamp with water and expect a brilliant light. And so, in addition to all else, there is early inculcated a distaste for the good, and the piercing blast of ridicule is turned upon the reader to destroy effectually all moral character.

Satan is more interested in the child than many parents are. Parents do not stop to think or look for their children in these matters, while the archenemy is thinking, watching, and plotting continually to effect their ruin.

Thoughtless parents, heedless guardians, negligent teachers, you are each of you just the kind that old Satan delights to see placed over each child. He sets his base traps right in your very presence, captures and ruins your children, and you are each of you criminally responsible.

Take further instances of the effect of this class of publications, and then say if my language is too strong. Does it startle and offend? To startle, to awaken, to put you on your guard, to arouse you to your duty over your own children, is my purpose. *Your child is in danger of having its pure mind cursed for life.*

From infancy to maturity the pathway of the child is beset with peculiar temptations to do evil. Youth has to contend against great odds. Inherited tendencies to wrong-doing render the young oftentimes open to ever-present seductions. Inherited appetites and passions are secretly fed by artificial means, until they exert a well-nigh irresistible mastery over their victim. The weeds of sin, thus planted in weak human nature, are forced to a rapid growth, choking virtue and truth, and stunting all the higher and holier instincts. Thus, many a child of dissolute parents is born with natural desires for strong drink, and early becomes intemperate. In his thoughtful moments he loathes drink, and yet there comes upon him a force he is powerless to resist. So, too, the incontinence of parents brings into the world children inheriting morbidly susceptible natures—natures set like the hair trigger to a rifle—ready to fall into shame at the slightest temptation.

We speak of youth as the plastic state—the period of all others when the human soul is most easily molded and character formed. Youth is the seed-time. Maturity gathers in the crop. Youth is the fountain from which the waters of life flow. *If parents do not train and instruct their children, the devil will.* Whether parents deem it important to watch the child or no, there is one who deems it so important that he keeps a constant watch. *The devil stations a sentry to observe and take advantage of every point open to an evil influence.* He attacks the sensitive parts of our nature. He would destroy the finest and most magnificent portion of our being. The thoughts, imagination, and affections he is most anxious to corrupt, pervert, and destroy.

I unhesitatingly declare, there is at present no more active agent employed by Satan in civilized communities to ruin the human family and subject the nations to himself than evil reading.

If gambling saloons, concert dives, lottery and policy shops, poolrooms, low theaters, and rumholes are allowed to be kept open; if obscene books and pictures, foul papers, and criminal stories for the young are allowed to go broadcast, then must state prisons, penitentiaries, workhouses, jails, reformatories, etc., be erected and supported. Expensive courts and high-salaried officials must be employed at the taxpayer's expense, to care for those youths who are ruined, or to protect society against them.

Parents do not permit their children to make a playhouse of a sewer, nor to breathe its poisoned gasses. It is not popular to set diseased meat before the public in any of our numerous hotels or restaurants. Infected clothing may not be offered for sale, much less hawked about the streets. Yet worse evils than these are tolerated and encouraged, even while they are scattering moral death and physical suffering among those whom it is the especial duty of every civilized government to shield and protect—the young.

NOTES

1. Food and Agricultural Organization, United Nations, *The Fourth World Food Survey, Statistics Series no. 11* (Rome: FAO, 1977), pp. 15–28.
2. These broad analytic categories were put together by David Hardcastle, Ph.D., a professor at the School of Social Work, University of Maryland-Baltimore, from the work of a variety of sociologists and other students of social problems. I have expanded them and added the details in the material that follows, creating substantial alterations to 1 and 4.
3. Other examples abound. Long stays in mental hospitals are said by some to not only worsen the condition of a number of the mentally disabled but also to create "insanity" in some patients who were never "insane" in the first place. Some welfare programs, such as AFDC, are said to create generational dependency—that is, to produce succeeding generations of children who will themselves be AFDC families.
4. Ibid. Of course, we must understand that Williams was writing for ordinary readers here and in the space allowed could not develop the complete analysis he would have done in an academic journal.
5. The reader may notice that these examples all concern individuals and may, thus, be concerned that this contradicts earlier statements that social problems concern *groups* and not individuals. That problem can be resolved by remembering that all the individuals here are assumed to be members of a larger group in which all suffer from the same problem.
6. U.S. Bureau of the Census, *Statistical Abstracts of the U.S.: 1991* (111th edition). Washington, D.C., 1991, p. 116.
7. Notice that this criterion for judging a policy or program is not entirely practical from the viewpoint of the government or society because the standard concerns what the policy or program does for *those in need.* Unfortunately, in any view the interests of the state do not always coincide with the interests of those in need, with those who suffer from a social problem. For instance, it may be easiest, and certainly the least costly, for society at large and a government to ignore the sick, the disabled, and the poverty stricken. The focus on the interests of those in need is a bias here and is consistent with the value positions of the social work profession. The profession takes as one of its goals the elimination of "barriers to human realization." Social problems of concern to the profession are those believed to be major barriers to many people. See "The Working Definition of Social Work Practice," *Social Work,* 3:2 (April 1958) pp. 5–9.
8. *Diagnostic and Statistical Manual of Mental Disorders,* 3rd edition. Washington, D.C.: The American Psychiatric Association, 1980. See also P. G. Janicak and S. N. Andrukaitis, "DSM-III," *Psychiatric Annals,* 10:43–56 (Aug. 1980).
9. Richard A. Musgrave, *The Theory of Public Finance* (New York: McGraw-Hill, 1961), pp. 111–112.
10. The subject of why such nonsolutions are implemented is important, very large, and interesting in its own right, but it is not the main topic of concern for the practical analyst.

CHAPTER 2

Creating the Context for the Analysis of Social Policies: Understanding the Historical Context

By Richard Spano, Ph.D.

Chapter 2 is used with permission of the author, Richard Spano, Ph.D. Professor Spano was asked to write this chapter because of the unique approach he offers to help understand the relationship between history and social problems and social policy. Not only is this approach unique, it translates easily into a method that yields practical results for those to whom it is important to understand why policy and programs are what they have become today.

INTRODUCTION

This chapter is concerned with the contribution history makes to our under-standing of how social problems are defined and social policies developed. It presents history, and more specifically historical context, as a critical factor in shaping specific thinking and attitudes in all elements of society. The intent here is not to educate historians, but rather to sensitize social workers to a view of social policy as shaped by prior as well as current efforts to resolve social issues.

THE IDEA OF HISTORICAL CONTEXT

To begin with, it is important to be clear about what is meant by *historical con-text* as it relates to social policy analysis. In most social work programs, under-graduate students take introductory courses in "Social Welfare as an Institution" and "Social Work as a Profession," each of which has some small portion of its emphasis on history. Sometimes these courses consist of a recitation of dates, people, movements, and structures that represent benchmarks in the develop-ment of social welfare and social work: the Elizabethan poor laws, the Social Security Act, the Civil Rights Act, Jane Addams, Mary Richmond, Florence Kelley, the Charity Organization Society, and the settlement house movement, xample. Assuming retention of only these facts, do they help a social work-anderstand social policy? Probably not.

Although this focus on facts and dates represents the dominant view of history in most social work curricula, at the other end of the continuum are those historians who suggest that the only way to understand history is to know everything about a society during a given era: its music, art, economics, politics, religion, and intellectual climate. Although this is important for historians, the assumption underlying this book is that readers want to prepare for a career in *social work*. Thus, there is the need for something less than comprehensive preparation in history. The way to do that is to learn to be sensitive to some of the more important historical aspects of social policy development without having to relinquish the viewpoint of a practicing social worker. Toward that goal, some ways will be suggested here for you to enrich your understanding of the complex issues associated with social policy analysis.

For our purposes we are not so much concerned with history as history but with the historical context of social policies and programs; historical context is the soil in which social policy grows and takes root. If social policy is viewed as a plant, historical context consists of the air, water, and ground in the immediate area that will shape the growth of the plant. So it is that the particular interaction of political, economic, religious, and social welfare systems becomes the ground that shapes our analysis of social policy. For example, two conflicting struggles in the 1960s—the domestic War on Poverty and the Vietnam War—illustrate the struggle that can occur when the political and social welfare systems make conflicting demands on the economic system.

One major dimension of historical context refers to the *people and/or organizations that hold a stake in developing social policy in a particular direction*. An example of how potent this aspect can be in shaping social policy is illustrated in the field of mental retardation. Rose Kennedy, President John F. Kennedy's mother, and Hubert Humphrey, a leader in the U.S. Senate, both had a personal stake in seeing to it that retarded children received social services. In both instances their concern came as a result of both having had retarded members in their immediate families: Mrs. Kennedy had a retarded daughter and Senator Humphrey a retarded grandchild. Both Mrs. Kennedy and Senator Humphrey worked tirelessly to improve the treatment and promote the cause of mentally retarded people.

Sometimes small groups of experts band together and organize to effect a social policy. An example of this is the work of Isaac Rubinow, a statistician and one of the founders, in 1906, of the American Association for Labor Legislation. Rubinow worked as a member of this group for nearly three decades to promote a conception of social insurance that was incorporated in the Social Security Act in 1935. Other examples of these constituent groups include such diverse organizations as the American Medical Association, the American Bar Association, the National Association of Social Workers, the Children's Defense Fund, the American Association of Manufacturers, and the AFL-CIO. What they share in common is that they seek to shape the process by which policy is developed to fit their own view of the most desired outcome.

From the foregoing it should be clear how important it is to establish a historical context as a precondition to understanding social policy development. To do that, the practical policy analyst needs to know how current conceptions of a social problem and current actors connect with prior conceptions and actors in a policy area. Having set out what we mean by the idea of historical context, let us now consider some more detailed examples. First, let's think about how historical context affects viewpoints on social problems. Then, let's think about how historical context affects social policy development.

USING HISTORICAL CONTEXT TO UNDERSTAND SOCIAL PROBLEM VIEWPOINTS

In sixteenth- and seventeenth-century England, the social problem of concern was pauperism. Most learned people then writing social commentary about poor people were either churchmen or were educated within theologically dominated institutions. They saw pauperism as an individual moral deficit related to some lack of "moral fiber": pauperism was the product of individual failure or laziness. In general, people were viewed as evil by nature and headed for serious trouble if not kept busy ("the idle mind is the devil's playground"). These attitudes toward the poor reflected the prevailing theology of that era and led to efforts to control paupers rather than poverty. George Herbert's *The Country Parson* illustrates this view. In his chapter "The Parson Surveys," he suggests that it is necessary for the parson to survey his parish to determine the "faults" therein, and that included the sin of "idlenesse."

> The great and nationall [sic] sin of this Land [the Parson . . . should] . . . esteem to be Idlenesse. . . . For men [who] have nothing to do . . . fall to drink, to steal, to whore, to scoffe, to revile to all sorts of gamings. . . . Idlenesse is twofold, the one of having no calling, the other in walking carelessly in our calling. . . .[1]

Given this social problem viewpoint, ensuring that everyone had some form of employment should serve to alleviate the problem. Furthermore, once the parson had surveyed his parish and determined the needs, he was to extract funds from the rich members of the parish and carry out his charitable works with the following admonition:

> But he gives no set pension to any . . . for then they will reckon upon it, as a debt; and if it be taken away, though justly, they will murmur. . . . But the Parson, having a double aime, and making a hook of his Charity, he wins them to praise God more, to live more religiously, and take more paines in their vocation. . . . [because they cannot foresee] . . . when they shall be relieved.[2]

Much if not most of this view can be found in the English poor laws of this era: the notion of the need to exert influence and/or control over the poor so that they would mend their ways and thereby take their rightful place in the kingdom of God, and the theological assumptions about the nature of man as

.azy and prone toward evil. These concepts legitimated the notion of
.trol *as a function of charity.*

.e Ypres Plan developed by Juan Vives for the Consuls and Senate of
.s (Belgium) in the sixteenth century, the blending of church and secular
/s with an eye toward social control is clearly illustrated.

> We have decreed by an open commandment that none of our citizens presume to let
> any house to a stranger without our knowledge and consent for else by the daily
> increase of poor folks greater charge might grow unto us than we were able to
> bear. . . . Now for all this no man is [hindered from doing] good deeds but every man
> if he will may give alms privately to who he listeth. . . . Let them not send only broken
> meats but let them rather send a mess or two of meat even purposely appointed for
> them so that citizen's children may learn to visit and love the poor men's little
> cottages. . . .[3]

This view takes note of the economic problems associated with caring for
poor people but draws heavily on the prevailing theology as the basis for
explaining the nature of poverty and the relationship of paupers to the rest of
society. In fact, this view of poverty was very nearly the only available explanation of the conditions of the poor. Even those few who advocated relief for poor
people focused, for example, on the lame, blind, and sick (the individual characteristics of the poor), rather than on social or economic structures, as nine-
teenth- or twentieth-century commentators might.

Were the seventeenth-century inhabitants of England unconcerned about
their fellow citizens? Were they significantly less intelligent than we are? Were
they malevolent? The answer to each of these questions is "Probably not." They
were probably not significantly different from their twentieth-century descen-
dants on any of these dimensions. However, they were different in that they
were products of their history and current social context, just as we are products
of ours. Remember, in that period there was no social science, which meant that
there were few explanations to rival individualistic and theological perspectives.

Approximately three hundred years later, in the early 1900s, the American
progressives John Spargo and Robert Hunter studied the problem of poverty in
America. They used newly developed techniques such as social survey research
methods, statistical and economic analysis, and political ideology to frame the
issues surrounding the causes, consequences, and cures for poverty.

Spargo was a radical among the progressives. When he wrote *The Bitter Cry
of the Children,* he was active in the Socialist party, although he was identified
with that party's moderate wing. In the preface to *Bitter Cry*, Spargo clearly
expressed his intent:

> The purpose of this volume is to state the problem of poverty and its effects on
> childhood. Years of careful study and investigation have convinced me that the evils
> inflicted upon children by poverty are responsible for many of the worst futures of
> that hideous phantasmagoria of hunger, disease, vice, crime, and despair which we call
> the Social Problem.[4]

To achieve his purpose, Spargo compiled an impressive array of statistical information about family income, occupation, number of children, and education and their impact on child nutrition. He took a view of "charity" and the poor that was quite different from George Herbert's (see p. 37). Spargo emphasized the inadequacy of charity as a tool to sustain poor people.

> But it is only too true that charity—that damnably cold thing called charity—fails utterly to meet the problem of poverty in general and childhood's poverty in particular. Nothing could be more pathetic than the method employed by so many charitable persons and societies of attempting to solve the latter problem by finding employment for the mother, as if that were the worst phase of all from any sane view of the child's interest. Charity degrades and demoralizes and there is little or no compensating effecting help. In the vast majority of cases [this kind of charity] fails to reach the suffering in time to save them from becoming chronic dependents.[5]

Robert Hunter was a contemporary of Spargo's, but he was more closely identified with social work. Hunter analyzed poverty, paying special attention to quantifying it and then identifying the factors that contribute to it. Hunter's analysis vacillates between careful study—reflecting the social science perspective—and polemic sermonizing—emphasizing a socialist perspective on the causes for poverty. One of the most interesting aspects of Hunter's analysis is that he takes great pains to separate poor people into different categories: paupers, vagrants, the sick, poor children, and newly arrived immigrants.

These distinctions play an important part in his analysis because they suggest different approaches to the problems of different groups. Hunter's view of the pauper is different in substance from that of George Herbert three hundred years earlier, even though it has a familiar ring. According to Hunter:

> In nearly all cases, he who continuously asks aid becomes a craven, abject creature with a lust for gratuitous maintenance. And he who becomes an habitual pauper undergoes a kind of degeneration. . . . In some cases he becomes almost incapable of self support; he loses all capacity for sustained effort. . . . Avoiding any useful effort, he becomes skilled in those activities which enable him to more perfectly retain his state of dependence.[6]

The significant shift in his view is that he uses a medical rather than a theological metaphor to view the pauper. He "diagnoses" the problem as a "disease of character" and suggests that it affects the actual physical condition of the pauper, using the Jukes studies to support his assertion.[7] The focus of concern is the body, not the soul, and it is to be understood "scientifically," not theologically.

Hunter expresses a good deal more sympathy for the working poor, who he believed made up about 20 percent of the total number of poor. In his conclusion he admonishes the reader not to believe that all those in poverty are "effortless beings" who make no fight and wait in misery for someone to help them. He concludes the analysis with a plea for social justice for the working poor that he translates into recommendations for our basic economic system.

If we placed these perspectives on poverty side by side, it would be difficult to find many similarities. Were these progressives antireligious? Were they unaware of the spiritual aspects of their fellowman, aspects so prized by George Herbert? Were they amoral? Probably not. Possibly they were quite similar to their English forebears on these dimensions. They were, however, part of the first generation of social scientists who were developing a rival set of ideas to explain poverty. They chose a "scientific" rather than a theological framework, which led them to very different conclusions about poverty, its causes, and its consequences. Note that this does not suggest that social science is a better or a more valid explanation, but simply that it leads to different formulations in a social problem analysis.

Hunter and Spargo's social science perspectives were early examples in a long line of scientific explanations of poverty. Hunter and Spargo used economic and political science concepts as useful tools, whereas others used newly emerging concepts from public health and "industrial sociology" to explain poverty. In the 1960s there was another popular conception of poverty, "the culture of poverty," as advocated by Oscar Lewis, a widely read anthropologist who studied intergenerational poverty cross-culturally. In part Lewis's anthropological notion of the culture of poverty was intended to bridge the gap between large-scale economic and political explanations and the individually oriented explanations of theology and psychology. For Lewis the poor family and its adaptations to the dominant culture were used to explain how this subculture of the poor developed as a response to poverty. Some of the traits embodied in the culture of poverty included a lack of effective participation and integration of the poor into major social institutions, a lack of productivity and marginal consumption, an espousal of middle-class values without the commitment to live by them, and a minimum amount of organization beyond the level of the nuclear family. At the family level the traits included the absence of a prolonged childhood, early initiation into sex, free unions, a relatively high incidence of abandoned wives, a trend toward mother-centered families, a strong disposition toward authoritarianism, and a lack of privacy. On the individual level, the culture of poverty included a strong feeling of marginality, of helplessness, of dependence, and of inferiority.[8]

The War-on-Poverty programs were consistent with notions embedded in the culture-of-poverty idea. At an institutional level, Legal Aid and storefront lawyers attempted to make structural policy changes through case law that would help the poor access goods and services and expand civil rights.[9] At the neighborhood level, the Mobilization for Youth program was designed to intensify participation and a sense of control over one's environment. At the individual and family level, community mental health services were provided to retard the "disorganization" within the family and the individual.[10] Clearly the War-on-Poverty programs represented a multifaceted approach that Lewis's conception suggested as the appropriate means to alleviate the problems resulting from poverty. (Note that Lewis himself would *not* always have agreed with this interpretation of his work.)

Questions to Guide the Search for the Historical Context of a Social Problem Viewpoint

These brief descriptions of social problem analyses of poverty illustrate the interplay of historical context with social problem analysis. Here are some questions that might guide your search to establish the historical context surrounding a modern social problem analysis.

1. **Why is this concern being raised as a problem at this moment in history?** For instance, in the prior examples, it is appropriate to ask: "Were there no poor people prior to 1601?" The answer is that there were, but poverty was seen as a condition, a simple fact of existence rather than a social problem. A condition does not call for a resolution unless the condition is connected to a value commitment to which existence of the condition is a contradiction. Examples of the forces that shape the problem are complex and often related to events in specific time periods. The 1930s was a period during which economic depression was sufficiently widespread to capture the attention of nearly all groups in America, when urgent economic problems were of such magnitude that they had to be addressed in order for American society to continue. At another time, in the affluent 1960s, concern about the oppression of blacks captured the public's attention. In that instance, blacks raised discrimination as a moral issue and gathered sufficient support from other minority groups and from segments of white society so that long-term changes in our social system resulted. Why were the 1960s ripe for such a change? Why not the 1950s or 1970s?

2. **Is this a "new" problem?** As we saw earlier in this chapter, our society has wrestled with the problem of poverty for centuries, employed numerous explanations, and developed a multitude of policies and programs. Each time a new formulation of the problem is put forward, we alter the service-delivery structure to account for the change, and sometimes we create a whole new structure. However, in every era new "problems" are put forward that may have little precedent; for example, the policies and programs regarding nursing-home care are a post–World War II problem that called for novel solutions. Never before had so many people lived so long or families been so loosely knit—both attitudinally and geographically. Those facts provided the historical context for the definition of totally new social problems.

3. **What are the precedents for the ideas and values (ideology) being used to define the problem?** Sometimes the current conception of a situation is just a narrow revision of an earlier conception. Note, for example, that there is a contemporary view that poverty is a condition perpetuated by mental mechanisms that develop to adjust to deprivation and are passed down through families. In some ways this is a view of poverty as a moral degeneration to which the poor become acclimated and that is perpetuated in new generations and by the charity of others. For example, the basic principles enunciated in the Elizabethan poor laws rather dramatically parallel the "individualistic" principles used in the

development of President Richard M. Nixon's 1970 Family Assistance Plan. Rightly or wrongly, validly or invalidly, this is an individually oriented view of poverty that has persisted intact for the last four centuries.

Sometimes the ideology used to define a problem is almost unprecedented. For example, although the social problem of poverty is defined as having its historical roots in the poverty of women—caused by their occupational segregation, job discrimination, and unequal access to public benefits and services—it comes very close to presenting a new social problem view. Although feminist viewpoints are surely not unique to the twentieth century, their ideological extension to advocating for a position of equality with men in employment and in child rearing probably is unique to this era.

4.   Who are the actors now defining this issue as a social problem and how are they different from past actors? Identifying the relevant stakeholders in the problem usually leads to identifying important constituent groups that seek to influence future policy and program development. For example, the battles waged around Medicare and Medicaid in the 1960s included many of the same groups that in the 1930s had argued issues pertaining to the provision of medical care. The beginning of these debates prominently featured points that eventually led to the Social Security Act. Many social service people, politicians, and interested private citizens saw this concern as an essential element in any social insurance package. However, the medical community lobbied hard against this aspect of the bill, and it was removed early in the political process. (The political process will be discussed later in this chapter.) Today, however, the American Medical Association (AMA) and a whole new health care industry are among the important problem definers and supporters of the public provision of medical care.

5.   If the issue currently being raised has some historical precedent, what conditions now exist that suggest different outcomes or make society more receptive to change? The suggestion that "history repeats itself" is somewhat misleading. Although certain basic social issues or problems such as poverty persist over time, the policy responses to those problems are never exactly the same. Social insurance provides a good example of a means to combat poverty that was actually not new in the 1930s when Congress passed the Social Security Act. Social reformers like Isaac Rubinow had already proposed various schemes for social insurance in the early 1900s. Those ideas made little impact on society then, in part because they were proposed in a period of relative economic prosperity when society was not threatened economically. Social insurance became a reality in America in the 1930s during the Great Depression, when the resolution of economic problems was central to society's survival.

Along the same line, blacks had been discriminated against in this country for nearly two hundred years before civil rights legislation was passed. Why, in 1964, did we get the Civil Rights Act? In part the answer lies in casting the treatment of blacks as a matter of social conscience rather than an economic issue. In other words, the civil rights movement, the War on Poverty, and the Vietnam War interacted in a way that made this society sensitive to the redress of grievances that had a longstanding precedent.

Although the answers to these five questions will not provide all the information necessary to develop a comprehensive understanding of the historical context of a social problem viewpoint, the questions do suggest some important areas that should yield valuable information with which to assess a social problem viewpoint. In summary, social problem viewpoints can best be understood as both a product of prior experience on the part of a society and as the unfolding of the current interrelationships existing in that society. The practical policy analyst's task is to identify some of the key factors that lead to the development of a particular problem formulation, rather than to a comprehensive understanding of history for history's sake.

USING HISTORICAL CONTEXT TO UNDERSTAND SOCIAL POLICY AND PROGRAM DESIGNS

Thus far, we have looked at a framework useful in developing an *analysis* of a social problem viewpoint and at how to ground such a framework in a useful historical context for thinking about social problem analysis. In this section we will use the concept of historical context to see how it affects the implementation of social policies and programs. We will look at policy and program implementations as products of the interaction of political processes and formal organizational structures.

Political Process

Earlier we described social policy as an expression of society's concern about the need to resolve a specific social problem or issue. For example, so long as there is sufficient clean air to breathe and clean water to drink, these critical aspects of our existence remain outside the purview of social policy. If clean air and water become scarce (whether because of pollution or increased population), their management, distribution, and protection will become subjects for social policy. The underlying idea is that social policy usually reflects society's attempts to manage a scarce resource. Accordingly, there are nearly always competing and conflicting demands made by various groups that shape public policy. These conflicts are expressed through our political system, which generates much of our social policy. The process by which claims are advanced for resources within the political system is called the *political process*.

Our political process has formal and informal dimensions. Its formal aspects are expressed through congressional hearings, public statements put forward by concerned individuals or groups, political platforms, and legislative bills—all of which culminate in social policy being enacted into laws.

Compromises may occur at any point in these formal activities. This happens when some group, organization, or individual exerts influence that alters the makeup of the policy proposals. For example, as a part of its platform a party may champion a specific proposal such as the Equal Rights Amendment. At any point from the time a bill is introduced, people will try to shape its policy in ways they believe are in their best interest. This effort can occur in congressional hearings, floor debates, public hearings, or joint conferences—all of which are part of the formal political process.

As you examine the political process and how it developed around a specific social policy or program design, two key notions can help guide you in establishing an appropriate historical context in which to understand social policy and program development: (1) the constituent groups—large and small—involved in the process and (2) the nature of the compromise reached. First, identify the various groups that had some stake in the policy. Some of the groups will be private and others public; some will be highly visible and some may keep a low profile; some will have a long history of involvement in the issue and some may be new to the battle; and some will represent special-interest groups whereas others may advocate based on their expertise. The important thing to remember is that each constituent group will have a stake in the process and will try to shape policy and program development to fit its own view of the best solutions to the problem.

The nature of the compromise reached is most often determined in the informal political process. The informal political process is somewhat more difficult to track because it refers to compromises arranged outside formal channels, such as conversations, confidential communications between people or organizations, or decisions made in closed meetings. This information is much more difficult to locate and often requires access to committee minutes, organizational memos, confidential reports and unpublished studies, private notes or diaries, and correspondence between crucial actors in the drama.

Formal Structure

Formal structure refers to the organizational mechanisms established and charged with responsibility for translating social policy and programs from theory to implementation. In some situations new agencies, bureaus, or divisions are created; in others, social policy is delegated to existing agencies or bureaus that may have similar goals or that in the past have served the population groups toward whom the policy is directed. Oftentimes the success of social policy depends on the two things: (1) choosing an appropriate organizational structure for policy delivery and (2) designating the appropriate level of government at which the structure is lodged. An example of an agency that played a crucial role—and an unprecedented one—in American history is the Freedman's Bureau. This structure was created at the end of the Civil War to meet the many needs of blacks during their transition from slavery to freedom. The Freedman's Bureau provided settlement, employment, and legal assistance. Furthermore, it was lodged in the federal government, the first time the federal government stepped in to provide directly for the welfare of a group of its citizens. The comprehensive structure of the bureau, coupled with its federal sponsorship, made it possible to achieve some of its objectives. Had the same agency been lodged in state government, its effectiveness most likely would have been severely hampered.

To understand the current role formal structure plays in policy and program development, it is necessary to look at the history of the organization or bureaucratic structure administering the policy or program design and to examine its relationship to various constituent groups. For example, Gilbert Steiner identifies nearly a dozen major organizations interested in the welfare of children. Each has a specific stake in the "children's cause" and defines its objectives in ways that often overlap. These organizations may share related objectives, but they often compete for the scarce resources available to meet them. Organizational survival can become as important as the objectives they seek to reach. Steiner does an excellent job of tracing the effect of these turf battles and personality conflicts in shaping various elements of policies and programs in the field of child welfare.

In *The Children's Cause* Steiner focuses specifically on tracing the role played by the Children's Bureau in the field of child welfare. The following brief overview of this organization illustrates some of the important aspects of formal structure in policy and program development. The Children's Bureau was created as a result of the first White House Conference on Children in 1909. Answerable directly to the White House, it had remarkably able leadership as well as stability and clarity of purpose. From 1912 until the 1950s it had only five directors, including such notable social workers as Julia Lathrop and Grace Abbot. The bureau consistently focused its efforts on research—on preparing solid evidence for the development of a policy in the public sector to benefit children. However, from the 1930s on, it was exposed to increasing competition from the newly developing public relief agencies that took over more and more of its turf. By the 1960s the bureau had become part of the Department of Welfare Administration of the U.S. Department of Health, Education, and Welfare (HEW) and subservient to HEW civil servants. HEW itself was absorbed into the U.S. Department of Health and Human Services.[11] As a result, the Children's Bureau was lost from the sight of its powerful constituent groups and deprived of its autonomous destiny. Formal structure can determine the destiny and influence of a program, and the Children's Bureau could no longer determine autonomously how it should serve children because it had to answer to other civil servants. In its early days it had answered directly to the White House.

According to Steiner, this loss was the result of the informal influence of Jules Sugarman, an aggressive associate director of the Head Start program, who opposed the assignment of Head Start (then in its early years) to the Children's Bureau. In a confidential memo to Mary Switzer, then administrator of the U.S. Division of Social and Rehabilitation Services, Sugarman was critical of the Children's Bureau and recommended that the solution to its problem was to reduce its role by incorporating it into a new organization or substantially modifying its leadership at all levels.[12] Sugarman's informal organizational activity doomed any chance for the Children's Bureau to assume a new leadership role by taking on responsibility for the Head Start program.

Subsequently, HEW Secretary Robert Finch received a memo from Switzer that further damaged the bureau's reputation and led to its incorporation in a new structure, the Office of Child Development (OCD). Eventually the Children's Bureau, once the most influential child welfare agency, became an obscure small department in OCD.

It is in this manner that social policy and social problem viewpoints reflect public debates about issues. The informal maneuvering that occurs within and between organizations uses the need to implement policy as an opportunity to provide their own interpretation of the social problem. It is no wonder that ordinary agency practitioners, the street-level bureaucrats, become confused and frustrated when asked to implement policy that reflects compromises at so many levels. Those compromises represent conflicting interests and different purposes all the way back to the time of the first legislative debates on the problem.

THE FOOD STAMP PROGRAM: AN EXAMPLE

Before concluding this chapter, it will be useful to see the interplay of historical context, social problem views, and social policy and program design by looking at the food stamp program. The origins of the U.S. food stamp program can be traced to Section 32 of Public Law 72-320 (known as the Potato Control Act of 1935). The last section of this act authorized the purchase of surplus commodities for distribution to needy church groups and families.

The surplus commodities distribution programs were controlled by the U.S. Department of Agriculture (USDA) and administered by the Federal Surplus Commodities Corporation (FSCC). FSCC's purpose was to support farm prices, not to feed the poor. The creation of the program caused concern among the various constituent groups that were claiming an interest in it, including recipients who disliked the distribution system, and the food retailers who did not want normal trade mechanisms disrupted. In this instance there were two problems existing side by side: widespread starvation and malnutrition caused by the Great Depression and disposal of surplus created by new agricultural technologies. On the surface the two problems appear to be compatible, but the policy goals of feeding the poor and reducing food surpluses proved to be embarrassingly awkward to achieve.

The organizational mechanism created to meet the two goals was a two-stamp system. In this system, welfare recipients were issued stamps that could be used to buy food at authorized retailers: orange ones, which were purchased at face value by recipients, and blue ones, which were provided for free on a 2:1 orange-to-blue ratio. The blue stamps could be used only to purchase surplus commodities designated by the secretary of agriculture. In theory the program would reduce food surpluses by making them more available to recipients and reduce malnutrition by increasing the amount of food available for recipients. However, in practice the program had mixed results. It did not appear to stimulate expenditures on food any more than would have been expected from a cash subsidy. On the other hand, it did expand the choice of foods beyond the prior commodity programs and was advantageous to food retailers as well as producers.[13]

The problem—and thus the policy—regarding these issues again came to public attention in the early 1960s, when surplus food and a concern for nutrition among the poor reemerged as social issues. This time new protagonists were brought into the fray. The goals remained utilization of the nation's food surplus and promotion of the nutritional well-being of low-income persons; however, the political process and formal structures were subject to new stress from politicians who were concerned about the relationship of states' rights to the federal government. A critical factor shaping the eventual food stamp program centered on compromises that needed to be made to ensure support from conservative members of Congress who were concerned about the expanding role of the federal government in the lives of their constituents. The eventual compromise that allowed conservatives to support the food stamp program was that the federal government would determine payment levels (how much benefit was to be given), but the states would determine eligibility standards (who was to receive benefits).[14]

Two social problems—the enormous farm surplus stockpile and feeding of the poor—and their solutions were clearly articulated in the food stamp program from the very beginning, and one structure, lodged in the USDA, was established to resolve both. This suggests some answers to three questions commonly raised about the food stamp program, for example:

1.   Why did poor people get so much peanut butter and lard from the food stamp program in the early years? (Answer: Lard and peanuts were glutting the market.)

2.   Why is there a stamp program instead of simply giving poor people the cash to buy their own food—especially now that it is clear that the costs of the two alternatives do not differ significantly? (Answer: Continuation of the program requires support of the congressmen from the farm states who have a loyalty and an ideological bent toward a program that was once a useful mechanism for reducing farm surpluses.)

3.   Why does the state control the administration of the food stamp program when the federal government pays all its bills? (Answer: The program was caught up in an ideological battle in the 1960s, at a moment in history when increased federal operation of programs was viewed as an encroachment on states' rights.)

To understand policy formulation and program development is to understand clearly the surrounding conditions: poverty in the midst of plenty; the various constituent groups with some stake in the process (poor people, farmers, food retailers, activist groups of the 1960s, and politicians); and the history of compromises meant to implement a specific program. These individual aspects came together in what we call the historical context of social policy and program analysis.[15]

SUMMARY

The study of history for the purpose of creating the historical context for the study of social problems and policy is different from the study of history qua history. For the purpose of the student of social problems at least five questions are useful in establishing the historical context surrounding a modern social problem:

1. Why is this particular social problem being raised as a matter of concern at this particular moment in history?
2. Is this a new issue?
3. What are the historical precedents for the ideas and values being used to define the issue?
4. Who are the actors now defining this issue as a social problem, and how are they different from past actors?
5. If the current issue has some historical precedent, what conditions now exist that suggest different outcomes or make society more open to change?

In analyzing social policies and programs there are two important issues to establish in creating the historical context:

1. The political process: How causes are advanced within the political system and how this leads to creation of a policy or program; what constituent groups were involved in the process; and the nature of the political compromises necessary to legislate or gather support for the policy or program.
2. The formal structure: The nature of bureaucratic and organizational competition that may have been instrumental in deciding where to lodge administrative responsibility for a new policy or program or in shifting such responsibility from one organization or department to another.

These elements of the historical context of policies and programs have important bearing on both the form that the program eventually takes and the extent to which it can be successfully implemented.

EXERCISES

The following exercise is intended to help you gain skill using the framework presented in this chapter. Pick an area of social policy that is currently being debated in your community or state.

1. Identify the relevant actors in the debate. Who are the people and organizations that stand to gain or lose in developing this particular social policy? What appear to be the major areas of contention among these groups? How do they define the problem?
2. Examine public documents, newspaper reports, committee reports, public speeches, and so on, and try to infer from them why this problem is being debated at this juncture in history. Is this a new problem? What, if any, specific events fueled the debate?
3. After examining the definitions of the problem, look behind the words to the ideology being used to shape the definition. What can you tell about the actors' views of the relationship between the problem and social and personal responsibility? Are these new or old arguments?

4. As you look at the surrounding social context, can you identify similarities or differences between these conditions and those affecting prior attempts to deal with this problem? Are there new technologies available? Is a new value commitment evident? Are the relationships among the contending parties different?

NOTES

1. F. E. Hutchinson, *The Works of George Herbert* (London: Oxford University Press, 1941), p. 274.
2. Ibid., pp. 244–45.
3. Karl de Schweinitz, *England's Road to Social Security* (New York: A. S. Barnes, 1939), p. 35.
4. John Spargo, *The Bitter Cry of the Children* (New York: Quadrangle Books, 1968), p. xlii.
5. Ibid., p. 54.
6. Robert Hunter, *Poverty* (New York: Harper & Row, 1965), p. 69.
7. Ibid., p. 318.
8. Oscar Lewis, *La Vida* (New York: Random House, 1965), pp. xlii–xliii.
9. Joel Handler, *Protecting the Social Service Client* (New York: Academic Press, 1979).
10. Leopold Bellak and Harvey Barton, *Progress in Community Mental Health* (New York: Brunner/Mazel, 1975).
11. Gilbert Steiner, *The Children's Cause* (Washington, D.C.: The Brookings Institution, 1976), p. 39.
12. Ibid.
13. Maurice MacDonald, *Food Stamps and Income Maintenance* (New York: Academic Press, 1977), p. 2.
14. Ibid., pp. 3–4.
15. The following books represent various ways in which historical context is written; the best single example is Robert Bremner's *From the Depths* (New York: New York University Press, 1956). Other examples are: Fred Best, *Work-Sharing, Issues, Options and Prospects* (Grand Rapids, Mich.: W. E. Upjohn Institute on Employment Research, 1981), pp. 1–9; Judith Cassetty, *Child Support and Public Policy* (Toronto: Lexington Books, 1978), pp. 5–14; Sar Levitan and Richard S. Belous, *More Than Subsistence* (Baltimore: Johns Hopkins, 1979), pp. 29–52; Theodore Marmor, *The Politics of Medicare* (Chicago: Aldine, 1970), pp. vii–ix, 1–82; and Gilbert Steiner, *The Children's Cause* (Washington, D.C.: The Brookings Institution, 1976), chaps. 3, 4, 5.

CHAPTER 3

The Judiciary as a Shaper of Social Policy, Program and Practice

INTRODUCTION

The judiciary (all federal and state courts) creates social policy that guides and constrains, gives freedom to, and charges practitioners with helping client/consumers of public services and benefits delivered by agencies that employ social workers in various clinical and administrative capacities. Virtually all fields of practice are affected by social and organizational policy made by judicial decisions; this includes social workers doing what the field has come to call "clinical practice," which serves individuals afflicted by various kinds of emotional conditions. Certain policy created by judicial decisions prevents social work and human service practitioners from doing certain things: for example, the ruling in *Goldberg v. Kelley* prevents practitioners from terminating public cash benefits without explanation to the beneficiary—an application of the citizen's right under the U. S. Constitution to due process, details of which will be discussed in a later chapter on issues relating to administrative and service-delivery systems.[1] On the other hand, a series of state court decisions has created policy that holds practitioners responsible for taking "due care" to notify people directly who have been specifically and personally threatened with violence or physical harm by the client/consumers of the social worker or human services worker (*Tarasoff v. The Regents of the University of California*, 1976).[2]

Some court decisions make public policy in the sense of holding social workers and human service workers responsible for their professional actions, the explicit policy being that they are accountable to their own professional standards for competent practice. Consequently, they can be sued for their actions (or lack thereof), to the fullest extent allowed by law. Besharov lists a whole catalog of legal horrors that can beset the unwary practitioner:[3]

- *Treatment without consent* (a social worker and her employer were sued by a service recipient who claimed that her [the recipient's] consent to treatment was given only because she was threatened with loss of her job if she did not complete residential treatment for substance abuse.)

51

- *Inappropriate treatment,* ". . . half the claims for erroneous diagnosis made under the NASW insurance malpractice program were based on a charge that the client's problem was actually medical. . . ."
- *Inappropriate release* of a client from hospitalization, confinement, or supervision.
- *False imprisonment* (a client is wrongly detained or committed on the basis of false or inadequate information given to a physician who recommended commitment.)
- *Failure to be available when needed.*

Social workers must be aware of these and other decisions in order to keep their practice within the law and to take advantage of social policies that are to the best interest of their client/consumers. In addition to exercising due care with regard to confidentiality, they must be prepared to take strong positions in clinical staff discussions about whether to recommend commitment of a client. Not only must they be wary of participating in agency decisions that may violate a client's civil rights, they must be wary of participating in those organizational decisions that violate social policy in their state. For example, public agencies cannot act arbitrarily and capriciously and must follow their own rules, so long as those rules are legal.[4] It is particularly problematic when public agencies deliberately change administrative rules and regulations, thereby changing laws that Congress has enacted to affirm specific social policies. That was certainly the case when hundreds of thousands of Social Security Disability Insurance (SSDI) beneficiaries were terminated "arbitrarily and capriciously" (illegally, the courts finally ruled) in the mid-1980s.[5]

Social workers and human service practitioners need to be aware of the judiciary as an instrument of social policy as they assist in the preparation of court cases that have the potential to serve and better the interest of their client/consumers. Practitioners can be called to testify in all manner of court proceedings—termination of parental rights, commitment and guardianship hearings, malpractice suits, disputes over public agency benefits, and so forth. It is always possible that their testimony may be crucial in court decisions that break new ground in social policy. In all these ways social workers must understand that as they interact with the courts they are molding their profession's destiny.[6]

Ordinarily, public policy is initially framed via the political process. Recall from Chapter 2 the origins of the Food Stamp program, which began as the Potato Control Act of 1935 when Congress legislated the distribution of government-subsidized farm surpluses (food products) to low-income households. This policy resulted from the awkwardness of having large government-owned food surpluses (created by the emerging agricultural technology) exist side by side with widespread hunger created by an out-of-control economic depression. Over the years, the legislation was shaped by political compromises between the competing economic interests of various social groups: the farmers, whose surplus production must be sopped up to decrease the costs of governmental farm subsidies that protected farmers' income; welfare beneficiaries, whose hunger was to be relieved by the free commodities of farmers' food; and the retail food merchants, who feared being dealt out of the low-income market. As new economic realities evolved, both the original intent and the competing interests changed in this small sociological drama: farm surpluses increased and disappeared cyclically, the poor became the economically marginalized (for example the aged or the disabled, rather than, simply, unemployed mainstream workers). The original intent was to dispose of agricultural subsidies in a useful way; the later intent was to feed the poor.[7] The legislative provisions that shaped the program changed as well.

But the judiciary can modify or completely negate legislation, so in effect the judiciary and the courts hold trump cards. This fact is simple evidence of the operation of constitutional checks and balances between the legislative, judicial, and executive branches of government. It is a mistake to be misled by the prevalent view that, somehow state and federal statutes (enacted legislation) are self-revealing; that the purpose and task of the courts is only to reveal the law. Of course they do that as a matter of course but in so doing courts produce effects far beyond those that legislators had in mind. As Ehrmann says:

> The authority of a court to declare laws and official acts unconstitutional is a practice that . . . gives to judges so obvious a share in policymaking that . . . there is little room left for the pretense that judges only apply the law.[8]

The judiciary both creates anew and reshapes old social policy. One example is the *Roe v. Wade* decision, which in effect made abortion a public policy by making it legal for the public sector to provide for the cost of abortions. Another example is the final *Cruzan v. Danforth* decision, which as public policy denied to parents the right to remove life support from their comatose daughter who over an eight-year period had been in a persistent vegetative state. Clearly those were not public policies made by an elected legislature, and yet they nonetheless were social policy in that they were decisions that literally meant life and death to actual persons. Not to be overlooked are the judicial decisions that mandated due process in appealing denials of public welfare benefits. Or consider all judicial decisions on the nature and distribution of education rights and resources: *Brown v. Board of Education* (1954)[9] and the hundreds of education desegregation court orders that followed, not to mention the court-appointed masters (administrators) who oversee reallocation of state funds from richer to poorer school districts. Of more direct relevance for human service and social work practitioners are decisions that (1) appointed Court masters to oversee the development of treatment programs for the institutionalized mentally retarded in Alabama (*Wyatt v. Stickney*),[10] (2) stopped the massive terminations of Social Security benefits (cash and medical care) for the disabled during the Reagan Administration of the 1980s,[11] and (3) established welfare benefits as a new form of property to which certain property rights are attached (under specific conditions—*Goldberg v. Kelley*).[12] As stated by Notes:

> The courts in their relationship with public policy, are also involved in an evaluative process . . . (which is) interpretive and not . . . political. It is impervious to electoral judgment, unrestricted by the constraints of partisan ideologies and relatively immune

to the requirement of (political) compromise. The public policy values the court is free to evaluate are related to but independent from the political values which motivated the existence or absence of a statute. Parliament passes laws, courts decide what the laws mean and in so doing courts react to what they feel are the public policy values that underlie the statute.[13]

Some, who take the view that such decisions deform the original, pristine intent of the framers of the U.S. Constitution, are likely to call such acts "judicial activism." To them the power to make public policy belongs solely with the legislative branch, using the constitution as a stringent framework. This view is popular in conservative circles and for elaborate discussions the reader might refer to journalistic accounts and editorials on the congressional hearings on the nomination of Robert Bork to the U.S. Supreme Court in the *New York Times,* the *Washington Post,* the *New York Review,* or *Harper's.* This chapter will assume that, whatever its merits or demerits or whatever is its historical status relative to the founding fathers' intentions, judicial activism is a reality that shapes social policy in this country and any analysis that fails to attend to it is incomplete at best.

Here are a few things to think about in understanding the judiciary as a shaper of social policy. First, in the United States, at least, courts must perform their interpretative magic on a concrete case, a dispute in which at least two parties have an interest at stake and go to court to establish which interest shall prevail under the law. In short, the courts cannot act on abstract issues. In many European countries the situation is quite the opposite: judicial decisions *can* be made in the abstract, absent any legislation, pending or otherwise, or absent any concrete controversy between interested parties. The policy varies worldwide: for example, in Britain the courts have no power of judicial review of legislation.[14] Second, courts can shape and frame social policy in regard to administrative rulings as well as legislation—administrative rules are interpretations made by public officials about how and when legislation is to be applied in concrete cases.

Finally, practitioners must understand the attitude taken by the courts toward social science and topics such as experimental psychology—an attitude social workers may find surprising; in fact the courts only reluctantly accept such findings.[15] Webster says that the courts are on unfamiliar ground in dealing with testimony of this kind, and that its plausibility is ". . . never taken for granted as is medicine or law itself. . . ."[16] Whereas some might not agree, Webster is probably correct that there are very few unequivocal social science findings and that because those few quickly find their way into common knowledge, they lose any potential status as scientific conclusions. Not only that, the typical social science finding accounts only for parts of the variance in the data so that individual variability is always an alternative explanation. That phenomenon creates a big problem because always and everywhere the court is concerned with unique, individual cases, not averages; the opposing legal counsel can always argue away the data of social science on the basis that her or his client is simply "the" plausible exception to the general case.

In court, human service personnel often make ambiguous responses, giving "it depends" answers because they are trained to make conditional responses.

However, courts want "the truth," definite answers, a categorical yes or no;[17] therefore, courts do not take social science findings or social workers' testimony seriously if either is offered in the context of "it depends" answers.

The power of the judiciary to shape social policy is embedded in its present power to review legislation and the decisions of public officials. That power was established in the 1800s by Chief Justice John Marshall, in his opinion justifying the majority ruling of the U.S. Supreme Court in *Marbury v. Madison,* [18] which is the cornerstone of U.S. administrative law. Marshall was concerned with (1) preserving the principle of strict limitations to government invasion of private affairs (thus the Marshall court ruled that the government couldn't *always* intervene) *and* with (2) constraining legislative majorities from changing the U.S. constitution outside the means provided for by the constitution itself (a constitutional convention, state-by-state ratification of new provisions, or modifications of old ones). Marshall's fundamental guiding principle was that the direct and current will of the people regarding laws and government must always be served. In part he feared that legislative alliances did not always represent the will of the people. On the other hand, judicial review was one possible way to remedy the problem when legislatures went so far that they intervened in private affairs in ways that were contrary to the constitutionally established rights of citizens.[19] Hence the Marshall court also ruled that in principle the court *could* intervene in private affairs, and so it became possible for the U.S. Supreme Court to concern itself with abortion—with what goes on even *inside* a citizen's body.

A Simple Framework for Examining Judicial Decisions

A few basic concepts (an analytic framework) will be of use in understanding the nature of judicial decisions as they bear on public policy of the kind that is of interest to human service and social workers. The following sections describe four analytic concepts that B. C. Canon thinks are useful in that regard:

1. Negating earlier legislative processes
2. Determining the type and effect of social policy to which a judicial decision pertains
3. Understanding the degree to which precedents are altered
4. Examining specificity of judicial decisions[20]

Negation of the Legislative Process: Canon suggests that if we want to think about how a new judicial decision affects public social policy, the first thing we ought to consider is ". . . the degree to which the policies adopted (by the court) negate those constructed (earlier) through strict democratic (legislative) processes."[20] In other words, Canon thinks that to properly appreciate the weight or importance of a new judicial decision, it is essential to know *whether and the extent to which it is a change away from whatever was directly legislated by a sitting or elected assembly* (e.g., the Congress, state legislatures, city councils). Marshall's original concern about judicial activism was that a group of judges (appointed, remember, not necessarily elected) might make public policy that bound and constrained citizens who had not directly elected them. For Marshall, the principle to be served was that the authority to govern was derived from the free consent of the governed. So in examining any judicial decision we must answer Canon's first question: "To what extent is this decision a departure from the public social policy enacted by a freely elected legislative assembly?" It is an interesting issue precisely because it demonstrates the interplay among the judiciary, the executive, and the legislative branches of government.

One good example is the U. S. Supreme Court decision in *O'Connor v. Donaldson*,[21] a case that marked the first time a Supreme Court decision recognized the legitimacy of the courts' involvement in activities that earlier legislation clearly had defined to be the exclusive domain of psychiatrists (*O'Connor v. Donaldson*, 1975).[22] What is relevant here is that up to the moment of the Supreme Court's decision, state statutes had clearly assigned to clinicians—psychiatrists in particular—the professional discretion to continue to confine citizens and determine when, where, how much, and what kind of psychiatric treatment was needed. A 48-year-old Florida man, Kenneth Donaldson, was committed to the Chattahoochee State Hospital at the request of his parents. Some fifteen years later Donaldson and his friends were still trying to obtain his freedom. They did so over the objections of his psychiatrist, who did not find Donaldson dangerous to himself or others; nor was Donaldson receiving treatment that he could not have gotten as an outpatient. At issue was that Donaldson was deprived of his liberty as a free citizen (a basic due process, constitutional, Bill of Rights issue), and the concern of the court was whether he was dangerous. Was he competent enough to avoid "the hazards of freedom," and could he receive the same treatment outside the hospital—all of which are conditions that might mitigate the citizen's right to liberty. The court decided that indeed he could and in doing so the *O'Connor v. Donaldson* court decision has fundamentally changed that public social policy so that

> . . . no longer can the professional base his decisions as to the most appropriate treatment modality solely on clinical grounds. He must become cognizant of such issues as whether the patient will be viewed as dangerous by a judge or jury, whether the recommended program will be considered adequate treatment or even treatment at all, and whether he will be considered liable for denying the patient his constitutional rights if he continues to hold him in the hospital because he considers him dangerous if a future court hearing finds the patient not dangerous.[22]

Notice how this court decision changed the usual relationships between the legislative and executive branches of government, which implement legislation. The court ruled that prior legislation was unconstitutional and required the administrative branch (in this case public officials and professionals—probably psychiatrists employed by the state hospital system, usually a state mental health or institutional service—in the employ of government) to follow the court order rather than the legislation.

Type and Effect of Policy Concerned: The second basis on which to evaluate a judicial decision with social policy relevance, says Canon, is the type of social policy the decision concerns and its practical effects on operating procedure and policy. This criterion will give direction to our inquiry about the practical effects of the judicial decision. The courts can and do make social policy of two types: (1) due process or procedural policy and (2) substantive policy. The type discussed above created by the judiciary concerns what we might call procedural issues. *Procedural policy* has to do with rights ultimately derived—indirectly or directly—from the Bill of Rights of the U.S. Constitution: for example, all citizens have a right to a fair trial, an opportunity to confront witnesses, be informed of charges against them, and so on. These rights apply in particular ways to social policies and the associated administrative procedures constructed by the executive branch of government by means of which assorted actions are taken and various benefits are distributed to citizens.

Goldberg v. Kelley, referred to earlier in this chapter, is a leading example here of how the judiciary creates operational social policy: in *Goldberg,* the U. S. Supreme Court held that once a benefit is legislated for citizens and administratively granted to them, that interest constitutes a type of property to which due process rights apply. Thus, in this decision the Court created for Mrs. Goldberg (and others who follow her) a substantive right to this welfare benefit. When welfare benefits are interpreted in this light it is clear that not all of them can be withdrawn by the simple act of administrative discretion. In fact, this judicial decision establishes that once welfare benefits are granted, to withdraw them after the fact the government must provide procedural rights: that is, the client/beneficiary must get advance notice of a hearing in which the action will be reviewed; furthermore, the client/beneficiary has a right to appear and argue his or her point of view, have benefit of counsel, the opportunity to confront witnesses, and so on.

The Supreme Court decided that Mrs. Goldberg had not been given such a hearing and ordered the (Texas) Department of Welfare to do so. Note that in addition to other constraints on their application, these procedural rights do not apply to all beneficiaries or to all benefit programs. Those issues will be discussed later in Chapter 8 on administrative and service-delivery systems. *Goldberg* is an important type of judicially created social policy if only because it obliges public organizations that administer benefits to establish fair hearing systems with precisely these kind of features.[23] Those features are neither trivial from the client's point of view—because they can restore benefits that were illegally or unjustly terminated—nor trivial from the organizations point of view—because they are expensive and complicated to administer.

In summary then, analysis of a judicial decision as a social policy document should always include clarification about whether the issue at hand is one that concerns substantive policy or due process (procedural) issues. It should also include an examination of the practical effects on organizational operating policy and procedures (such as the need to add to or modify fair hearing features as discussed above).

Judicial Precedents: The *degree to which the earlier court decisions are altered* is a different consideration from what kind of judicial decisions are made and how they affect social policy. In looking at degree, attention is not on legislation but on legal precedent, that is, on prior court decisions. Remember that in contrast to European judicial systems, the U.S. legal system as a rule is heavily oriented to and guided by earlier court decisions (precedents). So in principle, the greater the departure from prior court decisions, the more we ought to consider a judicial decision to be important, all other things being equal. Let us take as an example the 1969 decision of the U.S. Supreme Court, which found that state laws were unconstitutional in using a period of state residence as an entitlement rule for welfare benefits. Prior to this decision all states had very stringent residence requirements (usually a year) for a person to be entitled to a state welfare benefit (remember that no *federally* administered programs ever had such requirements). For almost two hundred years, local courts had repeatedly supported the legality of state residence requirements as a condition for expenditure of state funds for welfare benefits. In fact, this provision has its roots in the British Poor-Law system.

Residence requirements created all sorts of problems for poor and low-income citizens, many of whom were necessarily mobile and who qualified for welfare benefits but were not state residents. Consider what a hardship that might be if, for example, unemployed auto workers left Michigan with their families to go to Nebraska to look for work—perhaps an economically rational and otherwise virtuous idea. If they needed welfare benefits until the first check from the new job arrived, they would be out of luck—not because they didn't need it but because they hadn't lived in Nebraska for a year. In short, the Supreme Court ruled that such state laws are unconstitutional because they hinder the free movement of persons, a constitutionally protected right. Furthermore, labor must have the ability to move freely in order for the economic wheels of the country to grind efficiently. From the day of the Court's decision, states cannot lawfully deny access to welfare benefits simply on grounds of the applicant's residency.[24] In this decision the Supreme Court overturned 150 years of its own precedent (and perhaps 600 years of British Poor Law) as well as those of the lower courts in denying the right of states to terminate or deny welfare benefits solely on this basis.

It is an important example because it reveals that not only are abstract issues of freedom and legal rights at stake, but current and *concrete* agency operations are also at issue. Since the decision state welfare administrators not only must take the necessary administrative means to stop implementation but also must prepare budget estimates of what costs the Court's decision will impose on the state's welfare programs. For example, consider how eliminating the residency requirement would inevitably add more beneficiaries to a state's welfare roll—especially in California and Arizona, which have high worker in-migration rates on account of healthy employment markets and an attractive climate. The other side of the in-migration coin, of course, is that it reduces the welfare budget of other states. An influx of workers will benefit a state's economy, but a side effect is increased demand on general assistance and indigent medical care funds.

Inevitably, some workers will arrive without adequate funds to see them (and their families) through to actual employment or they will suffer medical and other disasters that deplete their resources. Such workers are "between jobs" and more than likely are uncovered by either unemployment or medical insurance. One substantive consequence at stake here is that the Court made public social policy that will effectively increase citizens' taxes.

By now, you might already have observed that another issue is relevant here: taxation without representation (remember, the Supreme Court is only an appointive, not an elective office).

Parameters for Agency Discretion: The fourth consideration in analyzing judicial decisions that influence public social policy is what Canon calls the specificity of the policy altered, that is, *the degree to which a judicial decision establishes policy itself rather than leaving discretion to other agencies or individuals.* It is clear that with reference to the residence requirements, the Supreme Court left *no* discretion to state administrators—the court order simply forbade use of this kind of entitlement rule. An example of how agencies are endowed with discretion is found in the Federal Appeals Court decision of the 1980s which forbade the Social Security Administration (SSA) to use its psychiatric classification as a basis for awarding or denying mental disability benefits.[25] It also ordered SSA to develop a new one based on more contemporary thinking. That instance is a clear example of the Court's leaving the discretion about the specific policy rule to the administrative agency and acknowledging the agency's competence and resources to do so.

Other examples abound, but one of the most extreme is *Wyatt v. Stickney,* a 1972 federal court order that established detailed standards of care that actually redefined public policy regarding institutionalized mental patients in the state of Alabama.[26] In deciding what has come to be called "the right-to-treatment rule," the Court determined that Mr. Wyatt did indeed have such a right, and did *not* place discretion with Alabama's mental health program administrators to decide what treatment had to consist of. The Wyatt standards have never been overturned. Not only did the Court mandate standards of care but it appointed a Court administrator for the state mental hospital in question, a magistrate or master responsible only to the Court, to enforce those standards. Part of the lesson of the *Wyatt* decision is about the limits of judicial activism, i.e., the big problem courts have in actually enforcing such detailed policy and program provisions.

Using the Canon Framework to Analyze Judicial Decisions That Create or Alter Social Policy

This section looks at some other examples that reveal how Canon's framework can help analyze particular court decisions. The issue of termination of parental rights is a good example for this purpose. Almost all states have statutes about terminating parental rights in cases of child abandonment. Widely varied, they are useful because they demonstrate how different state courts develop both very different and very similar kinds of social policies on this inherently private family matter. Here the long arm of the state intrudes into the very heart of the family, determining in the last analysis such a basic issue as who shall and who shall not remain a member of a family group. Traditionally, courts have relied on common-law criteria to make this determination—whether the parent provided materially for the child, or whether the parent was abusive, for example. These criteria proceed from what is taken to be "ordinary common sense," that is, socially inarguable standards for parental conduct. Of course the social world is a very different place these days, far removed from the simplicity of a tightly knit and traditional agrarian society upon whose long-established traditions common law is built. Small nuclear families, geographic mobility, and personal catastrophes such as marital breakup or drug addiction were not a part of the reality of those times; hence, common law does not speak to these contemporary realities. Therefore, the judiciary must consider criteria from other sources in applying its broad discretion in determining whether parental behavior is an indicator of intent to abandon or an indicator that parental responsibility should be terminated.

In terminating parental rights based on concepts that are beyond common-law traditions, courts must of necessity create new public social policy (negate earlier legislation). This is done in the name of public interest, for it is precisely the public's interest that courts are obligated to serve. In terms of parental rights, what is at stake is not only the private rights and interests of the child and the parents (and the family kin group), but the public interest in terms of guarding the integrity of a future citizen's (the child's) developmental life, avoiding public expenditures for foster care, ensuring that the child has not only a family identity to carry into adult life but a family or kin group that will socialize the child to dominant values.[27]

For example, a Connecticut court terminated the rights of the parents of three minor children because the parents failed to ". . . maintain a reasonable degree of interest, concern or responsibility as to the welfare of (their) child. . . ."[28] The Connecticut statute gave only the most general definition of abandonment: ". . . the parents' failure to maintain a reasonable degree of interest, concern or responsibility as to the welfare of their child. . . ." This court was forced to define it more concretely. Note the many very different, perhaps even opposing, interpretations that could be given this abstract definition. For example, some might define church attendance or corporal punishment as a necessary ingredient of "assuming parental responsibility" whereas others might not. Ultimately the Chignon court decided that ". . . maintaining a reasonable degree of interest . . ." means that a parent had to have continuous, face-to-face contacts with the child over time and thus this mother's average three visits per year to the child, infrequent phone calls and letters, and moving to a neighboring state (Maryland) did not meet that standard. In applying Canon's concepts for the analysis of judicial decisions, we first must think about the degree to which this decision departs from a directly legislated social policy. It is clear that the legislation (state statute) concerned with this matter leaves the crucial operating term "maintaining a reasonable degree of interest [in the child]" entirely undefined. The court then sets about defining the term and giving it concrete meaning, in effect acting to create law independent of the elected legislature. On that account and following Canon's advice, we would take note in our analysis that *In re Chignon* is surely an important court decision with direct impact on citizens in that it sets the basic policy by which state and other social agencies deal with citizens.

In analyzing this judicial decision the second thing we would consider is whether the legal issue at hand is one that concerns substantive policy or due process or procedural issues (social policy type and effect). It would be a due process or procedural issue if, for example, the case concerned *the way* in which the hearing to terminate parental rights was conducted, whether the parent had competent legal counsel, received timely notification of the hearing, had a chance to confront witnesses, and so on. As the reader can see, none of those were points at issue; rather, the issue was a substantive one: how should child abandonment be defined? This tells us that it isn't the judicial or agency procedures that will have to be reshaped but the way in which the agency decides which of its custodial children will be considered for termination of parental rights and, perhaps, placement in adoption with other kin groups.

In analyzing this judicial decision, the third thing Canon would have us consider is the degree to which earlier court decisions are altered. Unfortunately, the material in which this decision was reported does not give us that information.[29] To complete our analysis of this judicial decision we will have to locate the decision of this Connecticut court (with the help of our nearest and friendliest law school librarian) and review it for what it has to say about other earlier court decisions on related matters.

The fourth consideration, according to Canon, is the degree to which a judicial decision establishes policy itself rather than leaving discretion to other agencies or individuals. In regard to this decision, we can answer in the affirmative. Indeed the court went to great pains to establish policy itself and did not leave the matter of defining abandonment to other agencies nor to the discretion of individual state officials. Note that this is more than just an abstract point: in making a judgment about this analytic criterion, officials are alerted to the fact that the law will not sustain case decisions they make based simply on their own ad hoc criteria. An effective and efficient bureaucracy will take steps to know the law and incorporate it into its operating policy. On the question of abandonment, the above definition will serve as the important benchmark for the state child protective agency that must decide daily which parents of children in its custody must be severed from their parental rights. A good bureaucracy knows that it needs the specifics of such court decisions in order to decide which children are candidates for eventual adoption. This knowledge avoids fruitless ventures into court by agencies pursuing terminations of parental rights for parents who fail to meet the new court-established policy criteria about what parental behaviors constitute neglect or abandonment. Naturally a child protective agency can consciously pursue cases in court in an effort to extend or otherwise modify this judicial criterion but surely it would be best advised to do that knowingly, choosing precedents/cases in which it would be certain to have the strongest reasons to argue for some particular judicial innovation the agency favors.

Another case (this one in Kansas) created a new social policy when the court upheld termination of paternal rights of a father for the purpose of placing the child for adoption on the basis of his negligence as a parent in attending to the child.[30] Again the court had to make a decision as in regard to what counted as negligence. The decision was based on a Kansas statute, which specified that the court could grant adoptions without the consent of the natural parents where the parent failed or refused to ". . . assume parental duties for two consecutive years prior to the filing of the adoption petition. . . ."[31] The court decided that the parental effort over a two-year period was insufficient and therefore constituted parental abandonment. In this case efforts had been limited to Christmas and birthday gifts and a few telephone calls but no financial support, written communication, or other form of emotional support. The court created new social policy in the sense of deciding that absence of financial support, coupled with lack of emotionally significant contact, constituted parental abandonment for any practical purpose and so termination of parental rights was in order. The court was obliged to make such a determination because legislation did not define fulfillment of parental duty so that the Kansas supreme court had no alternative but to exercise its own judicial discretion. Because U.S. courts are guided by decisions of courts in other jurisdictions as well as by earlier court decisions and by higher court decisions, that will influence courts in other states.

Finally the West Virginia Supreme Court of Appeals created new social policy in that state when it upheld the parental rights of a father.[32] Whereas West Virginia Code §48-4-3 provides for termination of parental rights in the instance of abandonment, it does not contain a definition of same. The West Virginia court held that the prospective adoptive parents had *not* shown that the father had abandoned the child because failure to pay child support was not by itself sufficient to constitute child abandonment. The father had sent gifts, cards, money, telephoned repeatedly, paid for health insurance, and written the mother seeking visitation (subsequent to her refusal to allow visitation as a means of prompting him to pay child support).[33] In analyzing this decision following Canon's advice, we would conclude that the West Virginia court had indeed ventured beyond what the elected legislature had decided in such matters.

Canon's second analytic concept (type and effect of social policy) obliges us to consider whether what is at issue here is a substantive matter or a due process right. Clearly it is the former, because, once again, the concern of the court is with what constitutes child abandonment. Note that the father did not contest the procedures by which a lower court had arrived at its decision; rather, the entire focus is on what should be considered as child abandonment and whether the father's behavior conformed to that definition.

Using Canon's third analytic concept, (degree) we are led to conclude that in fact the West Virginia Supreme Court did not venture far from earlier court precedents but based their decision on them, citing an earlier court decision that provided precisely the definition of abandonment upon which they could base their work. This earlier case in a *local* (lower) court in effect defined abandonment as failure to provide support and maintenance, visit the child or exercise parental rights, responsibilities, and authority.[34] Notice that the West Virginia legislature could have (but did not) incorporate the standards for termination of parental rights from this case into legislation on the matter. Canon's analytic concept yields practical information because (1) once it is known, as in this case, that these criteria for abandonment are part of a whole set of precedents, they become even more important as operating policy in the sense that policy implementers have some certainty that the criteria will have continuity over time; and (2) the decision came (partly) from a state supreme court, which ultimately binds the lower courts with which agencies and officials have to deal.

Using Canon's fourth analytic concept we can conclude that, as in the earlier case law cited, the West Virginia Supreme Court did not delegate to other agencies or officials the responsibility to make general policy or case decisions but took responsibility to create their own. On that basis it is, as in the earlier cases cited, clear guidance to the official bureaucracy that later cases in which termination of parental rights is an issue will have to be forwarded to the court on the basis of precisely these (and not other) criteria for abandonment. In summary, then, from a quick review of only these cases it seems quite clear that in at least three states (Connecticut, Kansas, West Virginia), operating public social policy parental rights may be severed when there is very little direct or significant contact between the parent and child but that failure to pay child support is not alone a sufficient ground.

SUMMARY

This chapter has shown how the power of the judiciary to shape social policy is embedded in its present power to review legislation and the decisions of public officials. Judicial capacity can influence social policy of two types: (1) policy about due process and fundamental citizen rights and (2) policy about substantive matters—who gets what, when, in what form and under what conditions, and how benefits are financed. Some basic considerations about the judiciary were presented. For example, the judiciary must consider a concrete case that represents an issue between the vital interests of at least two citizens; courts can shape and frame social policy in regard to administrative rulings as well as legislation; and the courts view with reluctance the findings of social science and experimental psychology.

Based on the work of B. C. Canon, a conceptual framework for the analysis of judicial decisions with social policy relevance was given. This framework is founded on advising practitioners to be alert to four basic considerations:

1. The extent to which the judicial decision is a departure from legislation passed by a freely elected assembly
2. The extent to which the decision concerns a due process or procedural issue, or a substantive policy issue

3. The extent to which the decision represents a departure from prior judicial precedent
4. The extent to which the court delegated the responsibility to other agencies or officials or took responsibility to make general policy to create their own.

NOTES

1. J. Handler, *Protecting the Social Services Client* (New York: Academic Press, 1979), p. 31.
2. *Tarasoff v. The Regents of the University of California,* Sup. Ct. of California (July 1, 1976).
3. D. Besharov, *The Vulnerable Social Worker* (Silver Spring, MD: National Association of Social Workers, 1985), pp. 2–9.
4. E. Gellhorn, *Administrative Law and Process* (St. Paul, MN: West Publishing Company, 1974).
5. D. E. Chambers, "Policy Weaknesses and Political Interventions," *Social Service Review,* 42:87–99 (1987).
6. I am indebted to David Brown, J.D., of the legal staff of the Kansas Appeals Court, who kindly read this material and supplied this inviting comment.
7. M. MacDonald, *Food Stamps and Income Maintenance* (New York: Academic Press, 1974), pp. 2–4.
8. H. W. Ehrmann, *Comparative Legal Cultures* (Englewood Cliffs, NJ: Prentice-Hall, 1976), p. 138.
9. *Brown v. Board of Education,* 347 U.S. 483 (1954).
10. See note 26.
11. D. E. Chambers, "The Reagan Administration Welfare Retrenchment Policy: Terminating Social Security Benefits for the Disabled," *Policy Studies Review,* 2:207–15, 234–35 (1985).
12. *Goldberg v. Kelley.* See note 1.
13. J. Notes, "The Least Dangerous Branch, *Revue de Droit de McGill,* 34:1025–28 (1989).
14. C. N. Tate, "Introductory Notes," *Policy Studies Review,* 19:[1]76–80 (1990).
15. C. D. Webster, "On Gaining Acceptance: Why the Courts Accept Only Reluctantly Findings from Experimental and Social Psychology," *International Journal of Law and Psychiatry,* 7:407–14 (1984).
16. Page 410 in Note 15.
17. Page 412 in Note 15.
18. *Marbury v. Madison* [citation not provided].
19. D. W. Jackson, "A Conceptual Framework for the Comparative Analysis of Judicial Review," *Policy Studies Review,* 19:161–71 (1991).
20. B. C. Canon, "A Framework for the Analysis of Judicial Activism." In *Supreme Court Activism and Restraint,* edited by S. C. Halpern and C. M. Lamb (Lexington, MA: Lexington Books, 1982). I have chosen to use only some of Canon's analytical dimensions, omitting others when they seemed less relevant to the common practice of human service and social workers.
21. *O'Connor v. Donaldson,* 422 U.S. 563 (1975).
22. L. E. Kopolow, "A Review of Major Implications of the *O'Connor v. Donaldson* Decision," *American Journal of Psychiatry,* 133:[4]379–83 (1976).

23. Although the Social Security Act required fair hearings for all programs funded with federal money, the Social Security legislation did not specify their mandatory features.

24. D. E. Chambers, "Residence requirements for welfare benefits," *Social Work*, 14:[4]29–37 (1969).

25. *Mental Health Association of Minnesota v. Schweiker*, 554 Fed. Supp., 157 (D.C. Minn., 1983).

26. M. Levine, "The Role of Special Master in Institutional Reform Litigation," *Law and Policy*, 8:275–321 (1986).

27. What will be lacking in using this issue as an example is the history of its legislative politics in the initial framing of state statutes on termination of parental rights. This issue is seldom an occasion for high profile political compromise, nor are the constituent (interest) groups either obvious or very visible. Naturally parents themselves have a stake here, but the activist sentiments of most parents would not be engaged by a legislative proposal on an issue that for them is bound to be only potential, not actual. On that account the political issues tend to be much more ideological, dividing legislators along lines of commitment to either the rights of parents or the rights of children.

28. *In Re Chignon*, 1989, Connecticut General Statutes, §17–34a(b)(1).

29. Legal Analysis: "Infrequent Contacts with the Child, Grounds to Terminate Parental Rights in Abandonment Cases," 8 ABA *Juvenile and Child Welfare Reporter*, 157–58 (December 1989).

30. Matter of Adoption of B.C.S., 777 P.2d 776 (Kan. 1989).

31. Kansas Statutes Ann. §59-2101(a)(1).

32. *In the Matter of Adoption of Schoffstall*, 368 S.E.2nd 720 (W.Va. 1988).

33. Page 164 in Note 19.

34. Page 158 in Note 29.

PART TWO

A Style of Policy Analysis for the Practical Public Policy Analyst

... providence never intended to make the management of public affairs a mystery, to be comprehended only by a few persons of sublime genius, of which there seldom are three born in an age

Jonathan Swift (Gulliver's Travels)

INTRODUCTION: ANALYZING POLICY AND PROGRAM DESIGN

The first part of this book closed by showing how conclusions from the social problem analysis and the analysis of historical and judicial context might indicate for the practitioner/analyst how particular features of a policy or program were (or should have been) shaped. The next step is to look closely at an actual operating policy or program design to identify its major features. Thus, the first section of Chapter 4 will present a way of "looking closely at" (of describing analytically) social policies and programs. It proceeds by first searching for the six fundamental elements in social policy and program designs. These will be called *operating characteristics* and are fundamental in the sense that they can be found explicitly or implicitly, in one form or another, in every social policy or program. Each element will be discussed, examples will be given, and concepts and classifications will be presented so as to sensitize the observer to their various forms. Once these elements are identified, a judgment is made about each operating characteristic so as to answer the most basic question: Are these program or policy features "good"?

In Part Two will appear a separate chapter on how to describe and evaluate each of these operating characteristics.

CHAPTER 4

An Overview of a Style of Policy Analysis

A VALUE-CRITICAL APPROACH TO SOCIAL POLICY AND PROGRAM ANALYSIS

This chapter is intended to sort out several important issues that lay the groundwork for understanding the perspective on social policy and program analysis taken in this book and the basic tasks the practitioner/analyst will confront. Furthermore, this chapter will prepare the reader for a detailed description of those tasks by discussing the distinction between the value-analytic and the value-critical methods of policy analysis. Arguments will be presented for the value-critical style for the use of social work and human service practitioners, the audience for which this book is intended.

A number of evaluation criteria, essential for that style, will be presented and argued in this chapter. Some are argued as essential and others as optional but illustrative of how personal value preferences of the analyst can (and must) be taken into account. Note that these evaluation criteria are important because they will be used throughout the succeeding chapters of part 2, one chapter devoted to each important program/policy operating characteristic. Chapter 4 will close with a discussion of the important distinctions among programs that offer social services, public social utilities, and hybrids (those offering both simultaneously).

The reader should be alert to the fact that much of what will be said about operating characteristics is simply to show a way to generate an adequate description of a social policy of program. Martin Rein calls this endeavor the *analytic-descriptive* method of policy analysis.[1] The reader should notice that an analysis that proceeds (as advocated here) by dividing the whole of a social policy or program into parts labeled "operating characteristics" and social problem/historical/judicial contexts

> . . . takes as its task dividing an accepted whole into logically consistent categories; the intellectual challenge is to identify common features that are (or aren't) congruent or consistent with each other. . . .

But for the practical public policy analyst, description is never more than a means to an end because the most important step in analyzing program and policy features is to arrive at a judgment about them, i.e., whether they are, in a particular sense, "good," "right," or "appropriate." Policy analysis that remains at a descriptive level, leaving this question unanswered, cannot be a complete, much less a "good," analysis. Until analysts have attended to that task, analysis is incomplete. Coming to judgment is always a value-laden enterprise and a policy/program practitioner cum analyst should not apologize for that fact; a judgment that would try to be otherwise—somehow value-neutral, in the popular idiom—is hollow in that human judgment must use value criteria as a foundation. Martin Rein calls this *value-critical policy analysis* and uses that phrase to distinguish it from the analytic-descriptive approach described above. The value-critical approach stands this latter approach on its head, begins with parts and tries to understand the whole that they constitute, the whole that does (or should) integrate them.

The method of analysis presented in this book advocates using *both* approaches serially. It is analytic-descriptive in proceeding first to instruct the reader how to do close description by *disaggregating* the social policy or program into parts (operating characteristics and the three contexts) and examining them one by one. The method in this book thus follows Rein in advocating the crucial second step, which consists in critically evaluating all of the parts, using certain strong, value-based criteria by which to make judgments of their goodness, fitness, and appropriateness. In some ways the analytic-descriptive approach is a way to see clearly how things *should* work. Using Rein's phraseology, because in the real world things almost never work out as planned, this second-step, value-critical approach then throws the conventional view (how a program should work) into question and adopts a critical and skeptical view of how programs *actually* work—or don't work.[2] It seeks to uncover shortcomings, inconsistencies in logic, and ambiguities in the everyday program operations. Much of the policy analysis done by political scientists and public administrators does not—in fact cannot—do that, because their method of analysis is so focused on explaining how things *are*, rather than how things *could be* from some value-committed point of view.

Michael Howlett's summary of contemporary theories that attempts to account for public policymaker's decisions about the form in which welfare transfer benefits will be delivered to citizens is a good example of policy analysis that stops short of the value-critical appraisal.[3] At issue is whether poor people's need for low-cost housing will be relieved by benefits given in the form of cash (e.g., housing allowances for AFDC), tax breaks (e.g., tax credits for interest on home loans), loan guarantees (e.g., guaranteed home loans to investors in low-income rental housing for the poor), or in-kind transfers (e.g., construction of low-income public housing). Howlett's review shows that these theories leave no room for consideration of benefit forms in relation to what they are or are not likely to do for beneficiaries and stops short of considering how cash, as opposed to in-kind housing benefits, extends different kinds of advantages and disadvantages to beneficiaries. For example, these theories consider things like "complexity of operations," "level of public visibility," and "chances of failure." The point here is that the theories that Howlett's broad sample represents (from three countries, no less) cannot uncover policy short-comings or throw the conventional view into question, simply because they are not asking the kind of question that would move discussion in that direction. The reader should think of how the questions generated by concern with "complexity of operations" or "level of public visibility" *cannot* encompass how the form of benefit is positive or negative for the beneficiary. (Such factors as "level of intrusiveness" and "adaptability across users" are listed but the interest in them is relevant only to what problems those factors pose for administration, not for clients.) One can say that these theories cannot be used in service of a value-critical agenda because at their most successful they can only explain the given present situation and cannot cast its desirability against the issue of what any benefit form does or does not do for recipients. Although that fact might be defended on the basis that the theories are attempts at "value-free" or (at least) value-neutral social science, that won't do; examination of the details of how those theories concentrate on factors like those listed above points in the direction of a strong bias toward the concerns of the organization and its administration—what is on the minds of such folks are things like "complexity of operations," "level of public visibility" and the like. And in that sense, such theories can be said to prioritize organizational over consumer/beneficiary issues.[4]

Value-critical analysis seeks to ferret out policy problems using an explicit set of value-based evaluation criteria the function of which is to alert the analyst to specific and problematic policy and program features. In this and later chapters we will discuss those value-laden criteria, one set for each operating characteristic. Value-critical analysis seeks to make explicit the underlying values expressed by the social policy or program in its implemented and operational form. In just that sense value-critical policy analysis seeks to make explicit the "frames of reference" used by implementers of policy—middle managers and street-level bureaucrats among them.[5] The analyst should expect to encounter conflict and divergence between frames of reference of two opposing groups: (1) originating legislators or high-level administrators and (2) middle managers and practitioners. This kind of policy analysis is similar to what Habermas calls "cross-frame discourse."[6] Out of this dialectic implications for action arise and it is precisely the intention and purpose of this method of policy analysis to generate action from its results. Policy analysis cannot be content with creating abstract academic exercises. The hope is to present a method that will result in reader discontent with the old and a strong motive to create something new and better. The discontent should arise from the analyst's encounter with the operating frameworks of those who actually implement a policy or program. To the reader/analyst who is prepared for it, that encounter reveals the marvelous dialectic between what the legislature, history, and judiciary fondly hope for and the actual.[7] And of course, the practical policy analyst should anticipate conflict between these and his or her own frame of reference. The point of this analytic method is not simply to criticize but to develop a better (more useful-for-clients) way of doing things.

Actually Rein points out yet another approach to analyzing social policies and programs (one this book will not emphasize) called the *value-committed* approach. This approach

> . . . starts with a strongly held position about how things *ought* to be . . . [and why they aren't] and then works out the implications of this commitment for action. . . . Some Marxists [and many social activists], but definitely not all, fall into this category . . .[8]

On several counts, value commitment is an important dimension for social work and human service practitioners in that there are moments when they can be plausibly called by their professional commitments to all *three* of these approaches. A calling to "activism" is recognizable in the roots of the social work profession—a calling to actively pursue particular strongly held positions based on fundamental professional values about how things ought to be as against a very different real world. Note that in following that course, however, the policy discourse will then *not* be about operating details of policies and programs but about more fundamental social and structural problems—perhaps, for example, about how the whole broad social issue is wrongly conceived from the outset. Such arguments turn out to focus ultimately on values.

Under certain circumstances, a value-committed approach is irresistible. An example from Central America serves to clarify: from some particular value-committed points of view there is an inherent injustice in a society in which 95 percent of a nation's assets and income are received by 1 percent of its people, particularly in the face of unemployment rates of over 40 percent, a poverty rate which even by local standards approaches 50 percent, and a level of armed violence that makes death and civilian casualties a daily occurrence. For the value-committed analyst, then, the argument should *not* be whether a policy of in-kind benefits like governmental commodity distributions (beans, cheese, flour, or meal, for example) is the best way to keep people from starving (not that hunger isn't an important policy issue). Rather, for the value-committed practitioner the argument *should* be whether this kind of income maldistribution is basically just; the policy arguments should be over what is the best means to alter it. An appropriate comparison that expresses the futility of small-scale adjustments against a catastrophic environment is that it's like rearranging chairs on the deck of the sinking *Titanic* (an old and famous "unsinkable" Atlantic-crossing passenger ship that did indeed sink after an iceberg collision). Examples closer to home might be high-risk industries—coal mining, hard-rock mining, metal refining, lumber milling—or certain kinds of employees—migrant workers in fields sprayed with pesticides or workers involved in the production of nuclear power. For purposes of the value-committed approach, the argument *should not be* whether Workers Compensation benefits should be administered by a public or a private profit-making insurance system (as it is in most states) but about (1) whether some operations of high-injury industries should be permitted at all or (2) whether some industries produce injuries at such a high rate or level of seriousness that any Workers Compensation system design will be deficient. Or take another example: From a value-committed point of view and in the face of 15 percent poverty rates in the United States, one of wealthiest countries in the world, the social policy argument should not be about *which* measure of the poverty line is preferred, but about what is the maximum acceptable rate of poverty (*however measured*) in this country.

The value-committed approach will not take the world at face value but seek to impose its vision onto the world and change conditions so that they are more in keeping with the ideal world envisioned. Social workers and other human service practitioners need Rein's distinction among the three types of policy analysis in order to think clearly about which type they will opt for in any given situation. The decision is difficult because a number of questions must be weighed: "What is the 'real' state of the world with respect to the presenting social problem?" "How should the social problem be framed?" "What fundamental values are at stake?" "Is there plausible reason to believe that any audience exists to respond to the policy implications of a given activist approach to the social problem (that is, will the approach have any chance of success)?" Of course the same questions can and should be asked of any of the other types of policy analysis.

The merits and difficulties of the value-committed approach will not be discussed in detail here because it seems a better fit with pure political activism, which is beyond the scope of this book—although the professional practice of social work does include that aspect. The world needs all kinds of political activists, including those in the professions. The point here is that professional practice goes beyond exercise of strongly held ideological conviction. Certainly social work practice includes political activism, but the social worker who wears the policy analyst's hat cannot *simultaneously* wear the political activist's hat. In this style of policy analysis the two hats are mutually exclusive. Professional practitioners are called to commitment to a rationality that prizes alternative viewpoints and advocates taking them into account. They also are called to commitment to an objectivity that features multiple perspectives. However, *multiple perspectives are not a major feature of the value-committed approach because it assumes that the "truth" is already known and value choices are already made.* The profession is currently much enamored of practice using multiple perspectives about the human condition. So the value-critical approach has a nice fit with the current professional preoccupation in its emphasis on multiple perspectives on the human condition (Weick, 1987).

The value-critical approach also fits the current professional preoccupation in its assumption that no facts are independent of theories and value biases. Whereas certain kinds of facts are very unlikely to change, the value-critical approach takes the view that the *selection* of facts taken under consideration does vary with the theory used; the approach further posits that it is the very purpose of theory to highlight some facts and ignore (or suppress) others. Note that for the purpose of analysis the value-critical approach is, like all professions as a matter of fact, both conservative (in its view that the status quo might be worth saving) and radical (in calling the status quo into question).

The value-critical approach also has appeal because it can (and should be) grounded in practice experience. The questions practitioners raise are not just theoretical or just value-driven. In conducting the analysis of a social policy or program, social work and human service practitioners must bring to bear their own practice experience and that of others. Whereas clear value positions are an essential element in initiating the value-critical approach, such positions can be called into question on behalf of, for example, the experience and observations that other value positions are more beneficial or more relevant to clients' needs. For example, a practitioner might well be convinced that valuing a client's self-determination was the very highest priority in practice and that almost all social problems ought to be framed and social programs designed on the basis of what the problem or program did or didn't do in regard to this preferred value. However, if the practitioner is faced with clients who physically abuse children, then the danger to the child or the child's survival (precisely from the adult's exercise of personal autonomy) might quickly take first priority. Consider also that one valuational stance might set the practitioner in a very low-key, nonintrusive mode, while another might lead to strong interventionist strategies.

One element of the value-critical approach is that it requires "teasing out" the value biases and frames of reference that lie behind social problem analyses and their associated policy and program designs (ideology, causation, recall). It develops a useful skill in elucidating competing values and frames of reference, a skill practitioners might use when confronted with conflict at any level—personal, familial, organizational, communal, or political. Practitioners need to develop this skill to be able to sort out their own organizational world. After all, each practitioner conducts her or his practice surrounded by competing values and frames of reference. For example, as indicated earlier in this chapter, organizational administrators may have a frame of reference about implementing legislation or court mandates that differs completely from that of the practitioner (the street-level bureaucrat) whose frame of reference about the social program design and the social problem come from an entirely different world: street-corners, interacting families, or the corridors of public schools and hospitals. Part of the business of practice is to find some rationalization for practice behaviors or program designs to bridge these competing interests and frames of reference. Social work and human service practitioners at either administrative or direct service levels don't anymore "directly" implement legislation than do physicians "directly" implement medical care out of textbook solutions or Medicare, hospital, legal, even ecclesiastical regulations. Thus, one of the important and persuasive attributes of value-critical policy analysis is that it forces practitioners to analyze for multiple and competing values and frames of reference, to make hard choices among them and to take even their own frames and values into question as they confront the reality of both the social world in general, the world their clients live in, and the daily operating world of organizations, laws, and public expectations.

Still, there is a utility to all this ambiguity in public policy. Social workers and human service professionals need to realize that it is precisely the *lack of specificity* of legislation, court decisions, historical tradition, and organizational regulation that is, in some important sense, the source of their freedom to practice and remain faithful to their own values and within their own frames of reference. Where legislation and regulation is precise and specific, practitioners have no discretion and their tasks lie in direct implementation of, more or less, automated decision making. Although practitioners' freedom will be seriously restricted whenever it conflicts with or bursts the bonds of plausible relation to the general specification of legislation or regulation, nonetheless it is commonly the judgment of experienced practitioners that *there is almost always more freedom to practice at the limits of organizational rules and regulations than is ever used by most social work and human service practitioners.* The point is, practitioners can protect themselves as well as maximize their freedom to practice simply by having a keen awareness of the relationship between their own values and frame of reference about a social problem and the programmatic features designed to cope with it. A key part of the practitioner's task is to bridge the two, and it is both an offensive and defensive practice strategy to be prepared to do so. The general principle is that a practitioner who can give a rational account of the relationships between what she or he is doing and the various frameworks that administrative or political superiors are using, is less likely to experience a serious attack on their competence and autonomy. Martin Rein is very clear on this point:

> We more typically start with practice (action) and then design policies to justify what we do. The sequence is then from practice (action) to design to purpose. *Thus, policy rationalizes and legitimizes actions that arise from quite different processes....* (emphasis added).

The advice here is not to suggest that a seat-of-the-pants behavioral style is really the way social work or human service is best practiced but only to underscore that practitioners and organizations (and street-level bureaucrats) muddle through, work things out and try to do everything they can to be successful—then repeat what experience shows to be successful. Most likely they *did* begin with a guiding idea for practice but that idea was shaped by the lived realities (experiences) of both clients and helpers. (Conversations with practitioners in other professions will usually lead to the same conclusion.) Practitioners have their own "policy (and program design) positions"; they *must* have them to conduct a rational practice with clients. Whether they express them as such is variable, of course. The notion is that policy formed out of practice experience like this serves a useful function in helping to shape the resulting program and practice design basis into a more formal, more conscious product that meets three criteria:

1. It is more legitimate in the eyes of legitimating agencies, which fund and give the social and moral approbation necessary for practicing on behalf of vulnerable social groups.
2. It is more open to both control (in the sense of a desirable accountability) and change *of practitioners themselves*, hopefully for the better.

3. It creates a more honest stance from which to practice, relieving the practitioner and the organization from the necessity to take a stance as the rou-
   tinizing, bureaucratic implementer, the tool of higher powers.

Thus, this value-critical approach to policy and program analysis is advocated
here.

The major issue in this approach lies in locating and working with a set of
criteria by which to make the value-critical judgment. Particular sets of criteria
for each operating characteristic will now be advocated, criteria that seem to
be absolutely necessary (though probably not sufficient of course). Other, perhaps better, criteria could be proposed, certainly, but those proposed herein
will force the analyst to give attention to certain features of social policies and
programs that are absolutely essential if the analyst is to understand the
whole. It is left to the reader to ferret out the peculiar set of underlying, fundamental value biases in the criteria presented here. One such bias is the
assumption of rationality, that is, that the best social program and policy is the
one that is most rational in the sense of being logically and internally consistent—to wit, consistent with its history, with the judicial decisions that by law
it is obliged to follow, with whatever social problem analysis that has been set
forth (not, of course, necessarily that of others, the legislature or the organization hosting the program) but with *its own* carefully articulated, rationalized
social problem analysis, faithfully executed and taken seriously by practitioners and clients.

So, our list of evaluation criteria will begin with *whether the program and policy operating characteristics are consistent with the social problem analysis the
policy or program system claims*. It can be said that the solution to irrationality
or inconsistency of logic in a social problem analysis is not *necessarily* to change
the program features, but to change the social problem conception and its analysis. This is in line with two ideas: (1) Policy as well as social problem analysis
can emerge from practice, not always the other way around, and (2) theories are
not ultimate truth and should and must be shaped by practice and empirical
experience as well as abstractions.

The other evaluation criteria used here include traditional ones: equity, adequacy, and efficiency (originally developed for use in economics). Also included
are criteria that may be less familiar: trade-offs and access/coverage effects (as I
have labeled them). The reader will also note that whereas these criteria are
intended to be used for critical evaluation of *each and every one* of the various
operating characteristics, there are also subsets of criteria that are unique to *a
single* operating characteristic (e.g., merit for racial/ethnic diversity and program
overutilization and underutilization).

The section that follows will give a brief overview of how to do an analytic
description of policy and program using the six fundamental operating characteristics. It will then discuss how to do the value-critical aspect of the analysis,
using suggested evaluation criteria to judge the ultimate merit of the operating
characteristics.

The Policy and Program Analysis Process: An Overview of the Six Fundamental Operating Characteristics

Six operating characteristics form the cornerstone of every policy and program presented daily to citizens, program clients, and beneficiaries. It is these operating characteristics on which the practical social policy analyst ultimately will base judgments about a policy or program. Ordinary sources for information about them cannot always be relied upon; and, given the size and complexity of modern social welfare programs, agency staff members, administrators, and policy manuals are not always accurate or completely informed. The six operating characteristics to be discussed are as follows:

1. Goals and objectives
2. Forms of benefits or services delivered
3. Entitlement (eligibility) rules
4. Administrative or organizational structure for service delivery
5. Financing method
6. Interactions among the foregoing elements[9]

Why study these six rather than others? Because these are the six without which a social policy or program cannot be operated; that is, they are necessary to implement a program or policy system. It is simple enough to do a mental experiment to test out this idea: Suppose you have something very valuable to convey and you neither wish to bury it nor give it to kin or friends. How will you dispose of it? You will have to ask six questions so as to reach a decision.

1. What purpose or *goal* do you wish to achieve in giving this gift?
2. Given those goals, who is entitled to the gift?
3. In what *form* would the gift be given in that you could easily transform it into cash or some other gift?
4. Whom will you get to select who gets the gift and to *deliver* it?
5. Do you want to give the whole gift at once or just the interest earned from principal, or do you wish others to help with *financing* by putting up some of their own money?
6. If the gift is given in cash will recipient(s) spend it for the *purpose* intended?

These same choices have to be made whenever policies or programs for the general good are to be put into effect. In an ideal world, of course, no such choices are necessary because there is an unlimited supply of what everybody needs. Unfortunately, however, in our faulty paradise, a world in which it is *not* the case that everybody has enough, social welfare policy and programs are necessary. Absent an unlimited storehouse where money, goods, and services are in infinite supply, and where inefficiency and waste do not jeopardize resources, social policy and programs are necessary. Concern about efficiency and waste lies at the heart of the matter in regard to social welfare policy and program design because they are crucial to ability to cover human need.

Social policy is concerned with the six elements enumerated because, in the final analysis, they are the basis on which social policies and programs ration and distribute benefits and select beneficiaries and attempt to ensure that money, goods, and services are used efficiently, effectively, and without waste. Some public commentators remark sarcastically that social welfare policy and programs are futile because they attempt to bring paradise to an inherently imperfect world; the reality is quite the opposite—the benefits of paradise are self-selected, self-rationed, and occasioned by justice. *Social welfare policy is about selection, rationing, and the attempt to correct injustice.* Social welfare policy is about a concrete empirical world and the attempt to moderate its sometimes cruel and inhumane effects. We will talk more later about how the challenge to social policies and programs is to be successful in moderating one cruel effect without creating another, more cruel effect.

Table 4–1 lists two additional types of information for each operating characteristic: subtypes and evaluation criteria. When the practical policy analyst studies the operating characteristics of particular social welfare service and benefit systems, it becomes clear that there are only a limited number of ways in which those criteria are expressed; for example, only about a half-dozen (more or less) subtypes of entitlement or eligibility rules are apparent. That is not to say that an inventive mind couldn't think of others or that certain programs (domestic or foreign) might not have others. Column 2 of Table 4–1 summarizes the main subtypes for operating characteristics—for example, the main subtypes of forms of benefits are cash, commodities, personal social services, and so on. This summary provides a quick and handy reference for describing the main features of any social welfare service or benefit program. The subtypes listed in Table 4–1 are intended for use by the practical policy analyst who daily encounters a world full of new and old social programs and policies that he or she must evaluate in order to know whether they are useful to clients.

These subtypes are not mutually exclusive; that is, a particular social welfare program or policy may use more than one kind of entitlement rule or financing method. For example, most state Title XX programs that offer social services to various categories of citizens not only have a means test (in most states only those with incomes less than 125 percent of the state's average income are eligible for free services) but require (in most cases) the exercise of professional discretion—the potential consumer must have been referred for services by a professionally qualified person.

How each operating characteristic is evaluated is discussed in the following section.

Table 4–1.   Operating Characteristics, Basic Subtypes, and Evaluation Criteria for a Value-Critical Appraisal of Social Policy and Programs

Name of Operating Characteristic	Basic Subtypes or Concepts	Evaluation Criteria
Goals and objectives	1. Long term/short term 2. Manifest/latent 3. Abstract/concrete 4. Intermediate/ultimate	1. Concern with means, not end 2. Clarity, measurability, manipulability 3. Inclusion of performance standards/target group specifications 4. Fit of terms of objectives with social problem analysis: with problem definition, independent variables of causation, ideology regarding definitions of adequacy and equity 5. Analyst's evaluative perspective 6. Social control implications: fit with other evaluative criteria
Forms of benefit or service 1. General forms 2. Specific forms 3. Multiple and interrelated benefits	1. Personal social services (PSS) 2. Public social utilities (PSU) 3. Hybrid PSS/PSU 4. Cash, material goods/commodities 5. Expert services 6. Positive discrimination 7. Credits/vouchers 8. Subsidies 9. Government loan guarantees 10. Protective regulations 11. Supervision of deviance 12. Power over decisions	1. Target efficiency 2. Cost-effectiveness 3. Stigmatization 4. Complexity of administration 5. Adaptability across users 6. Political risk (political visibility) 7. Consumer sovereignty/reliance on free-market mechanisms 8. Substitutability 9. Coerciveness/intrusiveness 10. Fit with social problem analysis 11. Tradeoffs between criteria

Table 4–1. Operating Characteristics, Basic Subtypes, and Evaluation Criteria for a Value-Critical Appraisal of Social Policy and Programs, *continued*

Name of Operating Characteristic	Basic Subtypes or Concepts	Evaluation Criteria
Entitlement rules	1. Prior contributions 2. Administrative rule 3. Private contract 4. Professional and/or administrative discretion 5. Judicial decision 6. Means/asset test 7. Attachment to work force	1. Social problem analysis: fit to target specifications/ ideological constraints 2. Stigma and alienation 3. Off-target benefits 4. Overwhelming costs 5. Over/underutilization 6. Opportunity for political interference 7. Work disincentives 8. Procreational incentives 9. Marital breakup 10. Generational dependency 11. Special applications: personal social services and public social utilities
Financing methods	1. Prepayments and the insurance principle 2. Publicly regulated private contracts 3. Voluntary contributions 4. General revenue appropriations 5. Fees for service 6. Private endowment	1. Short-term/long-term funding continuity 2. Protecting against inflation/depression 3. Dealing with demographic change 4. Incentives and disincentives provided for client outcomes 5. Fit with social problem analysis

Table 4–1.   Operating Characteristics, Basic Subtypes, and Evaluation Criteria for a Value-Critical Appraisal of Social Policy and Programs, *continued*

Name of Operating Characteristic	Basic Subtypes or Concepts	Evaluation Criteria
Administrative or service delivery	1. Social program and policy design 2. Centralization 3. Federation 4. Case management 5. Agencies specializing in referrals 6. Indigenous worker staffing 7. Racially oriented agencies 8. Administrative ("fair") hearings and appeal procedures 9. Due process protections for clients' procedural rights 10. Citizen participation	1. Program design 2. Integration-continuity 3. Accessibility 4. Accountability 5. Client empowerment 6. Consumer participation 7. Fit with social problem analysis
Interactions between operating characteristics and between this policy or program and/or others	1. Coentitlement 2. Disentitlement 3. Contrary effects 4. Duplication 5. Governmental-level interactions	(Undesirable interactions are those that work against any of the criterial above; thus, interactions have no special evaluative criteria of their own.)

Criteria for a Value-Critical Appraisal of Social Policy and Programs

Column 3 of Table 4–1 lists evaluation criteria by which the policy analyst can judge how a particular program has implemented each operating characteristic and, ultimately, the worth of the program and policy system. For example, goals and objectives should be evaluated according to whether they are concerned with means and not only outcomes; whether they are clear, measurable, and manipulable; and other such criteria. A means test (entitlement rules) should be evaluated on the basis of whether it creates stigmatization or alienation, or off-targets benefits for example. The method of policy analysis contained in this book actually suggests three general but very different types of criteria for evaluating the features (operating characteristics) of social program and policy systems.

The first type are *those that use the social problem analysis as a referent*, the evaluation issue being whether the program or policy made any impact on the social problem it was intended to solve. In this mode, the practitioner asks certain questions:

- Do the entitlement rules (irrespective of their form in the program under judgment) direct benefits at the entire population defined to have the social problem, or do they only reach subtypes?
- Is there any anticipated reduction in the number of people who have the problem or in its seriousness or consequences?
- Do the goals and objectives of the program or policy system incorporate the defined social problem?
- Can this form of benefit produce an impact on the causal factors believed to produce the social problem?

The second type are *those traditional value perspectives—adequacy, equity, and efficiency*. For example, one might ask "Is delivery of commodities rather than cash as a form of benefit a more *efficient* (cost-effective) way to solve the problem of nutrition?" An example of the *adequacy* criterion lies in the question "To what extent does a voluntary contribution method of financing generate year-to-year funding continuity?" Similarly, a practical policy analyst might be evaluating a particular service delivery type against both an equity criterion and an adequacy criterion when she or he asks "To what extent does the case-management style of service delivery increase the ability of the policy and program system to relate to the ethnic and racial diversity of its target population?" It is more than a little useful for the practitioner to be aware of what root questions are being asked (whether adequacy, equity, or efficiency questions) when a program and policy system are being judged for merit.

It will be useful to note how questions differ depending on which evaluation criteria are used. A fundamentally different question is asked by one concerned with whether the *entire* defined population is receiving program benefits in contrast to one whose concern is whether the particular benefit is the least costly way to serve those in need. It is very important to question, understand, and evaluate the inner workings of a policy and program system—goals, entitlement rules, administrative arrangements, and such—but that kind of question can never raise the issue of whether the program or policy system actually made a difference with respect to a solution to the social problem of concern. On the other hand, using the social problem approach alone is a sure way to overlook internal inadequacies and inefficiencies in the policy system, inadequacies in operations that could work cruel inequities on human beings. Each question is important but for very different reasons; and those reasons are why it is so important to have a number of different kinds of evaluation criteria.

In summary then, the evaluation criteria for deciding the merit of each operating characteristic will always include (1) one that refers to the positive or negative impact of the particular operating characteristic on the social problem of interest and (2) those that reflect value perspectives other than, or in addition to, those specific to the social problem definition, causation, or ideology (equity, adequacy, and efficiency). We will save a more detailed look at evaluation criteria for the specific chapter on each operating characteristic. As a close to this introduction, let us give some special attention to an important distinction between personal social service programs and public social utility programs because evaluative criteria can apply differently depending on which program type is under analysis.

Personal Social Service Programs and Public Social Utility Programs: A Distinction

Before looking at the difference between personal social service programs and public social utility programs, we need to bear in mind the nature of *public social benefits*, that is, welfare transfers directed to meet communal and citizen needs and financed from taxation of all citizens. The reader might be surprised how broad and extensive this is, not only among social programs that readily come to mind—mental health counseling, family planning, public health services—but also programs *not* commonly considered to be welfare transfers— Social Security Disability and retirement insurance, Medicare, public roads and bridges, police and fire protection, agricultural subsidies, public schools, low-interest government loans to individuals and corporations, to name some. All of those involve welfare transfers precisely because many user/consumers have not fully paid for their use through taxes. For example, Social Security benefits are welfare transfers to the extent that nonworking beneficiaries are paid from the contributions of those currently in the work force. Were it not for the constant influx of benefits, Social Security funds would be exhausted before current retirees/beneficiaries die. A consequence of this welfare transfer is that by the time he or she dies the average retiree will have paid no more than about one-half the benefit received. The same principle applies in great measure to low-interest government loans to corporations and certainly to agricultural subsidies to farmers, both of whom receive public funds for which there has been no market exchange (money or work). The tax money that pays for that subsidy is just as much a welfare transfer as an AFDC benefit.

This is not an argument against welfare transfers. Many good economic and social reasons underlie welfare transfers and apply equally to agricultural and corporate subsidies, to AFDC mothers, and to unemployed persons or work-injured employees. Although fundamental similarities must be acknowledged, surely some important differences exist between a government benefit paid to a person who is impoverished and a government benefit paid to a large corporation with substantial assets and a huge work force. Both similarities (discussed above) and differences (discussed below) help determine how we go about evaluating these social policies. Let us now turn to the three major types of public social benefits: public social utility programs, personal social service programs, and hybrid programs.[10]

Personal social services (PSSs), also called "soft" benefits, are welfare transfers to which the following conditions pertain:[11]

1. The benefit is delivered face to face to a particular user/consumer. Examples are mental health counseling or public legal services.

2. The benefit is not standardized but highly individualized, varying by individual differences and hence delivered without regard to strict equity among citizens (that is, some beneficiaries get more than others). Examples are foster care, public legal services, and medical care where the recipient gets what the professional thinks is needed.

3. Entitlement is broadly discretionary, usually via credentialed professionals. Examples are medical care (from a physician or therapist) and foster care (from a social worker or administrator).

4. The benefit is intended to serve citizens with unexpected problems. Examples are child and nonroutine or spouse abuse hot lines or crisis counseling.

5. Beneficiaries of personal social services can be required by law to accept personal social services. Examples are court orders that direct a substance abuser or a spouse or child abuser to counseling.

6. Personal social services deliver intangible benefits that generate a benefit or change for recipients by actions taken on their behalf, by support extended to them, or by access to resources other than the PSS itself. Examples are advocacy services for the disabled or some of the highly individualized special education programs or information and referral services.

7. The purposes of personal social services are often (though not always or inevitably) in the service of the enforcement of social control or the amelioration of the effects of personal catastrophe (physical or mental impairment, family disintegration, or environmental disaster).

According to Kahn (1963), the following public social utilities (PSUs), also called "hard" benefits, are welfare transfers delivered under the following conditions:

1.   The benefit can be delivered without face-to-face contact with the user/consumer. Examples are agricultural subsidies, tax credits, public health services (sanitation or clean water supply), and Social Security Retirement (OASI) benefits.

2.   The benefit is standardized and delivered with strict respect for equity among citizens, without considering individual differences. Thus, every eligible person sharing the same characteristics gets (roughly) the same benefit according to administrative policy. Examples are public health services (sanitation and clean water supply), and government-subsidized loans.

3.   The benefit, therefore, is delivered under a set of policy (administrative) rules that leave very little discretion to either administrators or professionals. Examples are food stamps, and Social Security Retirement (OASI) or Disability benefits.

4.   The benefit is tangible: cash money; material goods that easily convert into cash; commodities; market advantages, whether delivered directly or indirectly by stamps or vouchers to suppliers. Examples are farm subsidies, roads and bridges, public recreation, food/commodities (cheese, beans, and such), food stamps, and Medicare payments.

5.   The benefit is intended to serve citizens with ordinary, predictable problems. Examples are Social Security Retirement (OASI) benefits and public recreation.

6.   Benefits are generally available only upon the initiative of the user/consumer. In general, they cannot be legally forced on a user/consumer because beneficiaries must apply for them. Examples are agricultural or industrial subsidies, tax credits, and Social Security Retirement income (OASI) benefits.

Let us turn now to look at whether and how these attributes of PSS's and PSU's distinguish between specific examples of current social programs and policies.

Consider the *face-to-face* service delivery attribute in the context of mental health counseling and public legal services. Both services are delivered, with rare exceptions, face-to-face with their intended beneficiaries. This is also true of the other common counseling services (marital, sexual, family, educational, and the like). Exceptions include the occasional telephone conversation that counselors and attorneys might have with clients.

Taking some broader social services—foster care and protective services—as examples, it would be inconceivable to deliver them indirectly because both depend heavily on the development of meaningful personal relationships to achieve their goals. For example, foster children need face-to-face interaction, as do children in need of protection. Even though mental health counseling or legal services sometimes are offered over the telephone or via correspondence, no one would seriously suggest that either is preferred or commonplace. Again, face-to-face does not necessarily rule out the occasional telephone conversation.

Unlike the PSU face-to-face attribute, the essence of personal contact here is to further a detailed and broad-scale understanding of the uniqueness and individuality of the user/consumer, particularly with a view of observing how a specific social problem impinges on him or her.

In contrast, PSU programs are not concerned with the whole person and his or her uniqueness, only with those aspects held in common with others. Thus, an applicant for Social Security Retirement benefits is of interest only to the extent he or she fits the eligibility criteria. Any contact with beneficiaries is simply to determine initial (or continuing) eligibility—which can be done via the phone or a computer terminal. Details about the individual other than these few facts are irrelevant to program administrators and staff.

To test our classification scheme, consider some hard cases that are marginal in the sense that they are rare types of social program. Police services, for example, are indeed a key public social benefit; but whereas police intervention is a face-to-face activity, the main part of the service action occurs face to face with the offender, not with the victim, the user/consumer on whose behalf the police officer is acting. Contact with the victim is only incidental to the main service action with the offender. Although there may be some face-to-face contact between an officer and the user/consumer during the original complaint, there is no need for later face-to-face contact with the same officer—any officer will do. On that account police services are public social utilities and not personal social services (or perhaps they are a hybrid, which we will discuss later in the chapter). Another lesson this case teaches is how important it is to be clear about who the client/beneficiary is or on whose behalf the benefits or services are instituted. This awareness can make a difference in understanding the fundamental nature of benefits or services.

Client advocacy services, such as those directed toward obtaining specialist medical services or a shelter for the homeless, present an interesting example precisely because face-to-face contact with others who "hold the key" to services is an essential ingredient of client advocacy. Indeed, advocacy cannot be done without consulting with the client on the nature of his or her problem so as to deal with questions from those who control delivery of the service the client needs. A practitioner, in speaking to a program administrator on behalf of a client who had been denied subsidized housing, would need to know details of the rejection. Only by face-to-face contact with the client can the practitioner get the full story.

The second attribute of personal social services is that *they are not standardized but highly individualized.* Perhaps their face-to-face feature is a consequence of this attribute. Thus, a physician giving medical services or a social worker doing client advocacy are fundamentally interested in what it is that makes a client or the client's environment and/or problem *different* from all others. The task of the PSS deliverer is to tailor a service (or services most likely) to the unique needs of individuals and to exercise discretion by modifying, mitigating, extending, or otherwise *individualizing* applicable administrative regulations. However, for a public social utility like a city recreation program, the standardized services are offered: basketball and handball courts, meeting rooms, dance floors, bingo facilities, craft classes for instance. Accommodating the needs of individuals is always a public relations and administrative problem for PSUs—precisely because ordinarily it is not in nature to offer individual services. Remember that beneficiaries of PSUs are entitled via a set of administrative (or legal) rules—OASI, food stamps, inoculations—in regard to which neither administrative nor professional discretion is exercised. Because of that feature entitlement is straightforward and mechanical and easily can be computerized.

PSUs and PSSs can also be contrasted with respect to the tangibility of benefits they deliver: Personal social services deliver intangible (or soft) benefits and services whereas for the most part public social utilities deliver tangible (or hard) benefits—cash goods, commodities, or market advantages that directly can be translated into tangibles. This contrast is dramatic when one considers the comparison between PSSs like counseling or child protective services and PSUs like food stamps, or Social Security, or farm subsidies. The contrast becomes less clear when it concerns personal social services received by AFDC mothers or others extended as a part of a day care program because in both cases a tangible benefit is received by a user/consumer: cash and food commodities with respect to the AFDC mother and her child's meals and the daytime shelter commonly associated with day care. However, clearly personal social services such as counseling or job training are identified as PSSs because the tangible benefit (cash) is to be delivered *in the context of* these accompanying personal social services. Further, even tangible benefits can be somewhat discretionary, i.e., delivered based on the assessment of professionals or administrators about whether they are needed or can be "used well."

Physical rehabilitation programs also are characterized by the thin line between tangibility and intangibility. They commonly deliver tangible benefits (orthopedic appliances for example), but they also deliver intangibles (counseling, medical consultation, vocational assessment, job placement—all believed to be essential) under face-to-face conditions, and to be influenced by individualization and professional discretion. The crucial detail is that *the tangible* orthopedic appliance or medical procedure cannot possibly be delivered like a mail-order catalog item; rather, it requires individualized measurement, fitting, supervision, and posttreatment consultation.

PSSs and PSUs differ with respect to their purposes and the possibility of their being *legally required* of user/consumers. Whereas PSUs always require the initiative of user/consumers to obtain the benefit or service, *user/consumers can be legally required to accept PSSs.* Although it may be strange to think of a service being forced on someone, in every state citizens are charged or convicted daily of substance abuse, spouse abuse, child molestation, exhibitionism, and so forth. The courts order (or otherwise constrain) offenders to attend various and sundry counseling and treatment centers, and they order certain paroled offenders who report to probation and parole offices to do the same. Juvenile courts send children from the parental (or kin) home to live in foster homes. On the other hand, as far as I can determine, neither tradition nor law makes it possible for someone to be legally obligated to accept food stamps or Social Security Disability or Retirement benefits. A marginal case that illustrates this contrast is that of an incompetent person whose application for Social Security Retirement benefits is pursued by a court-appointed guardian. Note that this happens only because such a person has been declared legally incompetent to manage his or her own affairs, an extraordinary situation by any standard. A person deemed competent must take initiative in applying for PSU benefits, whereas PSS "benefits" can be court-ordered.

Public social utilities are intended to serve ordinary citizens who encounter *ordinary and predictable* problems. Common examples are retirement from the work force or the need for housing or adequate nutrition. Old Age and Survivors Insurance (OASI) is the benefit program for retirement, whereas Section 8 of the U.S. Housing Act and the Food Stamp Program cover the latter two. Personal social services, in contrast, are intended to serve nonmainstream citizens who are encountering *unusual, unexpected, nonroutine* problems. Personal social service programs like protective services, probation or parole, or foster care are examples—all serving needs that current social norms dictate would not be among those most people (mainstream citizens) would expect.

This contrast highlights the differences in the basic program purposes. *PSSs are intended primarily to serve society in regard to the enforcement of social control, especially control of deviance.* Even a casual survey of those programs here identified as personal social services have that hallmark (for example, child protective services, the primary purpose of which is the child's protection by means of controlling the physical or sexual deviance). Naturally, human service practitioners bring more than that intention to their practice; but from the point of view of the broad public purpose, the basic intention and the reason public monies are appropriated to hire human service workers in the personal social services, is to enforce social control. Quite naturally, there is inherent tension between this purpose and that of social work and human service practitioners. For example, think of how child foster care is motivated by an intent to contain deviance on the part of parents (or older children) that constitutes the reason parents cannot care for their children or children cannot remain in their own homes. Other examples include family catastrophe (mental or physical illness or family disintegration), neglect, lack of supervision, "child-out-of-control phenomena," abandonment, parental imprisonment. All examples are unusual, or catastrophic, or problematic—clearly not within the range of what most citizens expect in their lives. It is precisely these features that constitute the hallmark of PSSs—individualization of the person in need, face-to-face contact, wide administrative or professional discretion to help people with unique needs (See Table 4–2). Public social utilities are designed as "programs for the masses," so to speak, directly in line with the public, not private, interest. *Personal social services are designed to bring public resources to bear on essentially private, idiosyncratic matters that are nonetheless of public interest.*

Hybrid Programs

By now, you probably have thought of examples of social programs (income transfers) that do not fit easily into either the PSS or the PSU category. Usually, such programs don't make a comfortable fit because they have characteristics of both; for that reason we will call them hybrids. The most obvious hybrids are public school programs. Generally speaking, on some grounds public school programs are clearly personal social services: They are delivered face to face with the children in attendance, instruction that is tailored to individual student needs is an ideal among teachers, the claiming of the educational benefit is not up to the initiative of the citizen/parent but is legally required up to a certain statutory age (usually 16), and learning is clearly an intangible benefit. However, on other grounds, public school programs have many characteristics of public utilities: Whereas individualized instruction is deemed an ideal, the benefit is standardized to a large extent (a single curriculum for all students in each grade); it is delivered with respect for equity among citizens (all citizens have a right to equivalent education for their children and—at least in principle—every student has an equal right to take advantage of whatever the school offers); entitlement to enroll children in public schools is a matter of administrative rules (school district boundaries, age, and the like); the discretion of school administrators is limited; and mainline public school educational benefits are designed for the ordinary child in ordinary circumstances. On that account, public school programs will be called *a hybrid public social utility/ personal social service* (HPSU/PSS). By definition, then, HYBRIDS are *public benefits that have at least one characteristic of a social utility and one characteristic of a personal social service.*

Other prominent examples of social program hybrids include police and fire protection; Workers Compensation; public health programs (inoculations and tests for communicable diseases); public day care or recreation; and family planning. Table 4–3 examines their attributes.

If we consider public health as an example of an HPSU/PSS social program, we must be careful because public health programs may be of more than one type. If we consider only inoculation and testing for communicable disease, we observe that these programs serve the public good by making tests and inoculations freely available for smallpox, overseas travelers, AIDS screening, and tuberculosis. One motive is to protect user/consumers, but another is to prevent their infecting the general population. On the one hand, public health services are not just pure personal social services because they deliver standardized benefits (i.e., every user gets the same inoculation for a particular communicable disease), and the benefit itself is tangible, as shown in Table 4.3. Furthermore, said benefits are made available at the initiative of the ultimate beneficiary, the user/consumer. On the other hand, public health services are not pure PSUs: for example, inoculations are (sometimes) delivered face to face and (sometimes) distributed equitably among individual user/consumers; the inoculation received depends on what, in the judgment of the public health officials, is believed to be

Table 4–2. Exemplars of Personal Social Service and Public Social Utility Program.[*]

Social Program Examples

(Attribute)	(Public Social Utilities)[**]					(Personal Social Services)				
	OASI	Food Stamps	Section 8 Housing	City Recreation	Public Health (Sanitation)	Vocational Rehabilitation	Day Care	AFDC	Client Advice	Mental Health Counseling
Face to face	–	–	–	–	–	+	+	+	+	+
Individual	–	–	–	–	–	+	+	+	+	+
Nonequity	–	–	–	–	–	+	+	+	+	+
Discretionary	–	–	–	–	–	+	+	+	+	+
Nonroutine problems	–	–	–	–	–	+	–	+	+	+
Intangibles	–	–	–	–	–	+/–	+/–	+/–	–	+
Can be legally required	–	–	–	–	+	+	+	+	+	+
Purpose: Social control	–	–	–	–	–	+	+	+	+/–	+
Supression of deviance	–	–	–	–	–	+	+	+	+/–	+

* Explanation of symbols:
  (–) program has that attribute.
  (+) program lacks that attribute.
  (+/–) some program aspects *do* and some program aspects *do not* have that feature.

** Notice that in the four programs immediately left, the tangible benefits are delivered only on condition that they are accompanied by a personal social service (in service of enhancing its use or being absolutely necessary to accompany its use). That is, client advocacy may result in the delivery of a tangible benefit but without the intangible face-to-face, individualized personal social service, the tangible would not have been attained; day care cannot attend to the intangible, developmental services it offers without also supplying food and shelter to the child.

Table 4–3. Examples of Hybrid Social Programs

(Dimension)	Police Protection	Fire Protection	Public Health WC	(Shots)	Day Care	Recreation	Birth Control	Education
Face to face	–	–	+	+	+	+	+	+
Individual	+	+	+	–	+/–	–	+	+/–
Nonequity	–	–	+/–	–	+	+	–	+
Discretionary	+	+	+	–	+	–	–	
Nonroutine problems	+	+	+	–	–	–	–	–
Intangibles	+	+	–	+	–	–	+	+
Potentially legally required	+	+	–	+	–	–	–	+

Explanation of symbols:
  (–) program has that attribute.
  (+) program lacks that attribute.
  (+/–) some program aspects *do* and some program aspects *do not* have that feature.

needed. Such officials also are expected to exercise some discretion in regard to the total health of the individual and the risk of negative reactions. Because a public health inoculation program contains at least one fundamental characteristic each of a PSS and a PSU, we will call it a hybrid. Note, however, that some other public health programs are unambiguously public social utilities—sanitation and the supply of clean water. These public health services meet all requirements of a public social utility: They are not delivered face-to-face (restaurant inspectors or laboratory personnel never have to see the users of their product); every citizen receives exactly the same service (product in this case); all beneficiaries are equally entitled; service delivery is at the initiative of the user/consumer; and public health officials have no latitude in deciding who receives clean water and eats uncontaminated restaurant food—all tangible products of a tangible service intended to address common needs to ensure the health of citizens it serves.

Personal medical care is different from public health services, though both share some of the same technology. Public health objectives are broad and universal; they are directed to the health needs of the whole community, whereas personal medical services are directed toward illness. Thus, public health is preventive in nature, and personal medical care is remediative. Focusing on the illness-health difference is crucial to understanding the distinction between the fundamental nature of these two services. In fact, doing so ultimately turns the one in the direction of a personal social service (personal medical care) and the other in the direction of a public social utility (public health). Note that personal medical care is a matter of (professional) physician discretion and is *not* discretionary on the part of administrative or professional officials in that it serves citizens in extraordinary medical emergencies, which clearly are unexpected circumstances. Personal medical care benefits and services are highly individualized, but they can be (although generally are not) legally forced on a user/consumer in emergencies and accidents; the benefit is itself intangible and is delivered face to face. Clearly, all are attributes of a personal social service, and whether it serves the ordinary needs of ordinary people (appendectomies, childbirth) depends on whether one considers illness to be expected or unexpected, common or ordinary, or an extraordinary event. It seems safe to assume that for most citizens in our culture, serious illness is still considered an extraordinary event for which medical care (as a personal social service) is considered the effective remedy.

If one thinks of police and fire protection carefully, the benefit will be seen as protection of person and property and exercise of social control. Protection is not a tangible benefit, although what is protected might be—peace of mind versus household furniture is an appropriate contrast. Using this logic, police and fire protection is not a personal social service because neither is delivered face to face with the user/consumer but is delivered against lawbreakers. On the other hand, many features of police and fire protection are characteristically personal social services: Think only of the radical counseling and mediation services that (good) police routinely perform in situations that involve violent or potentially violent domestic disputes, neighborhood disputes, street gang violence, personal-injury accidents, or child or spouse abuse. In those situations, police know that violence can be defused by radical individualization of the situation, and police and fire personnel are allowed (and must have wide discretion) in judging whether to apply force or constraint. All these situations are examples of services rendered in "extraordinary" or "unpredictable" cases. Therefore, police and fire protection is a type of hybrid type of program.

Chapters 5–10 will be devoted to examination of each of the six operating characteristics, and in each some attention will be given to the way operating characteristics vary depending on whether the program or policies under discussion are personal social services or public social utilities. Those concepts will be useful because operating characteristics vary with the "spin" given them by this variability. The chapters are organized around a discussion of the various forms that the particular characteristic can take—for example, each form of benefit and services is discussed in turn (goods, commodities, cash) in Chapter 6, "Analysis of Forms of Benefits and Services," which will provide opportunity to examine further the distinction between personal social service and public social utility programs.

SUMMARY

Chapter 4 contrasted three styles of policy analysis: the analytic-descriptive, the value-committed, and the value-critical. While recognizing that political occasions will arise during which it is essential, the value-committed approach is rejected as a basic practice because fundamentally it is not open to new data or conclusions. Thus there can be no agenda for changes or improvement. This fact argues for the value-critical style, which forces into the open whatever ideology is inherent in the analytic method used and the fundamental value commitments of the analyst in whose hands the method rests. Taken into the open, the effects of ideology can be observed and accounted for. Although useful, the analytic-descriptive method fails in policy analysis because it commits the analyst to untenable assumptions: for example, that judgments about the "goodness," or "merit" of a social policy or program can be made in a value-free way. Such assumptions are unrealistic because any judgment of social program merit requires judgment of social worthiness—which simply cannot be made absent a strong value commitment. The virtue of the value-critical method is that it forces value commitments into the open and therefore gives both the analyst and his or her audience great freedom in using (or not using) the data produced from the analysis. This approach also enables practitioners to decide whether they are in agreement with the conclusions, to sort them selectively, or to freely substitute their own value biases and draw different conclusions. That sort of freedom can be used at different levels—either in regard to particular social program or policy operating characteristics or in regard to summary judgments.

Value commitments inherent in this preferred method of policy analysis were presented: rationality and consistency of logic (logical fit between program and policy operating characteristics and details of the social problem analysis) and new conclusions reached by a dialectic contrast between various value perspectives on the social problem and the means used to resolve it. Other basic and general value commitments advocated throughout the presentation of the analytic method in succeeding chapters were also presented; that is, adequacy, equity and efficiency. This chapter also noted how evaluation criteria vary in their relevance depending on which operating feature of the social policies and programs is under discussion.

The distinction among personal social services ("soft" benefits), public social utilities ("hard" benefits), and hybrids was presented in terms of understanding and evaluating social policies and programs. Personal social services (PSSs) are welfare transfers that deliver benefits and services under conditions of (1) face-to-face contact with particular user/consumers, (2) high individualization among user/consumers, (3) broad administrative and professional discretion, (4) service to citizens with unexpected problems, (5) benefits the acceptance of which can be required legally, (6) delivery of intangible service, and very often (7) enforcement of social control or the amelioration of personal catastrophe. The opposite of all these defining dimensions (save the last) define public social utilities (PSUs). Hybrid social policies and programs contain a mix of PSUs and PSSs, and are referred to as HPSU/PSS.

EXERCISE

1. *Complete the following mental experiment*: Your physician has just told you that you have a fatal and incurable illness. You have just eight weeks to live. Upon returning home from the physician's office you decide not to go berserk today (perhaps tomorrow), at least not until you open your mail. There is an envelope with a strange return address on it, foreign stamps in fact. Opening it first, you learn that you have inherited several million dollars, being the last living heir to a European fortune. A quick calculation shows that you cannot possibly spend it all in eight weeks. Then you decide you do not want to give it either to friends or relatives—your closest friend recently offended you, and your closest relative died three years ago. Use the six basic policy elements to decide how you want to get rid of the money.

NOTES

1. M. Rein, *From Policy to Practice* (Armonk, NY: M. E. Sharpe, 1983), p. ix.
2. Page x in Note 1.
3. M. Howlett, "Policy Instruments, Policy Styles, and Policy Implementation: National Approaches to Theories of Instrument Choice." *Policy Studies Journal*, 19:1–21 (1991).
4. Pages 6–9 in Note 3.
5. M. Rein, *Value-critical Policy Analysis*, In *Ethics, the social sciences and policy analysis*, edited by Daniel Callahan and Bruce Jennings (New York: Farrar and Rinehart,

1983), pp. 83–111. See also A. Weick and L. Pope, *Knowing what's best: A new look at self-determination.* (Lawrence, KS: The University of Kansas, 1975), mimeographed.

6. J. Habermas, *Theory and Practice* (Boston: Beacon Press, 1976).

7. M. Piore, "Qualitative Research Techniques in Economics," *Administrative Science Quarterly,* vol. 24, December 1979.

8. Page x in Note 1.

9. Elements 2, 3, 4, and 6 were used by Evelyn Burns in a book titled *The American Social Security System* (New York: Houghton-Mifflin Company, 1949) and I assume that (collectively) they are original with her. Her ultimate sources may lie somewhere in the British tradition of social policy studies, of course. Many contemporary authors use Burns: *Dimensions of Social Welfare Policy* (Englewood Cliffs, NJ: Prentice-Hall Inc., 1974). I have added three new operating characteristics in the belief that they are crucial to a thorough analysis: Goals and Objectives and Interactions among Elements.

10. I am indebted to many authors for their work in distinguishing types of policies and programs but especially to A. J. Kahn and Sheila Kammerman and their book *Social Services in International Perspective* (New Brunswick, NJ: Transaction Books, 1980), pp. 3–6.

11. In drawing this contrast it is important at every step to keep examples in mind. As you work through the list of attributes that characterize personal social services and public social utilities, keep in mind a wide range of policy and program examples such as the following:

Mental health counseling	Social Security Retirement benefits
Farm subsidies	Workers Compensation
Child and sexual abuse (protective) services	Meals-on-Wheels (for the homebound and aged)
Public roads and bridges	Police protection
Case management	Sanitation services
Foster care for children	Public medical care payments (Medicare)
Tax advantages	
Client advocacy services	Social Security Disability benefits
Public education	Food Stamp Program
Information and referral services	Public recreation centers, play-grounds, and public parks
Clean water supply	
Public legal services	Public day care and Head Start programs

CHAPTER 5

The Analysis of Policy Goals and Objectives

INTRODUCTION

The method presented in this book proceeds by first obtaining a close description of social policy or program implementation and then evaluating its merit according to specified criteria. Six fundamental operating characteristics are essential to implementation of all social policies. Chapter 5 will consider the first—*goals and objectives*—along with the various forms in which they are expressed. The chapter also will describe the difference between goals and objectives, identify sources and problems in locating statements of program and policy goals and objectives, and review their components and functions. In addition, the way in which goals and objectives differ in the personal social services and the problems of setting them in that context will be considered. The chapter will close with an extensive discussion of the task of evaluating the merit of social policy program and policy goals and objectives. The discussion in this chapter is intended to set a model for later chapter discussions on other operating characteristics.

DEFINITIONS AND BASIC CONCEPTS FOR ANALYSIS OF GOALS AND OBJECTIVES

A goal is a statement, in general and abstract terms, of desired qualities in human and social conditions.[1] It is important to grasp the goals and objectives of a program so as to answer the question "What is the purpose of this program or policy?" In fact, all elements of the program or policy must be judged on the basis of their contribution to program goals and objectives; the extent to which program or policy elements make such contributions is a measure of the wisdom of choosing them as an instrument of policy operations. Therefore, the program or policy goals and objectives are the programmatic "measure of all things." Program goals and objectives are highly variable, as the following examples are intended to show. The goal of the Social Security program known as Old Age and Survivors Insurance (OASI) is to ensure that citizens will have income after they no longer can work. The goal of the Low Income Energy Assistance Program (LIEAP) is to reduce the impact of increased world energy costs on low-income households. The goal of most child abuse programs is to protect from abuse children who are too young to protect themselves. It is important to understand that when we describe the goal or objective of a policy or program, we are describing a desired end, *not a means to an end*. It is easy to confuse the two when speaking of social policies and programs because programs often are described according to the methods they use to achieve their goals and objectives. Thus, when asked to define the purpose of their program, staff members and executives often say, for example, that they provide counseling or money or nursing care to people who need it. That, however, is not a legitimate goal; by definition, services are means to ends, not ends in themselves. Thus, the provision of *services or benefits is never, by itself, a legitimate goal or objective of a social program*. To describe services and benefits is to describe program processes (inputs) or perhaps program designs, but certainly not goals or objectives. One of many reasons for *not* including service provision as a legitimate goal is that doing so makes it possible to consider perpetual service provision as a legitimate outcome by which to measure program performance. Think for a moment about how, under these circumstances, a social program can simply continue to give services forever and never have to look at whether it produces a tangible result in regard to the social problem to which a social program is intended to be a solution. In effect, to express goals and objectives as services rather than outcomes makes it impossible to evaluate a program against its outcomes, rendering such a program essentially nonaccountable. Neither public nor private programs can afford to be deemed nonaccountable, given the finite nature of resources and funding and the pressing need of human beings for goods and services. If a social program cannot produce results that meet human needs, the welfare system must direct funding elsewhere—which itself requires an accountability system.

Here is an example of how this means–ends distinction works in practice. Consider this common problem faced by those with responsibility for allocating funds for the delivery of social services. Assume you chair the board of directors of the Barrett Foundation, whose purpose is to fund social programs for general philanthropic deeds, and you exercise broad discretion in doing so. Assume further that while speaking with the director of a local program, the Great Plains County Counseling Service, the director argues that the organization is a viable, successful operation due to the following reasons:

- Great Plains has a full staff, each of whom is an expert in three types of therapy (behavior modification, psychoanalytic therapy, and Bowenian marriage counseling).
- The number of clients served has increased by 20 percent this year.
- The number of treatment hours has increased by 35 percent this year.
- New satellite clinic offices were established in six counties over the past year.
- New consulting services were contracted for in two new school districts and in three high schools.

You must decide whether your organization should fund this operation for another five years at an annual budget of around $500,000. Based on the viewpoint about goals and objectives expressed above, the answer is no, because the operations data that are given tell you absolutely nothing about program effectiveness, only about program inputs and processes (mostly counseling), not program outcomes. The data speak only about means to ends, not ends themselves. Goals are not about delivering services (treatment hours, treatment modalities, consultation, and the like), but about achieving a desirable outcome in regard to the targeted social problem(s). If this board of directors doesn't insist on this, they have no rational means by which to make a decision about funding this program. In an important sense, program outcomes are a public social program's "profit," without which program operations inevitably are taking resources away from opportunities to meet human need elsewhere. The key to the distinction lies in judging whether the program or policy goal or objective could be accepted as an end in itself. For example, could personal counseling be accepted as an end in itself? Not likely, for the mere fact of counseling does not by itself suggest any particular social problem that is being solved. That is, there is never a guarantee that counseling will be successful. The goal will be revealed by the answer to the question "Counseling for what, to achieve what purpose?"

DIFFERENT TYPES OF GOALS AND OBJECTIVES

The practical public policy analyst should be alert to the fact that goals and objectives come in a variety of forms. For example, sometimes social programs specify objectives as "long-term" or "short-term." This specification is useful because it can relate to funding—there may be enough money only for outcomes having short horizons and the program may not last long enough to be concerned about a long horizon. Consider a highly politicized social problem like substance abuse. For a time, a drug education program for grade school children was highly publicized and appealed to the general populace. When these programs were first funded they were fielded with very short-term goals—to increase children's knowledge about the effects of drugs. Once programs were implemented, change was expected to occur over a matter of weeks. In fact, the program was designed to be delivered and the information learned in a very short period of time because funding not only was limited but restricted to a few months' duration. When an intermediate step is crucial to a long-term goal it is only logical to test for whether the intermediate step is attainable; further dollars await the outcome. The long-term goal here was the reduction in adult, long-term substance abuse, but in that funding environment the long-term goal was irrelevant from a practical point of view.

Manifest and Latent Goals

A statement about a social policy or program goal is different from sociological statements about the social function served by a particular social program or policy. For example, Piven and Cloward (1971) conclude that the primary social function of the U.S. welfare system is to regulate the poor in two ways:[2]

1. To ensure a supply of cheap labor to the economic system
2. To ensure that discontent among the poor does not rise to levels where it becomes a major threat to social order.

These are theoretical conclusions about a social welfare system from the point of view of sociological analysis. Policy or program goal statements are much less global, less inferential, and they are traceable to sources that can be observed "directly"; they are based on evidence from statements in such visible sources as legislative bills, administrative documents, and/or judicial decisions. If sociological and social policy analysis are confused, the policy analysis will suffer because manifest and latent functions are being confused.[3]

A *manifest* function is an explicit, stated purpose. With respect to social programs or policy, manifest functions are discovered through examination of statements in primary documents of concern (legal or administrative) about goals and purposes. As sociologists and anthropologists have long been at pains to point out, social programs, policies, and institutions have purposes or functions (goals) other than those stated publicly, labeled *latent* functions. One of the most widely discussed latent function is served by mental hospitals, which, it is contended, serve the manifest (stated, legislated) function of treatment of mental disorders for the benefit of individual patients; they are also said to serve the latent function of the social control of deviance (control of the incidence of unusual, norm-defying behavior). Another common example is the federal government's Section 8 housing program, which offers substantial rent subsidies to low-income families. The manifest goal or objective of this program is to make safe, adequate, and affordable housing available to the poor. Section 8 housing, located in scattered sites outside the inner-city urban ring, is reasonably expected to be an environmental improvement for low-income families and to reduce urban minority populations. As laudable as these goals and objectives are, some policy analysts argue that their *latent* goal is to gradually depopulate housing projects in inner cities so that they can be torn down and redeveloped as luxury apartments and condominiums. This charge is plausible in that one can easily point to housing projects in metropolitan areas that would be prime real estate development sites. Chicago's inner urban ring is one example where housing projects are being vacated and discussions are being held as to their future. Whereas, ultimately, manifest and latent goals and objectives are very important (latent rather than manifest goals often drive program features and implementation), the first-order focus in policy and program analysis is on a description of the stated (manifest) goals. Observations about latent goals and objectives, even though speculative, are almost always useful but shouldn't displace focus on what is manifest. Even so, experience shows that when latent goals and objectives are the dominant forces in determining program decisions, operating features, and budgetary allocations, it almost always works *against* achievement of manifest goals and objectives.

DISTINGUISHING BETWEEN GOALS AND OBJECTIVES

A *goal* is an abstract and general statement of desired outcomes, and an *objective* is a specific, empirical, operational statement about a desired observable outcome. For any given goal, many different (apparently divergent) objectives can be written. For example, the goal of Literacy, Inc., a social program, can be stated as follows:

- To increase the ability of native and nonnative speakers of English so that they can accelerate their acculturation

That goal seems specific and in some ways it is. It certainly conveys a clear idea of what the program wishes to accomplish. Note how this goal *could* admit of several very different objectives:

- To increase reading competence to the sixth-grade level and to the point where employment advertisements can be read with comprehension.
- To increase the ability to understand spoken English at a level where conversation with the average U.S. high school graduate can be conducted to the linguistic satisfaction of both parties
- To increase the ability to read and speak standard English so as to eliminate any linguistic barrier to passing the GED high school certificate examination

The idea here is that any one of these statements of objectives would be sufficient to satisfy the goal statement of Literacy, Inc., in any one given program. (It is unlikely that such a program would adopt all three as objectives.) Taken together, multiple objectives cannot constitute the total meaning of goals, a direct consequence of the fact that a good, well-defined abstraction admits of an infinite number of concrete empirical instances. Put another way, a good definition of an abstraction is something whose meaning *cannot* be exhausted by a list of instances, no matter how long.

The nature of goals is that they are quite general and abstract; therefore, they are not ordinarily intended to be directly measurable. Objectives, on the other hand, are intended to be measured. It is not too far out of line to say that the importance of goals is to mark out the general scope (conceptual coverage, one might say) or the theoretical territory of a policy or a social program. The implication is that, for goals, their clear definition is their most important attribute. The importance of objectives, on the other hand, is their concreteness, their observability. When a social program or policy is evaluated by a carefully designed empirical study it is to objectives, not goals, that the evaluative measures are related.

OBJECTIVES (NOT GOALS) MUST CONTAIN TARGET GROUP SPECIFICATIONS AND PERFORMANCE STANDARDS

If objectives are to be of maximal use, they must clearly specify those to be affected, changed, or whose circumstances or surroundings are the target of change efforts. They must also make a reasonably clear statement about the *extent* to which effects or changes are expected. In specifying a *target group,* the phrase "serving the homeless of the city of Pocatello, Idaho," is not an acceptable target group specification. All terms of an objective need to be concrete: for example, "serving the homeless, those without permanent, warm, secure, sanitary shelter with running water and a stool and those older than 60 years of age . . ." and so on. It is a mistake to write objectives without that kind of specification. Although goals and objectives may seem remote and abstract at program initiation, they take on a serious import when it comes time to evaluate the program for effectiveness because program merit will be judged against the standards implied in objectives.

One would not expect a program with limited resources to serve a total population, but program auditors and evaluators will not make that assumption. Thus, a program objective that says it will serve the population of a city means exactly that. If target groups are not specified, goals and objectives will almost always be read to indicate that the program will serve a larger population than really intended or, for that matter, will have adequate resources to do so. Absent target group specification, program evaluators or auditors would conclude that the shelter would serve *all* the homeless in Pocatello. If a shelter has accommodations for only ten and there is a demonstrable demand for accommodations for fifteen, it will almost inevitably be given bad marks because it didn't do what it said it would, never mind after-the-fact arguments that the program really didn't mean what it said.

It is common for legislatures or United Way to cut social service budgets by some arbitrary percentage—arbitrary from the point of view of what it takes to deliver social services. When this happens with services that are mandated by law (child protection or public education), services may deteriorate or even become tainted. Because child abuse reporting is mandated by law, reports must be attended to by the authorized public agency. If staff is already limited and operating at full capacity, a 10 percent cut in the agency's budget will mean that the mandated function still will be performed but the cut will come out of other budgeted services (perhaps follow-up and treatment). Although such a scenario might be tolerable in some social services, in child protection agencies it invariably means that most resources will be expended on investigations—an exercise in futility absent ability to follow them up with needed services. The outcome is that children will be left unprotected, thus defeating the agency's very purpose. Another case is a venereal disease clinic for which budgetary reductions force it to focus on verifying cases of venereal disease (because it is mandated to do so) although the clinic cannot provide recommended treatment. Budgetary cuts often emphasize negative side effects, whereas the positive accomplishments of the program are left unfunded. For example, child abuse reporting *is* a good thing, but false and misleading reports can cause terrible social damage to innocent parties. If the focus of a child protection program is limited by budgetary constraints, investigation can be haphazard and create negative side effects without providing the positive benefits of follow-up and treatment for abused and neglected children. As we will discuss later, many social policies involve these kind of trade-offs, and funding must be sufficient to meet the problems created by social policy so as to be balanced by its positive effects. *When budget cuts occur, social program managers and practitioners should be ethically obligated to alter their publicly stated objectives so that it is clear how those fiscal reductions have affected the ability of the social program to serve its target groups.* One key reason for target group specification is to be able to alter objectives; without an established baseline for contrast, estimating the impact of fiscal reductions is very difficult to do plausibly.

All of this is to say that it is desirable to delimit objectives so that the program is never obligated to provide more service than allowed by the resources or technology at its command. An easy (though not necessarily ideal) way to ensure this is to set a percentage of a particular target group or a numeric parameter: "will serve 30 percent of the homeless" or "will serve an average of eight teenage homeless persons over a one-year period." Baselines may or may not be precise; absent "hard" information, parameters based on practice wisdom are better than none at all. Needs surveys usually can provide reliable guidance for anticipating service demand, but, unfortunately, funding is seldom available to conduct them. The most common way that target group specifications are made is simply to take the relevant resources into account and calculate the maximum number of clients who could be served. The downside to this approach is that, absent need/service demand data, nothing useful can be said about the expected impact of the program on actual need.

Too often, social programs are discontinued not because their program ideas and implementation were lacking or ineffective but because they failed to reach a target group that, with proper foresight, would have been known to be unreachable, given the resources at hand. This happens when administrators and social program innovators become so enthusiastic about their ideas and operations that without realizing it they overcommit their organization. This is unfortunate because good ideas are scarce. Finally, competition for social program funding is fierce, and interested parties will seize on the others' shortcomings like sharks in a feeding frenzy—all the more reason to avoid being careless about setting target specifications in building objectives.

Objectives (not abstract goals) must contain *performance standards*, which are statements about the extent of the changes or influence the program effort is intended or expected to have. A performance standard for a housing program might be "within five years to secure safe, up-to-standard permanent shelter for one-third of the low-income population of Compton, Mississippi, that is inhabited by no more than two persons per room, and has running water, sanitary toilets, and electric outlets in each room." Certainly the details can be argued, but the phrases "two persons per room" and "running water" are examples of performance standards. Any housing falling short of those descriptions does not meet the standard of performance and thus cannot count as a positive outcome of the program. Another example from the personal social services might be a program for integrating the severely emotionally disturbed into a pattern of community living where the objective is to have each "severely mentally ill person living in a private single-family residence, with the family in residence exercising oversight and with the person taking full responsibility for his or her nutrition, medication, and interaction with a non–family member who shares the dwelling for at least ten hours a week." In this case the phrases refer to explicit performance standards for the program. Wherever those standards are not met, that instance does not count as a success for the program.

PURPOSE OF GOALS AND OBJECTIVES

Why have both goals and objectives when, in one sense, they refer to the same thing? Because they serve different purposes. Statements about objectives are absolutely essential for two reasons.

1. They give the operational outcome toward which program operations are directed, and no administrator can make decisions about daily issues like constructing budgets, distributing money among various program operations, and hiring and firing without a concrete objective in mind.
2. Programs cannot be evaluated for effectiveness unless there is an objective to serve as a measurable standard against which data from actual achievements can be cast.

Program goals are also necessary in that they provide a crucial link between the more concrete and specific objectives, and the public documentary sources (laws, judicial decisions, administrative mandates) that establish the program or policy. Statements in such documents can never be sufficiently specific so that a program or policy can be constructed from them directly. Whatever their source, statements are quintessentially political, the product of political compromise; and political documents can never be truly explicit lest some party takes issue with them. If that happens, it may destroy delicate political, judicial, administrative, or organizational compromises that were necessary to promulgate the policy or program in the first place. Part of the art of politics is to avoid saying what will offend, and in that way both sides believe the issue is settled. As S. M. Miller states, ". . . behind every political agreement there lies a misunderstanding. . . ."[4] Program designers must translate these documents into operating programs, and to do that they need to translate the goal in the public document into a statement at a concrete level, i.e., a measurable objective. Such a statement at a general and abstract level will encapsulate the basic desired outcomes. Then they need to make a statement at a more specific and concrete level that will direct a choice of specific program operations and program provisions that will move events toward the stated general goal as well as allow observations to be made by which program success or failure can be judged.

Following is one example of how goals and objectives function to provide a link between legislative intent and program operations and to assist operations accountability. Consider the Social Security Retirement program's minimum benefit provision in contrast to the goal of the Social Security program. Social Security's broadest goal is to replace income lost through inability to continue earning at accustomed levels in the labor force and to do so at an income level that would provide at least for minimum survival.[5] An objective is to accomplish this goal through a self-financing insurance mechanism. When the Social Security system was begun in 1935, Congress worried because levels of unemployment were very high at the time—at least 30 percent—due to the Great Depression. The target population was likely to include many people who were either working at very low wages or had not been working for some years. Because an insurance system must work on prior contributions, there would be, for some years to come, many elders who had made no prior contributions or had contributed at very low levels—thus making their expected retirement benefits either nonexistent or very small, way below what anyone could expect to live on. The solution was creation of a "temporary" minimum benefit for those workers whose contribution history could not generate sufficient income for a living-wage Social Security benefit and creation of a means-tested secondary welfare system that would add to that income. The latter became the Old Age Assistance Program (later called Categorical Assistance because beneficiaries qualified by virtue of being in a category like "old" or "blind"). Together the two would create a minimum income at a survival level.

For a variety of reasons, this temporary solution continued to be a program feature long after its need was markedly reduced. It should have been phased out in the early years of the system when wage histories and worker contributions came up to standard under the impact of the full-employment conditions of World War II. To make matters worse, it became a handy way to solve other social problems; for example, Congress later extended minimum benefits to disabled and dependent youth, the disabled mentally ill, and the self-employed. However, this move ran counter to the goals and objectives of OASI because it had to be financed from the contributions of other workers and thus seriously contradicted the self-financing insurance principle on which the Social Security system was built. In burdening Social Security contributors with welfare payments to citizens whose wage histories could not generate a decent OASI benefit, the plan imposed on citizens problems that should be solved by the entire tax-paying public (not just wage earners but those who make their income from capital investment and the like). The objective of OASI is for benefits to be self-financing because they are proportional to contributions; setting a benefit below which no contributor will fall is contradictory to that objective. Any social program in a functioning democracy needs to guard zealously its roots in legislation, the ultimate expression of the will of the people, for that is the ultimate source of its legitimacy.

SETTING GOALS AND OBJECTIVES IN PERSONAL SOCIAL SERVICE PROGRAMS AND POLICY

Despite belief that evaluation criteria require a fair degree of consensus among those charged with responsibility for setting them, at many points we will call that implication into question. In fact, lack of consensus at various administrative, legislative, and program operational levels is exactly the divergence that this method of policy analysis seeks to exploit for purposes of new and improved policy formulations (as explained later in this chapter). Three issues are important here.

First, recalling the distinction between systems that provide personal social services ("soft" benefits) like foster care and those that provide public social utilities ("hard" benefits) like food stamps, commodities, cash, or housing, it is quite possible for a personal social service (PSS) program to function without expressing precisely the goals and objectives of its enabling legislation. The reason is that in the PSSs, expressions of goals and objectives in the enabling legislation is vague. In Chapter 3 (judicial context), we referred to state legislation in regard to child custody, which consistently referred to criteria like the "child's best interest." Such legislation leaves it entirely in the hands of the court and its operatives (social workers and others in this case) to define what that goal (child's best interest) means for a particular child. This discretion, although it does not necessarily impede the functioning of the program of awarding child custody, may be cause for trouble later (in some cases it may be downright illegal), but nevertheless it is common practice. Ability to draw personal social service goals and objectives that are clear, measurable, and manipulable is not impaired by their lack of fit at the operational vis-à-vis the legislative level. Of course, they could not be described as "good" goals or objectives on just that account.

Second, note that many argue that because it is sometimes difficult for program staff at the grass-roots level to come to a consensus on proper goals and objectives, *none* should be constructed. It is a weak argument on two counts: First, a strong consensus is entirely unnecessary when the broader program goal admits of many concrete outcomes—for example, if the goal is so broad as to say "to encourage development and experimentation with various service strategies to achieve community integration or independent living," then the objective is precisely to explore the feasibility of a number of ways of delivering services and to study their negative side effects, costs, and all other tedious and unrelenting problems that beset implementation of social programs. In an avowedly experimental venture, consensus on a much lower level is all that is required. Consensus can actually be antithetical to program intent. Frequently, the proper issue in the early stages of the development of social program and policy system designs is not what can be achieved in some ideal world, but rather what is practical, feasible, cost-effective, and implementable.

Third, PSSs require much more individualized objectives, perhaps for each client, tied together generally by their association with the broad goal. For example, in a residential care home for the mentally retarded, one would expect to have very individualized (probably behavior-oriented) objectives. Such objectives should have relevance to the general goals of the program—for example, socialization, self-control, verbal expression, and the like—and this general relevance should be public and explicit. It makes all the difference in the world *why* a program and its practitioners do one thing and not another. Individual practitioners might disagree on what the specific behavioral objectives should be, but indeed many sets might be satisfactory. Thus, lack of consensus on objectives at this level of practice is not a major problem; it might even be a virtue in early stages of program or policy system development and in regard to certain types of clients or beneficiaries. One example of how it might be a virtue is found in residential care centers where, given sets of specific behavioral objectives for each resident, payment for client care can be based on achievement of objectives, called *targeted reimbursement. Nontargeted reimbursement* in personal social service programs has dubious trade-offs. For example, if care providers are paid the same for all clients without respect to their disability or level of care required, there is every motivation for the facility to admit those clients who are *least* disabled. Another example is reimbursement of facilities based on levels of care provided. The trade-off here is that residents are often segregated by whether their care needs are "high," "medium," or "low,"—a situation that tends toward the creation of old-fashioned "back wards," where "difficult," "challenging," and "hard-to-manage" clients are "warehoused." The solution that seems to avoid most of these problems is to make reimbursement variable and dependent on client characteristics and level of challenges (a code word for special and often difficult behaviors in residential settings). Although creation of a policy and program system that will identify client characteristics and behavioral challenges is itself no small challenge, it may carry a handsome payoff, as suggested by recent research.[6] The point here is that to construct a policy and program system that can accomplish targeted reimbursement, clear and unambiguous goals and objectives are an absolute essential, even though precise consensus on these particulars is not.

There is no intention here to suggest that only policy system or program staff or legislation can set goals and objectives. In fact, in the personal social services there is (or should be) considerable room for clients or beneficiaries to shape and/or set their own objectives. In various counseling settings, clients present problems that are within the general range of the social problem on which the organization focuses. This makes for a nearly infinite range of possible routes out of the problematic condition. Take the example of marital disharmony. At least four general solutions are possible in this example: (1) transcendence (stick with it and take on a different mental set by which to deal with a bad situation); (2) personal adjustment (change one's own ways of acting and responding); (3) interpersonal adjustment (change both partners' ways of acting and responding; or (4) dissolve the marriage.

It would appear easier to set goals and objectives for a "hard" benefit program, one that delivers goods rather than services—food stamps, cash, housing, or commodities are examples. With regard to food stamps, for example, defining objectives is rather straightforward. The goal of the program is to provide essential nutrition and the objectives are phrased in ways that shape the buying habits of beneficiaries—thus junk foods, alcoholic beverages, and tobacco cannot be bought with food stamps. In Europe and other countries where the welfare commodity programs are heavily shaped by current agricultural surplus, the policy system to distribute it is based on a heavy subsidy to the retail grocery merchant (or surrogate); so prices for milk and cheese, for example, are significantly reduced.

GOALS AND OBJECTIVES VARY ACCORDING TO THE DEVELOPMENTAL STAGE OF THE PROGRAM

In program or policy analysis it is important to understand the developmental stages of the enterprise. It is reasonably common for social programs to go through a demonstration phase where the objectives are much looser than described above. In fact, social policy and program efforts probably would be better off were they routinely tested in one of (at least) three demonstration forms: pilots, models, or prototypes. Models (sometimes called prototypes) are social programs implemented as a trial under the *most desirable* conditions under which they are most likely to succeed. The idea is, if they cannot succeed under these conditions they will never succeed in "real life." Models are very tightly constructed and are not subject to change in mid course. *Pilot projects* are likely to be the loosest type of demonstration program and the ones whose objectives are most subject to change. A pilot searches for unexpected outcomes and the program design is changed on a simple trial-and-error basis "to see what happens" as a result. It is the strategy of choice where not very much is known about the social problem of concern. Although this approach is social "tinkering" in its most blatant form, there is a clear place for pilot projects in the absence of good guesses about the nature of a social problem. The actual objective of such a program is to gather more knowledge or information about the problem and the program, even though the explicit objective may be a specific desirable social outcome. If that is the case, it is important for the analysis to take that dichotomy into account and always to feature it in drawing conclusions about the integrity of the overall program.[7]

METHODS OF IDENTIFYING GOALS AND OBJECTIVES

Identifying program goals and objectives is not always a simple matter. There is no one source for the documents that are necessary to draw firm conclusions, even in the case of public social policies or programs. What follows, however, is a routine procedure that ordinarily will result in reasonably firm conclusions about the goal(s) and objective(s) of public policies or programs. Note that the procedure does not necessarily need to follow the sequence presented.

Step 1: Locate the Enabling Legislation

All public social programs are "public" because in one way or another they are funded from the governmental treasury. Any treasury expenditure must be authorized by the elected officials constitutionally empowered to do so. Authorizations for expenditures are almost always made in terms of "programs" under the administrative control of various governmental departments. Programs are set up by what is called *enabling legislation*, acts that contain some statement about the purpose or goal of the act and for the program.

Step 2: Locate Legislative History

It is important to gain a deeper perspective on policy goals, purposes, and legislative intent, and the best source for doing so is ordinarily called the "legislative history." *Legislative history* refers to a set of official documents or transcripts of legislative hearings and documents accepted as part of the background material studied by members of the legislative committees that considered the matter at hand and framed the legislation that subsequently was passed into law. Legislative history is more readily available for acts passed by Congress, but is also available at the state level. Legislative histories can be found in any law school library, statehouse library, or university library public documents department.

Step 3: Locate Staff and Committee Studies and Reports

Other sources of program goals (besides the preamble to the enabling legislation itself) includes *staff studies* prepared for use by congressional committees to study issues that may result in new programs or policies and amendments to existing legislation. Staff studies are usually considered reasonably authoritative sources for statements concerning the goal and purposes of public social policy and programs.

Step 4: Check Other "Official" Sources

There are two main authoritative sources for statements about the goals and objectives of social programs that entail federal funds or administration. One of those is the official biannual *Social Security Handbook,* published by the Social Security Administration and housed in all federal document repositories. (Nearly all university libraries are repositories or, if not, have this volume in their government documents collection.) Another main authoritative source is *The Green Book: Social Security and Income Maintenance Programs in the U.S.,* which gives exhaustive detail on these programs as well as legislative history.[8] Another source is the guide to means-tested income maintenance programs, published by the Food Research and Action and Council (FRAC) of New York City. The American Public Welfare Association also publishes a means-tested income guide. Other sources, more minimal in character, include brochures and fact-sheets available at local Social Security offices ("Understanding Social Security," for example); local social security employees are generally helpful sources for detailed information on programs if questions are specific (although they will not offer evaluative opinions on programs). Finally, the following Commercial Clearing House (Washington, D.C.) paperbacks are almost always part of the document collections of university libraries:

- 1991 *Social Security Explained* (248 pages, $12)
- 1991 *Medicare Explained* (192 pages, $15)
- 1991 *Social Security Benefits* (including Medicare) (48 pages, $4)

The National Underwriters Association also publishes authoritative handbooks on Social Security and Medicare: *Social Security Manual,* 31st edition (209 pages, $10.95).

In the search to document public social program goals and objectives, do not overlook the rich resource of official administrative rules and regulations. Although social program administrators commonly prepare public relations material intended to describe programs and program operations, these releases usually are of little help, and often are deliberately vague. Public program operations manuals, on the other hand, are very much public property, although they are not always easy to get (or to use, I might add). For example, the policy manuals for the public agency that operates state foster care and adoption programs routinely list thousands of rules and regulations. The *Federal Register* publishes into the public domain the multitude of rules and regulations and much else that pertains to federal agencies. Buried in these documents are explicit statements about goals and objectives, which, precisely because they are official, can be excellent sources of information on this point.

Locating Sources for Goals in Private and State-Administered Programs

Social programs that are entirely state administered have documentary sources that are somewhat similar to those for federal programs, although exact titles and sources will vary by state. All state legislatures maintain current legislative history sources, and they can be obtained by a simple inquiry directed to the state legislature's library, usually located in the statehouse. In regard to state-administered programs, look for official committee hearings, staff studies, and reports to committees. A simple inquiry to your local state legislator will usually net a short and helpful discussion with one of her or his aides about how to locate the documents desired. Checking amendments to bills as originally written will net information on what was *not* intended. A letter to the legislator who introduced the bill may also provide helpful data about intentions and will usually be answered quickly. Social programs in the private sector and those run by local governments, despite their importance to the total social welfare effort of this country, may not have easy-access official public documentary sources if such programs are not enabled or mainly financed by the state. Therefore, such goals are often fugitive and can be very difficult to identify. Usually, some kind of organizational document is available that supports or mandates the program and therefore can serve as "legislative history." Using a program administrator as a source is legitimate, but not only might goals change almost daily, they might be no more than a reflection of the administrator's casual, ad hoc style. Sometimes goals developed in this off-hand way have found their way into print and later influenced day-to-day operations in the organization—much to the surprise of the administrator, who never foresaw that his or her informal goals and objectives might develop lives of their own. In researching private sources, you may find instances of organizations that have no overall goal-guiding operations; rather, each staff member has personal and professional goals for her or his practice. You may also find instances of organizations that lack overarching goals, where the only goals and objectives are chosen by clients based on their own preferred outcomes. Based on certain assumptions, both cases are legitimate; note, however, that in neither case is a single social program or policy system in place. In effect, there are as many programs or policy systems as there are staff practitioners. From another point of view, *no* public social policy or program is at work here, and therefore nothing can be analyzed.

EVALUATING PROGRAM OR POLICY SYSTEM GOALS AND OBJECTIVES

Introduction

In a value-critical analysis of social policy and program features, fundamental value positions must be declared since, implicitly or explicitly, they are the source of the value standards against which the program or policy system features will be judged. To illustrate how this value-critical method of policy and program analysis works, particular value positions will be adopted and argued here. They will be set forth affirmatively and as persuasively as possible. Value neutrality is specifically rejected in the belief that it is a seductive ideal, one that is fundamentally negative in its effects because it seduces the expositor into believing that something said in a value-neutral way is somehow "scientific." Readers, however, may disagree and may give priority to other value positions. The best way to understand how this analytic method works is to substitute your own value commitments and repeat the exercise. Note that certain value positions already are implicit from statements about program and policy system features made earlier in this book. Let us now try to ferret those out (remember, what follows is simply an illustrative selection) and begin by noting some value positions that are inherent in the very nature of doing an analysis at all.

One such feature is the preference for *logical consistency and rationality*. To write a book about analysis is to announce a commitment to those virtues. For example, the first part of this chapter stressed the importance of logical and definitional links between goals and objectives and the problem definition given in the social problem analysis. In the Western tradition I—and perhaps the reader—have an a priori, ordinarily unexamined commitment to the virtues of logic and rationality. (Perhaps this is a legacy of rational western industrialism—witness the old factory and mill cities along the Eastern Seaboard or the worn-out hills among the nearly abandoned open-pit iron mines of northern Minnesota.) The point is, the rationality that produces good outcomes can also produce negative ones if it remains undisciplined by other value positions.

Two other examples of value positions are inherent in this method: public accountability, and the notion that product counts. All social programs (public and private sectors) must always be *accountable* to their relevant publics; in public sector programs that means taxpayers and their elected representatives. Accountability makes the program and policy provision directly connected to legislative mandates and thus the will of the citizenry whose taxes pay for it. Accountability has other virtues as well, such as ability to change and make "mid-course corrections" possible. The value position that *product counts*, i.e., that policies or programs that produce results (verifiable outcomes) or best results at least cost, should be preferred, has application in this method of policy analysis. Note that product is not *all* that matters, for concern with side effects is also an important issue here. To the extent that social policies and programs are implemented precisely to solve social problems, their performance in that role is the ultimate measure of their worth.

Rationality, accountability, and product (verifiable outcomes) in public social policy and programs serve other more fundamental social values. Rationality and logical consistency are required in order to have some grounds on which to believe *in advance* that the program will be a likely solution to the social problem of concern. After all, how could one argue successfully (other than from intuition) that a program might solve a problem (any problem!) unless there were rational grounds for it?[9] In the final analysis, it is our preference for control and prediction and the implicit commitment of our political process (social program funding is only one example) that demands a rational basis for public expenditures; legislative, judicial, and administrative accountability demands it. Public appropriations, in our North American way of doing things, are not given simply by virtue of having faith in the persons who will spend them. So it turns out that the political ideology of our society demands rationality because it contains a not-very-implicit assumption about rationality and logical consistency as an instrumental means to achieve just and fair dealings with citizens' money. That creates a necessity to have advance grounds for judging that a program will be adequate to answer the social problem of concern, equitable for prospective clients or user/consumers, and efficient in obtaining the most value for money expended. Whereas other societies have different commitments on this matter, North Americans are firmly committed to rational prediction and the rationalization of control; to be otherwise is to be unable to account for program or policy system operations or have a consistent standard for performance.

When we come to personal social services, there can be dramatic consequences to this commitment. As discussed in Chapter 4, personal social service programs are characterized by strong individualization and many involve a "treatment process." Treatment processes can be directed at mental, social, and/or emotional disorders, which belie specifying outcomes or end products on the view that a treatment process worth its salt serves to make possible outcomes that go beyond the scope of the social problem; the specifics of these outcomes are at the choice of the user/consumer of services (patient or client). Social services conceived this way do not necessarily serve as a solution to the presenting social problem but rather to make it possible for a person to choose a different course and not live a life driven by, or at the mercy of, a social problem. Chemical substance addiction is probably the clearest example that illustrates this point. Other, more controversial examples may be social problems like illiteracy, emotional disturbance, or children's behavioral problems. Some of these viewpoints can emphasize a general and radical freedom on the part of the individual in terms of the outcome preferred. One of the principles set out early in this chapter emphasized that providing services or benefits is never, by itself, a legitimate goal or objective of a social program, meaning that the preference here is that product, not process, counts. It is a biased viewpoint, of course, whose ultimate source lies in the assumption that because the personal social services that concern us here involve public funds, at some level they must concern the public interest. To do that, the service outcomes must be explicit and measurable so as to withstand judgment of their relationship to the public interest. Individually chosen outcomes concern private, not necessarily public, interests.[10]

Another issue here is the bias that personal social services that focus narrowly on the individual involved may fail to solve social problems and may even be detrimental. They can be detrimental in the sense illustrated by the following (admittedly extreme) example. Consider the social problem of children with severe emotional disturbance or severe mental retardation. Such children can be extremely demanding of families and others in their immediate environment. Routine temporary relief through respite care is absolutely essential for the family system to function over any given length of time. A treatment process that would assist persons to "choose" heroic sacrifice to that child over better adjustment to the situation is detrimental because it obscures the realities of the child's care needs (not to mention those of other family members)—realities that generally are beyond the endurance and capacity of ordinary families in a society that encourages nuclear families and thus isolates such a child's family from the resources of an extended kin group (respite care). Any treatment process so narrowly focused that it concerns itself only with the individual's (the child's) internal processes and how the child or the family (or even the school personnel) can alter their own attitudes or emotional reactions so that "choice making" somehow helps the child and the family "adjust," is not preferred here because it can fail to take account of the child's environment and the social needs of the whole social unit. This example shows *bias in favor of a person-environment viewpoint as well as a bias in favor of the social responsibility of social programs toward whole social units versus individuals and toward the maintenance of the social fabric itself.*

Overorientation to end product goes against the grain of service-providing professionals. In fact, *no* practitioner of high standards *ever* guarantees an outcome as a result of services given, even though they may express to clients their general optimism or pessimism. An experienced lawyer, for example, knows that she or he cannot guarantee to a client that their case can be won in court; an experienced physician or surgeon will not guarantee that an operation will be satisfactory. What professionals do offer is service expertise, a process of understanding a problematic condition and bringing their best knowledge to bear on it—they do not offer a product. Other than from an ethics standpoint, professionals are accountable to their own professional organizations and state licensing boards only for showing that they offer a knowledge-based, up-to-date, professional *process*. No lawyer was ever disbarred for losing a particular case, no physician's license was ever revoked for failing to cure a particular patient. True enough, lawyers and physicians might be investigated if they lose *all* their cases or if *all* their patients die on the operating table, but these situations only illustrate the principle: Licenses are withdrawn only upon showing that the reasons the failures occurred are those that, *in the process* of providing professional services, the licensed professional could have or should have foreseen. Understood this way, it is easy to see why professional practitioners are uncomfortable with being evaluated on the basis of their "product."

Other value positions are not so obvious. The value positions discussed below are my personal preferences. The fact that they are well within the scope of value commitments current within the profession should not obscure the idea that practical policy analysts must expect to bring their own value perspectives to an analysis. Such perspectives need to be very explicit because they help consumers, and indeed analysts themselves, think about how different value commitments might steer conclusions in important, and ultimately more productive, directions. The agenda here is to present a method of policy analysis that is sufficiently flexible so that it can accommodate a wide range of viewpoints.

Recall that in the introduction to this method of social policy and program analysis, two general types of evaluation criteria were cited for each operating characteristic: (1) fit with the social problem analysis and (2) evaluation criteria external to the social problem analysis and having their own definitional and ideological base (see Table 4–1). In regard to (2) we will discuss (A) adequacy, equity, and efficiency; (B) criteria with unique applications to goals and objectives, and (C) the analyst's own value perspectives as evaluation criteria. Let us first consider how we go about evaluating goals and objectives with respect to their fit with a social problem analysis.

EVALUATION OF FIT BETWEEN PROGRAM OR POLICY GOALS AND OBJECTIVES AND SOCIAL PROBLEM ANALYSIS

Because providing a solution to a social problem is, in our definitions, the manifest purpose of a social policy or program, the merit of any of its features must be judged by how they fit that purpose. Social policies and programs should *not* be designed in the abstract, no matter how strongly they stand as innovative or "good" ideas. This conviction also applies to features, such as policy system or social program goals and objectives, whose purpose is to keep the policy or program going in the desired direction, that is, toward solution (or mitigation) of the social problem. Thus, the fit, goal relevance, and objectives are of premier importance. Unfortunately, a number of social policies and programs are misdirected in this way.

Consider for a moment a program of public child care for working parents. Note at the outset how varied the objectives for such child care can be because definitions of the social problem intended to be solved by such programs can vary widely. Fairly common objectives for preschoolers (for example) include the following: to provide educational enrichment (develop preschool skills); to provide safe and dependable substitute parent care during work hours; to develop early cognitive and emotional creativity; to provide nutritionally sound, emotionally stimulating, and health-attentive care. Program features of a multitude of day care settings are recognizable in that list. A neighbor who tends to fewer than three children in her own home but provides no explicit educational or creative stimulation exemplifies day care with a minimum of objectives—safe and dependable care. Alternatively, a local franchise of a national day care chain may focus on educational enrichment and development of cognitive and emotional roots of creativity, as well as program components having to do with nutrition, child health, safe care, and the like.

Imagine how different will be the objectives and organizational policies within these different programs. Behind all that is an implicit social problem analysis. In what follows you will recognize the four elements of a complete social problem analysis (as described in Chapter 1): (1) problem definition, (2) causation, (3) ideology, and (4) gainers and losers. Thus, the favored definition of the social problem to be dealt with for the neighborhood scenario might be the parent's need to have a dependable person to be in charge of an infant during work hours and to feel at ease about the child's nutrition, physical safety, and health. Although this objective may preoccupy many (if not most) day care parents, that is not to say that other objectives are superfluous. The Montessori school scenario has a much more complex, theoretical, even elegant social problem definition in mind. Perhaps their basic concern here is expressed as the absence of age-appropriate stimulation to the child's cognitive and emotional capacities. Whereas preoccupation with a child's safety and nutrition, and the dependability of care may be present, the school may demand more.

The point here is that goals and objectives must fit the social problem viewpoint to which the program is intended to be a solution and so, for each different social problem/policy/program package, goals and objectives are likely to differ conspicuously. The "fit" is twofold. First:

> A good fit between social problem analysis and goals and objectives is a matter of demonstrating the similarity between the terms in which the social problem is defined and the terms in which the goals and objectives of the program or policy system are defined.

Unless this fit can be demonstrated, it is possible that the programmatic solution is irrelevant to the social problem declared to be of interest. Of course, that is a major flaw because it is then quite likely that public expenditures are purchasing essentially irrelevant goods or services.

Second:

> Demonstrating a good fit with the social problem analysis is a matter of showing the
> relationship between the terms in which the objectives (outcomes) are defined and the
> independent variables in the causal chain of the social problem analysis.

Thus, if the social problem analysis contains a causal chain in which the outcome (independent) variable is child abuse, the objectives of the program must
relate to child abuse in some way (of course there can be other objectives as
well), but it is important that the same definitions be used. If, as actually occurs
sometimes, program designers have developed a set or programmatic interventions targeted not on child neglect but on physical child abuse, then there a serious flaw is involved. It is not difficult to make this kind of mistake in a field
where ambiguous definition is commonplace. It might be made because many
social workers and human service staff continue to think of child neglect as simply a lesser version of physical child abuse—despite substantial research evidence
to the contrary (concluding that child abusers inflicting serious physical damage
are probably a breed apart). It makes no sense at all to contrive and implement
an elaborate intervention directed toward a phenomenon that is entirely different from the one intended. The following sections address the second set of
evaluation criteria—adequacy, equity, and efficiency.

Adequacy

Were this book written for economists or political scientists or students of public administration, it would seem strange to begin a discussion of evaluating public social program goals and objectives by speaking about "fit with the social
problem analysis." That is because the traditional concepts by which public
expenditures are evaluated are adequacy, equity, and efficiency, and that audience would expect to begin with them. What is at issue in this section is something that rarely is recognized: *The concrete definitions of what counts as adequate (or equitable) are embedded in the ideology inherent in the social problem
analysis.* On that account it is by reference to their fit with the social problem
analysis that even these traditional concepts work as evaluation criteria. The
questions to be asked by the practitioner-analyst should be whether the goals
and objectives as stated are adequate at a level that expresses the value biases in
the social problem analysis—for example, whether objectives as stated create an
impact on the social problems of concern to the aging retired, that is, on housing, food, transportation, and so forth. How far will this set of program or policy goals and objectives carry us toward solution? Making this type of judgment
also requires quantitative judgments, for example, what percentage is the target
specification of the total population affected? The traditional equity–adequacy
criteria were developed in regard to social programs of most concern to
economists, i.e., those delivering the public social utilities, otherwise known as
hard benefits: housing, cash in the form of retirement and disability benefits,
farm subsidies, mortgage subsidies, student loans or scholarships. As evaluation
criteria adequacy, equity, and efficiency leave a great deal to be desired when

judging the operating characteristics of personal social service programs. Consider how much more difficult it is to make equity–adequacy–efficiency judgments about personal social service programs than about public social utility programs delivering hard benefits. What constitutes enough "community integration" (of the mentally ill or developmentally disabled, for example) for there to be a significant impact on the social problem of community alienation, is but one mind-bending example. Plainly, some levels are negligible—a retiree's presence at one group luncheon at a senior citizens center certainly sounds insignificant. The answer turns on *both* the causal theory in the social problem analysis *and* its inherent ideology about what counts as "significant impact." How much easier it seems to make statements about how much and what kind of transportation is required for a social program to have an impact on the social problem of making outpatient medical care available to the frail elderly and disabled, for example.

Equity

Equity is a more complicated criterion in this context and in general has to do with whether citizens in equivalent situations are treated similarly by a social policy or program. There are two kinds of equity: (1) *proportional equity*, where citizens receive benefits or services that are proportional to their relative need for them, and (2) *absolute equity*, where citizens receive benefits or services in equivalent amounts regardless of their relative need. Whether the goal treats one user/consumer/beneficiary the same as others turns on how equity is defined. Two families who receive the same amount of food stamps or commodities even though one family earns $100 a week and the other $35 a week, is an example of absolute equity. If the $35 family receives more food stamps than the $100 family so that the buying power of both families' food stamps plus their earnings is identical, then proportional equity is the result.

Statements of goals and objectives need to be clear as to whether absolute or proportional equity is intended. An example of a statement of objective that embeds proportional equity is "The objective of the program is to provide transportation to the aged at a cost that, taking into account their earnings, assets, and/or other cash benefits, will not decrease their total spendable income for food and housing." If this program objective is implemented, program participants will get transportation at various costs, depending on what their other money resources are; those with high earnings or assets will have to pay and those with very low earnings might get a free ride. An example of a statement of objectives that embeds absolute equity is "The objective of the program is to make elderly transportation available at actual cost." If this program objective is implemented, all program participants can use the transportation service at a set fee—the per-user actual cost of providing it—with the consequence being that the fee will be a greater burden on those with low earnings or assets compared to those with high wage earnings or assets.

Equity cuts other ways as an evaluation criterion for goals and objectives. In specifying particular target subgroups in the statements of objectives, some groups will inevitably get more benefits or services or resources than others. Some statements of objectives might express an affirmative action sentiment: "Transportation services will be provided, first priority, for those sections of the community in which ethnic minorities reside." The equity question here has several dimensions. If the ideological position is that ethnic minorities have been historically and systematically deprived of transportation, then proportional equity would justify the priority service given them in the preceding statement of objectives. On the other hand, if the statement of objectives specifies transportation services operated at the county level of government and specifies that they are to be focused on geographic areas closest to the county seat so they can link up with existing city transportation, the system will expand transportation opportunities for those who live on the city fringe but systematically deprive rural residents. The basic question is not answered solely by judging whether equity exists but, if inequity exists, whether the stated value positions rationally justify it.

Efficiency

The efficiency criterion cannot be applied logically to the goals and objectives, basically because the concern of goals and objectives is restricted to *outcome*, whereas the concern of efficiency always lies with *means* to an outcome. The center of the efficiency question is always whether there is a better (least costly, more cost-effective) means to achieve a given outcome. Because goals and objectives must refer to ends and not means, the efficiency criterion hardly applies.

OTHER CRITERIA FOR EVALUATING THE MERIT OF GOALS AND OBJECTIVES

Statements of goals and objectives can be evaluated for substance and for inclusion against the following criteria: clarity; measurability (which only concerns objectives, of course); manipulability; concern with ends, not means; standards for expected program performance; and specification of the target group at which intervention is aimed. These criteria are specific to goals and objectives, not to other operating characteristics.

Clarity

A statement of a goal or objective is clear if its terms are well defined; a well defined term easily distinguishes examples of things to which the term refers from those to which the term is closely related. In other words, meaning of the terms is not left to the imagination. Goal statements or statements of objectives must be accompanied by definitions for terms whose meanings are uncommon or terms not in general use among the intended public. The following goal statement is unclear because its terms are not subsequently defined and probably are not familiar to most: "The goal of this policy is to raise the level of consciousness about work sharing and its benefits for the unit work group." Note that if the terms *work sharing* and *work group* were defined the statement might be clear. For example:

> *Work sharing* means splitting one standard 40-hour week of a paid, skilled job into several parts of a workday, each part held by a different employee who works only part-time.
>
> *Work group* refers to a group of people who are employed by and earn wages from the same employer, working in close proximity to each other at the same workplace.

What we have done here is simply to change the goal statement into what we could now call a statement of objective simply by making it concrete and observable.

The second definition holds a number of definitional options: One could loosen the definition (and include more people) by removing the qualifier "working in close proximity to each other." That would increase the number in the work group but, more important, it would scoop up a very different set of people than is referred to in the first definition. The first would likely include people in relationships usually defined as primary, the second would include those usually defined as primary *and* secondary social relationships. It is easy to see how fundamentally arbitrary definitions are. Choices here depend on the purpose for the definition: Is the interest actually in primary or secondary relationships? Of course the phrase "raise the level of consciousness" is more abstruse, but it is still capable of definition. The difficulty is that it could mean so many different things that any one definition probably will seem arbitrary and strange to the ear. A handy idea to remember about definitions is the ancient distinction between genera and specie: One acceptable way of constructing definitions is to have the definitional statement tell the general class (genera) to which the thing defined belongs and then tell the things that make it different from all other members of that class (specie). For example, "raise the level of consciousness" means acquiring the cognitive grasp (genera, the general class of things to which this thing belongs) of the contemporary social realities that make work sharing a desirable work option (specie, the feature that makes this different from all other kinds of cognitive grasps).

Measurability

Unless statements of objectives are *capable of being measured,* they are of little use in administering or evaluating a program or policy. Remember, it is only objectives, not goals, to which the criterion of measurability applies. We will not talk about goals because it is in their nature to be so general as to be immeasurable in principle (as discussed earlier in this chapter). To be measurable means to be quantified, even if only in crude fashion ("none, some, much"). In practice, it seems likely that any term can be measured; all that is required is to give it definitional substance. The most general problem in regard to measurability is that definitions are neither given nor carefully constructed.

Manipulability

Some objectives are expressed in literally unmanipulable terms: "The goal is to develop in military service personnel the capacity to publicly criticize their superiors in the civilian press." Or "The goal is to enable preschoolers to objectively evaluate parents' restrictions on their behavior." The terms in which goals are expressed must refer to factors for which there is a basis for reasonable expectations for change under the impact of some plausible range of interventions. The preceding examples would appear extremely resilient to manipulation. What would it take to induce a military person to do the one thing that would be most likely to destroy a military career (i.e., publicly criticize a superior)? In regard to the second example, isn't it true that most empirical data on the judgment processes of very young children do not support its plausibility? Everyday experience with such children suggests that the mechanisms of identification with parents (logically) destroys any notion about the children's objectivity about their parents. It seems safe to suggest that the preschooler's dependency needs would obscure even the simplest objectivity. To suggest an intervention (a goal) that would interfere or challenge that dependency seems quite unlikely. The research of Walter Miller provides an example quoted by Martin Rein. After conducting a lengthy research study of delinquency, Miller concluded that delinquency was mainly a function of age and sex—under 18 and male. Neither, of course, is manipulable and if Miller is correct, juvenile delinquency is essentially beyond the reach of social interventions.[11]

Of course, most of the above arguments against manipulability appeal to the illogic of the ideas as against everyday experience. The more common use of this criterion calls for some kind of evidence from empirical research—historical, experiential, experimental—that would give some basis on which to rest belief that the variables in which the objectives are started are open to influence. Consider an objective common among child abuse programs—to prevent incidents of child abuse. Any preventive program must successfully predict who will be at risk so as to target program interventions. However desirable this might be, to date no empirical study has done so successfully.[12] So at present, goals and objectives centered on child abuse prevention would have to be judged negatively because they refer to factors not yet shown to be manipulable.

The demand for evidence of manipulability is not overly constraining—if such evidence isn't available, one would not always have to give up the programmatic or policy idea, rather simply increase awareness that the program is setting out on an entirely unique experimental adventure. The consequence for action is not to abandon the concept, but to loosen the expectation of achievement *and* to administer the program with an eye to other alternatives, i.e., more manipulable and achievable objectives that are still within the scope of the general goal set for the program. The attitude counseled here is to adopt doubtful objectives as *hypotheses* rather than as firm expectations in preparation for abandoning the program or policy idea should they fail. Later on in this book, an argument will be made that social policies and programs ought to do more of just that kind of thing. All kinds of good reasons exist for being clear about what one is doing. For example, no program or policy system can be accountable in any important sense unless there is this kind of clarity, an absolutely indispensable virtue in public social programs. Further, the likelihood of obtaining important results is, without doubt, increased by consciousness of its experimental or exploratory nature. Frequently, serendipitous findings from exploratory and experimental research will be overlooked if social program managers are not conscious of these possibilities. And, because we are speaking about programs and policies that affect human beings, being clear that a program effort is experimental or exploratory is a necessary condition for alerting program participants to that fact; often it is a legal obligation. Finally, it is only ethical to be straightforward about such matters in dealing with those who make program and policy funding decisions. Too often and ultimately to our misfortune, policy and program advocates have promised more than they can deliver.

Concern with Ends, Not Means

Concern with ends that are outcomes, not means to ends—essentially "inputs"—is another standard that statements of goals and objectives should meet. If you want to make coffee from coffee beans, you put *into* the grinder (inputs) coffee beans, then you place the ground beans into the coffee maker and *out* comes brewed coffee (outcomes). No one would confuse the solid beans with the liquid coffee. The standard that must be met by statements of objectives or goals is that they must concern *outcomes, not inputs.* An example common in social work practice in the personal social services is making home studies, that is, those evaluations of the "goodness" or "fitness" of a home for a child in adoptive or foster family care or decisions having to do with which of a child's divorced parents the child should live. It is *not* acceptable to say that the objective of this social program is to "make home studies." Home studies are a means to an end, not an end in itself. A home study is surely not an activity that could stand on its own and be justified. There is simply no use for home studies unless they are necessary for a decision about a child. It is in this sense that we can say, in a commonsense way, that objectives and goals should be able to "stand on their own" as justified.

THE ANALYST'S OWN VALUE PERSPECTIVES IN EVALUATING THE MERIT OF GOALS AND OBJECTIVES

At some point practical public policy analysts will find that their own personal value positions will intrude on their enterprise. Recall a point made earlier that such value intrusions are important sources of bias and can only be made public to others and the audience for the analysis if analysts themselves are aware of their existence. So let us use some of the author's value commitments as examples of how these are likely to show up in judging the merit of social program or policy system operating characteristics. The concept of client empowerment refers to the idea that the fullest development of human potential takes place in an environment in which it is possible to bring one's choices (empowers those choices) into reality; taking charge of one's life is a common description. It is, at root, the simple idea that one's life can be filled with circumstances that grind into dust the ability to act on the choices one makes: too little money, time, opportunity, training, the moral support of others, skill, vision, energy, health. Valuing client empowerment implies strong medicine, strong constraints on social work and human service policy and practice goals and objectives.[13] For example, in one instance it might mean that in preference for doing things for people, a practitioner will work toward helping a client take charge, but it also may mean in another instance that the practitioner will take charge of organizing resources for people who (at that moment) cannot do that by themselves. Making available those resources is a means by which it becomes practically possible for the person helped to take charge. Without direct assistance from a practitioner (or others) in providing resources or access to them, taking charge of one's life in regard to housing and education is unlikely. Without training or skills or job opportunities, taking charge of one's work life is impossible.

Goals and objectives of social programs and policies will be preferred by the author-as-analyst when they reflect that idea—when they reflect the value commitments preferred. Now think of this example of a shelter program for the homeless the goal of which is to help its consumers avoid exposure to the elements; contrast it to one that *also* has goals and objectives reflecting empowerment goals, for example service consumers learning how to do the following:

- Access medical care (empowering service consumers to maximum physical capacity)
- Access housing market facts and resources (empowering service consumers to search out their own housing)
- Access welfare income maintenance benefits plus skills in applying for a job (empowering service consumers to an independent income and all that implies for their ability to make other life choices)
- Support others who have social problems that are similar to their own (empowering them to help their own)
- Form political constituencies for the homeless (empowering service consumers to exert political control over their own problems and work for political solutions of housing shortages, for example)

The latter program or policy system will be preferred over the former simply because it has empowerment goals and objectives whereas the other does not. Do not be misled—the intent is not to imply that helping homeless people to survive is somehow trivial. The issue here is to stress how much better is the solution for the social problem whose goal also seeks to empower the homeless in a way that goes a distance toward assisting people to the point where they can work changes in their own lives and live in circumstances that allow them to pursue the choices they make freely. The fact that it might be preventive is important to me only because it reduces preventable basic human pain (always a value preference for almost anyone involved in delivering human services and because less recurrence is an efficient use of resources—it makes available those resources for better work with fewer people or for work on other important social problems).

Such value choices can be complicated because they are not benign in every respect or they sometimes impinge on the delivery of "best" or "better" services to everyone. That happens because a broad objective (like empowerment) requires so much in the way of additional program services. In a world where finite resources and demand for services exceed availability, doing more for some client/consumers necessarily means doing less for others. When some get so much that others may get nothing, those with nothing are unlikely to agree that my value choice is a better one. Although I don't believe the above choice is always the best, in this instance I am persuaded it is and here is the best case I can make for it. When a social program does only a little for everyone in need, it may be that a little can be worse (or at least not better) than nothing—that is, its contribution to the solution of the problem is either minuscule or may create even worse problems. Under many conditions, homeless shelter programs are good examples of the potential for that result. It is one thing for a shelter program to provide benefits in the aftermath of community disaster—tornadoes, hurricanes, earthquakes; it is another when the disasters are personal (or perhaps singularly economic). If a homeless shelter can't provide enough services or benefits to make it possible to escape from the shelter, it can create a permanent resident population of those who cannot deal with the circumstances that brought them there in the first place; being "institutionalized" is not far around the corner. Before the advent of psychotropic medication for psychosis, mental institutions were very much in that same position. Income maintenance programs like SSI, which currently has a maximum grant of $407 per month for a single person, will help people survive but not move beyond that level of existence. The viewpoint in this book is that one aspect of the empowerment idea is that it assumes that people are continuously changing organisms, so that new paths (sometimes, but not always positive and growthful) are necessary as environmental conditions, experience and social circumstances change around us all. The idea is that social programs, policies, and practitioners *ought* to keep that in mind and see their work, their goal, as a continuous effort to rescue human potential from under the grind of circumstance—and perhaps even from the outcomes of what we tentatively call not very wise or good choices.

Readers might want to repeat this example using their own cherished value preferences—the result might be quite different in terms of the implications for implementation policies and program activities. Take, for example, how a homeless shelter program would work out if it were devoted to exercising the common value preference for self-determination. Let us emphasize a very traditional, limited meaning for the concept in order to illustrate the point at issue here: how different value preferences create quite different evaluations of the merit of program and policy goals and objectives. So it is useful to take into account Keith-Lucas's critique of self-determination and view it not as a principle but as a preference for "social work's liberating role."[14] Sporting a long history embedded in social work and human services, self-determination as a value preference concerns valuing personal autonomy and the exercise of personal individual choice.[15, 16] One way to put it is that this idea of self-determination drives practice toward the actual act of personal choice making. Let us use McDermott's concept: "the function of self-determination is to provide a moral restraint upon social workers . . . springing from the client's right to go his own way not because it is constructive, good or socially acceptable but simply because it is his own."[17] The self-determination concept has a strong linguistic implication, a person-centered focus. Weick and Pope conclude that this traditional idea of self-determination ". . . carries with it hope of happy endings . . . a degree of contentment and self-satisfaction . . ."[18]

So how would it turn out if one used the concept of self-determination as a first-priority value in order to evaluate the merit of some homeless shelter goals and objectives? If the objective of a specific program or policy system is to solve the problem of exposure to the elements for the homeless, then the contrast of interest is between a shelter program for the homeless with an objective of only relieving the danger of exposure to the elements and one that has that objective plus others that look toward maximizing the choice making of the homeless. Following are some objectives, in terms of service consumers during the course of their shelter stay, that are consistent with that position.

- To be protected from exposure to the elements and be fed by accepted nutrition, housing, and public health standards
- To define a range of possibilities that they feel psychologically or interpersonally free to choose
- To identify a range of desirable possibilities that they feel are ordinarily accessible to others but, for psychological or interpersonal reasons, they deny to themselves
- To increase the range of those possibilities from which they feel free to choose
- To make choices among those possibilities, including when and under what conditions they will leave the shelter

These objectives differ from those that are consistent with the empowerment value emphasis: The focus of the objectives, driven by self-determination objectives, is on "what it takes . . ." to choose in contrast to the focus of empowerment-driven objectives on "what it takes . . ." to make it possible to make choices *come into being* in the real world. The empowerment concept, it seems, takes choice making for granted, not as problematic. Its objectives then focus not on the process of choice making, not on what it takes to "liberate" a person to expand the range of choices from which he or she can select, but on what it takes to work them out in the real world with which they are faced and to *endure the consequences* (not always or necessarily happy or sanguine). At a deeper level, empowerment has as its roots the ideal that goal is growth, not happiness, and that "the challenge lies in creating the conditions which will allow, to the maximum extent possible, the expression of that hidden power (to grow and develop). . . ."[19]

SOME SPECIAL PROBLEMS IN EVALUATING GOALS AND OBJECTIVES IN PERSONAL SOCIAL SERVICES

Aside from the aforementioned criteria for goals and objectives, there are some special problems in applying criteria such as these in the personal social services as opposed to applying them to the delivery of public service utilities or hard benefits like cash and commodities. In hard benefit programs (food stamps or housing), the steps in delivering benefits are reasonably direct with few if any intermediate steps. Many personal social service programs or policy objectives can have many *intermediate steps* in a whole social treatment process. For a personal social service agency that deals with the social problem of unemployment, its plausible objective might be the teaching or retraining of unemployed workers in certain high-demand skills for a particular local job market. Thus, learning to operate a word processor might be one of several objectives; others might include learning how to read city maps to find addresses of employers or learning interviewing skills and how to fill out job applications. If obtaining employment is the ultimate objective, then the examples above are clearly intermediate to the ultimate objective. Note carefully that this is not the ultimate objective itself, simply a necessity pending outcomes that could be justified as useful in themselves, even detached from the idea of getting a job. But they are still concrete observable outcomes, not processes.

Processes refer to things like psychosocial treatment, which can be described by the various steps that constitute the process. Think only of the process steps commonly referred to in speaking of psychological treatments—"beginning a relationship," or "terminating a relationship." Note carefully that they are very difficult to describe as tangible outcomes. Many personal social service programs or policy objectives contain *intermediate steps* in a whole social treatment process. Processes cannot be legitimately included as terms in a statement of objectives—not because they are unimportant, but rather because they cannot "stand by themselves" as outcomes deserving of serious consideration as such *if no other outcome happens* as a result. (Indeed, such treatment processes are not unimportant; rather they are so important that they will feature prominently in Chapter 8.) As soon as a tangible outcome can be concretely specified, for example the outcome of a psychosocial treatment—higher morale or less anxiety—it is exactly the tangible, and measurable outcome that can then legitimately be thought of as an objective. Indeed there might be several such intermediate objectives. Thus, although in everyday language these might be referred to as a type of means to an end, it could clearly stand on its own as an outcome—almost no one would argue these days that it isn't ultimately a contribution to a worker's skill to be able to use a word processor. They "stand justified on their own" in a sense for which foster home studies could never qualify. There is no use for home studies except for decision making. There *is* a use for word-processing skills almost anywhere in today's employment market. When intermediate objectives are present they must be accompanied by other objectives to which they contribute with the full expectation that the program or policy will achieve both the intermediate *and* the ultimate objective.

Another problem in constructing program and policy goals and objectives in the personal social services is that objectives will, of necessity, be highly individualized because, after all, that is precisely one of the defining features of personal social services. Recall how PSU programs such as OASI (Social Security Retirement) are governed by strict entitlement rules and that entitlement is a matter of demonstrating one's membership in large groups (over age 65, Social Security contribution history)—no individualization there! Those rules govern everyone who applies and the objectives of the program are the same for all beneficiaries. Contrast that with personal social service programs like day care for the aged, in which the main feature is to set client/user goals that are unique to the elderly individual—increase social interaction, increase attention span, reduce anxiety and disorientation. Whereas many user/consumers might share some of these goals, not everyone would. So, it turns out that for each client there may well be an individual program; the individual learning plan for the education of the developmentally disabled is just another example. What is important is that in the abstract, the program has some goal that is applicable to all user/consumers. Increasing the socialization skills and personal comfort of the aged person might be one example; increasing learning levels for the developmentally disabled might be another. This interesting twist that characterizes personal social service programs adds an additional complexity to evaluating their goals and objectives, i.e., the practical policy analyst must judge whether there is a fit between these highly individual objectives for user/consumers and the general goals to which the program is committed. And, of course, that is exactly the kind of value-critical judgment that the practical public policy analyst should be prepared to make.

Two special problems confront the practical public policy analyst in making value-critical judgments about public social programs and policies. The first concerns the evaluation criterion we called measurability, actually a twofold problem. First, recollect that the paramount requirement for measurability is that the objective be concretized but still recognize that what the personal social services offer are intangibles so that objectives are usually expressed in terms of mental states or attitudes or learning, for example, rather than in terms of increases in income, physical states, housing conditions. The former "soft" human factors create special difficulties. One such is human reactivity—that the object being measured can react to the fact that measurements are being taken, among other things. It is also important to keep in mind, in another regard for recall, that in the personal social services, services can be mandatory, not offered in response to the user/consumer's own initiative. Measurability is a special problem in that case for there is always a built-in bias in that it is in the user/consumer's self-interest to show that they are "responding" to the service. In that sense, measurements are always suspect under these conditions. That is particularly true with regard to consumer satisfaction measures. It is recommended here that consumer satisfaction measures, important as they are, never be considered the only data on which to make judgments about the program or policy but that other measures be available. No matter how "soft" they may be, they are likely to be more dependable than data from a user/beneficiary who has a built-in response bias.

Finally, the practical public policy analyst should keep in mind that the personal social services often have obvious *social control* objectives. On that account, personal social service goals and objectives should express them explicitly. For example, the organizations (courts and other legal and quasilegal agencies) that probation counselors work for have explicit social control objectives: mental institutions, youth detention centers, and camps are not very different. In fact, mental health clinics often have explicit social control tasks when they work with clients whose attendance at the clinic is court-mandated, whether for preliminary diagnostic evaluations or for treatment. Where that is the case, organizational goals and client objectives should clearly express that. Where a client is legally committed to residence at a state mental institution and the problem for which he or she was committed is, say, exhibitionism, then that behavior should be included in any statements of treatment objectives. While it seems obvious, in practice the principle often is violated in favor of others that ignore the very problem that created the basis for legal commitment. For example, a treatment program that increased self-concept, as desirable as that might be, will not have acceptable goals if it cannot show that it is plausible to believe that such increases influence exhibitionism. No one would seriously suggest that it be the only objective.

Human service and social work practitioners frequently are uncomfortable with social control purposes and they are easy to ignore. To conduct a value-critical analysis of personal social service programs, the analyst should look to see whether the program expresses those explicitly lest this feature be lost from sight. There is nothing intrinsically negative about the idea of social control or using public funds on its behalf. It is, after all, likely to be the reason the program is funded! To be clear on that matter with clients and organizational personnel is taken as a value position here in the belief that to obfuscate it only leads to serious problems with user/consumers who eventually will encounter it anyhow. Few of them are confused on this matter. Few adoptive parent/clients are confused about the fact that their friendly social worker who is supervising the last few months of their adoption actually can take their child away under certain conditions. Few children who are clients of social workers and human service workers in mental and penal institutions are confused about the fact that those workers exercise considerable control over whether and when and under what conditions they will be allowed to leave the institution. The value bias at work here opts for honesty and openness with clients; believes that "putting everything on the table," so to speak, is one of the conditions required for being helpful to people. It may be that this may rule out the possibility of achieving certain objectives with clients, objectives that require close personal, trusting, nonauthoritative relationships. Nothing is gained and perhaps everything can be lost by avoiding the issue of the existence of the authority factor in relationships when in fact that is the case. Social program goals and objectives should reflect that.

SUMMARY

A goal is a statement, in general and abstract terms, of desired qualities in human and social conditions. Goals are an answer to the question "What is the purpose of this program or policy?" All elements of a program or policy must be judged on the basis of their contribution to the program goals and objectives. The program or policy goals and objectives are the programmatic "measure of all things." When the goals or objectives of a policy or program are described they point to desired ends, not means to ends. That is essential because a program or policy system without a commitment to explicit (and public) outcomes could never be held accountable but could continue service provision indefinitely. Goals can be manifest (public and explicit) or latent (unstated). Whereas a goal is an abstract and general statement of desired outcomes, an objective is a specific, empirical, operational statement about a desired observable outcome. For any given goal, many different (apparently divergent) objectives can be written. Goals can also be long-term and short-term.

There are four types of evaluation criteria the practical public policy analyst should use in judging the merit of goals and objectives: (1) those that concern their fit with the relevant social problem analysis (from which the meaning of the traditional criteria of equity, adequacy, and efficiency are drawn); (2) the traditional criteria of adequacy, equity, and efficiency; (3) those that are specifically relevant to operating characteristics under analysis; and (4) the personal value commitments of analysts themselves.

A good fit between the social problem analysis and the goals and objectives of a program or policy system is a matter of demonstrating the similarity between how their terms are defined. A statement of a goal or an objective is clear if its terms are well-defined; a well-defined term is one that easily distinguishes actual examples of things to which it refers from those to which it is closely related. Unless statements of objectives are capable of being measured they are of little use in administering or evaluating a program or policy. The criterion of measurability applies only to objectives, not goals. Many personal social service programs or policy objectives contain intermediate steps (not necessarily ultimate outcomes) in a whole social treatment process. Goals and objectives in the personal social services create special problems because they must be highly individualized. After all, that is precisely one of their defining features. The fact is that, different from public social utilities, personal social services can be and often are mandatory and operate with quite obvious social control objectives. Personal social service goals and objectives should express them explicitly where that applies.

EXERCISES

1. Two of your friends are arguing: One says that the reason for high schools
    in the United States is to keep teenagers out of the labor market for as long
    as possible so there will be less competition, better pay, and more jobs for
    adults; the other says that the school district charter says that the goal of
    high schools is to teach teenagers the skills they need to get a good job.
    What does the material in Chapter 5 teach you about goals that would
    help you sort out that argument? Is one or the other or both right, and
    why?

2. The Indian Child Welfare Act (P.L.95–608, 95 Stat. 3069, passed 11/8/78)
    (Sec. 3), says that "it is the policy of this Nation to protect the best interests
    of Indian children and to promote the stability and security of Indian tribes
    and families by establishment of minimum Federal standards for the
    removal of Indian children from families and placement of children in foster
    or adoptive homes which will reflect the unique values of Indian cul-
    ture. . . ." It also says (Sec. 101[a]) that "in any State court proceeding for
    foster care placement of or termination of parental rights to an Indian child
    . . . the court . . . shall transfer such proceeding to the jurisdiction of the
    tribe (Tribal court) . . . absent objection by either parent or the Indian
    child's tribe. . . ."

    Write a one-sentence goal statement and a one-sentence statement of objec-
    tive from the preceding quotations, using your own words. Write a short
    paragraph justifying the difference between the two statements, telling why
    one is a goal and the other an objective.

NOTES

1. P. Rossi, *Evaluation: A Systematic Approach* (Beverly Hills, CA: Sage Publications, 1979), p. 58.
2. F. F. Piven and R. Cloward, *Regulating the Poor* (New York: Pantheon Books, 1971).
3. R. Merton, *Social Theory and Social Structure*. (Glencoe, IL: The Free Press of Glencoe, 1957) pp. 51–53.
4. M. Rein, *From Policy to Practice* (Armonk, NY: M. E. Sharpe, 1985), p. xii.
5. Although there is a tendency in the literature to conclude that Congress in the 1930s never intended OASI to provide a living wage but to be a supplement to workers' savings, that is plainly not the case as a reading of the legislative history of the Social Security Act will show. It defies common sense as well because Congress was well aware that almost no worker in the depression of the 1930s would have savings in this amount, either then or in the expectable future.
6. S. Geron, "Regulating the Behavior of Nursing Homes through Positive Incentives: An Analysis of the Illinois Quality Incentive Program (QUIP)." *The Gerontologist*, 31:292–301 (1991).

7. J. A. Pechman and P. M. Timpane, editors, *Work Incentives and Income Guarantees* (Washington, DC: The Brookings Institution, 1975).

8. Joint Commission on Labor, U.S. Congress, 1991, 2nd Session (Washington, D.C.: Government Printing Office, April 21, 1991).

9. In fact, that is the function of any "theory" or causal analysis in a social problem analysis on which social programs are based.

10. Recalling the earlier distinction between goals and objectives as one in which goals are abstract and objectives concrete (among other things), note here that in that spirit it follows that empowerment is an abstract value and thus always in the nature of a goal, whereas those particular concrete activities or behaviors that exemplify empowerment are objectives.

11. W. Miller, "The Impact of a 'Total Community' Delinquency Control Project." *Social Problems*, 10:168–91 (1962).

12. D. E. Chambers and M. K. Rodwell, "Promises, Promises: Predicting Child Abuse," *Policy Studies Review* (Summer 1989), 8:[4]749–93.

13. This narrow definition of self-determination is one of which Keith-Lucas, among many others, is quite critical and I wouldn't wish to mislead. Still, the narrow and historical definition serves well our purposes here. Those interested in the controversy or the current status of the concept should consult F. E. McDermott, editor, *Self-Determination in Social Work* (London: Routledge and Kegan Paul, 1975) and J. K. Bramann, *Self-Determination: An Anthology of Essays and Poetry* (Rochester, NY: Adler Publishing Co., 1984). The reader might want to consider that, doubtless, the concept can be defined so that one can speak of self-determination at any or all of several levels of social organization: families, organizations, small groups, and communities. At that point and when one works out the full implications of that change, the difference between empowerment and self-determination becomes ultimately quite unclear.

14. A. Keith-Lucas, A Critique of the Principles of Client Self-Determination. In F. E. McDermott, editor, *Self-Determination in Social Work* (London: Routledge and Kegan Paul, 1975), p. 47.

15. H. H. Perlman, Self-Determination: Reality or Illusion. In F. E. McDermott, editor, *Self-Determination in Social Work* (London: Routledge and Kegan Paul, 1975).

16. B. C. Reynolds, *Learning and Teaching in the Practice of Social Work* (New York: Farrar and Rinehart, 1942), p. 24.

17. F. E. McDermott, editor, Against the Persuasive Definition of Self-Determination. In *Self-Determination in Social Work* (London: Routledge and Kegan Paul, 1975), p. 136.

18. A. Weick and L. Pope, *Knowing What's Best: A New Look at Self-Determination* (Lawrence, KS: The University of Kansas, 1986), mimeographed.

19. Ibid.

CHAPTER 6

Analysis of Forms of Benefits and Services

INTRODUCTION

It would seem a simple matter to choose a type of benefit or service that would yield an effective solution to a particular social problem, but unfortunately that is not the case. Social welfare benefits include any income transfer in a nonmarket exchange. Such benefits can be anything from a free school lunch to a government guarantee of a corporate loan. Benefits can also include such things as increased "power" over policy decisions, positive discrimination in resource allocations (giving preference to the hiring of minority group members), and expert services. Therefore, Chapter 6 will be devoted to a discussion of an operating characteristic we will call *benefit and service types,* types that can be used as proposed solutions to the social problems with which we are concerned. We will look at the particular problems posed by making decisions about benefits and services in the personal social service (PSS) programs as compared with those in public social utility (PSU) programs or hybrid programs. Criteria that can be used to judge the merit of a particular benefit form will be discussed and some examples will be given of benefit packages to illustrate the fact that benefits can come in sets as well as singly.

A CLASSIFICATION SCHEME FOR BENEFIT AND SERVICE TYPES

It is of some use to the practitioner to have a clear grasp of the most common social policy benefit and service alternatives. This classification scheme will assume that any of these benefit forms can be interchangeable—which may mean positive or negative consequences.[1] A benefit form can only be judged *relative to* the available alternatives so it might help to see how, in very different ways, each benefit form could be used to solve the same social problem.

Assume that a low-income, working-class family is using the public system of treatment for mental illness. Derek and Drusilla Orkney, both in their mid-thirties, have four children and live in a moderate-size urban area on the Eastern Seaboard. Derek is a welder in a manufacturing plant, and Drusilla is a waitress at a neighborhood tavern. The Orkneys' children range from age seven years to eight months. Drusilla is suffering from a recurring psychosis, an illness first diagnosed when she was fifteen. This is her fourth episode. She has delusions of being pregnant with the second Savior, fights with those who frustrate her low tolerance for contradiction, and hallucinates about visitations by the Holy Spirit. When agitated, she paces the floor and pays no attention to her appearance or to others around her. She cannot care for her children now; nor can she work. It is difficult to predict how long she will be unable to function. Derek has her admitted to the state hospital, fearing that she will injure the children.

One issue of importance to the practitioner in this case is what different types of benefits could remedy or reduce the harm of this situation to family members. Let's consider Drusilla and her problem first. The public remedy that Derek chose for his wife was a (psychiatric) service, an "expert." *Expert services* include such things as care in a state hospital for the mentally ill. The reason the state hospital program is available to Drusilla (and others similarly afflicted) is that public policy is committed to providing this particular kind of solution for this particular kind of problem. Many other solutions could have been chosen; for example, the government could choose not to run hospitals at all, at least not hospitals for the treatment of mental illness. Most state governments, in fact, don't operate many hospitals of any kind, except for mental illness. (It is instructive to question why that is the case.) Public policy could provide a public remedy for the problem of mental illness in any number of other ways. One way is to pay directly the costs of citizens' care in private mental hospitals. Note that there are several methods by which that payment could be made, each featuring differences that could influence the desirability of the benefit from the point of view of the service provider or the consumer. The state could simply issue a check for the amount of the bill once the citizen submitted a claim and met eligibility requirements. That would be a *cash benefit*. Even though the benefit is in the form of a check, the issue that defines a cash benefit is how negotiable the benefit is. If the benefit can be exchanged for cash directly, with no loss over the face amount, then it is a cash benefit. Of course, another form of benefit is involved here: Recall that the cash is exchanged for expert services, the services involved in treating mental illness. Thus, such policies and procedures involve both cash and expert services as benefit forms.

The policy options can become much more complex. Suppose that the public policy was to pay private hospitals to provide care for citizens afflicted with illnesses like Drusilla's, but rather than giving the citizens cash for Drusilla's care, the public treasury gave a certain amount of money directly to the hospital. If this amount of money in this case was directly related to the costs incurred by Drusilla, then this type of benefit is a *credit*. The public treasury *credits* the Orkneys' account at the hospital with a certain amount. Derek will pay the rest of their bill (if the government doesn't pay it all). As in the preceding example, there are two benefit forms here—expert services and a credit. If the public treasury pays the hospital for anticipated costs of the "average patient,"[2] a cost related to a group and not to any one citizen, the benefit looks more like a subsidy (more on this later). *Credits* and *vouchers* are prepayments or postpayments to a purveyor of benefits and services. The difference between a credit and a voucher is that a voucher is a written authorization to receive a benefit or service, and the choice of purveyor is left with the consumer or beneficiary. The distinction is important because vouchers retain a good bit of consumer sovereignty. A credit is prearranged in such a way that the benefit or service can be received only by the purveyor chosen by the organization that provided the credit. An example here is the "grocery order" given to an applicant for local county funds, an "order" that can be redeemed only at particular grocery stores.

There are still other benefit forms that could be used as instruments of public policy. For example, a public policy could adopt a *subsidy* approach to help its citizens gain access to expert services for the treatment of mental illness. In return for a guarantee that the particular facility would serve all or a stated portion of low-income clients, the state could give hospitals 50 percent of their start-up costs and 70 percent of their net operating costs (or some fixed percentage of each). Even though the state is not directly paying the Orkneys' hospital bills, it is paying them indirectly through this institutional subsidy. The hospital bills the Orkneys only for those costs not covered by the subsidy or else agrees to accept the government subsidy as settlement for the account of any low-income patient. Once again, two benefit forms are at work here—expert services and a subsidy. There are a number of public subsidies at work in the United States. Government payments to purchase computers for university centers; passenger railroad service operations; national, state, and local highway construction; the operation of community mental health centers; many day care centers; and the education of developmentally disabled children are all examples of public subsidies.

Note especially that what makes the subsidy a distinct benefit form for our purposes here is the fact that the intended beneficiary may be several steps removed from receipt of the actual cash transaction. Also note that, as is the case with most other benefit forms, many citizens—other than those for whom the subsidy is directly intended—indirectly and substantially benefit from public subsidies. With respect to government subsidies to purchase computers for universities, students obtain a substantial benefit—they gain marketable computer skills they might not otherwise have. The computer industry is a gainer because it probably sells more machines, given the government subsidy. The Medicaid program, which subsidizes medical expenses for low-income patients, also benefits the hospital industry by picking up costs for services that hospitals cannot deny, services for which they cannot expect to obtain payment from patients. Hospital employees—including social workers—also benefit.

There is a small but useful distinction between market and wholesale subsidies. Those we've discussed so far are *consumer subsidies*, those in which the public treasury supplies monies to provide an indirect benefit to a particular population sector or group so as to serve the national self-interest. The focus of consumer subsidies, their intended purpose, is to benefit consumers, not producers. Consumer food subsidy is a common form of social welfare benefit worldwide. In Britain in past years, the price of bread, cheese, and milk has been subsidized at rates that reduce the price to the consumer some 21 to 40 percent. The government picks up the difference between the price grocers pay to the producers and the price received from consumers. All consumers, regardless of income, receive the benefit of this subsidy.

Market subsidies, on the other hand, focus on benefits for producers, not consumers. In a market subsidy, there may be no one who receives goods or cash supplied by the government treasury; nor is there always an identifiable product involved. Agricultural market subsidies are a good example because the subsidy here is not cash or the availability of a product, but a guarantee of a particular price to farmers for specific crops they raise. Under certain conditions, market forces generate a satisfactory price, and in that there is no need at all for the subsidy, none is provided. This means that wheat, corn, and soybeans, for example, have a "support price," and when market price goes below that, wheat growers will get the difference between the support price set by the government and the market price.[3] Note now that the intention of farm support prices is not only to benefit individual producer/farmers (though there is much disagreement over the issue), but in part (as declared) to ensure that the "family farm" remains as a viable unit in the U.S. economy and that those producer/industries that depend heavily on farmers as consumers are assured a strong market for their products (farm machinery, steel, rubber, fertilizer, and such). On that account, some kinds of market price supports for farm products can be called market subsidies. There are market subsidies in industries other than agriculture, of course. Scarce defense materials (such as uranium and tungsten and even tanker ships) are often in line for government subsidies because of their wide use in the economy and the government's wish to have them available should need arise.

None of the above exhausts the benefit forms by which the government could pursue its general policies. It could choose to provide expert services only to those who, because they were denied in the past, are in very special need. *Positive discrimination* is a benefit form that attempts to restore equity where inequity has prevailed in the past. Applicants for the benefit are not treated identically or equally. They get special treatment now as a way of remedying unequal treatment in the past. Affirmative action laws and certain administrative procedures are examples of positive discrimination, a special benefit made available to three groups—racial and ethnic minorities, disabled persons, and women—membership in which is, by public policy, deemed prima facie evidence of past discrimination in regard to employment. These groups are commonly given hiring priority for university faculty and many civil service positions. Clearly, there is little debate about the intent, although widespread public debate in the Unites States continues on whether the benefit of positive discrimination is a useful and/or effective means by which to right a wrong.

Three other types of benefits common in the United States are loan guarantees, material goods and commodities, and protective regulation. *Loan guarantees* have been a public policy favorite when the population sector of concern was the middle class or the business community. A common example is the FHA Program, which provided federal government guarantees of mortgage loans for private dwellings. If the home owner defaults, the U.S. government will pay off the loan. If no money changes hands, how can the loan guarantee be a benefit? It turns out to be a significant benefit because it will often result in a substantial loan from a bank where, without the guarantee, no money would be forthcoming. As with all other benefit forms, of course, others will benefit nearly as much as the home owner (the primary intended beneficiary): the home builder, the banker, the materials supplier for the home builder, to mention only a few. Loan guarantees are not made to individuals only. The U.S. government has made massive loan guarantees to businesses and whole sectors of industry. The 1990 bailout of the U.S. savings and loan (S & L) industry is perhaps the most extravagant example. It is clearly the most expensive federal intervention ever, with cost estimates currently running around $230 billion. It makes prior ventures along this line (including investment subsidies to the poor and middle class) pale by comparison. Note especially that these financial guarantees to S & Ls do not necessarily produce a single job or build a single unit of private family housing (arguably a predictable result of other government loan guarantees mentioned below). Nor are main beneficiaries either the poor or the middle class, few of whom are large savings and loan investors. Indeed, S & Ls may once again be a financing resource for middle-class housing, but at the present moment no one is making the case that there is shortage of such housing or no other financing resource available. Of recent memory are also the federal guarantees of loan monies to the Chrysler Corporation, absent which the auto maker would probably have gone bankrupt. Even New York City was bailed out of financial difficulties by a government guarantee of its debt. Slightly more removed in time is the loan guarantee to the Lockheed Corporation, without which the aircraft industry would have been minus one of its oldest and largest members. In the case of Lockheed, once again the primary economy is not the only beneficiary; aircraft suppliers and related materials industries also benefited.

An example of *material goods and commodities* (in-kind benefits) is the distribution of surplus farm products like cheese, flour, and bacon. Goods and commodities are as tangible and valuable a benefit as a direct cash grant. *Protective regulation* is a form of protected access to a market. The most familiar examples are public utilities (an electric or natural gas company), but regulation is also applied to telephone companies and airlines. Protective regulation is a welfare benefit because some regulations virtually guarantee the utility an annual profit; an exclusive franchise to sell a product people believe they can't live without implies that the company cannot help making money if only it prices its product at more than its anticipated costs, year by year. There are benefits to the public-at-large that result from protective regulation. When utility companies were first formed in the United States, many went bankrupt in the process of trying to meet the intense competition that emerged, and in some cases the public had no service at all. One of the major justifications for protective regulation rests upon preventing a repetition of that history. Airline deregulation, which allows virtually free competition among airlines, has resulted in a mixed bag of disadvantages and advantages: sometimes ultracheap fares but a worrisome reduction in service.

Finally, there is another benefit form that entails no transfer of money: *the delegation of power over decisions*. A typical example is the allocation of board of director positions to persons who are consumers of services or in some way are particularly well suited to represent consumers. This benefit encompasses the right to make decisions that serve the self-interests of the group with which the decision maker is affiliated. Of course, such a benefit is intended to benefit a group, not a particular individual. The issue of how much power is given in such instances and how much is necessary to make the benefit effective (what constitutes token representation and how much representation is required to constitute an effective bloc of power) will be discussed in Chapter 8 on service delivery systems. Notice here that these last benefit forms are not likely to be useful as a solution to Drusilla Orkney's problem; it would be an unusual social problem analysis that would suggest protective regulation, loan guarantees, or power over decision making as solutions for the Orkneys' problems. So, protective regulation is probably the limiting case with respect to benefit and service forms regarding the social problem of mental illness.

Some types of responses are considered by some to be the chosen instruments to deliver social policy. Some of these instruments are indirect means, and if they are of any significance, they are more in the nature of steps necessary to the process of enacting and implementing public policy. They are worth noting here because they can be examples of the substitution of shadow for substance—that is, examples of how effective policy action is delayed in lieu of relatively cost-free "window dressing." Some political scientists suggest that the gamut of governmental response can be thought of in terms of a continuum running from simple exhortation to the government actually conducting service programs or even operating businesses (market enterprises).[4] Doern says that a legislator can respond to a policy issue by giving a speech pointing out the problem or proposing a careful investigation into the nature of a social problem. (Do not misread Doern's commentary to mean that he thinks that investigations and speeches are useless—they certainly aren't. The point is that they represent no real commitment, and under some conditions may actually represent a lack of will to solve the problem.) Alternatively, the government or the legislature or Congress can make a maximum response and actually conduct enterprises to meet social need, in fact enterprises that are usually operated by the private sector. During the depression even bridges, post offices, and river dams were constructed by the government (under the title "public works").

SUMMARY OF FORMS OF BENEFITS AND SERVICES[5]

At least nine major forms of benefits and services are common in the U.S. social welfare system. They may be used singly or in combination; very often a single benefit may represent more than one benefit form. Whereas one form of benefit may appear to be obviously superior, the merit of any particular benefit form ultimately depends on the logic of its connection with details of the social problem analysis and the program or policy goal. The forms of benefit are summarized in Table 6–1.

Table 6–1. Major Forms of Benefits and Services

Benefit/Service	Definition
Material goods/commodities	Tangible benefits (e.g., food, shelter, clothing)
Cash	Negotiable currency, exchangeable without loss in value
Expert services	Skilled, knowledgeable perfomances by credentialed professionals
Positive discrimination	Benefits directed to protected groups to redress past inequities
Credits/vouchers	Prepayments or postpayments to purveyors of benefits and/or services. A *credit* can be used by a beneficiary only at purveyor(s) chosen by the organization providing the credit. A *voucher* can be used at purveyor(s) chosen by beneficiary.
Subsidies	Payments made to a third party (e.g., federal funds to private hospitals)
Government guarantees	Government promise to repay loan in event signatory defaults
Protective regulation	Grants of exclusive or near-exclusive right to a certain market as a resut of lack of competition
Power over decisions	Right to make decisions that serve self-interests of a particular group with which decision maker is affiliated

MULTIPLE AND INTERRELATED BENEFITS

It would be a mistake to leave the reader with the conclusion that most social policies and social programs pursue their objectives through single benefit or service strategies. Although there are instances of that, it is not the general case, especially in relation to programs that intend to deal with the social problem of poverty. It is common for citizens to think of programs like Social Security or even unemployment security as providing only a single benefit, but in fact eligibility for one benefit form very often automatically qualifies a person for multiple benefits. The fact of interrelated benefit packages certainly makes the analysis of social policy with respect to benefit forms, in particular, a lively and complex venture. It is not surprising that programs and policies should have more than a single kind of benefit; after all, we have already seen that multiple goals or objectives are commonplace. Where that is the case and where such goals are diverse it would be expected that different benefit types and thus multiple benefits would occur. Lewis and Morrison found that multiple benefits can occur in two major forms: (1) benefits from one program can alter benefits in other programs and (2) program benefits can change personal tax liability.[6]

The U.S. Unemployment Insurance (UI) program is an example of a benefit that generates multiple benefits: eligible, involuntarily unemployed workers receive both a cash payment, services from the state vocational and rehabilitation service, and referral to employers searching for workers. The purpose of rehabilitation services is to retrain the employee and to provide trained and ready-to-work employees for employers. Maintaining the stability of a large work force for the economic enterprise of the country as well as for relief of unemployment is a goal of the UI program. The AFDC program (Aid to Families with Dependent Children) is another example of a highly complex package of benefits and services. It is difficult to elaborate because of interstate variation, but the list that follows characterizes the most general case: a cash benefit, a medical card, special food allowance for infants and pregnant mothers, vocational training, family planning services, and so forth. Notice that not all elements in this benefit package are voluntarily chosen, but some are compulsory: Work Incentive Now (WIN) vocational training programs are compulsory for AFDC mothers after children are five years of age and in school. Sometimes "benefits" can be used punitively against clients: sterilization, family planning, and abortion. Further, some program policies automatically disqualify a recipient from benefits from another program. We will discuss those complex examples in Chapter 10, which deals with program and policy interrelationships.

CRITERIA FOR EVALUATING TYPES OF BENEFITS AND SERVICES: CASH VERSUS IN-KIND BENEFITS

Although we have reviewed many of the common benefit types, we have not paid sufficient attention to the differences between them. Argument about the "best" form of social benefits dates back to the Elizabethan Poor Laws. We also will examine evaluation criteria for forms of benefit. Three common criteria help determine the merit of forms of benefit: cost-effectiveness, target efficiency, and stigmatization. This is also a good place to consider several other evaluation criteria, in particular those close to the interests of politicians and public administrators (such as complexity of administration and political risk).[7] We must also use fit with the social problem as an evaluation criterion, one which we have said earlier applies to all operating characteristics of policies and programs. Finally, let us look at consumer sovereignty as an evaluation criterion—to which I am personally committed. Close examination of the contrast between cash and in-kind benefit forms will show how these evaluation criteria are used in an analysis of policy or program features.

CRITERIA FOR EVALUATING THE MERIT OF BENEFIT FORMS: STIGMATIZATION, TARGET EFFICIENCY, COST-EFFECTIVENESS, CONSUMER SOVEREIGNTY, SUBSTITUTABILITY AND IDENTIFYING CRITERIA "TRADE-OFFS"

Wherever there is a benefit to be given in remedy of specific tangible need, it can be given in the form of cash or it can be given it in the form of directly consumable articles (food or clothing for example). The question is "Which form is best, why, and from what point of view?" Almost all U.S. public benefits available in maintenance programs could be given in-kind. The issue touches on more than income-related benefits. Think for a moment about the delivery of medical care benefits and services. A cash approach would give dollars directly to families in need, that amount equivalent to whatever was the price of the necessary medical care. This benefit is most commonly given not in the form of cash but in the form of a credit or voucher—a strategy that is more related to an in-kind benefit than a cash strategy.

Such examples serve to illustrate how the evaluation criteria apply to this general question. From the consumer's point of view the major difference is the degree to which a choice can be exercised in regard to the goods or services delivered—the evaluation criterion we earlier called *consumer sovereignty*. From the benefit giver's point of view the major difference is the ability to exercise control over the nature of the article and the way it is consumed—the evaluation criterion we earlier called *target efficiency*. If a family needs cheese and you give them $5 to buy it, the family can decide whom to buy it from, when to make the purchase, under what conditions, and at what price—an example of maximum consumer sovereignty. If you give the family a letter telling the cheese store to give the family $5 worth of cheddar and to add it to your bill, the choices that can be made by the family are thereby limited. But notice that from the point of view of the benefit giver (the person who is paying for the cheese), it may be very important to restrict the choices. For example, the benefit giver may get a special price from the cheese dealer because, all told, a great deal of cheese is purchased this way and our cheese dealer can purchase more economically if he can count on volume sales. Not only that, the merchant knows that no advertising expense is incurred. Thus, the benefit giver is able to help more hungry people because cheese can be purchased for less in an in-kind, rather than a cash, benefit form. Under this condition (but *only* this condition), giving the benefit in an in-kind form satisfies the evaluation criterion of cost-effectiveness—the benefit is delivered at a cost that is effectively the lowest relative to the other available and practical forms and means of delivery.

Note that it is also true that the benefit goes directly for the specific social problem of concern—hunger. This is an example of the evaluation criterion called target efficiency, a virtue here because the efficiency involved makes it possible to benefit more hungry people. There is not much else to do with cheese except eat it, though a genuinely imaginative person might use it to catch mice, sell it to a neighbor at a cut-rate price, or trade it for another commodity.

There are those who argue against the above conclusions. With regard to the lower expense of in-kind benefits, they say, it is not entirely clear whether economies of scale work in a way that inevitably yields a lower unit cost than cash (and thus generate a cost-effective benefit form). A person can take the view that the only way to establish a true cost is through an exchange in a free market, even a cheese market. How can the benefit giver really know that the price charged by the cheese merchant was the best price on that day for that amount of cheese of that particular kind? Whereas the price quoted the in-kind benefit giver may have been the best price the benefit giver could have gotten that day, suppose there was a cheese crisis the day following; if the family had cash to deal with, they might have gotten twice as much cheese for half the price. On the other hand, the cheese merchant may have had bad luck selling his Swiss that week and would've sold twice as much to the family for half the price. (Of course, it might also have worked in exactly the opposite direction.) The same argument raises an objection to an extension of social control via the purchase of cheese. The cost to the family is a lack of consumer autonomy, and that makes them even more dependent and less able to cope with the stresses of life. After all, this argument goes, independence and self-reliance are built on experience in such small matters as deciding whether to buy cheddar, swiss, or mozzarella. Notice how important are the details, for it is on them that the ultimate conclusion depends—the wisdom is that it is when one contemplates the program *as implemented* that program features such as benefit forms can be truly evaluated against our criteria. On that account, much of the abstract debate about cash versus in-kind benefit forms is irrelevant.

Notice the *trade-offs* operating here between the various evaluation criteria: Regarding the delivery of benefits in the form of cash, consumer sovereignty is maximized and target efficiency is minimized. Conversely, benefits delivered in an in-kind form minimize consumer sovereignty and maximize target efficiency. Thus, the trade-off is between consumer sovereignty and target efficiency, because to get one advantage, the policy system has to suffer some disadvantage. In another example of trade-offs between certain kinds of evaluation criteria, in the social problem of poverty, low unemployment levels (a virtue) will produce price instability, but as unemployment decreases and as consumers acquire more money, a possible effect is inflationary price increases (a vice). Although considered a "side effect"—which certainly it is in the sense that it was not intended—the evidence for such a trade-off is very solid and could be anticipated as an ordinary consequence.

Somewhat more serious is the argument that the price of in-kind benefits is *stigmatization*. Where the consumption or acquisition of benefits is public, certain kinds of items become associated with "being on welfare," and negative attributions are made to those so identified. Although someone seen eating a slice of cheddar cheese attracts little attention, it certainly is the case that disparaging comments are made to people who spend food stamps in grocery stores (a mild form of in-kind benefit). And it certainly is the case that children are cruelly insulted when "welfare tickets" are required to be presented in school lunch lines. According to Terkel, local welfare agencies bought certain kinds of shoes and dresses during the depression, and those who wore them were sure to inspire negative comments from others.[8]

Some of these objections to in-kind benefit forms do not apply in all instances; it is surely not the case that all noncash forms stigmatize recipients—not all consumption or delivery of the article or good is public. For example, one way to avoid public consumption or delivery of foodstuffs in a noncash form is to use a subsidy method that was common in England. If the U.S. government wished to increase the nutritional level of its low-income citizens it could subsidize the price of a popular food to the point where it could become the least expensive, most nutritious food available (bread or milk products, for example). The public treasury could subsidize the bakers or grocers, perhaps 40 cents a loaf; every month those vendors would tote up how many loaves they sold and submit a bill to the public treasury. In return they would agree to sell bread for half the former price, maybe 35 cents a loaf. Thus, the consumer gets bread at a reduction and the baker or grocer still makes a profit. Would the consumption of bread increase? Very likely. Would consumers be stigmatized for buying bread? Not very likely, because everyone pays the same price. Would the benefit go only to those who "really" need it? No, because there would be considerable "seepage" to those not in low-income brackets (again, a question about the target efficiency criterion). Would this form of the benefit be more cost-effective than cash? That question can be answered only through the empirical study of increased nutrition as a result of the increased use of the subsidized foodstuffs. The increase in nutrition resulting from the cash benefit strategy would also have to be studied and the net results of the two compared.

Note that the cost of achieving the nutritional goal is the cost of the subsidy for the foodstuffs actually bought by the poor; the cost of the destigmatization of the in-kind strategy is exactly the cost of subsidizing the foodstuffs bought by the nonpoor. Thus, in this case the exact cost of the "trade-off" can be specified. Those who strongly support cash benefits argue that such a benefit form clearly has an advantage along the lines of ensuring consumer sovereignty by means of which receivers maintain control over when, what, and how things are bought. From the consumer's point of view, that autonomy is a major issue.

CRITERIA FOR EVALUATING THE MERIT OF BENEFIT FORMS: THE POLITICAL AND PUBLIC ADMINISTRATION VIEWPOINT (VALUE PREFERENCES)

The political and bureaucratic contexts in which choices about benefit forms are made generate evaluation criteria of their own. Here we will rely upon Linder and Peters, who suggest criteria such as *complexity of administration*, for example.[9] It's only natural to expect that public administrators will value a benefit form that is simple rather than complicated to administer. It would seem preferable to administer a fairly simple program delivering a partial cash subsidy to the elderly to pay part of their winter heating bill rather than administer an in-kind commodity program for the same purpose—one in which the benefit would be gas or oil or electricity (or cow chips for that matter), which the government owned and would deliver directly to consumers. Think of the problems of storage, delivery, services, and all the rest. A cash benefit places the responsibility on the beneficiary for obtaining the product needed and thus avoids the administrative complexities. Or, consider a program that delivers services for severely mentally ill children. Such a program may involve such complexities as administering income or asset tests to a wide variety of income levels (to determine whether to charge for hospitalization, for example); coordinating the program activities of a wide variety of professionals; facing high costs per case and "treatment" strategies of uncertain and sometimes controversial validity to consumers potentially capable of deviant and antisocial behavior. On the other hand, the public policy may choose to deliver this benefit in a form that simply subsidizes the costs of such services in the private sector by the consumer. In this case, the public administrator looks to the cost issues and struggles with determining whether charges are fair and whether services were actually delivered, but certainly that is less complex than taking responsibility for their actual delivery. The form taken by the benefit is determining here. Material, hard benefits are obviously simpler to administer than personal social services, which are often intangible and often controversial as to their effectiveness. It is quite likely that less complex business forms also entail *low administrative cost*, another evaluation criterion of preference to public administrators and political figures who must account to the public in such matters.

Another evaluation criterion common to public administration and the political context is the extent to which the benefit form is *adaptable across different kinds of users*. A subsidy (equivalent to cash) is obviously quite adaptable to different kinds of users: those who heat with gas versus electricity; those who live in apartments versus their own homes; those who live in rural areas versus central cities. An in-kind benefit may not be so adaptable across the diverse users in those examples. *Political risk* is also an evaluation criterion in this context; for example, the level of public visibility of the benefit form may be an issue here. The cash-equivalent subsidy for the winter heating program for the low-income elderly is quite invisible in that such programs can be handled via the U.S. mail. Note, however, that even if benefit receipt were visible, in this case it might be a political advantage rather than a liability; the viewpoint in our society is that the low-income elderly are surely "deserving poor," and that a politician who helps them projects the image of a social and moral conscience—good political images, no doubt. Contrast the level of political risk via the high public visibility of a program that generates benefits in the form of psychiatric services for severely mentally ill children. Because such children are capable of social deviance, they can be highly visible to a sensitive public and if the benefits (no matter how great or obvious the need for them) are delivered to a population group that is considered deviant, the political risk is high. It is widely believed among social historians that the popularity of mental institutions as a benefit form for the severely mentally ill or shelters for the homeless are, in the first instance, appealing to politicians and public administrators simply because such institutions effectively reduce their visibility to the public (hence the political risk) of the targeting social problem and the people who are subject to it.[10] Finally, another evaluation criterion—*potential for failure of the benefit to reduce the social problem successfully*—surfaces frequently for many of the reasons just enumerated.

CRITERIA FOR EVALUATING THE MERIT OF BENEFIT FORMS: PERSONAL VALUES OF THE PRACTITIONER—CONSUMER SOVEREIGNTY, COERCION, AND INTRUSION INTO PRIVATE AFFAIRS

This section considers an evaluation criterion that is preferred by this author/analyst: *consumer sovereignty*. One argument for its generally positive effects allows for making choices. Thus, it seems reasonable to believe that it defuses the demoralizing effect of the stigma commonly associated with receipt of in-kind benefits. Also, the cash expended contributes to the support of the general public economy in ways that in-kind benefits cannot. Cash benefits support ordinary businesses and ordinary employers and employees. In-kind benefits, if they are to achieve their major advantages of economy of scale and expense reduction, must enter a special market at the producer and wholesaler levels—certainly not the same retail market corridor used by the ordinary citizen/consumer. Support of that market "bypasses" many "free markets" and in a way that costs jobs because employers will not need the employees that are created by the additional cash demand for goods and products. In the long run, this argument speaks to the appealing idea of creating more employment and more taxes paid by a mechanism that remains faithful to a cash market system and ensuring that "the consumer is king". One also might realistically argue that, in this way, cash benefits reduce (ultimately) the need for them as a social welfare expenditure. It seems safe to generalize here and conclude that one appeal of consumer sovereignty lies fundamentally with a preference for *reliance on free-market mechanisms* as a way to relieve social problems.

Still there are those who seriously advocate for in-kind benefits. Alva Myrdal, the 1983 Nobel Prize winner in economics, is an example. Most of the arguments discussed above can be read in greater detail in her work.[11] However, Myrdal makes two other points we have not covered in the above and that are worth noting because they concern cogent arguments from an advocate for in-kind benefits about their limitations. The first is that the issue of consumer choice is not very relevant when it comes to benefits targeted primarily toward children; children seldom exercise much consumer choice in poor families. The second is that in-kind benefits cannot be seriously preferred where family income is not adequate in the first place. In the last analysis, Myrdal comes out for restricting in-kind benefits to secondary needs, nonbasic food, shelter, and clothing. On that view, then, it would seem that the kinds of benefits Myrdal really advocates as appropriate for in-kind forms are items such as medical care, education, perhaps clothing, but surely expert services. The issue of *substitutability* of goods, also important to Myrdal, refers to the possibility that a public policy or program the intent of which is to increase food purchases, for example, may not do so because more food is *not* purchased because the family uses food stamps to purchase the same amount of food they would have bought ordinarily; the money released by the availability of food stamps can then be used to buy other commodities of choice; the net gain, then, is not necessarily in food items. For example, the socially conforming family may use the extra purchasing power to buy books or more vegetables for their children. The less socially conforming may use it to buy illegal drugs, clothes, or a good time. Substitutability is an important idea because it shows how the in-kind benefit, when it concerns items that are vitally necessary for survival, may not always be an effective way of controlling the consumption pattern, amount, or kind of benefit received. The same argument might be made with respect to the provision of vouchers for medical care, physician prescriptions, and credit for child care or work clothing, for example. Substitutability is probably a criterion that has wide relevance to the evaluation of the merit of benefit forms, whatever those benefit forms might be.

Finally, in some ways the consumer sovereignty issue can be understood as a preference that public benefits *not* be in forms that are coercive and/or intrusive into the lives of private citizens. *Coerciveness and intrusiveness into private lives* should be considered important evaluation criteria. At certain levels, of course, intrusiveness into private affairs can be illegal, sometimes even a constitutional issue, because a citizen's right to privacy derives from the U.S. Constitution.

CRITERIA FOR EVALUATING THE MERIT OF BENEFIT FORMS: FIT OF THE BENEFIT WITH THE SOCIAL PROBLEM ANALYSIS AND WHAT TO DO IF THE ANALYSIS TURNS OUT TO BE WRONG—PERSONAL SOCIAL SERVICES

Much, though not all, of the distinction between the personal social services (PSSs) and the public social utilities (PSUs) turns simply and straightforwardly on the benefit form: for PSSs the benefit is an individually tailored, nonmaterial service, whereas for PSUs it is uniform and material in nature. Three of the five distinctive features of PSSs are simply a consequence of that difference: that PSSs are offered face to face, are unique in some respect to each consumer, and are entitled via administrative or professional discretion. Thus, these features are only a consequence of their nonmaterial character.

An important issue for evaluating the merit of a personal social service is whether it is truly substitutable for a material benefit in the sense of being a solution to the social problem of concern. The history of the provision of social welfare benefits in the United States shows that important and very costly mistakes can be made in that regard. In legislating the 1962 amendments to the Social Security Act, social workers and other human service proponents convinced Congress that PSSs should be institutionalized as a major strategy against the problem of poverty. It wasn't a totally new idea—the emergency relief legislation of the depression era in the early 1930s had provided for special units of social workers to be available for difficult cases on an individualistic basis to those who were poor and/or had personal problems.[12] Prior to that time, private charitable agencies included social workers as part of a system to tailor cash assistance to individual characteristics and to plan and implement service and benefit delivery. In its 1962 amendments, the Social Security Act provided the first federal statutory instance in the United States for the general provision of personal social services to families on relief. According to Morris, at the same time Congress increased the federal dollar match (to state funds) to 75 percent for this purpose as if to underscore their commitment to the "rehabilitation" of the poor via PSSs. This effectively put into practice the idea that services were an inextricable part, if not the major strategy, for a solution to the problem of poverty. The social problem viewpoint was that the cause of poverty was an interaction between lack of material resources and some personal attribute (attitude, cultural approach to work) and was amenable to change by a service strategy: family, group, and individual counseling; job and parent training; referral agencies; and service coordination, which avoided duplication of services. Indeed, the very name of the federal agency responsible for basic income maintenance programs (AFDC for example) was changed to the Family Service Administration.[13]

Congress was convinced to increase appropriations by hundreds of millions of dollars for services and the training of personal social service workers on behalf of those ideas. Federal expenditures for personal social services increased from $194 million in 1963 to a billion and a half dollars by 1972.[14] Needless to say, services weren't successful in reducing poverty. The money was directed at what was perceived to be the shortcomings of individuals rather than the shortcomings of the economic system. The mistake was to think that these services could somehow substitute for the problems of an economy that created the poverty in the first place.

Here is an instance of a social problem analysis shown by subsequent events to be dead wrong and it reveals, on the one hand, the limitations of the criterion of fit with the social problem analysis and, on the other hand, how important it is to remake the social problem analysis when that is the case. An obvious alternative hypothesis is that the error is caused by external and environmental, not personal, attributes. Such errors are common mistakes, evident in much of social welfare history of the Western world. Modern instances include comprehensive job training programs and quintessentially personal social services that offer training in job skills, job search, and job application. These are relevant examples when offered such that the anticipated employment is either nonexistent or comprises only minimum wage jobs and when costs for transportation and work uniforms reduce net earnings to well below those of many income maintenance program benefits. The best training, education, and job referral systems can't make up for a bad job market or low earnings combined with (for example) high child care and transportation costs. Barbara Wootten puts it this way: "It is always easier to put up a clinic than tear down a slum . . . we prefer today to analyze the infected individual rather than . . . the infection from the environment."[15]

But it isn't that difficult to take all this history into account and then recreate a social problem analysis based on a broader economic and social system viewpoint. If one did, the implication would be reasonably clear that the most obvious cause of poverty is lack of money and the most obvious remedy is via material benefits: cash and adequate paid, full-time jobs. History shows that such jobs can be increased by a wide range of governmental public policies including (but not limited to) the following:

- "Trickle-down" policies that give tax cuts to employers and investors to invest in new industrial plants and equipment to create new jobs (very slow in producing effects and with heavy unintended benefits to the wealthy)
- Governmental policies to place new orders to private business for military equipment, roads, bridges and hydroelectric power dams in employment-distressed regions (quicker effects for the middle class but expensive and controversially cost-effective for the poor)
- Projects directly administered by the federal and state government to construct public buildings, roads and bridges and national park facilities (like the Works Progress Administration (WPA) and the Tennessee Valley Authority (TVA) during the 1930s depression) (quickest for the poor but controversially cost-effective for the product produced and politically very controversial in the United States, though not in Europe)

And of course there is an incident in world history that, while not so intended, dramatically demonstrates the effectiveness of public policy remedying poverty by hard benefits like money or food or the access to opportunity for the ordinary jobs that produce it. In the 1800s, Great Britain, stubbornly ignoring the relationship among crime, poverty, and general economic distress, decided to solve its problem of an immense overload of civil prisoners by shipping them off to their colonies in Australia and New Zealand—out of sight, out of mind, out of trouble. No one believed that colonial societies would be successful social and economic failures. As hindsight shows, not only did that happen but successful modern social and economic structures were built on a populace of convicted criminals. The desire to work and the ability to compete and survive are shown by this example not to have been lacking in the convict society. The economic and social development of these countries is the premier example of the importance of having available sufficient economic opportunity created by public social utilities (when the private sector can't provide it). Given a PSU in the form of abundant land made available by explicit public policy in the form of subsidies, land grants, transportation, and settlement, a society made up of convicted criminals created a hard-working, ordered, socially conforming and economically productive life.[16] The mistake in the British approach to their social problem of crime was an ideological error in the British understanding of the problem of criminal behavior—the problem was thought to be one of moral lack, not of economic opportunity. However, when given a labor market that provided opportunity, these early Australian and New Zealand settlers took advantage of its benefits and turned them to their own self-interest. Personal social services were not required. At the most concrete level one might say that the lesson to be learned from this history is that the problem of overcrowded prisons is simply to find new, undiscovered continents or vast ocean islands as resettlement sites for criminals; a wiser conclusion is that it takes very dramatic, hard-benefit–oriented mechanisms (jobs and money) to produce a major impact on serious national poverty and crime and no personal social service strategy—training, rehabilitation, job search sophistication, however well financed or conceived—can substitute for it.

There are examples of failed social problem analyses in other social problem areas as well. In the 1970s, when federal payments to states for child foster care were raised to 100 percent of state costs, it was done based on the entirely innocent motive to protect children by making available to states essentially cost-free family foster care. The threat to children was the lack of same for those in institutions and in need of protection from abuse and neglect, among other things. This truncated view of the social problem of such children led to massive increases in the numbers of children placed outside their homes in public foster care facilities.[17] Many believe that the open-ended funding contributed substantially to children being "stuck" in foster care for interminable periods ("foster care drift"), neither returning home nor finding a permanent environment as families re-formed around their absence. The problem was created by a faulty social problem analysis, which defined the problem simply in terms of the child's need for protection. The obvious alternative is to define the problem in terms of the child's need for permanent and nonneglectful kin. Defined that way the solution is unlikely to be state-financed family foster care, which has a poor track record as a permanent arrangement. In fact, that kind of problem definition might lead to considering how much cheaper it would be to pay the prospective foster care costs (thousands of dollars per month) to a child's relative (for example) rather than to a foster family who is essentially a stranger to the child and the child's family. Foster family care provided as a public personal social service by the state often has no margin of excellence over the ordinary families from which these children come, even in protecting them from neglect or from sexual or physical abuse.

SUMMARY

The discussion of benefit types began with a consideration of the rise of the cash benefit as a norm in the 1930s coincident with the early days of the Social Security Act. Nine types of benefits and services were presented for use in the analysis of social program and policy provisions: material goods and commodities, expert services, positive discrimination, cash, credits and vouchers, market or wholesale subsidies, government loan guarantees, protective regulation, and power over decisions. The interrelationships between benefit and service forms were reviewed, particularly the offering of several benefits and services in whole packages: unemployment security and AFDC were discussed as examples. The problems of multiple benefits, in the sense of benefit packages that accrue from more than a single program, were noted (with further discussion reserved for Chapter 10 dealing with the overall interrelationships between social policies and programs). The cash versus in-kind debate was reviewed as an occasion to illustrate how to use evaluation criteria in judging their relative merit: potential for stigmatization, target efficiency, cost-effectiveness, consumer sovereignty, substitutability, and fit with the social problem analysis, and examples of various personal criteria that might be used by the policy analyst. Multiple and interactive benefit forms were also discussed, as was the issue of trade-offs between evaluation criteria.

EXERCISES

1. Review the exercises in Chapter 5. Now think of a way the government could provide emergency substitute care for children without a government agency recruiting and selecting foster homes.
2. Write a paragraph expressing some conclusions you have drawn about whether the alternative benefit forms you have proposed in answering question 1 do better or worse on the four evaluation criteria for forms of benefit discussed in the chapter.

NOTES

1. M. Howlett, "Policy Instruments, Policy Styles and Policy Implementation: National Approaches to Theories of Instrument Choice," *Policy Studies Journal*, 19[2]1–21 (1991).
2. Of course, the U.S. Medicare system had reached that point by 1990 and now finances hospitalization under a diagnosis-related group (DRG) system where the same (average cost) payment is made for patients whose diagnosed medical conditions lie in the same DRG.
3. Of course, sometimes the U.S. government has worked out agricultural subsidies in ways that require direct federal ownership and handling of grain: for example, there have been times when the federal government would actively take ownership of wheat, corn, rice, and soybeans and store them for years in their own granaries located across the country. They would do this as a way of "artificially" creating low supply (acting to "corner the market" and thus control prices), so as to increase demand and therefore increase prices paid to farmers for what grain they either retained or grew next year. That is still a market subsidy because its purpose is directed toward producers, not consumers. This is only a different mechanism for working it out.
4. G. B. Doern and R. W. Phidd, *Canadian Public Policy: Ideas, Structure, Process* (Toronto: Methuen Company, 1983).
5. The reader might wish to consult Martin Rein, "Poverty, Policy and Purpose: Dilemmas of Choice," in *Social Policy: Issues of Choice and Change*, M. E. Sharpe, Inc., Armonk, NY, 1983, for a somewhat different and more abstract classification of benefit forms: social amenities (what here were called public social utilities), investment in human capital, welfare transfers, rehabilitation, participation (of the poor), and aggregative and selective economic measures. Whereas Rein calls these benefit "strategies," ultimately that is what Table 6–1 amounts to. Rein's list is useful but in the list presented here, the benefit forms are more mutually exclusive and concretely descriptive of exactly what the benefit is.

6. G. Lewis and R. J. Morrison, *Interactions Among Social Welfare Programs* (Discussion Paper No. 866–88) (WI: Institute for Research on Poverty, University of Wisconsin, September 1988).
7. S. H. Linder and B. G. Peters, "Instruments of Government: Perceptions and Contexts," *Journal of Public Policy*, 9:[1]35–38, 56 (1988).
8. S. Terkel, *Working* (New York: Avon, 1992).
9. Page 56 in Note 7.
10. L. Stone, "Madness," *New York Review of Books*, July 10, 1988, 8–12.
11. A. Myrdal, *Nation and Family* (Cambridge, MA: MIT Press, 1968). See also Gilbert and Specht, Op. Cit. pp. 81-102.
12. Robert Morris, *Social Policy of the American State* (New York: Harper and Row, Publishers, 1979), p. 120.
13. Page 121 in Note 12.
14. P. Mott, *Meeting Human Needs, a Social and Political History of Title XX* (Columbus, OH: National Conference on Social Welfare, 1976).
15. B. Wootten, *Social Science and Social Pathology* (London: Allen and Unwin, 1959), p. 329.
16. M. A. Jones, *The History of the Australian Welfare State* (Sidney: George Allen and Unwin, 1988).
17. A. Kadushin, *Child Welfare* (New York: Macmillan, 1986).

CHAPTER 7

Analysis of Types of Entitlement Rules (Who Gets What, How Much, and Under What Conditions)

INTRODUCTION

Fifty years ago textbooks on economics referred to air and water as examples of "free goods." So far have we come from that more plentiful time that it is now difficult to cite any example of a free good: free in the sense that it is neither rationed, regulated, nor priced. Because no social welfare benefit is a free good, rules and regulations allocating such benefits abound. Such rules and regulations are not dispensable. So long as the demand exceeds the supply of benefits and services, some rule or principle must be used as a guide for deciding who gets the benefit or service and who does not.

Social work practitioners need to understand eligibility and allocation rules because they work daily within the context of these guidelines and use them at all levels of complexity. For example, the practitioner may need to seek exceptions from those rules to meet a client's special need. The practitioner may need to understand the eligibility rule to decide whether to advise the client to seek an administrative hearing on the issue. As an agency representative, the practitioner may need to help a client or another practitioner understand the details of the rule and its associated principle so the client has an equal chance to receive a benefit.

Social work and human service practitioners must also live with the fact that they are in the business of denying as well as qualifying clients for benefits—a hard fact of life that is a consequence of scarce resources. In an earlier chapter the argument was made that finite resources was one of the reasons that social policies had to be invented; social policies are the vehicle by which social resources, services, and benefits are rationed when there isn't enough for everybody under every condition. So, as long as there are insufficient resources for every conceivable social need, social and human service workers must keep in mind that every time a benefit or service is given to one user/client, it takes away the opportunity to give it to another one in need.

Entitlement and eligibility rules are the vehicle for rationing benefits and services. On the positive side they seek to target resources on those who need them or those who need them most. If they are off-targeted and go to clients who don't need them then, at some point in time someone who does need them will go without.

It is a mistake for practitioners to think they can just "work harder" somehow to deliver services to clients so that *no one* will go without. Practitioners' time is also a scarce and expensive resource, every bit as scarce and expensive as cash. It is tempting to think that a way around this problem is to deliver services via a "first-come, first-served" entitlement or eligibility rule. Although that rule has qualities of "rough justice" that are somehow appealing, the justice involved is probably illusory. Think of how a "first-come, first-served" rule gives a not necessarily merited advantage to those who *by chance* hear of the rule or the service first; there is no particular justice in that. At some point those who implement that rule will run out of resources, so that denying clients has only been postponed. First-come, first-served is not inherently a bad entitlement rule, but it has no great virtue either—why shouldn't it be preferable to give preference to those who are, on some basis, most needy? Indeed, the practitioner may even be responsible for constructing such rules at some time later in his or her career.

In any of those instances there is at stake a professional responsibility for good service to clients. Where a policy does not meet the needs of clients adequately, neither the exercise of simplistic eligibility or entitlement rules nor a large dose of moral indignation will suffice to discharge professional responsibility. Practitioners are responsible for advocating their clients' needs even to their own administrative superiors as well as to their colleagues in other agencies who have resources that clients need. Furthermore, practitioners are responsible for joining with others in pursuing legislative or judicial advocacy where these strategies have a possibility of success.

SPECIFIC TYPES OF ELIGIBILITY AND ALLOCATION RULES

The decentralized disarray of the U.S. welfare system creates literally hundreds of public and private programs that offer welfare services and benefits. Each has a somewhat different set of rules for determining who gets what, how much, and under which conditions. Faced with this bewildering variety, we must reduce its complexity by some kind of scheme that will render it understandable. The purpose of this scheme is to group together eligibility rules so that we can talk about "types" of eligibility rules without the trouble of weighty discussions about lightweight differences. Many schemes serve this purpose—none perfect—so we will borrow heavily from one scheme that seems well suited to the purposes of this book. It was devised by Richard Titmuss, a student of social policy in the British tradition of Beatrice Webb, Beveridge, and others.[1] Titmuss was tentative about this analytic scheme: "This represents little more than an elementary and partial structural map which can assist in the understanding of the welfare complex today." Thus, we might hope Titmuss would be pleased with the additions and modifications in the classification below:[2]

- Prior contributions
- Administrative rule
- Private contracts
- Professional discretion
- Administrative discretion
- Judicial decision
- Means testing (needs minus assets and/or income)
- Attachment to the work force

Entitlement Rules Based on Prior Contributions

Entitlement to many important social welfare benefits is established by rules about how much advance contributions have been made to the system that will pay the benefit later. A prominent example is a benefit paid by the U.S. Social Security system: retirement income for workers and survivors (OASI), disability income for workers and dependents (DI), and payments for medical care services (HI) for both the disabled and the retired. Exactly how much prior contribution is required varies with the age at which benefit is drawn and the type of benefit in question; but some *prior contribution* is always necessary. The prior contribution of which we are generally speaking comes from two sources, the worker and the employer. Each pays an equal share, calculated by a formula written into the law and expressed as a percentage of workers' wages. As of 1991, 7.35 percent of wages (on wages up to $53,000) was paid by both employer and worker as a contribution to the Social Security Trust Fund (SSTF) from which workers' benefits will later be paid.

Note that in the case of Social Security retirement or disability benefits, some citizens receive payments although they have never made payments to the SSTF. That might be because they are (or were) dependents of a worker who did contribute to the Social Security system. The basic ideas behind the prior contribution method of establishing entitlement are the same principles that lie behind all private insurance schemes: (1) payment in advance provides for the future and (2) protection against the economic consequences of personal disasters is best achieved by spreading the risk among a large group of people. When Social Security was first established, it was intended to be based on just such insurance principles and benefits were to bear a strong relationship to contributions. That relationship has eroded over the years so that in 1981 the benefits received by the average Social Security recipient will equal his or her payments in only eighteen months (nor is it very different in 1991).[3]

The insurance principle has come upon hard times in the Social Security system lately, largely because Congress has continued to enact larger benefits than were ever anticipated in earlier years when financing was being planned, and the ratio between the number of working contributors and the number of retiree beneficiaries has changed substantially (more on that later). The prior contribution strategy is subject to a number of problems, one of which is the fact that it is insensitive to demographic changes. There are also strong inequities for employed women whose spouses also pay Social Security contributions: Upon retirement she and her spouse will receive no more than 50 percent more benefits than if she had never paid Social Security contributions at all (the maximum family benefit is approximately 150 percent of the benefit of the spouse who has the best earning record). In an insurance scheme that was absolutely faithful to the insurance principle, the married couple's benefit upon retirement would be based on the contribution of both husband and wife, plus whatever interest and dividends accrued over the years during which the contributions were made. It must be said, however, that to date there is little actual loss on this account in that the average Social Security beneficiary has actually paid for only about half of what is received in benefits. On that account and contrary to a common myth, *it is impossible for any present Social Security beneficiary household to have come out better had they paid the same amount as their total combined Social Security contributions into a private insurance scheme.* If you study that statement, you will see that it is true because private companies must not only "break even," they must also show a profit. No private insurance company will pay out more total benefits to policyholders than are received in premiums (of course that is exactly what happens, or is expected to happen, when insurance companies go bankrupt). The feature that makes Social Security work to the advantage of those who are retiring now is that (1) there are income transfers at work and (2) profitability is not a factor (at the least because there are no sales or marketing costs). The Social Security system is, in fact, transferring income from those who are now working to those who are no longer working—the retired, disabled, or users of Medicare benefits.[4]

Entitlement by Administrative Rule

Although entitlement rules for public social programs may be laid out in some detail in the law, seldom are they sufficiently detailed so that no administrative interpretations need be made. Thus *administrative rules* are made to clarify the law. This is an advantage to client/beneficiaries because it gives social workers and other human service staff members a means by which to administer the benefit or service program even-handedly and reliably, so that people similarly situated are more likely to be given similar benefits. On the other hand, administrative rules restrict the freedom of staff members to use their discretion, that is, to judge need for the benefit or service in individual circumstances. So even though administrative rules may work toward greater equity, they may also be a less effective response to unique individual circumstances. There are some entitlements that are almost fully spelled out in the law, and the Food Stamp program is probably the best example. Almost all of the details necessary to determine whether a citizen is entitled to food stamps are built into the law. The exact amount of assets, as well as income, is specified by family size in the text of the act, along with definitions of what constitutes a household. Consequently, no discretion is needed in determining whether (for example) a live-in friend of either sex should be included in determining household size. The administrative rules for the AFDC program, on the other hand, are so numerous and concern so many different topics that most states bind them into ponderous "manuals." These administrative tomes not only include the state and federal statutes relevant to the program, but (mainly) they address how those laws are to be interpreted. One reason for the complexity of entitlement rules in the AFDC program is that it is a "means-tested" program, meaning entitlement is established by a test of whether a person's assets and income are greater than some official standard of need for a family of some designated size. Apart from all of the administrative rules that concern counting assets and income, the AFDC program also has to be built on numerous administrative rules that tell the staff who sign the entitlement documents how to interpret the law. It is in the character of administrative rules that they can be modified over time; if they are devised by administrators, they can also be changed by administrators. Therefore, it is important to know whether a certain entitlement rule originates with judicial decision, administrative rule, or individual staff discretion, for upon that fact depends the probability for change—staff decisions certainly are changed more easily than are formal ("manualized") rules or statutes. Further, as you might imagine, the method, resources, and time used to effect changes differ for each rule source. Chapter 8 (administrative and service delivery system operating characteristic) will discuss the details of administrative appeal hearings, which are required by law for all social programs established under the Social Security Act and for many programs that receive federal funds.

Entitlement by Private Contract

Strange as it may seem, it is possible to become entitled to a public benefit through the provisions of *private contracts*. The Workers Compensation system is constructed this way.[5] In every state employers are required to purchase insurance policies from private insurance companies (or, as is rare, a state insurance fund) to pay to workers money for income and medical costs to replace what is lost through work injury. There is nothing optional about the law, and employers are subject to substantial fines for noncompliance. In this case the benefit form is a cash payment plus a voucher for medical expenses.

Another source of entitlement to public benefits in which private contracts are involved is purchase-of-service contracting (POSC). In the past decade more and more welfare services—counseling, legal advocacy, special education, day care, and some transportation services (for the elderly and/or disabled for example)—are delivered by private contractors. In the case of purchased services of various kinds, the state actually pays the bill (or some of it) directly to the private purveyor of the contracted service. Because the state is the purchaser of services, the state can insert conditions into the contract concerning who can obtain the service, for how long, and under what circumstances.[6] Not only state and federal governments subcontract for services; private charitable organizations do so as well. For example, private hospitals "contract out" to private profit-making corporations the operation of psychiatric units—Horizons Corporation and Humana operate many such units nationwide. Another example is a midwestern private social agency that operates a "high-tech foster care" program for its state. This program serves severely emotionally disturbed children who cannot be cared for in the ordinary family foster home setting. In both these examples, the entitlement rules embedded in the private contract determine who is eligible for services.

Services provided under Title XX of the Social Security Act is another example of the extensive use of POSC. Title XX is intended to provide services ". . . aimed at the goals of: (a) Achieving or maintaining economic self support to prevent, reduce, or eliminate dependency, (b) to prevent or remedy neglect, abuse or exploitation of children and adults unable to protect themselves, (c) to provide services to individuals in institutions."[8] Although Title XX did not require POSC from private contractors, it certainly anticipated it, because specific provisions in the act (subpart G) set out what had to be included in such a contract. In fact 33 percent of all Title XX expenditures were purchased from private purveyors under this act rather than being provided directly by the state welfare agencies. Payment for services under POSC arrangements can be either by fixed-price, reimbursement-at-cost, or performance contracting. In *fixed-price* contracting, the governmental body pays the contractor a price that remains stable over a set period of time; the main reward for the contractors depends on their ability to estimate costs accurately and to administer the program within those constraints. A *reimbursement-at-cost* contract insulates the contractor from unexpected costs and is often used for research or program development for which it is difficult to estimate costs. *Performance* contracting rewards contractors for achieving program objectives at certain levels and penalizes them financially for failing to do so. Incentives for goal attainment are built into the performance contract in various ways. For example, Wedel and Colston cite job training, job placement, maintaining frail elderly in their own homes, and so on, describing in detail a performance-based contract between the state of Oklahoma and local community mental health centers. The contract featured the use of financial awards for those centers delivering services that exceeded the contracted amount of service provided and the assessment of financial penalties for those centers whose performance was not up to par.[10] Performance contracting is not without some problems, one of which is the ruling of Michigan's attorney general that contractors could not be held responsible for failure to meet performance goals specified in the contract. Among other problems is the difficulty in always being able to specify some numerical criterion by which good and bad performance can be distinguished and the potential conflict over how the enduring profit motive in performance contracts creates incentives to shave services in ways that, while not mentioned in the contract, may degrade them.[11] Clearly all POSC and performance contracting require participants, both government and contractors, who are particularly sophisticated in pricing, administrative controls, and close monitoring.[12]

Entitlement by Professional Discretion

One of the most widely used sources of entitlement is the *professional discretion* of individual practitioners. A common and concrete example is entitlement to medical benefits, which is always contingent on the discretion of the physician (or physician surrogate). Almost every licensed profession controls part of the entitlement to some kind of social welfare benefit: dental care for AFDC children is entitled in part by the judgment of dentists; foot care for veterans is entitled in part by podiatrists; legal advocacy for low-income people is entitled in part by the judgment of lawyers; eyeglasses for low-income mental patients are entitled in part by optometrists; foster care for children is entitled in part by social workers. In each case, the entitling profession whose judgment is necessary is presumed to have some expertise about the matter. More often than not, such a presumption is correct, though there can be exceptions. Social work and human service practitioners must keep in mind that such discretion can be challenged in an administrative or judicial hearing, and where such discretion seems prejudicial to their clients practitioners have a professional obligation to help their client challenge it. Sometimes professional discretion is the leading evidence that severs children from parents, as in child physical abuse, sexual abuse, or neglect cases. The opinions of therapists and diagnosticians (both physicians), clinical psychologists, and social workers are commonly used. No doubt those opinions are important and often accurate, but social workers and human service workers should be wary of a blanket assumption about the validity of those very difficult judgments. Clientele may consist of accused parents as well as children, and practitioners are obligated to advocate for their client first and foremost.

Entitlement by Administrative Discretion

Another kind of discretion that serves as a source of entitlement to social welfare benefits is *administrative discretion*. A common example of this is the policy in some states and counties that allows a county welfare worker to distribute small amounts of cash and credits for food, housing, and utilities to poor people who apply. This kind of policy is characteristic of the General Assistance programs of the twenty-seven states that have them. General Assistance is financed by the local government and is usually oriented toward short-term emergency budgets. The staff member must account for the funds only in the fiscal sense; administrative judgment is seldom called to account, and there is little systematic effort to document its accuracy. However, there are more important examples of administrative discretion. It is indeed widespread and the source of such extensive power throughout modern public organizations that, according to Michael Lipsky and Michael Brown, there may be serious question as to whether staff members at the lowest level or the chief executive actually controls the organizational operations.[13,14] All general organizational policies and administrative rules must be interpreted and applied to individual situations, so it is important to understand that such interpretation and application necessarily involve significant personal judgment—a form of administrative discretion—on the part of the staff member. For example, a state patrolman sees a person stopped at the side of a highway and diligently applying a willow stick to the bare rear end of a five-year-old child. In a hairbreadth, the patrolman is duty-bound to make a serious decision about whether to stop and make inquiries. His decision is essentially administrative because it comes out of the role he fills as protector of persons. Later he may have to make an even more serious decision. Was what he saw simply a child who had tried the parent's patience and was being disciplined within acceptable bounds? Or was it a cruel physical attack that will leave black-and-blue bruises or break the skin of a child too young to defend himself? The discretion entailed here concerns interpretation of the state child abuse statute. Does this instance, and the data selected to report it, constitute an example of what the statute delineates? The statute will not reveal to the patrolman what rules he should use for its interpretation; it will not say how inflamed the bruises should be—or even whether black-and-blue rather than red bruises count. Nor will it always protect the officer from consequences if the parent claims illegal detainment or false arrest. The same situation is faced by the social worker or the physician while examining a hospital emergency room patient. Here, however, it is *professional* discretion that is being asked for. Their task is to render a professional opinion about the matter, and they are prepared by training and experience and specifically empowered by law to make that judgment. The difference between professional and administrative discretion is source of authority of each: professionals exercise discretion because of the authority of their professional preparation and training, whereas administrators exercise discretion because they are appointed by their superiors to do so.

There are important examples of administrative discretion gone amok, so that social work and human service professionals should be aware that administrative discretion—as important and humane as it can be—also can be used in ways that work to the detriment of their client's welfare. Few cases are so flagrant as the massive disentitlement of the chronically mentally ill from Social Security Disability benefits during the early-1980s Reagan administration. Although it is not a common case, it is useful to summarize briefly here to illustrate this point. At that time, the Social Security Administration (SSA), ostensibly concerned about the rising costs of the Social Security Disability system, began a systematic effort to reduce approved benefit claims and to terminate the benefits of the chronically mentally ill whom the SSA believed to be unable to prove their illness. Some 150,000 beneficiaries had their benefits canceled during those few years. Not only the mentally ill were disadvantaged; there are documented cases of rejected applicants with severe cardiac conditions who died in the waiting rooms of Social Security offices.

The mechanisms by which this was accomplished included changes in the standards used for mental disabilities and attempts to impose a "quota" on SSA hearing judges for benefit denials—judges were expected to hand down a constantly increasing number of benefit denials. If the quota was not met, they were subject to considerable harassment: reassignment, or mandatory attendance at lengthy "educational seminars," for example. The Association of Social Security Administrative Law Judges appealed these measures on the grounds that they constituted unlawful interference in the fair-hearing appeals system established by the Social Security Act as independent of administrative authority. The Association won on those grounds, after verifying that indeed there were systematic, illegal, plainly political attempts to influence the outcomes of the fair-hearing system. Thousands of appeals of disability denials ensued, sizable proportions of which were successful. It is clear from the data available that disabled beneficiaries who persevered in challenging the administrative decisions of the SSA, increased their chances of a favorable decision to nearly 80 percent. The higher the federal appeal court rendering the decision, the more likely was a decision against the Administration.[15] Only through the efforts of both legal advocates and social work and human service advocates were these reversals accomplished. This example should give heart to practitioners that advocacy can succeed and, when conditions warrant, be a part of their daily work.

Practitioners who advocate in these matters should understand that the most important issue in these cases was whether the SSA had *followed its own rules* in denying disability claims. That is the standard required by administrative law, and it is the most common ground for appeals. The law does not often call into question the substance of an administrative criterion for eligibility or entitlement for benefits or services, but it does require that when specific criteria are established for public benefits, the agency must adhere to them. If rules change, the changes must be made public and published in certain ways. In a very concrete way, administrative rules are the "rules of the road," and justice requires that citizens know about them so that they can equitably pursue claims to which they may be entitled. On that account many (though not all) rules of due process apply, such as notice, opportunity to know the grounds for denial, opportunity to present testimony in a fair hearing, and the like. (Some of these rules will be discussed in Chapter 8.)

Entitlement by Judicial Decision

Judicial decisions are important sources of entitlement, virtually ruling applicants in or out of program benefits and services. (So important is it that all of Chapter 3 was devoted to the whole issue of the judiciary as a source of public policy.) After a program has been in operation over a period of time, it is very likely that a contention will arise either about a point in the enabling legislation, or whether an administrative rule or discretionary judgment was faithful to the spirit and intention of the law under which the program or policy was established. Appeals to the judiciary for clarification of the law are routine and in the end they can become as important as the legislation or administrative rules themselves. Sometimes judicial rulings prevent administrative rules from excluding people from benefits. An example is the 1969 ruling of the U.S. Supreme Court on the constitutionality of what were then called "residence requirements." Under residency rules in effect at the time, citizens of a state had to establish permanent residency over a specified number of days, weeks, months, or years (usually one year for AFDC) as a condition of entitlement. (Residency is an ancient eligibility requirement going as far back as the Elizabethan poor laws in England.) In 1969, the U.S. Supreme Court held that such requirements were unconstitutional infringements on citizens' right of free movement between states.[16]

Some judicial rulings operate not only to prevent exclusion from a program, but to positively assert an entitlement where none existed before. In one of the most familiar, *Brown v. Board of Education* (1954),[17] the U.S. Supreme Court ruled that all children are entitled to an equal opportunity for education, regardless of race. It was truly a landmark decision and marks the beginning of a whole era of efforts to establish civil rights, benefits, and services. Paternity determinations serve as a source of judicial entitlement to the child support payments by nonsupporting fathers, even though such entitlement may be viewed by some as a mixed blessing. There is now available a clinical test, the human leucocyte antigen (HLA) test, which will rule out, with 97% accuracy, whether a given individual is the father of a particular child. Nearly two-thirds of all courts accept use of the HLA test in paternity cases, with full confidence in its results.[18] When evidence is accepted and decisions are rendered about paternity, entitlement to child support payments from the adjudged father is established by court decision. Another kind of judicial ruling that represents a source of entitlement is somewhat unusual, but it occurs in the process of the judicial review of all children in "temporary" foster care and is now required by law in most states.[19] Begun in New York State in 1971, that state's court review statute provides that for eighteen months the Family Court will review cases of all children in involuntary placement and determine whether they shall be discharged to their biological families, continued in foster care, freed for adoptive placement, or placed in an adoptive home. In essence, this is a decision by a judge as to whether a child is entitled to parental care, adoptive placement, or foster home services.

Entitlement by Means Testing

One of the best-known and most widely used of all sources of entitlement is a *means test*: Income and assets are totaled to see whether they are less than some standard for what a person is believed to need. If the assets and/or income exceed this standard then no benefit is given; if assets and/or income are less than that standard, the person is given a benefit in such an amount that total assets and income are equal to the standard. The central idea is that where assets and income are up to the standard, the person "ought" to have enough to meet his or her needs.

Despite its apparent simplicity, the whole idea turns out to have enormous complications. For example, there is the issue of what to consider as income. Some means tests concern both assets and wages (AFDC), whereas others concern wages alone (Workers Compensation). Benefit amounts and types of beneficiaries turn out to be very different depending on which version of the means test is used.[20] Note the world of difference in terms of administrative complexity between income only versus income and assets with regard to the test. Income is almost always a matter of record (often public), is often in the form of cash, and, therefore, can be immediately valued. Assets are usually held privately and, because they are seldom a matter of record, determining their valuation is often problematic. Then there is the question of how to establish a standard of "need" against which to cast income and/or assets. Even determining what minimum nutritional need is can be very controversial; the same goes for "minimum" need for housing, clothing, and on it goes. As a result of the difficulty of arriving at a consensus on these issues, a different "standard of minimum need" applies in almost every state. In 1984, the state standards of need for AFDC—by any standard never a princely sum—varied by nearly 400 percent! For a family of three (two children, one adult) in the contiguous 48 states, the standards varied from the lowest in Kentucky ($218 per month) to the highest in Vermont ($930 per month). Means-tested entitlement procedures also vary with respect to whose income and assets are being considered when the means test is calculated. For some programs, focus is on individuals (SSI) or on children (AFDC); in others it is on workers (Workers Compensation); in still others it is on households "who purchase food together irrespective of blood relation" (Food Stamp); and in still others focus is on blood-related families (Title XX, Child-Support-Parent Location services). Table 7–1 summarizes some of the wide variability that can be found is concrete, selected social programs with respect to means-testing policy. Means are tested along three major dimensions: (1) type of resource counted (wages and/or assets), (2) concept underlying needs, and (3) beneficiary unit (child, household, worker, and such). These dimensions be useful in knowing what to look for in analyzing means tests as entitlement rules.

Table 7–1. Variability in Means-Testing Procedures for Selected Social Programs

Program	Type of $ counted Wages	Assets	Concept underlying idea of "need"	Beneficiary unit of concern
AFDC*	Almost all	Almost all	Absolute minimum subsistence	Child
Food stamps	Almost all	Almost all	Nutritional adequacy; income less than 125% of poverty line	Household: those who buy food together
OASI	Half of wages earned ages 62–70	None	Low–adequate living standard	Worker
SSI*	Almost all	Assets over $2,000 in general	Absolute minimum subsistence	Individual
Title XX	Almost all	None	Income less than average family	Family or household

* Varies somewhat by state, but these are the best general rules.

Establishing Attachment To the Workforce

Where social welfare programs are aimed at the primary workforce, that is, the working populace, it is of crucial importance to determine entitlement by a means that will qualify *only* those who are part of the workforce (lest benefits go astray). This is done by setting a minimum to be contributed (via wage deduction at a workplace) that will entitle a person to benefit. Note that in many programs that require prior contribution for entitlement, not just *any* prior contribution will do; it must be a particular minimum amount, over time, that counts up to entitlement. The U.S. Unemployment Insurance (UI) program is a major example of this mechanism of entitlement. The goal of the UI program is to benefit those who have some significant work history—the program does not now intend, nor has it ever intended, to benefit those working part-time, only in casual employment, or only for insignificant wages. Although specific rules vary state by state, UI typically requires the worker to have received wages for at least six months and to have received at least $200 in wages during each prior three-month period. The purpose of such entitlement requirements is to establish that the worker has some significant "attachment" to the workforce. The Social Security Disability (DI) program has a similar policy built into its prior contribution policies, but Workers Compensation is concerned with limiting coverage, only to those with attachment to the workforce. If a worker is injured on the first day of the first job ever, and the employer carries Workers Compensation insurance, that worker is entitled to benefits appropriate to the injury as provided by law.

CRITERIA FOR EVALUATING THE MERIT OF ENTITLEMENT RULES

Fit with the Social Problem Analysis

Correspondence between the Entitlement and Eligibility Rules and the Target Specifications of the Social Problem Analysis: For a program or policy to be a coherent solution to a social problem, those who receive the program's benefits and/or services must be included within the group whom the social problem analysis identifies as having the problem. Recall from Chapter 1 on social problem analysis the necessity of social problem definition, which generates ". . . concrete observable signs by which the existence of the problem can be known," including "subtypes" and "quantifications" of the size of the problem. *Those concrete indicators, subtypes and quantifications are main sources from which entitlement and eligibility rules must be drawn.* Entitlement rules that don't correspond to those indicators will off-target the program benefits and services. If poverty is defined as annual cash income less than $13,500 for a family of four, then at least one of the entitlement rules must restrict the benefits of a cash assistance program to those with that level of income. If inability to attain a university-level education is defined as one problem for families with annual incomes less than $20,000, then the same stricture applies. If the social problem of providing income support for the physically and mentally disabled is defined as applying to those with a verified disability and proven inability to work for the next six months, then indeed the entitlement rules are about verifiable standards for determining disability and the inability to work for that period of time. The quantifications embedded in the social problem definition are the basis for the target specifications that must be a part of well-formed goals and objectives and it is to those that entitlement and eligibility rules must be relevant.

Also recall that definitions in the social problem analysis can always be changed to widen those target specifications. Note, however, that doing so has serious consequences; changing the description of those who have the problem will very often work considerable changes in the factors (antecedents, independent variables) in the causal analysis. Because those factors are the targets for the specific activities (interventions) of the program designed to effect change in the problem, it may well change the whole program design. This is a consequence of featuring the social problem viewpoint as the central basis for the rationality and coherence of the social policy and program system: Changing one feature of the problem analysis changes the entire social program. Do not necessarily interpret this position as advice against changing the social problem viewpoint once it has been established; instead, know that it is simply advice meant to alert the unwary to a potentially serious consequence. As social practitioners gain experience, their viewpoints on the social problem they are trying to solve become more sophisticated and, hopefully, better.

Correspondence Between the Entitlement and Eligibility Rules and the Ideology of the Social Problem Analysis: Eligibility and entitlement rules do more than just reflect target specifications, they also reflect general ideological positions that underlie or are associated with the viewpoints from which a social problem is defined. An example is commitment to the work ethic, an idea that refers to the common belief that work is inherently virtuous and that the virtue of a citizen is related to work effort and work product. English poor laws required work tests as a condition for entitlement; that is, one way a person proved he was poor was to be willing to accept placement in a nineteenth-century workhouse. The modern U.S. equivalent is the requirement that unemployed food stamp recipients be registered for work referrals at their local state employment agency. That requirement is itself a condition of eligibility and thus an eligibility rule. It reflects an ideological commitment to the idea that citizens should expect to work for their own bread and that if they don't, they should have to show that no work is available or that they are unable to do the work that is available. The "relatives responsibility" policy is another instance of eligibility ideology. England's Elizabethan poor laws, as well as U.S. judicial decisions, provided relief for the poor but it was constrained by the common ideological commitment to the idea that families were always primarily responsible for their members. Thus, the underlying practical understanding of the social problem of poverty was that three descending generations in the family group—grandparents, their adult children, and their children's children—must be poor before any individual member was deemed poor. The entitlement rules for the expenditure of public funds for the poor reflected that ideology: Parents were financially responsible for the relief of the poverty of their children, and children were responsible for the relief of the poverty of their own parents.

Good entitlement rules for personal social services must have an ideological fit with the relevant social problem analysis. For example, in the field of mental health there is an interesting split between ideological positions: One implies that severe and chronic psychosis is a problem of greatest concern, and the other implies that prevention of mental health problems is the premier priority. Thus, for the entitlement rules to be consistent with ideology here, the former would have entitlement rules for mental health services and would give priority to those with psychotic behaviors whereas the latter would give priority to those considered to be major "at-risk" groups—those considered to have high potential for the development of mental health problems (however those problems are defined). Of course, that applies only under conditions where resources are insufficient to provide services for both, but that is almost always the case for social policy and program systems. For a different example, consider child protective services. If the ideological position implies that children should never be considered to be a cause of their sexual abuse by an adult, then the rule that entitles them to protection by state intervention also entitles them to remain in their own homes while the adult perpetrator is required to leave. That is a modern practice, of course, not universally followed as a matter of public policy on child protection.

SOME SPECIAL CRITERIA IN EVALUATING ENTITLEMENT AND ELIGIBILITY RULES FOR THE PUBLIC SOCIAL UTILITIES AND HYBRIDS

Stigmatization

The manifest purpose of entitlement rules is to ensure that only those whom the program intends to provide with benefits are in fact included as beneficiaries. Certainly there are also latent purposes to entitlement rules, and some social scientists believe these have clearly negative effects as well. Side effects of some eligibility rules may have such serious consequences that they outweigh benefits received. Some argue that these side effects are intentional, the sign of true latent (and negative) purposes of a social program. Two of the most widely discussed side effects of entitlement rules are stigmatization and alienation. To be *stigmatized* means to be marked as having lesser value, to bear the burden of public disapproval. There are many meanings of *alienation*, but here the term refers to the subjective sense of being estranged from the mainstream of the society in which one dwells. How is it that an entitlement rule or mechanism can produce such strong negative social effects? Both alienation and stigmatization are serious side effects that are believed to be associated with many consequences (suicide, social deviance, tendency toward serious crime, and chemical addiction).

To understand how entitlement rules can produce these strong side effects, think for a moment of what is entailed in an application for a means-tested public assistance program like AFDC, a hybrid of PSUs and PSSs. (Recall that AFDC offers both cash benefits for all citizens whose income is less than some standard *and* personal social services designed to do such things as increase parenting effectiveness, offer children foster care, and help single parents get jobs.) Basically, the application requires a person to lay bare the details of his or her financial and work history in order to document income and assets. Thus, it requires a person to reveal all details about when jobs were left (for whatever reason), when spouses or children were abandoned—without regard for whether the details are flattering to the applicant. The application requires a person to say some or all of the following: "I'm broke. I can't keep a job. I left my last job because I had to go to jail (or the mental hospital). I couldn't be enough of a success in school to get the credentials that would persuade people to hire me. My parents, relatives, husband have all left me and don't care enough about me to help out." Revealing such details to a stranger cannot help but make the strongest constitution quiver in the telling. The ordeal is self-stigmatizing because the teller can no longer hide what may be humiliating facts—at least one other person knows. The more a person believes he or she is regarded negatively, the more likely will that opinion be believed and the stigma accepted as real. The stigmatization that appears to result from entitlement rules associated with the AFDC program is widely discussed in the literature.[22,23,24] The Pettigrew article contains an excellent survey of the studies of labeling and stigmatization of welfare recipients.

It is important to observe that not all entitlement rules are associated with this kind of stigmatization. Few elderly feel stigmatized by the application process guided by the entitlement rules of the Social Security Retirement or Disability program. Nor do people feel stigmatized by the means tests involved in the application for student loans (BEOG [Basic Economic Opportunity Grant] or NSDL [National Student Direct Loan]) or, for that matter, the means test inherent in payment of income tax (if your earned income is more than $15,000, for example, and you have no more than three dependents you are "eligible" to pay some income tax). Two factors distinguish a means test involving an application for AFDC from a means test involving a loan for attending college or university and illustrate how stigmatization occurs. (1) The reason for application for AFDC (say) is most likely to be something that must be apologized for or explained. In contrast, the reason for applying for a BEOG or NSDL loan is almost never the occasion for an apology or explanation; to the contrary, it is likely to be occasion for congratulation or recognition that a person is about to embark on a path of high social regard—going to college. The same applies to the instance of the means test entailed in paying taxes: The very fact that a person struggles over filling out forms and takes a long time at it suggests a person who has considerable assets and income.

The *worst* consequence of the means tests involved in a BEOG loan application is that a person would have to look elsewhere for funds or delay going to school for a year. Contrariwise, the *best* consequence of the means test for AFDC is that a person will receive a poverty level income and medical card.

Some years ago, George Hoshino suggested that, in a phrase of Gilbert and Specht, the means test did not have to be mean-spirited.[25] Hoshino suggests that one of the main reasons for the negative effects of the means test as a way of determining entitlement is that it places great stress on determining unique individual needs when all that is really required is to determine average need for categories of family size, age, and so on. Verification of these assets is a process filled with arbitrary and specious judgments of the market value of mundane goods. As any experienced social worker knows, the administrative cost of such determinations far outweighs the relatively small misplaced benefit that might be given were the verification of the value of highly personal assets simply ignored. It was a considerable step forward when the means test for the Food Stamp Program cleverly avoided these pitfalls and determined need on exactly the basis Hoshino suggested in earlier years—that of some concept of average need (for food, in this case) and by "average" deductions for major items like cars, houses, and insurance policies.[26] Although there may be the rare applicant who has a house full of expensive new furniture and who might not declare it when applying for food stamps, this would certainly not characterize the majority of food stamp applicants. The administrative cost of tracking down that odd exception far outweighs any saving that might result.

Every entitlement rule for PSU or hybrid programs needs to be scrutinized for potential stigmatizing potential. One important thing to look for is the extent to which receipt of benefit is a matter of public knowledge. Free school lunches are a good example: If a student is required to show a voucher, a form, or a ticket that can only be obtained upon demonstration of inability to pay, then having to show that voucher in public to receive the meal is stigmatizing in our society where the general social norm disvalues people with low incomes. This entitlement rule would be judged to be deficient on this criterion. There are ways to "de-stigmatize" the meal benefit: If the ticket for a free lunch is issued for an amount that is larger than a single meal—so that it is a credit that is spendable on diverse goods and services provided by the school (books and athletic fees) and which must be purchased by *all* students—then the fact of who paid for the ticket is withheld from the public and so fails to be stigmatizing.

Off-targeted Benefits

Another criterion for judging eligibility rules and their associated procedures for PSUs and hybrids is the extent to which benefits are directed to population groups who are not the main object of the program. One example from the early 1980s concerned the NSDL funds for college and university students in the United States. NSDL loan funds were very attractive to students in those years because their interest rates were far below the existing market rate of around 7 percent. The difference between the interest rate on the loan (some as low as 3 percent) and prevailing high interest rates in 1981 on such things as long-term savings accounts (12 to 17 percent) was so much that some students who already had sufficient school funds took out an NSDL loan simply to make a little money by banking it at a higher interest rate. Every year the cost of the interest on the loan was $300 (3% of $10,000), whereas the long-term savings account yielded perhaps as much as $1,700 (17% of $10,000). The net profit on this no-effort enterprise would have been the difference between the dollar yield of the two interest rates, i.e., $1,700-$300, or $1,400 total. It would be hard to think of a way to earn more than $100 a month more easily. Because NSDL loans didn't have to be repaid for eight years, the total profit was eight times that $1,400, or $11,200. Not bad.

There aren't many examples of porous entitlement rules as outrageous as that and, in fact, that gaping wound in the design of this social policy was closed after several years by raising interest rates on loans to competitive levels. But entitlement rules such as this should be judged negatively since the off-targeting is significant and has no obvious impact on the social problem. In fact, it represents off-targeting of the worst kind in that it takes away money for income transfers from those who are most clearly in need of them and because the government that made the loans possible had to borrow at market rates, the profit for those who took advantage of the opportunity was and probably still is being paid for by you and me. It is important, nevertheless, to notice that some instances of off-targeting are intentional and that the targeting criteria cannot be used without discrimination.

In fact, some social policies are operationalized in ways that purposely produce "seepage" of benefits to nonmembers of the target group.

Perhaps the best example of off-targeting intended to produce positive results is the Social Security Retirement program. As noted earlier, the program is non-stigmatizing, in contrast to many other social programs. Because financing and entitlement for the program was based on insurance and prior contribution principles, the designers ensured that nearly the whole population was covered by Social Security in one way or another and that fact made it impossible for stigmatization to be an issue for beneficiaries. But it is possible to argue that the designers created an enormous amount of off-targeted benefits ("seepage") of program benefit funds to those who actually don't have economic problems in retirement. Think of it, a billionaire could apply for and probably does receive a Social Security Retirement benefit. What is given to all as a right of citizen or prior contribution can never be stigmatizing or alienating.

With respect to issues of the off-targeted benefits and universal program coverage, two other alternative program designs provide income support. Although neither of these programs has been implemented directly in the United States, both have been set forward as plans for "solving the welfare mess," a phrase frequently used in election years by support-hungry politicians. One design is to abolish all existing cash and cash-equivalent programs (AFDC, Food Stamp, SSI, and UI programs) and replace them with a cash benefit that will provide a minimum subsistence standard of living for those who, for whatever reason, do not have a minimum amount of income and/or assets. The program would use the regular IRS administrative procedure for collecting income tax as a means of distributing benefits to the poor, a system generally called a negative income tax

(NIT). Originally called the Family Assistance Program (FAP), the program was first sponsored in Congress in 1974 by the conservative Republican Nixon administration. The basic idea is that every three months people would file an income tax statement. If their total income and assets were less than some designated poverty line, they would receive over the next three months a monthly amount which, when added to their past three-months' income, would equal the poverty line for their household size. When income exceeded the poverty line, that household would incur a tax liability and be required to pay the government additional tax dollars. This scheme was neither clearly universal nor clearly selective. In fact, the system carefully selects and benefits most those in greatest need, even though all citizens can potentially benefit and the system is nonstigmatizing in that there is almost no public revelation of benefit receipt. The Nixon administration scheme was automatic in that it was operated by the Internal Revenue Service and had a built-in work incentive feature. Using 1980 figures, if there was no earned income, the family would get a standard "base payment," a fixed-dollar amount. Families could work and still keep part of the "base payment." For example, the first $2,000 of earned income was excluded from consideration and doesn't affect the base payment at all. The next $2,000 of earned income, however, reduces the base payment by $1,000 because for each earned dollar above $2,000, the base payment is reduced by 50 cents. The base payment is reduced even more for earned income above $4,000—for each earned dollar in this range the base payment is reduced by 75 cents. More and more of the base payment is taken away as earnings climb, but each dollar earned up to $6,000 will still continue to add something to the family coffers and thus continue a work incentive. A point is reached where finally the base payment is totally wiped out by the reductions for earned income.

Using arbitrary figures, the following example shows how this would work if the objective was to be absolutely sure that incomes for a family of four would never fall below $7,500, still maintaining an incentive to work so long as the worker's income remained below $11,200.

1.   The basic income guarantee is set at $2,500 per adult and $1,250 per child. This nets a guaranteed income of $7,500 for a family of four ($2500 X 2) + ($1250 X 2) = $5000 + $2500 = $7500.

2.   All income up to $2,000 is disregarded. Thus, if a family wishes to work to earn $2,000 they can increase their net spendable income to $9,500 by their efforts.

3.   The basic wage guarantee is reduced by a "clawback," a reduction of the guarantee by 50% of all wages over $2,000 and under $4,000. Thus, if a family chooses to work and earn $4,000, the first $2,000 is disregarded but the family nets only $1,000 of the other $2,000 earned since half of the next $2,000 reduces their income guarantee by $1,000. Their net income under these conditions is $7,500 minus the $1,000 earned income clawback, plus the $4,000 earned income, or a total of $10,500.

4.   The basic income guarantee is reduced by 75% for all wages between $4,000 and $6,000. Thus, a family's income guarantee is reduced by half of all wages earned between $2,000 and $4,000 (that is, by $1,000) and is further reduced by three-fourths of all wages earned between $4,000 and $6,000 (that is, by another $1,500). Their net income under these conditions is $7,500 (NIT guarantee) less $1,000 clawback less $1,500 clawback plus the $6,000 earned income, or a total of $11,000.

In contrast to this design, which targets benefits heavily on those presumed to be most in need, there is a program whose design is in the nature of a public social utility and is called "Children's Allowances." It is almost universal in the sense that it benefits every household having children, irrespective of their level of need. Some form of Children's Allowance is operating in nearly every industrial country in the Western world except the United States. Canada has had a children's allowance scheme since the 1930s and Great Britain since 1945, when it was called "family allowances." Since 1977 the allowance in both countries has been called "child-benefit." Whereas the benefits are usually small in each country, they are a significant addition to family finances. Proponents sometimes argue that it targets benefits directly on children and their needs, in that such allowances often go directly to mothers.[27] In 1990, Great Britain's child benefit was 2-1/2 pounds (£) per week for the first child, and one and two pounds per week for each subsequent child. The March 1992 exchange rate was about $1.72 U.S. per English pound. With respect to off-targeting of benefits, the Children's Allowance strategy involves considerable seepage, depending on how one perceives the program objective. If the objective is to supplement incomes, the seepage is very large—more non–target groups than poor will receive the benefit. If the objective is to increase the standard of living of all families with children, whatever their present income level, then there is probably much less off-targeting. However, there can hardly be any sense, from any point of view, of increasing the standard of living of those families already at the top of the income distribution scale. Finally, note that the NIT idea must always involve some kind of means and asset test. It is the presence of this feature in NIT and the lack of it in Children's Allowance that always generates controversy over whether there is strong off-targeting in any Children's Allowance scheme. An additional point of vulnerability for Children's Allowance proposals is that the benefits must be very low per family or else the cost is enormous; otherwise, the cost becomes overwhelming. Simple arithmetic will show that a payment of $100 per week per child in a nation with 50 million children would cost $260 billion per year—more than the cost of the U.S. defense budget. Though child advocates would not find that unseemly, there is no doubt it would be an unacceptable division of the pie to the advocates for other constituent groups, like the American Association of Retired Persons (AARP) or AIDS advocates. It is important to note that Children's Allowance schemes are not inherently bad proposals, but they are neither cheap nor insignificant in that their redistributive qualities would require a radically different consensus in the United States about the importance of children and whether justice is involved in large-scale income redistribution programs.

TRADE-OFFS IN JUDGING THE MERIT OF ENTITLEMENT AND ELIGIBILITY RULES FOR PUBLIC SOCIAL UTILITIES AND HYBRIDS

So, if off-targeting has both "good" and "bad" effects, how is the practical public policy analyst to judge between them? It is an important question and doesn't yield to a simple answer. Let us use the concept of "trade-off" to characterize what we will be considering here. It is not an exotic idea, rather one we all use in working out our everyday lives: to get one or another good thing sometimes means having to endure some bad things. Usually, we choose so that the good outweighs the bad—but not always: If I have only enough money to buy badly needed new household appliances—perhaps a refrigerator, a washer-dryer, and a stove, but I also need a better used car, the choice is not so simple. Here is the trade-off: If I buy the appliances, I buy freedom from having to go to the laundromat, enjoyment of a new stove, ability to store food longer and therefore shop less often. In return, I have to endure an unreliable car that spends weeks in the repair shop, which forces me to depend on friends or public transportation. So, how does the ordinary person living an ordinary life make that decision? The answer ultimately depends on the relationship to what one values and disvalues—in a word, preferences. Now let us consider what those value/preferences might be and how a person might go about making decisions based on them.

The most obvious decision rule rests on a preference for getting the "best-value-for-money." Taking into consideration only the most obvious costs and savings, one might add up the costs and savings of choosing (in this example) to buy appliances: Suppose their total cost is about $2,000 and from that I can subtract the savings from avoiding laundromat costs (say $200 a year). But I must also add in the expected cost for car repairs (about $800 a year) and the extra public transportation costs (about $600). If a better used car will cost about $6,000, then (using out-of-pocket costs as a standard) I would be about $2,400 better off to buy the appliances and forgo the better used car: $2,400 = $6,000-($2,000-$200-$800-$600). A notable feature of the best-value-for-money standard is that it can depend on whether I want to make it work for the long or short term (these figures only take into account the first year). With every passing year I lose another $1,400 in transportation costs. Simple arithmetic shows that in three years I am $1,800 the net loser. Furthermore, when my appliances begin to need repair, I will go deeper into the hole. Thus in the long run, I would be better off, dollar-wise, in choosing the better used car; but in the short run, I am better off choosing the appliances. Still that doesn't take into account those preferences that are more difficult to put a dollar value to—my preference for saving time and trouble by having a dependable automobile. Best-value-for-money is an obvious standard for choice, but it won't sort out whether I would prefer the convenience of a reliable car compared with the convenience of new appliances. Choosing among trade-offs that involve social programs is no different in principle—whereas costs are important, they are not always (and in all ways) the crucial issue.

When we think about public social utility benefits, trade-offs are ultimately cost *and* value issues—is the public interest better served by exercising a preference for avoiding stigma and increasing costs (as in Children's Allowance or Guaranteed Income Programs) or by exercising a preference for lower costs (in which case the monies saved can be spent on reducing other social problems, for example) at the expense of creating stigma for beneficiaries (as in the means-tested AFDC program)? There are many other examples of trade-offs; in fact, almost all policy and program choices involve trade-offs of one kind or another and because they ultimately are settled on value/preference grounds, it is one additional reason a value-critical perspective is essential for the practitioner. Table 7–2 summarizes some of the many trade-offs concerning entitlement rules. Two concepts are used to examine some types of trade-offs: vertical equity and horizontal equity. *Vertical equity* refers to the extent to which resources are allocated to those with the most severe need—the kind of close target efficiency spoken of earlier in this and other chapters. *Horizontal equity* refers to the extent to which resources are allocated to *all* those in need (Danziger & Portney, 1988, p. 124). The point here is that, given scarce resources, there is almost always a trade-off between vertical equity and horizontal equity—the difficult (sometimes tragic) choice between meeting a little of the need of *all* those afflicted and adequately meeting the need of those in *most serious* difficulties. There is no consensus on the value/principles on which that decision can or should be made. Other important criteria for evaluating entitlement and eligibility rules involve trade-offs are discussed below.

Overwhelming Costs, Overutilization, and Underutilization

Cost consideration is an important criterion because overutilization, of course, creates cost overruns. Bad entitlement rules can create severe problems in generating overutilization and thus overwhelming costs or cost overruns that far exceed expectations. Medicare is a leading (and interesting) example in that cost containment is a major problem for Medicare and, on some views, a problem due to an overly generous entitlement rule. The entitlement rule for Medicare is universal in the sense that all beneficiaries of OASI are automatically coentitled to Medicare. Naturally, medical care for an aging population is an expensive business because there is a rising proportion of the elderly in the population. Whereas Medicare is paid from Social Security contributions, the ratio of beneficiaries to contributors is dropping. Not only that, but the absolute and relative costs of medical care have risen exorbitantly over the past decade.

But the problem is also due in part to the rising success of medical technology. For example, such procedures as bypass operations for heart disease are now routine. Kidney dialysis is at present included as an acceptable medical procedure for Medicare beneficiaries. The problem is even more complex because the long-term health benefits for both are debatable—kidney dialysis will extend life about ten years and heart bypass procedures last on average about five years before death or before having to be repeated. The debate is about whether adding zero to five years onto the life of a post–65-year-old citizen is the best expenditure in view of

Table 7–2. Trade-Offs in Analyzing Entitlement and Eligibility Rules

	Evaluation Criteria					
Entitlement Rule	Stigma	Cost overrun	Underutilization	Overutilization	Work Disincentive	Individualization of Services
Prior contributions	–	+	+	–	+/–	–
Administrative rule	+/–	–	+/–	–	+/–	+/–
Private contracts			(depends on provisions of the contract)			
Professional discretion	–	+	–	+	+/–	+
Administrative discretion	+/–	+/–	+/–	+/–	+/–	+
Judicial decision	–	+	–	–	–	–
Means testing	+	–	–	+	+	+

Explanation of symbols:
(+)   rule will create that effect.
(–)   rule will not create that effect.

the pressing health needs of children and adults in the United States. Recall that all policy systems operate under a condition of finite resources, so that every dollar spent for kidney dialysis and heart bypass procedures is a dollar that cannot be spent on disease prevention for children: The United States still does not make routine immunizations for smallpox, diphtheria, and typhoid available to its children, even though many Third World countries do so. The value-critical policy analyst must search for the value stance from which this policy choice is made. Universal entitlement to debatable medical procedures for the elderly was never discussed widely from a value-critical point of view; rather the choice that was made was quintessentially political, a result of overwhelming lobbying when the legislation was being considered in Congress. Note that many similar issues currently attend the Medicare system—research and care for AIDS being only one other example. The issue is for whom should scarce research and care money be spent—for AIDS, Alzheimer's disease, mental retardation, chronic mental illness, or for very premature babies? Whereas the latter does not concern a medical problem for the aging, it is an interesting example of social program costs that apply to the costs of providing medical care for the poor. It concerns newborns (neonates) born very prematurely, at less than one pound, ten ounces. Here are some quotes about the nature of neonatal care:

- "About half will live but three-quarters of those will have serious neurological damage."
- "All stops are pulled out, . . . we are doing virtually everything that can be done to keep these children alive."
- "One national study in 1988 revealed that a third of neonatologists said they had changed their medical practice and were treating babies they thought had nothing to gain and a lot to lose from aggressive medical care."
- "After three months in the hospital, which cost close to a million dollars . . . the triplets came home. All had grade 4 brain-bleeds making it virtually certain that their brains were damaged." (*New York Times*, September 30, 1991, p. A1)

These data are an example of an overwhelming and uncontrolled cost burden on the medical system in general. Because recent estimates suggest that such care is extremely expensive and that the babies' chances for surviving into adulthood as fully functional adults are quite slim, on what value/preferences shall such choices be based?

The basic value problem is highlighted because public policy has avoided the basic value issue. It is not (even mostly) a "scientific" choice when decisions are made about the kind and amount of medical technology and the level of care that can be prescribed. Clearly some public benefits create their own increased demand (and especially medical care) for which there is no limit. Where private physicians control treatment and where physicians fear legal suit for not providing maximum care and treatment, neither the patient nor the government is in a position to curb the use of modern technology. One of the reasons that Medicare and Medicaid costs have risen so rapidly is that nearly all the aged can qualify for benefits under one program or another. (Even in 1975, more than 95 percent of the elderly did so qualify.) Marmor says that universal coverage would never have happened had the original proposal to restrict medical coverage to fully insured Social Security beneficiaries been written into the Act.[28] Choosing an entitlement rule that focuses on age rather than the various factors that count for Social Security entitlement (prior contribution, attachment to workforce) has created a public obligation to pay for medical care for the aged, which has proven to be an overwhelming expenditure. But it is quite clear that the issue is not simply *who* is entitled, but also for *what benefit. The basic question U.S. social policy has not yet answered is "On what value premises shall medical care, indeed life and death, be rationed?"* And that involves both *who* and *what benefit.*

Some instances of entitlement rules create underutilization; that is, program benefits are not taken up by the people for whom they are intended. There are several important examples of underutilization in the United States, some more serious than others. One that perhaps is less serious is the low "take-up" rate of the 1980–1981 Low Income Energy Assistance Program (LIEAP), a federally financed program initiated by the Carter administration with the object of subsidizing increased energy costs among the low-income population. The entitlement program rules rested heavily on a reasonably flexible and nonstigmatizing income test, but there the public was poorly informed about exactly how much benefit was possible. In fact, in many states the LIEAP benefit was certainly more than a trivial amount—sometimes covering an average of 150 percent of the total cold-weather energy costs of the average household.

One more serious example of underutilization of a public benefit program is the SSI program offering cash income maintenance benefits for which a means-tested entitlement rule is in place. The take-up rates for this program run between 55 and 60 percent.[29] Although it is not entirely clear that this underutilization is totally an entitlement rule problem, there are suspicious signs: SSI is a program for which both the aged and the disabled qualify and, for complex reasons, much of the underutilization concerns the disabled. The entitlement rules have a very complicated procedure for entitlement determination, which appears to qualify only those completely and totally disabled for long periods; also, it was originally designed for physical, not mental, disabilities. For example, it ordinarily disqualifies those who can only work some of the time, which of course applies especially to those disabled for reasons of mental illnesses like psychosis, manic-depression or schizophrenia. Reestablishing benefits takes as long and is as complex and demanding as the original application—seldom less than several months and often more than a year. Also, it is well known among the disabled population that the outcome of application is unpredictable at best. It is reasonable to expect that rational people will hesitate before committing themselves to pursuing such benefits, especially when they involve heavy expenses in time and long-term doggedness in documenting medical treatment and diagnosis and not trivial monetary sums for a population that has no discretionary income. The mentally ill are not the largest proportion of the homeless, but they are a significant group. Homelessness creates public costs, an illustration of the point that underutilization doesn't automatically create cost savings in tax dollars.

WORK DISINCENTIVES AND ENTITLEMENT RULES

Almost all agree that entitlement and eligibility rules should be evaluated against their potential for work disincentives. The argument about whether cash benefits in social welfare income maintenance programs cause people to choose benefits over work for wages is at least two hundred years old. A major concern during the Speenhamland experiment in England in 1795, it is presently a concern of U.S. economists and politicians as they attempt to cope with rising social welfare costs in an inflated and stagnating economy.[30] Both economic theory and common sense would seem to indicate that cash benefits from the public treasury could strongly reduce work effort on the part of the ordinary citizen—why would anyone work if they didn't have to? Both the question and the answer are complex issues that for years have eluded practical resolution. Who, after all, would give money to someone just to see whether he or she would continue to work, work less, not work at all?

In fact, that experiment has now taken place and the full results are readily available. The economic theory behind the recent income guarantee experiments runs a little like this:

> One person can view time as being divided among three activities: working for wages, working at home, and enjoying leisure time, depending on relative opportunities and rewards. The reward for market work is money income, which ultimately is used to buy goods and services. One of the goods that people may "purchase" is leisure, but each person pays a different price, one equal to his or her wage rate. Economists theorize that the amount of nonworking time "bought" by a person depends on two factors: (1) the wages that must be forgone and (2) the amount of nonwage income that is available to the person. As a person's wages rise, leisure (non-work) time becomes more expensive. So, besides the question of whether public benefits cause less work effort, two other questions arise: (1) whether if there *is* less work effort, it is due to the fact that leisure time becomes more expensive as income rises, causing people to regard increasing leisure costs as "expenditures" or (2) whether with more income, people value increased income less and are willing to substitute leisure for work.

These questions have vexed discussions of welfare reform for many years. Kermit Gordon, one-time president of the influential Brookings Institution, speculates that what he characterized as "myths" about work disincentives contributed heavily to the failure of the Congress to enact the Family Assistance Act proposed by the Nixon administration in 1969. The U.S. Office of Economic Opportunity (OEO) undertook a series of large-scale experiments beginning in New Jersey in 1968. Later experiments were also fielded in Iowa, North Carolina, Colorado, and Washington state. These experiments, all long term (five years for the most part), were carefully designed and instrumented, and strong attempts were made—not always successfully—to insulate them from external contaminating influences. We will focus here on the Seattle-Denver Income Maintenance Experiment (SIMDIME) because it was the last in this series and provides the best data. It had the largest sample among all the experiments, in that it included around 5,000 one- and two-parent families of black, white, and Hispanic ethnic origin. In SIMDIME, the families were assigned either to one of several experimental groups receiving cash assistance payments at various levels, or to one of a control group of families who received no experimental payments but continued to receive whatever benefits they were eligible for under current governmental programs. Hours of work of experimental families were compared with hours of work of the control-group families during the course of the experiment. First, the results showed no significant difference between responses by racial or ethnic background, holding all other characteristics constant. Next, some noticeable decrease in work effort was shown when people got an income guarantee, but the difference was small and differed significantly for women compared with men. The report has this to say about the results:[31]

> The results for husbands show, for example, that if a family's preprogram annual income was $4000, a cash benefit that raised income by $1000 would cause the husband to work about an hour less per week . . . the effects on a wife in a family with the same income would cause her to work two hours per week less. . . . However, since wives usually have lower wage rates than their husbands, a given benefit reduction rate usually would have a smaller dollar effect on the wife's net wage than on the husband's.

The experimenters note that these results are as expected since "wives probably feel the greatest necessity to work when other family income is low and have more freedom to respond to changes in income or wage rates when the family income is initially high." Husbands, on the other hand, are more likely to feel that they "should" work, no matter what the circumstance. Table 7–3 presents the results of the effect of the income guarantee on work effort for all four work incentive experiments. Although some of the wives' reduction in work hours appears large, observe that the authors interpret this as a relatively small-scale response. "Since wives in poor families usually work relatively few hours to begin with, the large percentage change in their labor supply effort amounts to relatively small numbers of hours".[32] The net result, as stated above, is that a $1,000 increase in the family's income "causes" the wife in a poor family to work only two hours less per week. Recall that at the time of this experiment, the minimum wage was around $2.75 per hour and that was the prevailing wage for those women. So what should be our conclusion about the work disincentives of social welfare programs offering cash benefits like this one? A conservative conclusion, faithful to the facts the experiment reveals, would be that the effect is there, but is very slight, probably insignificant to most people. The experimenters believe that the results from all four of the experiments show a "striking similarity," particularly considering that the experiments provided different sets of benefit levels and benefit reduction rates, that they took place in

Table 7–3. Estimated Percentage Reductions in Work Hours in Four Income Maintenance Experiments.

Control/Experimental Group Differences as a percent Control Mean[a]			
	New Jersey (white only)	Rural wage earners	Gary, Indiana	Seattle– Denver
Husbands	6 %	1 %	7 %	6 %
Wives	31	27	17	17
Total	13	13	8	9
Female heads	[b]	[b]	2	12

(a) These estimates are weighted averages of the response in hours worked by different study groups. Because of the technical problems in estimating the response of black and Spanish-speaking groups in the New Jersey experiment, estimates reported here for New Jersey are for whites only. Recent reanalysis of the New Jersey data provides evidence that the response of these groups is similar to that of whites. Total responses (and base hours) include only husbands and wives in the Gary and Seattle-Denver experiments; in the other experiments they include other family members as well.

(b) None included in the experiment.

Source:"The Seattle-Denver Income Maintenance Experiment, Midexperiment Results and a Generalization to the Natural Population," Stanford Research Institute and Mathematical Policy Research, Inc., Stanford, CA, February 1978, Table 2, p. 64. Reprinted by permission.

states with widely differing tax and transfer systems, and that different criteria were used to select the four samples.[33]

One result of the Guaranteed Income experiment should not go unnoticed: There was a marked increase in the proportion of marriage dissolution under the impact of an income guarantee. It was about the same for whites as for blacks but noticeably greater for Latinos.[34] One important consequence here is that if an income guarantee program were put in effect, the proportion of female-headed, single-parent families would increase substantially, particularly for whites and Latinos. Remarriage rates for blacks under conditions of income guarantee is sufficiently high, so it would not affect the proportion of single-parent families among that subpopulation. Taken at pure face value, many U.S. citizens would probably agree that this is a negative feature of an NIT or any guaranteed income program. Note, however, that these facts can also be interpreted to mean that greater good prevails when women (and men) have the economic support that allows them to make free choices about ending "bad" marriages.

PROCREATIONAL INCENTIVES, MARITAL INSTABILITY, AND GENERATIONAL DEPENDENCY

Other criteria for evaluating entitlement and eligibility rules for PSUs, especially cash benefit programs, are the extent to which they provide incentives for procreation, marital break-up, and/or the dependency of the children of families who receive public benefits. The possibility that citizens conceive children in order to become entitled for, or to increase, welfare benefits, surfaces regularly as a matter of public and political discussion. For some, the issue is the amount of benefit per additional child, and for others it is simply that where benefit entitlement is tied to the number of children in families it is possible that it serves as a significant childbearing incentive. The latter issue is usually argued from a social problem viewpoint that is ideologically committed to the notion that work is a highly valued instrumental activity and that citizens have a predominant propensity *not* to choose work if there is an available alternative—no matter how grim. It is certainly possible to conceive of a person who would endure the physical discomforts of bearing children as the preferred alternative to working, but even if the standard of living it afforded was considerably less than a poverty line existence and if the attached stigma was extreme, such a choice is neither economically nor socially rational. What are the costs of bearing and rearing a child, when measured against the welfare benefit gain? Where such calculation is made, only the person who could *never* expect to work at all would find it to her advantage to bear children just to become entitled to (or obtain an increase in) U.S. public benefits at the present levels. In many states with generous AFDC benefits, that would amount to about $80 per month, and the costs of rearing children—even by modest standards of living—are many, many times $960 per year. Surely there will always be a few people who continually make irrational choices that work strongly against their own self-interest, but to rebut such an argument, one only need assume in this case that the ordinary person acts in ways that will be of most economic benefit to herself. Furthermore, there is every reason to believe that few people, especially poor people already acquainted with the realities of life at the poverty level, do that in the serious matters of everyday life. It is possible, of course, that some persons who come from circumstances of such great deprivation and social chaos would act in just such an irrational way.

And it is equally possible that there are people who are simply not rational about their appraisal of either themselves or their situations for purely idiosyncratic reasons. But in both of these instances we are speaking of the marginal case; there is no evidence that this is the general rule. In fact, Goodwin's study suggests quite the contrary: His data clearly show that poor people wish to work, believe that work itself is virtuous, and expect to work profitably most of their lives.[35] Probably the most persuasive evidence against the notion that financial incentives stimulate childbearing is found in the results of programs in countries which have needed to increase population rapidly and have purposely tried to do so by granting benefits, often sizable, to citizens who bear children. The most massive of such programs was the French attempt to raise their birthrate in a population decimated by World War I (from which France lost half of its male population). Both Sweden and, more recently, Canada, have also had Children's Allowance programs, conscious attempts to stimulate birthrate. *In all these instances, there was little success.*

In summary, does the fact of entitlement to welfare benefits from public social utilities and hybrid types serve as an incentive to procreation? Given the evidence reviewed above, it is very unlikely that there is any such effect in a population or even any of its sub-groups, though there may be some marginal and individual instances. There is, of course, no wisdom in forming large-scale public policy around small marginal effects. We are left with the conclusion that basing benefits entitlement on the fact of children's presence in a family and entitling citizens to larger benefits as a consequence of increasing family size does not create an incentive to further childbearing. Another widely discussed issue is that entitlement rules for public benefits like AFDC create marital insta-bility: Families may split in order to meet the condition that the major wage earner be absent from the home. Nancy Murdrick studied that issue directly through the use of data on when AFDC applications occurred relative to the marital split and observed differences between high- and low-income families with respect to the same issue. Study results are clear. Whereas one would expect an application to be seen in the same year as the split occurred, or at least in the year following, it seems beyond plausibility that a split aimed at creating the conditions necessary to qualify for AFDC would not occur very close to the time of the actual application. Indeed, the data show that AFDC applications peak nearly two years after the split. Murdrick concludes that the AFDC appli-cation is a response to the consequences of the split, not a premeditated out-come. Nor does it matter whether the applicants had an above-average or below-average income prior to their split.[36]

Earlier studies support Murdrick's conclusions. It does not appear that AFDC applicants contemplated applying for AFDC before the split, nor that possible entitlement somehow stimulated it.[37] Further, it appears that the expected wage rate, rather than expected AFDC benefits, is the significant factor in predicting marital splits. Given these results, it seems that the contention that AFDC active-ly creates marital instability is doubtful. However, there is no doubt that for children it eases the financial crisis caused by the marriage breakup—which of course is the main program intention.

Yet another problem said to be a consequence of entitlement to public wel-fare benefits is that, generally speaking, citizens who now receive public benefits were reared in families who depended on public benefits, and that this current generation will produce children who also will live at the expense of public ben-efit. In its most rational form, this argument over generational dependency (as it is sometimes called) asserts that social and personal identity are crucial in deter-mining the choices made about work and "getting by." It assumes that a child who grows up in a family in which there are no models of working to make a living will simply follow the pattern set by adults, that he or she will search out the welfare option. In its more unsympathetic form, the argument asserts strong antisocial, deviant motives to both parents and children in poor economic cir-cumstances. In order to make this argument plausible, it would seem necessary to assume that generational dependency must involve primarily those children whose families spent long periods as beneficiaries of the public treasury, since the learning of role models and the socialization process referred to is not a mat-

ter of casual training. No current explanation or approach to socialization suggests otherwise. If that is the case, the data from the Michigan Panel Study of
Income Dynamics bear strongly on the plausibility of the generational dependency argument.[38] This study, which has no challenges to its methodology or
conclusions, shows clearly that only a very small proportion of all welfare beneficiaries had received benefits for as long as four years (12 percent of total welfare ever, as a matter of fact). The authors conclude that there is little support
for the existence of a sizable welfare class, that the most characteristic welfare
recipient receives public benefits for about two years in succession, and then
may move on and off benefits for two considerably shorter periods of time later
in their lives.[39] If there is no sizable "class" of welfare recipients, there is no large
number of persons who spend long years on welfare benefits, and it seems
unlikely that the necessary conditions are available in which the mechanisms can
work that are said to create generational dependency. Of course, this only shows
that if generational dependency exists at all, it is a small-scale problem. Other
studies, based on less extensive data than the Rein and Rainwater study, support
the general conclusions. Podell's extensive study of a large sample of New York
City welfare beneficiaries concludes that about 15 percent of the group in the
mid-1960s were reared in families that were publicly assisted at one time or
another.[40] Less than 10 percent of the group had both parents and siblings who
had been public welfare recipients. It is noteworthy that in both the Rein and
Rainwater and the Podell studies, the definitions of *welfare dependency* are very
loose ("receiving over half the total income from public funds" in the latter case
and simply "to have received any income from public funds" in the former).
Finally, a study by Baumheier in the early 1970s draws the conclusion that the
magnitude of second-generation public assistance dependency is quite small.[41]
Whereas some might consider a 10 to 15 percent rate of intergenerational
dependency a significant problem, it would not seem to be a good characterization of the AFDC recipient group as a whole.

OPPORTUNITIES FOR POLITICAL INTERFERENCE VIA WEAK
ENTITLEMENT RULES

At one level there is every reason to believe that political influence is one route
to the entitlement to public benefits for individuals and groups—of course social
programs are a vehicle by which political interests are (and should be)
expressed. But once the program or policy is implemented, it becomes bad social
policy for citizens, or groups of them, to be either entitled or disentitled simply
because of political influence that circumvents the legislative or judicial processes that keep social policy as an expression of the will of the people in a democracy. Equity is the value issue here. Citizens in a democracy should have equal
access to public benefits, and that access should not depend on who one knows
or doesn't know. Nor should it depend on the desire of the executive branch of
government to shape a social program in ways that it couldn't achieve through

the regular channels of the legislative or judicial process. There is an unusual modern example of the latter, which we will briefly review for its value in illustrating the great danger posed by entitlement rules that are vague and uncertain in administration. Well-formed entitlement rules are not valuable just for their tidiness, rather that they might avoid the occasion for political intervention in the operations of social programs, an intervention of a particularly vicious sort for vulnerable people. This example, from the mid-1980s, concerns the Social Security Disability (DI) program.

Probably the premier policy problem of any social program for the disabled is to construct a useful and stable definition of *disablement*, and the DI program is no exception. Robert Ball, chief actuary for the Social Security Administration for many years, reports that the slippery DI definition of disability allowed opposing biases to be used within one rather short period of time.[42] The reason for its "slipperiness" is that it leaves one part of the entitlement rule to medical and administrative discretion—the determination of whether a disability exists in fact. Thus, administrators and physicians were left to liberal interpretation of medical facts. One has only to look at the sizable proportion of initial application decisions that were reversed and "re-reversed" at every stage of reconsideration and appeal to realize that what is technically called "inter-judge reliability" was a hallmark lack in this entitlement process.[43] Over a ten- to twelve-year period beginning in the 1970s, reversal rates on disability denial appeals rose to nearly two-thirds of all appeals; in regard to mental disabilities, reversal rates reached as high as 91 percent of all appealed denials of benefit applications.[44]

In explanation, Robert Ball noted that in the early years of the program, ". . . I can assure you gentlemen, that the general attitude . . . [was] wanting to pay claims."[45] To the point, it is notable that in this climate, even though Congress expressly forbade the Social Security Administration (SSA) from reversing the findings of state disability determination units, it did so regularly (to the advantage of applicants).[46] However, under the prodding of a Congress worried about rising program costs and a presidential administration looking with disfavor on most welfare benefits, SSA began by a variety of means to administer a very different definition of the term *disability*. Clearly, SSA was able to turn the DI system around simply by the strength of its own ability to reinterpret the definition of disability and change some of its procedural mechanisms: In five years DI benefit allowance rates were cut in half, terminations increased, and total costs slowed significantly. ". . . [D]isability examiners have become more conservative in the way in which they interpret and apply standards [for DI awards]."[47]

Despite the significant changes that had already occurred, with the 1981 inauguration of President Reagan, who had made explicit campaign promises to reduce the size of entitlement programs, not only were new applicants under fire but the disabled who already received benefits were affected as well. Unprecedented terminations of thousands of DI beneficiaries took place between 1980 and 1985: 71,500 in 1980; 98,800 in 1981; and 121,400 in the first five months of 1982—with 360,000 expected to be terminated in 1984.[48] "In the 1960s, the loose and ambiguous definition of disability could not constrain a [Democratic, neo–New Deal] political administration determined to expand the program any more successfully than it could in the 1980s constrain a [Republican, conservative] political administration determined to reduce the size and costs of the DI program."[49] Now another highly placed Social Security administrator could say, mimicking Robert Ball's earlier statement, ". . . I can assure you gentlemen, the general attitude [in the Social Security Administration) is to deny, deny, deny. . . ." [50] Intelligent programs cannot be administered under such conditions of radical changes in entitlement programs as exemplified above. Seriously disabled beneficiaries have had reason to expect that they could count on their benefit income in one year, only to learn a few years later that despite no change in their condition, benefits will be withdrawn. Worse, they learned a few more years later that many if not most terminations were illegal in the first place, so that if they reapply there is good chance that their benefits will be reinstated *(Minnesota v. Schweiker*, 1983; Social Security Regulations no. 83-15, 16, 17s, 1986). On such grounds as outlined above, it is clear that this policy system is in ragged disarray.

The definitional ambiguity of disability with which the DI has (and still does) operate has been used by parties of opposing political persuasions to expand and contract the program at will. Further, it is possible to increase substantially the clarity and reliability of medical disability determinations as Mashaw (and Nagi before him) have clearly shown and by fairly simple (albeit a mite more expensive) attention to definitional clarity about this entitlement rule and by use of means that are faithful to what is now known from modern research and investigative practices on the making of judgments. It is also clear that there is no reason *not* to expect that further political adventures into the Social Security system will occur absent the correction of this policy problem. "If the same policy weaknesses that made possible the political intrusions into this social program are still in place when the next liberal administration comes into office, it will simply use the very same weaknesses to restore the system to its former condition."[51] Such a political scenario would continue into infinity, a prospect that is not in the best interests of the country or its disabled citizens.

This example teaches two key lessons: First, it highlights for us from Mashaw the conclusion that there is nothing inherently wrong with using expert judgments as a basis for entitlement rules. Second, however, it shows that if that is the case then some conditions are necessary to keep the process on track and functioning for the advantage of client/consumer/beneficiaries. Researchers doing surveys have learned of those requirements. First, if you want reliable judgments you have to define very carefully the thing to be judged. Next, you have to train and orient judges to apply only that definition within a specific procedural context. Finally, you have to indoctrinate new judges into that system, a few at a time. This process is not inexpensive but almost any trained researcher can achieve a 90 percent agreement with almost any set of judges in making even complicated judgments, given sufficient care and perseverance. Costs will likely be less than the direct administrative costs of disentitling and re-entitling disabled beneficiaries time and time again.

SOME SPECIAL CRITERIA IN EVALUATING ENTITLEMENT AND ELIGIBILITY RULES FOR PERSONAL SOCIAL SERVICES

Do special criteria that are used with entitlement and eligibility rules for PSS programs differ from those used for PSU and hybrid programs? Probably not, but the *way* in which those criteria are evaluated does differ. In the following (extreme) example, the program doesn't involve cash or material benefits at all; rather, it is directed toward the social problem presented by the deviant and antisocial behavior of children. Such a program may have as its objective the increased socialization of children; for example, to reduce aggressive and non-defensive assault on other children. One common program design is to introduce problem children to overwhelming numbers of "conforming" children in a funded summer camp program that provides round-the-clock interaction between the two groups. Conforming children are recruited with the offer of a free camp, and into each group of approximately five recruits is placed one nonconforming child whose behavior is the real target of the effort. The program is expensive but can be shown to produce the desired result without simultaneously producing negative effects for the conforming children. Feldman, et al. show that in fact, "one bad apple doesn't spoil the barrel."[52] Notice that the causal analysis that rationalizes this program design calls for two quite different entitlement rules, one for conforming children and one for deviant children. Notice also that some of the previously mentioned evaluation criteria apply here. Clearly, the eligibility rule for conforming children will (intentionally) off-target benefits: five-sixths of the program cost per child may be charged to children who do not suffer from the problem of concern. At the same time, their inclusion will destigmatize involvement in the program.

Overutilization and underutilization criteria have special applications in the personal social services. A leading example of eligibility rules that create unintentional underutilization are programs that deal with the serious social problem of minority children who, otherwise available for permanent adoption, nevertheless remain in foster care for lack of parent/applicants. Despite more flexibility with regard to adoption rules over the past decade, some child-placing agencies that have adoptable minority children in their custody in fact "victimize" them by holding to certain eligibility requirements. For example, some require separate bedrooms for children, typical middle-class income levels, a nonworking mother for infants, and/or formal in-office interviews held in a distinctively white middle-class office environment. Such entitlement rules will actively disentitle minority and ethnic parent/applicants from consideration in two ways. First, minority status generally means absence of average incomes, and working mothers; therefore, if an eligibility rule is based on average income or presence of a nonworking mother, it disentitles all minority applicants except those with incomes above the average compared with their own racial group. Such a rule offends against the *equity* criterion because it systematically disentitles based on social class status that has nothing to do with any feature of the social problem the program is intended to solve.

This example also demonstrates underutilization of the worst kind in that its consequence imposes a penalty on children who need adoptive parents as resources for their personal development as human beings. That being the case, it offends the *adequacy* criterion because children are deprived of adequate adoptive placement services.

Second, some people from minority and ethnic groups have limited experience in making "formal applications"—in fact, the whole idea of "applying for" children and having their parental and social competence judged is an experience outside the realm of their cultural expectations. For most such groups, not only is taking responsibility for others' children not unusual—whether children from their own families or otherwise—it is usually negotiated in face-to-face encounters and in familiar surroundings with little or no expectation that motives are under scrutiny. Whereas there is good reason for adoption agencies to be concerned about applicants' motives for parenting, any good eligibility rule will take cultural practices into account, not run hard against them. Agencies have dealt with this by featuring initial contacts in the applicants' home, church (or other religious site), or lodge; sometimes these contacts have been initiated by friends or acquaintances. In that way the whole encounter in adopting a child occurs in the context of a familiar social network where the agency staff member, although a stranger, is at least "vouched for" by someone already trusted.

Here is another extreme example, this one from the eligibility rules apparently in common use by some public Central American child-placing agencies: Part of the application process involves psychological testing via such measures as the Minnesota Multiphasic Personality Inventory (MMPI). First-hand interview data suggest that the results of such tests have serious implications for adoption placement decisions.[53] In fact, a requirement for MMPI screening is listed in the administrative documents of one Central American public adoption agency. Screening is an issue because local Central American adoption agencies commonly have in their custody a number of local children of color (indigenous Indians and Caribbean blacks, for example), including infants and preschoolers, children whose only hope for kinship associations of their own are non-Indian (most frequently Latino) families. Those agencies report that adoption by local non-Indian citizens is uncommon. Psychological screening of this kind as an eligibility rule creates underutilization because it is so alien to the applicants' experience (leaving aside the cogent argument about its cultural transferability to a Hispanic culture or the doubtfulness of its ability to predict good parents or screen out the mentally distressed). That alien nature of psychological testing discourages scarce applicants (thus offending the *adequacy* criterion). And, news about agency experiences spreads widely in minority communities by word of mouth, especially among potential adoptive applicants, and that further discourages applications.

These considerations probably apply equally well to other personal social services such as mental health and counseling services where their delivery takes place in formal clinics and office buildings. That is one reason why "street workers" and "outreach" programs were invented—to place access to the services where they could be encountered in the everyday and familiar lives of the people for whom they were intended, rather than limiting formal application to unfamiliar, hard-to-get-to office settings. In small communities, it can be stigmatizing to enter a building known to be the community mental health center. Certainly that applies to more controversial birth control and/or abortion locations.

Clearly, eligibility rules for services that involve fee payment can be sources of underutilization and overutilization. Insurance companies find entitlement for mental health services to be problematic for two reasons: (1) lack of direct fee for certain services and (2) dearth of conditions for which there are standard treatments or treatment courses. Both are subject to large-scale overutilization because providers (therapists) may be tempted by a strong financial incentive to continue service indefinitely. After all, it is difficult to argue that there is no definable point at which a client is not helped (or no longer helped) by further "self-awareness"—a common objective of mental health counseling. The general solution insurance companies have resorted to is to place arbitrary dollar or time limits on mental health and/or counseling service—$1,000 a year for outpatient services or fifteen days of inpatient services is not an unusual standard. Costs are an issue and insurance companies have a telling point, one that the psychotherapy industry has yet to answer, coincidentally, because the insurance principle requires ability to forecast use (via some actuarial design) in constructing rate schedules for prepaid insurance premiums for health coverage. On the other hand, the health insurance industry is not noted for its leadership in this regard either; between the two, sizable underutilization and overutilization continue because of the arbitrary nature of the "caps" placed on mental health and counseling services. Note that in these examples of the personal social services, the way in which entitlement rules create underutilization are quite different from what occurs in public social utilities and hybrids (food stamps for example). In the former, underutilization is created by an arbitrary entitlement rule; in the latter, it is created by lack of awareness that benefits are available, by stigma, and by the probability of low benefit.

The prevailing entitlement rule for mental health and counseling personal social services that use arbitrarily low caps and other service restrictions offends the *adequacy* criterion for those who have serious mental disabilities. Overutilization of mental health and counseling services, where the financial rewards are generous to therapists continuing services to essentially healthy individuals for personal growth and fulfillment, may have contributed to this situation.

SUMMARY

This chapter presented concepts to assist the practitioner in understanding the variability among common entitlement rules and procedures. The following types of entitlement rules were discussed:

- Prior contribution
- Administrative rule

- Private contracts
- Professional discretion
- Administrative discretion
- Judicial decision
- Means testing
- Attachment to the workforce

Whereas the ultimate test of the merits of any particular entitlement rule is its "fit" with the social problem conception that underlies the program or policy under consideration, special problems are likely to be created by entitlement rules. The practical analyst should examine the available data and the general workings of the policy or program to search for evidence of the following special problems:

- Stigma and alienation
- Off-targeting of benefits
- Overwhelming costs
- Overutilization and underutilization
- Political interference
- Negative incentives and disincentives (work, procreation, marriage, and so on)

The presence of any of these special problems works against the achievement of a functional policy and programs—against adequacy, equity, and efficiency.

EXERCISES

1. What is the difference between the entitlement rule known as administrative discretion and the one known as administrative rule?

2. What are the consequences of basing entitlement to social welfare benefits solely on the type of entitlement called "attachment to the workforce"?

3. There are three branches of U.S. government: legislative, executive, and judicial. What role does each play in establishing the entitlement rules for AFDC benefits? What may each branch do to affect entitlement once the AFDC program is established? (Remember, no state is required to have an AFDC program.)

4. What is the major difference between professional discretion and administrative discretion as methods of entitlement to social welfare benefits or services?

NOTES

1. The scheme concerns only "selective" eligibility rules. However, this book will not consider the traditional selective versus universal distinction in regard to (among other things) eligibility rules, siding with Titmuss in his belief that its utility for the practical analyst is only marginal.
2. R. Titmuss, Welfare State and Welfare Society. In *Commitment to Welfare* (London: George Allen and Unwin, Ltd., 1968), pp. 130–134.
3. Statement by John Svahn, chief administrator of the Social Security Administration in a press conference October 3, 1981 (National Public Radio).
4. H. Aaron, *Economic Effects of Social Security* (Washington, DC: The Brookings Institution, 1982), pp. 12–16, 67–73.
5. Only in the United States is the Workers Compensation system operated as a private enterprise.
6. K. R. Wedel, Designing and Implementing Performance Contracting. In R. L. Edwards and J. A. Yankee, editors, *Skills for Effective Service Management* (Silver Spring, MD: NASW Press, 1991).
7. K. R. Wedel and S. W. Colston, "Performance Contracting for Human Services: Issues and Suggestions," *Administration in Social Work*, 12:[1]73–87 (1988).
8. "Social Services Programs for Individuals and Families, Title XX of the Social Security Act," *Federal Register*, vol. 40, No. 125, June 27, 1975, p. 27335, section 228.
9. *Annual Report to the Congress on Title XX of the Social Security Act, Fiscal Year 1979* (Washington, DC: U.S. Department of Health, Education and Welfare, Office of the Secretary, February 1980), pp. 38, 45.
10. K. R. Wedel and S. W. Colston, op. cit., p. 75.
11. Ibid., p. 81.
12. K. R. Wedel, op. cit., p. 348.
13. M. Brown, *Working the Street: Police Discretion and Dilemmas of Reform* (New York: Basic Books, 1981).
14. M. Lipsky, *Street Level Bureaucracy: Dilemmas of the Individual in Public Services* (New York: Russell Sage Foundation, 1980).
15. D. E. Chambers, "The Reagan Administration Welfare Retrenchment Policy: Terminating Social Security Benefits for the Disabled," *Policy Study Review*, 2:207–15 (1985).
16. D. E. Chambers, "Residence Requirements for Welfare Benefits," *Social Work*, 14:[4] 29.
17. *Brown v. Board of Education*, 347 U.S. 483 (1954).
18. H. D. Krause, *Child Support in America* (Charlottesville, VA: The Mitchie Company, 1981), pp. 330–40.
19. T. B. Festinger, "The Impact of the New York Court Review of Children in Foster Care: A Follow-up Report," *Child Welfare*, 55:[8]515–44 (1976).
20. AFDC beneficiaries live below the poverty line and seldom during their whole lives work at jobs that pay more than minimum wage, whereas Workers Compensation beneficiaries almost always earn average incomes and do at least semiskilled work.
21. *Characteristics of State Plans for Aid to Families with Dependent Children*, U. S. Department of Health and Human Services, Social Security Administration, Office of Family Assistance (1989), p. 385.

22. J. Feagin, *Subordinating the Poor* (Englewood Cliffs, NJ: Prentice-Hall, 1974), pp. 103–18.
23. T. F. Pettigrew, Social Psychology's Contribution to an Understanding of Poverty. In V. T. Covello, editor, *Poverty and Public Policy* (Cambridge, MA: Shenkman Publishing, 1980), pp. 198–224.
24. Susan Sheehan, A Welfare Mother (New York, N.Y.: Signet Books, 1976; *Social Security Benefit Rates* (Leaflet #NI 196), 1990. Department of Health and Social Services (HMSO).
25. G. Hoshino, "Simplifying the Means Test," *Social Work*, 98–103 (July 1965).
26. N. Kotz, *Hunger in America* (New York: The Field Foundation, 1979), pp. 28–29.
27. *Child Benefit* (Leaflet #CH1), 1990. Department of Health and Social Security (HMSO).
28. T. R. Marmor, Public Medical Programs and Cash Assistance. In I. Lurie, editor, *Interpreting Income Maintenance Programs* (New York: Academic Press, 1970), pp. 271–78.
29. J. Menefee, B. Edwards, and S. Scheiber, "Analysis of Non-participation in the SSI Program," *Social Security Bulletin*, 44:3–21.
30. Speenhamland was an English town whose council solved its poverty problem by providing bread—not cash—to needy persons. There was a public outcry from those who believed it would destroy all incentive to work.
31. "The Seattle-Denver Income Maintenance Experiment, Midexperiment Results and a Generalization to the National Population," Stanford Research Institute and Mathematics Policy Research, February 1978, p. vii.
32. Ibid, pp. 11–12.
33. Ibid, pp. 12–14.
34. M. T. Hannan, N. B. Tuma, and L. P. Groeneveld, "Income and Marital Evidence from the Income Maintenance Experiment," *American Journal of Sociology* (May 1977).
35. L. Goodwin, *Do the Poor Want to Work?* (Washington, DC: The Brookings Institution, 1972).
36. N. Murdrick, "Use of AFDC by Previously High and Low Income Households," *Social Service Review*, 52:(1), 110 (1978).
37. B. Bernstein and W. Meezan, *The Impact of Welfare on Family Stability* (New York: Center for New York City Affairs, 1975), p. 99.
38. M. Rein and L. Rainwater, "Patterns of Welfare Use," *Social Service Review*, 52[4] 511–34.
39. J. N. Morgan, et al, *Five Thousand American Families: Patterns of Economic Progress*, vol. 1 (Ann Arbor, MI: Institute for Social Research, 1974), pp. 1–9.
40. L. Podell, *Families on Welfare in New York City* (New York: The Center for Study of Urban Problems, 1968), pp. 28–29.
41. E. C. Baumheier, "Intergenerational Dependency, a Study of Public Assistance in Successive Generations." Ph.D. diss., Brandeis University, 1971.
42. M. Derthick, *Policy Making for Social Security* (Washington, DC: The Brookings Institution, 1979).
43. Chambers (1985), op. cit., p. 4.
44. U.S. Congress, Senate Subcommittee on Oversight of Government Management of the Senate Committee on Governmental Affairs, "SSDI Reviews: The Role of the Administrative Law Judge," Hearing Report, 98th Congress, 1st Session (June 8, 1983), Appendix, memo from Carl Fritz to Louis Hays, Chief of the Appeals Division of the Social Security Administration.

45. Derthrick, op. cit., p. 310.
46. Goldsborough, et al., "The Social Security Administration: An Interdisciplinary Study of Disability Evaluation" (Washington, DC: George Washington University Law Center, 1963), mimeographed, pp. 98–100.
47. M. Lando, A. Farley, M. Brown, "Recent Trends in the SSDI Program," *Social Security Bulletin*, 5:[2]50, August 1982.
48. J. Mashaw, *Bureaucratic Justice* (New Haven, CT: Yale University Press, 1983).
49. Chambers (1985), op. cit., p. 7.
50. Mashaw, op. cit., p. 37.
51. Chambers (1985), op. cit., p. 15.
52. R. A. Feldman, J. S. Wodarski, M. Goodman, and N. Flax, "Pro-social and Anti-social Boys Together," *Social Work*, 26–36, September 1973.
53. Data were gathered by author in personal interviews with public (and private) child-placing staff and administrators while conducting research on exportation of Central American children to Europe and the United States for adoption in Honduras, El Salvador, Guatemala, and Costa Rica (July 1991 through February 1992). Documents are available detailing administrative rules and regulations of the Costa Rican public child-placing and adoption agency that refer to the observation made in the paragraph to which this footnote refers.

CHAPTER 8

Analysis of Service-Delivery Systems and Social Program and Policy Design

He who would do good to another must do it in minute particulars. General good is the plea of the scoundrel, hypocrite, and flatterer.

William Blake, 1784

INTRODUCTION

This chapter will consider a social program operating characteristic we shall call the administrative and service-delivery system. First, the heart of the social service delivery system, the social program design, will be described and discussed. The discussion on design will encompass the relationship between program design and program theory as well as the other important functions of program theory in administration. Next, a distinction will be drawn between program theory and social problem causal analysis. Then, concepts and evaluation criteria essential for analyzing and judging the merits of service-delivery systems will be presented and exemplified.

Social Policy and Social Program Design

In the most fundamental sense, providing a solution to a social problem is the only reason for being that a social program or social policy can claim. And the only manifest reason for being of an administrative or service-delivery system is to provide the means by which that solution can be implemented. To be sure, there are many latent sociological reasons as well (see Chapter 5 on goals and objectives), though we will not focus on those here. Let's call the basic root of the means to that solution *program or policy* design (for the sake of simplicity, hereafter referred to as a *program design*). The program design consists of sets of carefully defined program activities that the staff or the implementing organization intends to deliver or undertake on behalf of its consumer/beneficiaries. These activities are the heart of the social program; however, the program has many other parts because programmed activities must have a context—a theater, a supporting cast, a stage to play on, so to speak. Thus, a program must have a geographic location and administrator(s) to oversee every aspect of program implementation, from window cleaning and trash disposal to accounting and public relations operations. Although administrative activities are important, this chapter will focus only on the program activities—the heart of the drama to which the rest of the cast plays. Let's call the set of ideas on which this drama is based a *program or policy theory*. Figures 8–1 and 8–2 show (respectively) an example of a common theory concerning the physical abuse of a young child and a sample program design based on that theory.

The word *theory* is being used loosely here to mean only a rough-and-ready sketch of a sequence of activities performed so as to make a difference and achieve the desired outcome(s). The logic of these connections (that is, how and why certain activities are sequenced) is not given here, but if it were it would set out basic premises about the events described and the reason they are connected to the desired outcomes. These rough-and-ready sketches are the fundamental ideas that highlight the cause-and-effect relations that are presumed (whether on good evidence or not) to lead to the stated outcome that represents—wholly or in part—a social problem solution.

This section will describe this fundamental aspect of social policy and program service delivery so that a judgment can be made as to whether a clear and credible program/policy theory and design are present and accounted for. *The presence of a clear and credible program theory and program design is an important evaluation criterion, one by which the merit of a program of service delivery*

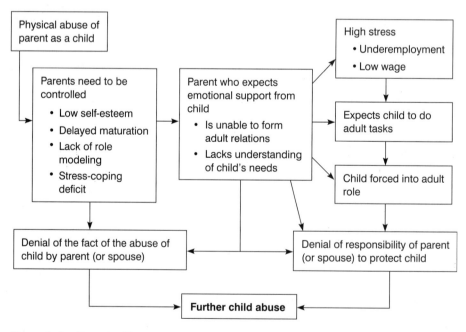

Figure 8–1   Program Theory.

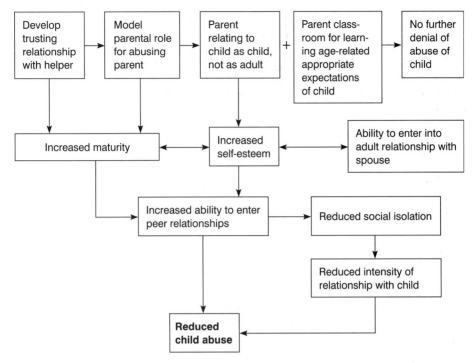

Figure 8–2   Program Design (Essential Program Elements Involving Child Abuser).

should be judged. Note that we will stress this aspect of service delivery and administrative systems for reasons that express important biases. The direct administration of such systems is beyond the scope of this book but, more important, the text is directed to social work and human service practitioners, those whose primary task it is to implement program design features rather than to provide organizational context in which that activity occurs.

Program theory is important for obvious and nonobvious reasons. First, it obviously is the source from which the program activities are drawn; absent a program theory, program activities would probably amount to random choices at best, assorted and uncoordinated "good ideas" at worst. If we care about the people who suffer from social problems, then it seems only right that we care enough to program a sensible and coordinated set of activities we have reason to believe will make a difference (and for which we would want to be held accountable) and then see to its implementation.

Second, for nonobvious reasons program design is essential to program management in that it is required as a measure of observing the program in order to assess the quality of its implementation. What would one monitor (observe) without some idea of what program activities are intended to produce the desired outcome? For example, it is possible to observe ("merely") *whether* the program performs accountable tasks, has credentialed staff, files reports, pays bills, completes other paperwork, and observes staff communication protocols to specification and on time. However, the heart of such observation in terms of quality assessment is whether program activities were in fact implemented *to specification*, i.e, in a way that makes it plausible that it will achieve its stated outcome(s) (the partial or whole solution to the social problem). That assessment is of more than passing interest to program managers because overseeing the program essentials is key to their task; it is on such observations that management decisions about personnel, organizational change, allocation of program resources, and the like, are made.[1]

Third, and perhaps even more important, unless one knows whether the program was implemented successfully and with sufficient intensity so that positive outcome could be expected, even outcome data that show success cannot be attributable to the program effort. Put simply, just because the program occurred prior to the positive outcome is not sufficient reason to think that the program caused the outcome. It is possible that any number of other factors about clients and external conditions were responsible. Recall here the standard distinction between correlation and causation: Correlation is not sufficient reason to attribute causation. The scientific standard for attributing causation is "control" over factors that the experimenter hypothesizes will produce change, control in the sense of ability to consciously manipulate them, put them in place in conjunction with things to be changed. That, as well as other things, is what implementing a program design achieves. [2]

Fourth, a good program theory will contain statements that are essential to high-level planners whose role is to decide when and where else such a program might be successful.[3] Good program theory speaks about the *conditions* required in order for it to achieve the desired outcomes. That is important because the kind of theory social programs use is generally very specific, perhaps even local—dealing as it does with the particulars of problems, people, and cultures. The specification of those conditions is an important function of program theory. Notice in Figure 8–1 that one of the factors is "high stress (under-employment/low wages)," which is an example of a factor so important that failure to attend to it in the program design may result in failure to reduce or eliminate child abuse, the desired outcome. On that account, such attention might be a necessary condition (alluded to above). It is difficult to specify all such conditions because very often we simply don't know enough to do so. Our theories soften in the face of hard unyielding realities of the everyday life of program users and program personnel. For example, even the most clever and devoted case manager or social work practitioner working with the chronically mentally ill cannot do his or her main job—acquiring resources for clients—if (as is too often the case) basic housing, public income support, and essential medical care are simply unavailable to this population. This instance is, of course, just another example of how services are no substitute for food, shelter, and medicine. It is critical to understand those as basic conditions for successful outcomes for a case-management program. Good programs have been dismissed as bad theory when they don't show positive outcomes, when in fact the conditions for positive outcomes are absent. Good intervention ideas are too scarce to let that happen.

Chapter 1 referred to causal chains in a social problem analysis. We should take some pains to distinguish causal chains from program theory. Understanding the causes of social problems does not necessarily guarantee knowing enough to do anything about them—the factors that created the problems may be beyond reach of ordinary programmatic interventions. That is particularly true in regard to the "soft" benefits of personal social services (though it also can be true of "hard" benefit programs). For example, no act of intervention will restore the loss one suffers from the death of a family member. Nor can anyone identify the exact factor that creates most chronic mental illnesses. Knowing so little about such imponderables means that the program objective may be simply remedial—taking the hardest edges off the consequences. That may be what program theory is and should be about. On that account, theoretical causes of social problems differ notably from the causal sequences observed in the social problem analysis. That difference will also be the case when social program or policy objectives are intended to deal only with a partial aspect of the social problem (the stresses and reactions of family members to an alcoholic parent or spouse, for example).

Finally, the idea of multiple causation is important in understanding why causal sequences at the social problem level may be different from those at the program design/intervention level. Multiple causation holds that there may be more than a single cause (or a single causal sequence) for any given human problem. Thus, *it is quite possible to assist people with problems other than by working just to reverse the same factors that were causal in the first place*. It is a fortunate idea because—again—the historical roots of certain social and personal problems are beyond our interventions; we can no more restore dead family members to life than we can go back and undo personal tragedies, cataclysmic weather, or catastrophic economic events. Note that the route *into* poverty is not necessarily the way out. For example, the route back to a solid and sustaining marriage is not necessarily to redo the past, but rather to help a relationship reestablish itself on an entirely different basis—changes in role descriptions, occupations, preoccupations, and the ways of the loving heart. The good program designer and the wise and witty interventionist understands that human beings have wings as well as roots, as the saying goes.

CONCEPTS AND EVALUATION CRITERIA FOR SERVICE-DELIVERY SYSTEMS

Neither love, money, nor good intention alone is sufficient to get benefits and services to masses of people who need them. Some kind of bureaucratic, organizational system is necessary to deliver benefits or services that will bridge the gap between problem and solution. Surprisingly, perhaps, the more an organization resembles a bureaucracy, the more effective and efficient it should be. That is because in its original sense the term *bureaucracy* referred to its rational nature, so to describe something as bureaucratic was to call it rational or thoughtful in pursuing logical, effective, and efficient means to specific ends.

Indeed, that is all we would wish of an organization that delivers benefits or services intended to alleviate the social problem of poverty. It is instructive to remember that the original conception of a bureaucracy was of people working together in a set of logically defined roles, where clear divisions of labor and authority enhanced the effectiveness and dispatch with which the assigned task was accomplished. That is still the ideal of organizations, certainly of organizations that deliver services and material benefits to people with social problems. Speaking from a client/consumer's point of view, Gilbert and Specht note three kinds of outcomes that characterize organizations good at accomplishing tasks with effectiveness and dispatch.[4]

1. Services are integrated and continuous.
2. Services are accessible to clients.
3. The system can be held accountable for its actions and decisions.

Let us look at each of these characteristics but add still another:

4. The system has the ability to relate to the racial and ethnic diversity in its client population.

(Recall that we discussed the presence of a program design earlier in this chapter as a *first* criterion for good service-delivery systems.) The following sections consider the presence or absence of these outcomes as the basic criteria for judging the merit of a service-delivery system.

INTEGRATION AND CONTINUITY

A social welfare program seldom delivers only one specific program benefit or service, in the same sense that some businesses handle only one product. On that account, problems of integrating different program operations, benefits, and services become an issue. For example, if program parts are not integrated, clients may be continually sent from one office to the next without understanding the reasons for being shuffled around, and may experience increased frustration over the loss of time. A benefit-delivery system can be constructed to avoid that situation. For example, the Food Stamp program is funded entirely by federal money but uses state agencies for delivery of benefits. In most states eligibility for food stamps is determined by the same personnel who work at the same location as the AFDC program. An example of a service-delivery system that increases program integration is the location of an income maintenance worker (a "welfare office" worker) on the grounds of a state mental hospital. Many mental hospitals treat numbers of inpatients who could maintain themselves in their own communities and who do not necessarily need to remain as inpatients.[5] A number of such persons have been residents of closed institutions for many years and have lost family that ordinarily would have provided them with either a home or funds to live nearby, albeit in a separate household. These persons might remain in institutional care (which may cost the state as much as $3,000 per month) simply because psychiatrically disabled persons, if left on their own, may not be able to follow through on an application procedure for the $500-$600 per month general assistance and food stamps necessary for a marginal existence. Locating an income maintenance unit on-site so that eligibility for food stamps and cash (general assistance) is determined prior to discharge is a delivery-system maneuver that integrates the income maintenance system with the health care and psychiatric care system in ways that would appear beneficial to both the client and the state.

This example shows how a service-delivery system increases integration of services by coordinating policy and procedures. It avoids duplication of services (e.g., determining eligibility twice for the same purpose) and attends to issues of physical location. Also, it is obviously administratively less costly. Many state social service-delivery systems discharge long-term patients into the community in such a way that they are forced to live for weeks until they can become eligible for cash benefits; or, they must make a long and expensive trip back to a mental hospital to receive routine medical or psychiatric care and medication. These systems are examples of service-delivery organizations that have serious problems in both integration and continuity of care. Where a service-delivery system continues to have such problems, the system is said to be fragmented. Child care services in the United States are one of the most fragmented service-delivery systems in all of the social services. Typically, child care agencies offer only one of three types of service—day care, temporary foster care, or adoption. Furthermore, delivery is complicated by strange situations, like the fact that many local juvenile courts—which usually have the greatest need for temporary foster homes—don't administer such a program themselves but depend on other agencies to provide them (the local welfare department for example). Some believe that this state of affairs is a major factor in creating "foster care drift," where children spend long periods (literally years) going from one set of foster parents to another. In fact, with careful planning and coordination of services, these children might never have entered foster care in the first place. It is not unusual that children are placed in 24-hour-a-day foster care for a long period when in fact their needs could have been met by a day care center that provided care for preschoolers as well as afterschool supervision for school-age children. Integration of substitute child care services in the United States is badly needed.[6]

Coping with Integration and Continuity Problems of Organizations and Service-Delivery Systems

Program coordination is one of the strategies by which these kinds of integration problems can be solved. Three types of program coordination are centralization, federation, and case management.

Centralization: *Centralization* refers to combining several agencies, programs, or services under one administrative head or controlling authority. Large urban hospitals have sometimes taken control of nursing-home facilities so that medical supervision can be achieved under the auspices of the hospital's medical staff.

Another large-scale example of centralization has been the amalgamation of nearly all state-level income maintenance and public social and medical services under the administrative control of a single agency (the Social and Rehabilitation Services in Iowa and Ohio, for example). Under this structure, state mental health clinics and mental hospitals have sometimes been placed under one administrator in an effort to integrate mental health services. In some states, the Vocational Rehabilitation agency was placed under the same umbrella.

These reorganizations have been accompanied by considerable political conflict because they inevitably entail significant loss of organizational power and influence by some agencies and power gains by others. Centralization has been a major feature in the changes in U.S. health, education, and welfare service-delivery systems since the end of World War II, prior to which income maintenance programs were the major responsibility of local units of government (counties, cities, townships, and villages). The general assistance (GA) programs run by these governmental units, which were the basic "relief" programs of the twenties and thirties, are today only a small portion of the income maintenance system in this country. This GA program was replaced (in the main) by the emergence of OASI, AFDC, SSI, and the medical programs associated with them. GA remains a viable program in thirty-two states, but the portion of all income maintenance benefits it provides is very small and continues to decline. A look at current issues of the *U.S. Statistical Abstract* will show this comparison, a change that represents centralization as it occurs nationally. That trend in program centralization has often been called "federalization" because the change involved a transfer from state and local authority to federal authority.

Federation: Another type of program coordination is *federation,* which entails a change in authority structure but only partially and much less extensively. Remember that centralization entails a change in authority structure, by moving separate organizations under a "super" authority that presides over all of them. When two or more organizations attempt to coordinate services by federating, they agree to cooperate in certain limited and precisely specified activities. For example, the day care centers in an urban community may agree to divide responsibility for the day care needs of the total community among themselves in certain ways. The objective is to serve the total need and serve it in a way that avoids duplication of effort and makes best use of available resources. With that in mind, each center may claim certain geographic areas so that no segment of the city population is more than ten blocks away from a day care center. All persons residing in a given segment are required to use a particular center, with some exceptions made for special cases. This makes it necessary to close some centers that, because of too-close proximity, make their operation financially ineffective. Sometimes the centers may choose to remain open so as to serve children with special needs (children intellectually disabled or children who need emergency shelter care).

Note that unlike centralization, with federation no center gives up authority over its internal program workings. What is given up is a part of the authority to decide who its clients will be. In a federation, no center makes a commitment that it cannot revoke after the period covered by the agreement is over. Because of the three reasons enumerated below, federation is a less extensive restructuring of authority than that involved in centralization.

1. The authority is released voluntarily.
2. The program operations that are released to the authority of another are clearly limited in scope.
3. The release of authority is time limited and can be revoked upon expiration of the agreement.

A useful description of the various kinds of interagency federative and cooperative efforts has been presented in terms of the following six types:[7] loaning of staff, colocation, joint delivery, combined delivery, outstationing, and consultation. Solving difficulties in integration and continuity by centralization or by federation is not without problems. Recall the general principle that any change in one element of a service-delivery system or organization almost inevitably will cause changes in some other organizational sector and that sometimes those changes will constitute problems as serious as those the original effort was intended to solve. Here are some of the important problems of centralization:

1. Because centralization almost always restructures authority by imposing another higher authority on existing executive layers, it almost always increases the distance between clients and policy decision makers. As we shall discuss in greater detail later, that almost always reduces organizational accountability.

2. Centralization is very likely to increase short-term intraorganizational conflict, in that some will gain and some will lose authority. Early conflict will occur as losers fight centralization; once it is in place, losers will attempt to minimize their losses. Gainers will seek to maximize their gains and work out new relationships with others in authority.

3. If authority is not delegated, the time it takes to make decisions can increase markedly, forcing clients to wait interminably for needed services or benefits.

Federation also has unique problems that continue over time, two of which are as follows:

1. Because coordination is achieved only issue by issue as authority is ceded over a specific operational particular, other program aspects in dire need of coordination must be put on hold. Thus, federation cannot provide timely response to emergencies or catastrophic events.

2. Federation creates difficulties in solving organizational conflict. In fact, there is no efficient way to resolve conflict in a federated service-delivery system. The federated organization exists by virtue of voluntary cooperation, and

should the thread of cooperation be broken by conflict, a stalemate ensues and the whole organizational enterprise is lost.

Case Management: Centralization and federation rely on changing the way organizations do business with each other as a way to get service and benefit packages to clients in need. One of the most popular strategies for solving integration and coordination problems in the complex system for service and benefit delivery is case management. *Case management* relies on settling the authority and responsibility for organizing and delivering services and benefit packages on a single person—the case manager. This practitioner must assess client need, plan for the provision of services and benefits to meet those needs, identify and acquire commitments from other organizations and service providers to deliver those services and benefits for a whole range of client needs (housing, medical care, employment, legal services, child day care, nutrition, personal counseling, and so on). Case management can go beyond just assembling "packages"; it can range from constant monitoring for quality to responsibility for seeing that clients get to the right places at the right times. It can also extend to actively advocating for clients' rights on behalf of benefits and services that may be unjustly withheld. Case management is also a product of extensive frustration in the field with the high degree of specialization in the functions performed by different agencies. So specialized have these functions become that differences between services and eligibility rules virtually mystify the uninitiated. One of the case manager's tasks is to clarify for clients the service and benefit choices available and what is necessary to gain access to them.

Although there are many versions of how case management should be pursued, three styles illustrate the variability. The most simple approach proposes that the case manager act as a broker of services, one who has little direct contact with clients but simply identifies needs based on clients' direct requests, locates organizations that offer relevant services and benefits, and refers clients to them. Responsibility for making direct contact rests with the clients' own initiative. A second version of case management views the case manager as a therapist devoted to healing but one who actively pursues, monitors, and evaluates the provision of treatment, services, and benefits other than what the case manager can provide directly. That pursuit, monitoring, and evaluation occurs in tandem with the therapist/case manager's treatment/services. A third version, taking exception to the presumption of client "deficit" or "pathology" implied in the second version, seeks to organize and orchestrate resources focused on an assessment of client and client social network strengths and assets. This is done in an effort to support and augment these strengths in service of the client's greater functioning in an ordinary community.[8] Thus, the case manager's assessment of need is focused on social "coping" rather than on diagnostic implications for "treatment." Resource acquisition is done with a dual focus on person-environment interactions and with a strong commitment to client participation in both decision making, resource acquisition, and quality monitoring. Deitchman describes these contrasts in the following way:[9]

The client in the community needs a traveling companion, not a travel agent. The travel agent's only function is to make a client's reservation. The client has to get ready, get to the airport and traverse foreign ground by himself. The traveling companion, on the other hand, celebrates the fact that his friend was able to get seats, talks about his fear of flying and then goes on the trip with him.

As Rapp and Chamberlain note, "The travel companion is an enabler engaged in a human relationship with the client but is not a therapist focused on the internal dynamics and psychiatric symptoms."[10] Case management has been a significant strategy in a number of different social problem and policy system areas—chronic mental illness, child welfare, and developmental disabilities, to name only the most prominent examples. There is some indication that case management is a successful strategy. Rapp and Chamberlain's pilot study shows that therapists and treatment staff as well as clients express high satisfaction levels with the case-management program, that rehospitalizations of a group of the chronically mentally ill are nil (at least over the short course of the study), and that a "high" proportion of case goals were achieved for this very difficult client group.[11]

ACCESSIBILITY

Another ideal that should characterize all service-delivery systems is that of accessibility of service, which refers to the extent to which obstacles block entry to the service-delivery network. Such obstacles may include geographic location, administrative rituals, selective eligibility policies, ethnic and linguistic characteristics of client populations, and outright racial or ethnic prejudice. One of the most common obstacles for many client groups is that of language. If agency personnel cannot speak the language of potential clients, services and benefits are not fully available to them. This country always has significant immigrant subpopulations who almost always concentrate in particular regions or in particular cities. For example, nearly every major metropolitan area has a sizable group of Southeast Asian refugees, and many East Coast cities have sizable Cuban or Haitian subgroups. If practitioners cannot overcome the language barrier in expediting delivery of benefits to these peoples, accessibility is severely impaired.

Cultural (but not linguistic) differences also hamper access of needful clients to important benefits and services. Certain programs have been ineffective in persuading Latino or native Americans with severe medical or psychiatric conditions to adopt treatments prescribed by Anglo physicians. These medical services were inaccessible to some of these groups because Western technology and medicine and its style of healing differ notably from their own healing traditions. Native healers (*curanderos*) are commonplace among Latino cultures of all regions and certainly are common to the tribal groups of North America.[12] One method of making the services and benefits of modern Western medicine accessible to these cultures has been to employ native healers as part of the treatment staff for relevant clientele. If the native healer then recommends further treatment by Anglo physicians, use of Western procedures is likely to become more acceptable. This service-delivery system innovation deals with the problems of access created by cultural clash.[13] It does so by providing continuity between the medical practices of the system to which the person is acculturated and the practices of the "alien" medical care system.[14,15]

Coping with Accessibility Problems of Service-Delivery Systems

Generally speaking, two strategies are used by service-delivery systems to remove obstacles to client use of, or entry to, the service-delivery system network: (1) staffing with indigenous workers and (2) constructing agencies that specialize in referral services.

Indigenous Workers: An *indigenous worker* is a nonprofessional who has had personal experience with the social problem of the clients being served.[16] As used here, the term *indigenous* refers to its common dictionary definition: originating in, growing or living naturally in a particular region or environment. Thus, with respect to poverty an indigenous worker is one who "lives naturally" in an environment of poverty. With respect to criminal deviance, an indigenous worker is a person who has been convicted of a crime and spent some time in prison. The classic example of the indigenous worker is the reforming alcoholic who is an active member of Alcoholics Anonymous (AA). The theory behind the indigenous worker strategy assumes that some social problems generate a particular culture or life-style or, according to Oscar Lewis, a "design for living" that has the social problem as a central reality to which life adjustments and responses must be made.[17] Those who have lived with a particular social problem have in fact become intimately acquainted not only with its reality but with the cultural response to it. Such people know its customs, its language, and its common patterns. That knowledge, born out of experience, enables that person to establish communication more quickly and effectively with those who continue to live with a given social problem. Alcoholics readily speak of the unique subculture of the alcoholic experience—how it yields a common pattern of life and a common language for those life experiences and how difficult it is for an alcoholic to believe that anyone who has not experienced alcoholism can understand it.

There are other social problems that develop a strong subculture. The most obvious example is that of substance addiction, the habitual use of chemical substances. Heroin addicts tend to form a discrete social group in their communities (though, as is the case with alcoholics and all other subcultures, loners exist among them); the life of individuals and the cultural group center on the central fact of demand, supply, and use of the chemical. Language, manners, and customs grow up around its use and are shared among group members. Knowledge of those cultural features of the addict's community gives the indigenous helper the critical edge in establishing communication and credibility more rapidly and more effectively. Perhaps less common—but certainly not less serious—is the use of indigenous workers to defuse encounters with staff of service-delivery systems that clients experience as humiliating, abusive, or traumatic. Keep in mind that social class, racial differences, prejudices, and biases can be the source of experiences that are so humiliating and abusive that clients will do terrible things to themselves to avoid repetition of the experience: They will go hungry, refuse to seek medical care, or refrain from seeking redress when innocent and convicted of crimes that carry serious penalties.

Also understand that in some geographic areas where racial minorities comprise a very large proportion of the population, the actual encounter between such minorities and outsiders may be infrequent; after all, the literal meaning of ghetto is "an isolated section." Children of ghetto minorities may have their first encounter with people different from themselves only upon visiting or being visited by a staff member of a social service agency. The encounter may be particularly revealing; having a black or Latino child feel the visitor's skin to see whether the white rubs off is not a scene that whites are particularly prepared to understand, much less handle well. The extensive use of indigenous workers can facilitate service provision without the interference of misunderstandings, trauma, and abuse that can result from tense encounters between ethnic groups and naive whites. Use of the indigenous worker seeks to increase the probability that the staff member whom the client first encounters will be able to respond in ways that are culturally and socially sensitive and empathetic with the client's problem. Whereas the primary intent of using indigenous workers is to produce better service for consumers, there is good reason to believe that there also can be specific benefits for the indigenous worker as well. For example, the helper-therapy principle asserts that those vulnerable to a problem who set out to help others with the same problem are very likely to benefit simply by being involved in the helping process.

There is no clear understanding about why this is so; the principle is simply an empirical observation of outcomes. The helper-therapy principle may be just another version of the common observation that when one helps another to learn, one learns as much in the process. To the extent that "helping" entails learning (and to some degree it surely does), the analogy is appropriate. The indigenous worker approach as a service-delivery strategy does have some basic problems and some limitations despite its appeal. Clearly, the indigenous worker idea is effective only with social problems that generate a subculture that is sufficiently unique so that it cannot be easily learned, understood, and incorporated by the ordinary nonindigenous helper. Also, it turns out that the career of a particular individual who performs in an indigenous worker role is fairly short. The tendency of the indigenous worker is gradually to take on the attitudes and values of the professional staff of the nonindigenous organization. That process goes by other names—socialization and co-optation, for example. It is certainly natural enough that a person should assimilate to the norms and outlook of those positioned to befriend, reward, and punish. It is not necessary to refer to a conscious motive on the part of organizations that employ indigenous workers to accomplish this, it is sufficient to cite socialization as a natural process in human groups.[18] Close observers of indigenous workers in Head Start and Community Action Programs (CAPs) report that it takes about eighteen months for the indigenous worker to be acculturated to the organization that pays the worker's wages. In other words, eighteen months is about as long as one can expect an indigenous worker to retain a view of the social problem of concern that is sufficiently allied with client views so that it gives the indigenous worker a unique value perspective.

Agencies Specializing in Referral Services: The system of agencies and organizations involved in delivering social welfare services and benefits can be maze-like for clients and helpers attempting to solve problems. In any given metropolitan area, hundreds of agencies, programs, and organizations offer multiple services and benefits under widely varying conditions for diverse target populations. This feature of variety can become one reason why benefits and services are inaccessible to people who need them. Sometimes the organizations are so numerous and the nature of their services and entitlement rules so ill defined and difficult in terms of distinguishing one from the other that it requires direct experience to judge exactly where a certain client with a certain problem should be referred for services or benefits. Where this has been identified as a problem, one solution has been to create a special agency whose sole purpose is to ensure that clients get to the appropriate agency. Such a solution is the embodiment of an attempt to solve a problem of accessibility—a problem created by the fact of agency overlap, duplication of services, and the general disarray of the social welfare service-delivery system in the United States.

Referral agencies often assume a client advocacy role as well, viewing their responsibility as extending further than the simple supply of information to clients about the "best" source of help for their problem. Most referral agencies are also committed to advocating their clients' needs to the agencies to which the clients are referred. The purpose of this advocacy is to ensure that once the application is made, the clients get the services and/or benefits to which they are entitled by right, policy, or law. In this sense, then, the referral agency acts as both a "front-door" for all the community's agencies and as a "door-widener" for clients to get what they need and what they are entitled to. Advocacy practices vary widely—following up with a phone call on each client to ensure that the client-agency contact was made, helping a client file an application for a "fair hearing," referring a client to legal counsel to get a special judgment as to whether the agency's actions or policy interpretations were correct. Some referral agencies broaden their functions to include what are commonly called "door-step" functions; that is, the agency's reason for being is to serve all persons who "appear on their doorstep." They are free to serve as just a referral agency and, commonly, that is the most frequent service, but where services are not available or cannot be made available by some combination of expert choice of referral and client advocacy, the agencies' commitment is to serve the clients' needs. It is in fact a radical professional commitment to undertake to serve all clients' needs. One of the stated functions of "door-step" agencies is that of constant monitoring and assessment of the adequacy and range of social services in the community, and of planning for additions or extensions where indicated by experience. In Great Britain a whole program has been devoted to the development of referral agencies and is directed toward the development of "Citizens Advice Bureaus" whose purpose is to provide referral services and, where necessary, client advocacy.[19]

ACCOUNTABILITY AS A CRITERION FOR THE SERVICE-DELIVERY SYSTEM

Accountability is the third ideal characteristic of a service-delivery system. The following example examines a service-delivery system, an agency concerned with child abuse as a social problem. Suppose a report was made to this agency of a case of suspected child abuse but that the report remained uninvestigated for two months. Meanwhile, the child was beaten to death by one of the parents. The agency's accountability in this turn of events must be questioned. Be clear that the thing for which the agency is accountable is not the life of the child but the lack of response to the report.

The service-delivery agency can be said to have a system for accountability if the following conditions are met:

1. It is possible to identify which staff member decided not to respond to the abuse report.
2. It is possible for both the staff member and the immediate superior to identify the specific organizational policy that justified that decision.
3. It is possible to identify the staff member's immediate superior for a quick supervisory review and opinion of the staff member's decision not to respond to the report (or lack of attention to it at all) with respect to its conformity to agency policy.
4. If there is substantive disagreement with the above opinions by outside third parties, there is a regular procedure (e.g., administrative hearing) by which such disagreements can be heard and resolved.

These are the minimum standards if accountability is to be a factor in the operation of a service-delivery system; more and better features might be involved. If organizations and service-delivery systems can respond to criticisms simply by denying that any overall policy is in operation, the organization cannot be held accountable. In other words, if *no* particular staff member can be held responsible, then of course no one can be held responsible. Where failure to respond to a report of child abuse is associated (causally or not) with the subsequent death of a child, it is a travesty of justice to try to affix responsibility only to find that "no one was responsible." That is why accountability is such an important feature in the character of an organization; without it, irresponsibility and injustice go unmended.

Coping with Accountability Problems of Service-Delivery Systems

Although many mechanisms are used to render service-delivery systems accountable as discussed earlier, three of the most prominent will be detailed: (1)

administrative ("fair") hearings and procedures by which clients can appeal decisions that affect their benefits or services, (2) constitutionally derived due process protections of clients' procedural rights, and (3) client empowerment and citizen/consumer participation.

Administrative ("Fair") Hearings and Appeal Procedures: Fair-hearing procedures are a common part of the service-delivery system of many social service programs. In fact, the Social Security Act requires a fair-hearing procedure for all programs established by the act (OASI, AFDC, UI (unemployment insurance), DI, Medicare, and so on). A fair-hearing procedure is one in which a client or applicant is given the opportunity to appeal to an administrative tribunal or a judge (or a panel of judges) who hears arguments of both sides. This tribunal reviews agency policy, practices, and enabling legislation and then renders a decision for or against the agency or the complainant. The administrative judge is duty-bound to hold the agency to decisions and actions that are consistent with agency policy, tradition, or legislative mandate. The judge can require the agency to reverse its prior actions or decisions and/or change its policies and procedures.

Fair-hearing systems most commonly use judges employed by the system that is being questioned. On that account, the U.S. fair-hearing system is not entirely independent of those who must submit to its scrutiny. On the other hand, the job performance of the administrative judges who operate the Social Security Administration (SSA) fair-hearing procedure are subject to review only by other administrative judges. However, during the early 1980s, judges were subject to unusual scrutiny by a new (Reagan-appointed) chief judge—clearly the first historical record of blatant presidential political interference with the administrative apparatus of Social Security or the congressional power to set public policy for the agency. The judges association filed suit in federal district court asking for a desist order against such practice. The conclusion about presidential political interference was supported by the entire bipartisan committee including prominent Republican congresspersons. State welfare departments administering income maintenance programs also have fair-hearing procedures, but note that in many state systems the "judges" often are no more than agency administrators with no supervisory responsibility for the decision being questioned and are pressed into auxiliary service as administrative judges. Clearly, such judges cannot freely make decisions that go against the interests of the organization that employs them. Every social practitioner should be able to counsel clients on use of the fair-hearing procedures in force in local social service and health agencies and income maintenance agencies. If they feel that policy decisions affect a client adversely and that a decision is inconsistent with past policy, is arbitrary or capricious, or is blatantly prejudicial or discriminatory, practitioners can help clients access fair-hearing/procedures.

Practitioners should be prepared to help clients get fair hearings even if the policy interpretation that works to their disadvantage was made by the very agency the practitioner works for—which is not uncommon. The first loyalty of a professional is to the client, and where there is a conflict of interest between client and organization, the professional obligation is to ensure that the client's interest is served. That may mean that the client's advocate may have to be someone other than the practitioner, and if that is the case, it is not difficult to secure the services of another professional to advocate for the client on this one issue.

Due Process Protections for Clients' Procedural Rights with Respect to Social Welfare Benefits and Services and Administrative Discretion: Unfortunately, scholars and practitioners are in virtual agreement that policy rules are never entirely adequate as a guide to action or decision in concrete, practical, day-to-day situations. The human condition is too variable, so that even the best policy statements fall short of accommodating the complex and finely tex-tured relationships between organizations and the people they serve. Absent a rule to guide action, staff members use the only recourse left to them, their own "best judgment," which can be wrong in any given instance. Among writ-ers and researchers on policy and organizational problems, such recourse is called *administrative discretion*. But, like strange and marvelous lights in the night sky, it needs careful watching. Administrative discretion can be a threat to the substantive rights of citizens, whether or not they are social service beneficiaries or service consumers. Administrative discretion can also be a threat to the procedural rights of citizens in claiming social welfare benefits or social services. *Procedural rights* are those elements in a decision-making pro-cess that are believed to be required for decisions to be made with the open-ness, fairness, and impartiality that natural justice demands. In the United States, federal and state constitutions provide for due process of law where interests in life, liberty, or property are at stake. Prior to the 1970s, social ser-vices or social welfare benefits were viewed as gratuities in which citizens had no property interests. These benefits were granted at the discretion—not the obligation—of the government. Reichs's concept of "new property" interest became ascendant, and the crucial case was *Goldberg v. Kelley*, decided in 1970.[20]

The key issue in that case was whether the constitutional due process requirements applied to welfare benefits. The U.S. Supreme Court held that they did indeed. Note that the Court did not find that citizens have a substan-tive right to welfare benefits, only that once a statute grants an interest or a right in a welfare benefit, then that interest must be protected by the constitu-tional due process requirements.[21] The Supreme Court recognizes that adminis-trative discretion can indeed threaten the procedural rights that protect the possibility of just and equitable decisions. What does constitutional due pro-cess require of administrative decisions about eligibility for, continuance of, or changes in welfare benefits or services? Whereas it is true that the Social Security Act has always required programs to have a fair-hearing procedure as a way of redressing grievances, it was little used and the procedures were vari-able prior to the 1970s, when they became one of the principal battlegrounds for the welfare rights movement.

Following is Handler's appraisal of what is required of a fair-hearing procedure:[22]

- The right to timely and specific notice of the action taken by the agency and its basis. The norm is that the written notice must be in a form that the person can understand and allows reasonable time to prepare for the hearing.

- The right to appear at the hearing, to give evidence, and to argue a point of view. Sometimes allowing a recipient to present his or her story only in writing and not orally in public will not satisfy the due process standards. The Supreme Court has noted potential lack of writing ability by welfare clients. The right to call witnesses exists generally, but is not unlimited.

- The right to counsel. In recent years the Supreme Court has retreated on this matter, though some precedent still stands.

- The right to confront and cross-examine witnesses.

- The right to an open or public proceeding. "Due process does not require an open hearing in certain kinds of administrative hearings (prison discipline cases and school cases)," according to Handler.

- The right to an impartial decision maker. The crucial issue is how much prior exposure to the case biases judgment. It appears that in some cases the Supreme Court has allowed decision makers to have substantial involvement.

- The right to a decision based on the record and to written findings of fact and conclusions of law. It is very important to understand that in granting the application of due process requirements to "government largesse" (like welfare benefits and services), the Supreme Court conditioned the grant in important ways. The general principle is that due process requirements apply in any given specific instance only to the extent that there is a balance between the following three elements:

  - the seriousness of the grievance to the person receiving the welfare benefit

  - the need for any particular due process procedure in order to resolve the grievance fairly

  - the costs in time, money, and other resources to the administrative agency

This means that the balancing test described above is the most explicit guide available to the "general rules" in determining what constitutes an acceptable attention to due process requirements.

Citizen/Consumer Participation as a Criterion to Evaluate Service-Delivery Systems and as a Strategy for Accountability: Citizen participation is the involvement of consumers and citizen representatives in policy decisions of a social service delivery organization. Citizen participation is intended to increase the accountability of the organization to its consumers and the general public who pay its bills. Involvement of laypersons or consumers of agency services in policy decisions is believed to curb the career and professional self-interest of staff members. Such involvement exposes professionals to fresh viewpoints and, in the case of citizen participation by consumers, to a view of service from the receiving end. The point of consumer involvement is to constrain policy decisions toward the needs of clients rather than the needs of the community or the service-delivery staff. The problem with citizen participation as a strategy to increase organizational accountability is twofold. One, it doesn't happen very often; laypersons or service consumers are not given significant power over policy-making decisions. Two, if they are, they may not be very interested in taking that much responsibility. Nearly every author who writes about community participation notes the frequency with which citizen participation actually refers to token representation. Not only have observers of the scene in the United States—like Arnstein, Kramer, and Weissman—included this style of participation in their typologies of community participation, but British policy analysts and observers note it with regularity.[23, 24]

It should be clear that because power is the crucial factor, meaningful citizen participation cannot be said to occur unless it is actually exercised. The conditions for its exercise are as follows:[25]

1. Citizens must constitute a significant (perhaps 1/3) voting block, not just a token portion, of the whole.
2. Citizens must have the right to initiate actions, not just respond to the agendas of executive managers.
3. Organizations must help citizen board members cope with formal procedures (like Roberts's Rules of Order) and technical language they may find unfamiliar.

The War on Poverty of the late 1960s and early 1970s featured citizen participation as a central element in program strategy. The CAP (Community Action Program) agencies were a central administrative device by which program benefits and services were delivered to neighborhood target areas. CAP agency boards of directors were elected by the neighborhood areas they served. One of the five major Head Start program areas was parent-participation in the policy-making and program evaluation efforts of Head Start, which itself was "governed" by an advisory board made up of citizen consumers. It seems safe to say that the War on Poverty programs spent remarkable effort and energy orchestrating citizen and consumer participation. The net gain in citizen participation of any kind, let alone effective participation, was disappointing in most instances in both programs. One of the facts about which there is little debate is that volunteer participation in organizational decision making is a strongly class-biased trait. Citizen participation is essentially a middle-class phenomenon; middle-class people take to it naturally, apparently, whereas blue-collar people do not see it as either very important or potentially very productive (though they surely might not express it in exactly those words).[26, 27] Neither Head Start nor CAP programs serve middle-class populations, so it should not be surprising that participation efforts were not productive. As Jones, Brown, and Bradshaw point out, it is not so much a matter of "apathy" as an essential pessimism about the likelihood of assuming an influential role.[28] Given documentation of the high probability that citizen participation was nothing more than tokenism in Head Start and CAP, it is a fair conclusion that blue-collar attitudes are in fact a correct assessment of the situation! Blue-collar people seem to have a grasp of this issue that neither professionals nor middle-class "joiners" seem to have. To balance the disappointing performance of the massive efforts by Head Start and CAP agencies to succeed in a full and serious citizen participation program, let us now turn to a description of a successful effort. Many believe that The Family Centre Project (also known as the Laurence Project) was the most significant antipoverty program ever undertaken in Australia. Perhaps it is best that Director David Donison speak for the project:[29]

> Radical, pioneering and iconoclastic in theory, and in practice full of human drama, the Family Centre project appeared to its staff to embody the very heart of the issues facing social work in the Australia of the mid-70s. The following description of the Project used by the Brotherhood of St. Laurence in its publicity material, outlines the Project's essential elements. In 1972 the Brotherhood took the major decision to terminate its established Social Work Service and the Youth and Children's Services, and to set up an innovative and experimental anti-poverty program designed to test new ways of assisting poor families. The overall objectives of the Family Centre Project were to demonstrate, with a small group of poor families who had been long-term clients of the Brotherhood, that changes in their economic and social conditions and opportunities were a pre-condition for change in their family and societal relationships, and that it was toward such changes that social work intervention would be directed. Through the first three years of the Project, the emphasis was on the redistribution of resources and power within the programme, with the implication that such changes are necessary in the wider community if power is to be effectively attacked. Among the features of the Project were:
>
> (a) A universal income supplement scheme in which every family was entitled to a weekly subsidy to maintain its income at a set level;
> (b) The use of a multi-disciplinary staff team as "resources" to the families rather than as conventional social workers, and an emphasis on "development work" rather than "casework";
> (c) A resource centre in Fitzroy and an extensive mobile camping programme;
> (d) A commitment to the "de-professionalisation" of the relationship between social workers and clients;
> (e) The introduction of programme in which the families ultimately took over the control and running of the Project both through a committee of management and through the gradual replacement of professional staff with members of the Project;
> (f) A growing emphasis on welfare rights, self-help and social action;
> (g) A comprehensive research and evaluation component and substantial range of publications.

Of course, there is no way to know whether the success of this radical experiment could be duplicated anywhere else. Those who observed it closely believe it to be successful, and in terms of citizen participation there seems little doubt that it was. Clearly the Laurence Project is unique among this type of effort. Another interesting and more recent example of citizen participation and empowerment as an accountability mechanism is the rise of citizen review panels for the purpose of monitoring, case by case, foster placement of children in long-term care. The function here is to keep a constant public tab on children in public care to ensure that they do not somehow get lost from sight. These "external" reviews can occur either alongside the more ordinary case review systems that have been put in place in many states or can occur independently (in addition to them). Citizen review systems of this kind have been put in place in Missouri, Arizona, Nevada, and New Jersey (to name some states), stimulated by provisions of the 1980 Child Welfare Act.[30] Although their net effect on accountability awaits a future study, they have certainly stimulated considerable discussion and been effective in raising public consciousness of the problem of accountability with respect to foster care programs.

ABILITY TO RELATE TO ETHNIC AND RACIAL DIVERSITY IN CLIENT POPULATIONS AS A SERVICE-DELIVERY SYSTEM CRITERION

Earlier the point was made that the use of indigenous workers is intended to increase the access of ethnic and racial minorities to welfare services and benefits. Access can also be increased by developing separate organizations to serve their needs exclusively. Instead of simply ensuring staff members who either have a special cultural understanding or who speak a special language, a whole organization can be developed that is exclusively devoted to the special social welfare needs of specific groups. Various kinds of such service-delivery organizations currently exist: some state income maintenance programs have established special units to serve Oriental populations; at one point in the early 1970s, the Black Muslims were frequent sponsors of child care and emergency relief agencies for black inner-city populations; many metropolitan inner cities have had medical facilities that traditionally served only blacks. Probably the most common example of ethnic- and race-oriented service-delivery organizations are the black adoption agencies that responded to local black communities whose children were embedded in the public foster care systems. As Fanshel (and Maas before him) has shown, the likelihood of these children leaving "temporary" foster care before they are self-supporting is distressingly small.[31]

At one time it was believed that the black community did not have the foster parents or adoptive parents needed to serve these children. Those who pioneered black adoption agencies believed that the reason black people were not forthcoming to serve these children was the barrier to application posed by confrontation with an all-white staff and the formal nature of foster care or adoption application forms, as well as interviews required in a formal office setting instead of in the home or even in a familiar neighborhood. Also problematic were the extensive discussion of past psychological history and the high fees required. The black adoption agency was created to construct a program that would give black applicants more reason to believe that their applications and life circumstances would be received without moral judgment. Further, it would avoid a confrontation with all-white personnel on unfamiliar grounds in unfamiliar neighborhoods. In fact, these agencies have been dramatically successful in increasing both the number of foster and adoption applications from black families and individuals and the number of permanent placements of black children. They demonstrate clearly that prior statements about the barriers presented by an all-white staff and the application process of the traditional child-placing agency were probably correct. It is worth noting that even though this service-delivery innovation seems to be one of the few undeniable successes in the delivery of child welfare services in years, it still lacks widespread support and is still controversial. Nevertheless, in some places where black adoption programs have been operating for a few years, healthy black infants are all being placed in adoption and no longer face interminable years in "temporary" foster homes as was routinely the case ten years ago.[32] As important as these special ethnic agencies are in the solution of some severe social problems, this service-delivery strategy was not alone a sufficient answer. Availability of "adoption subsidies" was an important factor in the recruitment of black homes for black children.[33,34]

Black adoption agencies are a special contemporary example of the private voluntary program, which has been so prominent a part of the U.S. social welfare scene for so many years. It is easy to forget that before the 1930s the major burden of the social welfare effort was carried by private voluntary agencies. Many of those voluntary agencies were ethnically oriented, oriented to alienated and often stigmatized subcultures that were similar in social status to today's U.S. black population. Out of that social position grew ethnically and religiously oriented social welfare agencies intended to serve the needs of their cultural parent group. The black adoption agencies are an independent but parallel development, an interesting commentary on the hardiness of the ethnic self-help, mutual-aid phenomenon. There has also been the contention that special agencies to serve ethnic and racial interests are prohibitively expensive because they duplicate the efforts of the mainline social agencies. Certainly there is little question that they are duplicative; whether they are "expensive" from a cost-effectiveness viewpoint (from the result obtained) is another question.

Nothing could be more clear from our examination of the efficacy of the black adoption programs. Such programs find black parents for black children where the mainline public child-placing programs have failed to do so over a very long period of time. Duplication of services in this instance must be more cost effective than non-duplication simply because it can produce a result where non-duplication cannot.

SUMMARY

Chapter 8 presented a set of ten concepts and implied evaluation criteria concerning social welfare benefit and service-delivery organizations and systems and judged their merit. These concepts represent issues determining the effectiveness with which social service organizations or systems deliver benefits and services to those who labor under the impact of social problems. These ten basic concepts are:

1. Program and policy design
2. Centralization
3. Federation
4. Case management
5. Indigenous worker staffing
6. Agencies specializing in referrals
7. Administrative ("fair") hearings and appeal procedures
8. Due process protections for clients' procedural rights
9. Client empowerment and citizen/consumer participation
10. Racially oriented agencies

The merit of service-delivery systems is always to be judged against their ability to contribute to the solution of the social problem with which the policy or program under analysis is concerned. However, a set of standards generally serves as criteria for the inherent quality of the service-delivery system. The practical analyst should use the following as evaluation criteria for service-delivery systems and organizations:

- The presence of a clear and credible program design
- Integration/continuity of services and benefits
- Accessibility of services and benefits
- Accountability mechanisms in place in the service-delivery system
- Ability of the service delivery system to relate to ethnic and racial diversity within its client population

EXERCISES

1. What is the difference between centralization and federation?
2. What practical difference would it make which organizations you chose to work in, and with respect to the day-to-day conditions under which you would work?

3. To what does due process refer? What does it have to do with human service or social welfare clients, programs, and policies?

4. How would you determine whether a fair hearing meets due process requirements of the law?

5. What are the major differences between administrative and professional discretion?

 6. What is citizen participation with respect to social welfare service-delivery systems and organizations? What is its main purpose?

7. In applying for a job at a social welfare organization you are told the agency surely has "a lot of citizen participation." What question(s) would you ask to determine whether that is really the case?

NOTES

1. K. Conrad and T. Miller, Measuring and Testing Program Philosophy. In. L. Bickman, editor, *Using Program Theory in Evaluation.* New Directions for Program Evaluation Series (San Francisco: Jossey-Bass, 1987) (pp. 19–42).

2. Of course, the fact of successful program implementation will not guarantee proof that the program features "caused" the outcome either. The only claim here is that it is a necessary condition for such an attribution, even though insufficient by itself.

3. L. Bickman, The Functions of Program Theory. In L. Bickman, editor, *Using Program Theory in Evaluation.* New Directions for Program Evaluation Series (San Francisco: Jossey-Bass, 1987) (pp. 5–18).

4. N. Gilbert and H. Specht, *Dimensions of Social Policy* (Englewood Cliffs, NJ: Prentice Hall, 1974).

5. F. N. Arnhoff, "Social Consequences of Policy Toward Mental Illness," *Science* 188 (June 1975).

6. M. R. Burt and L. H. Blair, *Options for Improving the Care of Neglected and Dependent Children* (Washington, DC: The Urban Institute, 1974).

7. D. J. Tucker, "Coordination and Citizen Participation," *Social Service Review,* 1980 54(1), pp. 17–18.

8. C. A. Rapp and R. Chamberlain, "Case Management Services to the Chronically Mentally Ill," *Social Work,* 1985.

9. W. S. Deitchman, "How Many Case Managers Does It Take to Screw in a Light Bulb?" *Hospital and Community Psychiatry,* 31, November, 1980, p. 789.

10. Op. Cit., p. 5.

11. Ibid., Rapp and Chamberlain, pp. 11–13.

12. D. D. Sharon, "Eduardo the Healer," *Natural History,* November 1972, pp. 32–49.

13. W. McDermott, K. Deuschle, and C. Barnett, "Health Care Experiment at Many Farms," *Science* 175:(January 1972), pp. 23–30.

14. E. Ginzberg, "What Next in Health Policy," *Science* 188: (June 1975), pp. 1182–86.

15. J. Goering, and R. Coe, "Cultural versus Situational Explanations for the Medical Behavior of the Poor," *Social Science Quarterly* (1970) 51(2), pp. 309–19.

16. G. Brager, "The Indigenous Worker: A New Approach to the Social Work Technician," *Social Work* (1965) 10[2].

17. O. Lewis, "Culture of Poverty," *Science* 188 (April 1975), pp. 3–54.

18. D. A. Hardcastle, "The Indigenous Nonprofessional in the Social Service Bureaucracy: A Critical Examination," *Social Work* (1971) 16[2].
19. J. Baker, *The Neighborhood Advice Project in Camden* (London: Routledge and Kegan Paul).
20. J. Handler, *Protecting the Social Services Client* (New York: Academic Press, 1979), p. 31.
21. Op. cit., p. 32.
22. Op. cit., p. 28.
23. S. Damer and C. Hague, "Public Participation in Planning: A Review," *Town Planning Review* (1971) 42(3), p. 224.
24. D. Phillips, Community Health Councils. In K. Jones, editor, *The Yearbook of Social Policy in Britain, 1974* (London: Routledge Kegal Paul, 1975), p. 106.
25. K. Jones, J. Brown, and J. Bradshaw, *Issues in Social Policy* (London: Routledge and Kegan Paul, 1979), pp. 106–108.
26. K. Newton, *Second City Politics* (London: Oxford University Press, 1976), p. 84.
27. For a dramatically convincing elaboration of this theme see George Orwell, *The Road to Wigan Pier* (London: Golancz and Song, 1937), p. 37.
28. Ibid, Jones, Brown, and Bradshaw, p. 106.
29. D. Donison, *Power to the Poor* (London: Basil Blackwell & Sons, 1979), pp. 12–13.
30. L. B. Costin and C. A. Rapp, *Child Welfare Policies and Practice* (New York: McGraw-Hill, 1984), pp. 370-71.
31. D. Fanshel and E. Shinn, *Children in Foster Care: A Longitudinal Investigation* (New York: Columbia University Press, 1978).
32. Kansas City black Adoption Program, J. Hampton, Director, personal communication to author, May 22, 1985.
33. A. Shyne and A. Schroeder, *National Study of Social Services for Children* (Rockville, MD: Westat, 1978), p. 125.
34. S. Katz and U. Gallagher, "Subsidized Adoption in America," *Family Law Quarterly*, (Spring 1976) 10, pp. 3–54.

CHAPTER 9

Concepts for the Analysis of Methods of Financing

By Rosemary Chapin, Ph.D.

INTRODUCTION

The way services are financed has profound impact on service provision. For example, services funded through voluntary contributions may cease to exist if contributions decline. On the other hand, services financed publicly through general revenue appropriations may be subject to legally mandated restrictions on service eligibility and method of service delivery that do not reflect professional standards of "best practice."

Service access and provision are also dramatically shaped by reimbursement, or payment methodology used to reimburse service providers. Public agencies are increasingly moving away from direct service provision; instead, public money is used to contract with, or purchase needed services from, private providers. This shift amplifies the importance of understanding how provider reimbursement or payment methodologies influence service access and provision. For example, if private providers are reimbursed the same amount for serving clients with intense service needs as they are for serving clients with minimal needs, providers could be expected to target service to clients with less intense needs. This often overlooked influence of reimbursement design on services is highlighted in this chapter.

To be effective, social service practitioners need to understand how methods of service financing shape service delivery and, ultimately, clients' lives. Some basic types of financing are common to social welfare benefit and service systems the world over. The following five classifications can be used to analyze financing of social welfare benefits and services in the United States.

1. Prepayments and other variations on the insurance principle
2. Voluntary contributions
3. General revenue appropriations
4. Direct out-of-pocket payment by consumer
5. Corporate/employment-based funding of benefits

To analyze a social policy or program adequately, it is necessary to grasp which of these types of financing (or combination thereof) are used to fund the social program or policy under consideration. However, that analysis alone will not provide enough information for the analyst to draw conclusions about the relative merit of the financing method and what changes might be needed; therefore, certain key questions (outlined below) on eight special aspects of financing will be germane to nearly any type of financing and will provide the additional information needed. These questions also need to be considered so as to judge the implications of a particular type of financing for a specific policy or program.

1. What is the immediate source of funds?
2. Are funds adequate to pay for the cost of providing needed service?
3. How is fund security and year-to-year funding continuity ensured?
4. What mechanisms are used to ensure funding stability in the wake of economic and demographic changes?
5. What is the distributional effect of this method of financing?
6. How are funds transferred from point of collection to point of service or benefit provision, and at what cost?
7. What methodology is used to reimburse the service provider?
8. What is the impact of this method of funding and provider reimbursement on the client?

The relevance of a question will vary based on the form of financing under consideration. In the following examination of each major financing type, these eight questions will provide the basic framework for the analysis.

THE INSURANCE PRINCIPLE: PREPAYMENTS AND OTHER VARIATIONS

The insurance principle enjoys wide use in the financing of benefits and services. Any financing method that relies on a "share-the-risk" mechanism and the payment of premiums before benefits can be received is, by definition, making use of an insurance principle. The basic concept of the insurance principle involves a group of people banding together and pooling some portion of their assets so that when an uncommon but disastrous event befalls one of the group, that person can recover the loss from the pool of assets. Life, health, and fire insurance are only a few examples of the insurance principle commonly in operation in our society.

Early insurance pools centered around commercial ventures. The intent was to provide some protection against loss of cargo or other property to a specific disaster such as fire or the sinking of a ship. Gradually, the insurance concept was expanded to protect individuals against a larger variety of losses and eventually to individual personal disasters, such as disability or loss of health. Even predictable, universal, and financially influential events such as old age are now covered by insurance. The insurance principle, originally developed in the private sector, is currently at work in the public sector protecting citizens against illness, unemployment, old age, and work injuries that interrupt the capacity of workers to support themselves and their families.

In the United States, a number of the public social welfare programs established under the Social Security Act employ the prepayment insurance principle. These include the Old Age and Survivors Insurance (OASI) program, the Social Security Disability (DI) program, and hospital insurance (HI) under the Medicare program. The first question to be examined when attempting to analyze these programs is "What is the *immediate source of funds for social welfare programs?*" The source is prepaid contributions from both employer and employee of a given percentage of wages collected with the total Social Security payroll deduction.

The question of *adequacy of funding for Social Security* has been hotly debated. In the early 1980s, a great deal of press coverage was devoted to the idea that Social Security was going broke. Although political motives were undoubtedly present, one of the reasons that the balance between Social Security contributions and benefits was getting out of hand was that Congress was trying to protect aged and disabled beneficiaries from inflationary depletion. In a period of rapid inflation, retired and disabled workers living on Social Security benefits experience severe reductions in their living standards if benefits do not increase along with the cost of living. In response to this problem, Congress *indexed* benefits, that is, passed a law that increased benefits in proportion to the increase in the Consumer Price Index (CPI). Although this strategy does help to mitigate the problems faced by the retired and disabled workers and their families, the trust fund from which benefits are to be paid is drawn down when wages do not increase as fast as the cost-of-living index (or even when they decrease). Recognition of this problem resulted in amendment of this method of adjustment. Now, in any year that the combined reserves of the OASDI trust funds fall below 20 percent of expected benefits, the cost-of-living adjustment is limited to the lesser of the increase in the CPI or the increase in national wages.[1] In fact, there was no genuine crisis, even though there were some technical problems that needed to be resolved (as discussed above), and some funding decisions that needed to be made. In one sense, what was presented as a crisis was simply the widespread recognition of what had been the case for years. The system operated on what was essentially a "pay-as-you-go" basis. Since 1960, about 90 percent of yearly contributions to the trust fund were being used to pay current beneficiaries.[2]

The Reagan administration moved to deal with these problems soon after taking office. The original Republican proposals were radical, including elimination of cost-of-living increases, elimination of all minimum benefits, and reductions of benefits across the board. By the fall of 1981 widespread grassroots opposition to those proposals, combined with weak congressional support, was apparent.

There are several lessons to be learned from review of these political maneu-
vers. First, they illustrate the widespread support for the Social Security system,
a major reason for optimism about its continuing soundness. The American people clearly want the problems solved and the system continued. Proposing
reduction or elimination of benefits is done only at considerable political peril.
Second, it is very difficult to predict consequences of changes in a system as massive as the Social Security system. Additionally, administrative expense of
undergoing changes can be prohibitive, and changes can take a very long time to
implement. Third, the system has shown resilience in the face of politically
motivated attempts to reduce benefits. Because the system is nonstigmatizing
and almost universal in its coverage, citizen beneficiaries are willing to defend
the program. Social Security withholding tax is an example of what are called
earmarked revenues. By earmarking or restricting taxes to certain uses, resources
are often protected against the uncertainties of the annual political process of
appropriation.

When considering issues of *fund security and year-to-year funding continuity,*
it is simply impossible to predict precisely the economic vagaries of the next seventy-five years. Projections of the adequacy of the system are made by Social
Security actuaries, based on certain economic and demographic assumptions
considered likely to occur. Given these assumptions, it is expected that large
reserves will continue to develop in the combined OASDI trust fund during the
1990s and the early part of the twenty-first century. Projections over the next
seventy-five years anticipate a small deficit (approximately 5 percent), which
may require a modest benefit reduction or payroll tax increase after the year
2020.[3] These mechanisms may ensure *funding stability* in the wake of economic
and demographic change.

The Social Security trust fund is the major mechanism used to collect and
hold prepayments. The guarantor of the soundness of that fund is the government of the United States. The dollars collected *each day* are invested in U.S.
Treasury Bonds, and interest is accrued at regular ongoing long-term rates.
Investment policy for Social Security funds is a complicated issue. Some
economists have illustrated how investing such enormous funds could result in
severe disruption in the financial world if they were invested in ordinary ways
and could affect the capacity of the Federal Reserve system to manage the economy.[4] *Year-to-year continuity* of the programs is dependent on the U.S.
Congress, which specifies the percentage of wages to be taxed for each program,
the relative employer–employee share, and other possible changes.

The method of financing used to provide Social Security benefits is particularly prone to problems because of *changes in national demographics.* When
there is low birthrate among the workforce and, simultaneously, large-scale
retirement of older workers, it means that there are fewer active young workers to pay for more retirement benefits. This is a problem not usually associated with financing based on the insurance principle because prepayment methods ordinarily deal with this by storing up funds in advance. It is a problem
peculiar to this prepayment type of financing because benefits are ultimately
tied to workforce wages.

The *distributional effects of Social Security* are often misunderstood and merit careful attention. Substantial *income transfers* are involved in the Social Security programs, and the presence of these income transfers is one reason Social Security can be deemed a social welfare program. It also must be noted that many economists have concluded that ultimately the worker's *and* the employer's share of the Social Security withholding tax is paid by the worker. At a certain level the employer's contribution may be considered additional wages that would have been paid to a worker had the payroll tax not been in effect.[5] Social Security contributions currently collected are used to pay benefits to current retirees, many of whom have not paid in anywhere near the amount of their long-term benefits. Based on this information, it is clear that a major income transfer is taking place. Money is being transferred from those presently working and paying Social Security withholding to those now retired and drawing benefits. Another important welfare transfer occurs because retired married women who have worked outside the home typically draw on their husbands' earning record and seldom on their own. A married woman who meets basic eligibility requirements is entitled to one-half of the amount of her husband's benefit. Because many women earn much less than their husbands, benefits based on their work history are less than the spouse's benefit. In that they cannot receive both benefits, these married women who draw on their husbands' earning record never draw more in benefits than if they had never worked at all. This is a direct violation of the insurance principle. One explanation given in defense of this striking inequity is that it was enacted as an attempt to pay benefits proportional to what a *couple* "needs" and not proportional to what they contributed.

When analyzing the distributional effect, it is important to consider not only the costs but also the indirect monetary benefit that may accrue to those paying the direct costs of Social Security. Most current Social Security beneficiaries have not fully paid for their retirement or medical benefits. However, the children and grandchildren who are now paying into the program do obtain a "benefit" in the sense that Social Security pension and Medicare health benefits help their retired parents maintain their independence without added financial support from their children. This facet of the program can be overlooked by those who currently pay Social Security taxes and who feel burdened by Social Security payroll deductions.

The federal agency that administers the OASDI program is the Social Security Administration (SSA). The Medicare program (HI) is administered by the Health Care Financing Administration (HCFA). There are differences in the way money is *transferred from point of collection to point of service or benefit provision* under the various parts of the OASDHI program. Social Security taxes are forwarded to the federal government by the employer, and benefits in the form of monthly checks are sent directly to eligible recipients by the U.S. Treasury Department. However, hospital benefits provided under the Medicare program, which was added to the Social Security Act in 1965, are paid out in a different manner. Medicare provides prepaid insurance primarily for the elderly, as well as voluntary medical insurance. Health benefits, paid under the Medicare provisions of the Social Security Act, do not go directly to the beneficiary but rather are paid to the health service provider. This makes it necessary for the federal government *to devise and implement payment or reimbursement methods to determine how much to pay providers for what services.* As Medicare costs continued to climb, cost-control strategies received increased attention. There is now little argument that cost control must be central to any publicly funded health care program if it is to survive. However, the way in which reimbursement methodologies are designed has profound impact on the client. For example, elderly patients may find that physicians in their area will not accept Medicare patients because they consider the accompanying paperwork too demanding and the payment level too low. Reimbursement design issues are discussed in more detail in the following section.

Additionally, any treatment of the *impact of the Medicare reimbursement* on recipients must include discussion of the significant reduction in poverty resulting from the elderly no longer being overwhelmed by hospital costs.[6] For millions of elderly Americans, their only defense against the crippling costs of health care is Medicare. Researchers also point out that during the ten years immediately following enactment of Medicare (1968-1977), mortality rates dropped sharply. In fact, the increase in life expectancy during that ten-year period accounted for almost one-third of the increase that the elderly as a group experienced from 1900 to 1975. Although factors in addition to the advent of Medicare influenced this increase, the access to health care that Medicare made possible—especially for the elderly poor—was an important ingredient in this change.[7]

At the same time, many elderly people believe (incorrectly) that major portions of long-term nursing-home care will also be covered by Medicare, whereas in fact, Medicare pays for approximately 2 percent of those costs.[8] In fact, elderly people in need of long-term nursing home custodial care still must be impoverished before they can be eligible for long-term care assistance under the means-tested health care Medicaid program.

How Social Security programs are financed has profound impact on recipients in a number of other ways. First, financing the program with payroll taxes based on the insurance principle has removed the negative stigma from recipients. Second, social insurance programs, especially Social Security, have done much to reduce poverty for the elderly in the United States. A U.S. Bureau of the Census report (1988) indicated that these programs have done more to reduce poverty and income inequality than either the American tax system or public assistance.[9] Although most people who receive monthly Social Security benefits are middle class, millions would drop below the poverty threshold without the health and income security benefits provided through OASDHI. Additionally, lower-income beneficiaries receive a greater portion of their retirement income from Social Security. The program was designed to pay a greater return in relation to amount contributed for the lower-income worker. Thus the program is even more crucial to the survival of the low-income retiree.

On the other hand, it also must be remembered that the Social Security payroll tax is a substantially regressive tax. That is, people with higher income do not pay a higher proportion of that income for Social Security tax purposes. In fact, the Social Security payroll tax may be the largest tax paid by low-income workers. This fact has special significance for minority workers. Because minority workers typically enter the workforce earlier, work at lower-paying jobs, and generally have a shorter life expectancy, the charge has been made that Social Security discriminates against minorities at risk.[10] As Kingson points out, this charge fails to recognize that minority members are more likely to receive survivors and disability benefits under Social Security. They also receive *proportionately* larger benefits because of the special low-income provisos described above. This discussion is not meant to suggest that Social Security could not be improved. However, it is important that attempts to reform Social Security are made with a clear understanding of the enormous benefits as well as shortcomings of the current program.

Besides OASDHI, there are other public social welfare policies that are pursued through programs financed through a prepaid insurance-type scheme. Unemployment insurance (UI) is a good example and is, in fact, also established by the federal Social Security Act. UI financing can be understood using the same general set of ideas as those used to analyze OASDHI. Although space does not allow for that analysis here, it is worthwhile to notice that there are as well several important differences. First, unemployment insurance is a *joint* federal–state program financed primarily by unemployment taxes levied by both the state and federal government. The source of the prepaid contribution is primarily the employer, although in some states the employee contributes. Second, *adequacy of the program varies from state to state*, for it is the state that sets the amount and duration of UI benefits. Although states are not required to have UI,[11] all states do because the federal government simply taxes them for the program anyway, even if the states' workers receive no benefits (a sizable inducement, indeed). Third, each state collects the advance payments made by employers and deposits them in the federal UI trust fund, administered by the secretary of the Treasury. The U.S. Congress can lend or give money to the state when the state fund is in danger of depletion. Such crises may result from inflation, recession and economic hard times, or poor advance planning by the state. Fourth, in contrast to OASDHI, employers contributing to the UI program are "experience rated," that is, if an employer has a history of high unemployment among its workers, the mandatory prepaid payments to the UI will be set at a higher level. OASDHI has no such feature; people paying DI withholding tax are not required to pay more if they work in hazardous occupations and are thus more likely to be disabled or in occupations (like construction) where employment is unsteady or seasonal.

The impact on the beneficiary of UI financing via state and federal taxes is complex. In that states set amount and duration levels, the result is inequitable treatment of workers from state to state. Also, legal requirements are placed on the worker as a condition of receiving these public funds. Although UI is a work-related benefit, recipient behavior is regularly monitored to make sure that the beneficiary is applying for work. The benefit received is proportional to the salary earned before the recipient became unemployed. The benefit typically equals about 50 percent of previous earnings up to a statutory maximum.[12]

However, it never is equal to previous earnings and is paid for a limited time period. Thus UI is actually a vehicle only for aiding recently employed persons who have lost jobs through no fault of their own. It can be used to empower workers in the short term in that they can (legitimately) spend some time looking for a job that pays at least what their previous job did without suffering a total loss of support for themselves and their families. It is not a vehicle for dealing with chronic long-term unemployment in a changing job market. In areas experiencing a shrinking job market in their manufacturing sector, people who lose their jobs may find their benefits have run out in six months to a year and before they find a job that pays anything close to previous earnings. Then, when the breadwinner takes one of the more plentiful jobs in a fast-food restaurant or a convenience store, the family's standard of living may drop dramatically; often no health benefits are provided.

Other social welfare programs that the ordinary citizen may fail to recognize as social welfare transfers are financed through the insurance principle and prepayment. These include federal flood insurance and crop insurance for farmers, for which prepayment is required. Such programs are experience rated and subsidized by the U.S. Treasury general fund.

VOLUNTARY CONTRIBUTIONS

Historically, private voluntary financing has been the predominant way of funding social welfare benefits and services. However, public financing now overshadows voluntary financing to such an extent that despite continuing assertions about the potential of the voluntary sector to assume more of the social welfare burden, there is little real expectation that the private voluntary sector will ever again play a dominant role in social welfare. However, voluntary financing continues to be the source of funding for many important new *initiatives* that advance the cause of social justice and are used as prototypes for some of our most successful public programs. For example, voluntary financing was crucial for the civil rights movement. Although help in the form of legal assistance, moral support, and use of the U.S. National Guard was eventually forthcoming from the federal government, money to fund the early civil rights movement came in the form of voluntary contributions. Additionally, some of the early work on which Head Start was based was financed by the Ford Foundation.[13] These are examples of controversial and experimental initiatives that resulted in vital contributions to the social welfare effort in the United States. Voluntary contributions are crucial because it seems unlikely that controversial, experimental, and political initiatives such as those cited will receive significant public funds during their formative stages. Indeed, voluntary contributions may be the *only* way of ensuring financing for such social welfare efforts.

A few examples of publicly financed controversial client advocacy programs come to mind, but they seem to have shared a common fate of lost funding and obliteration. One such example is Mobilization for Youth (MFY) (an early effort that supplied some of the important program models used in the old War on

Poverty programs); the Community Action Programs (CAPs) of the War on Poverty, and Model Cities. In retrospect, Model Cities was especially political and controversial in that *it totally bypassed the states* and put money into the hands of powerful political figures in cities. That meant that state-level political figures (i.e., the governors and legislative leaders) could not control and direct funds in ways that could serve as political rewards and punishments. State political administrations soon successfully lobbied Congress to change the process.

Legal aid is a well-known example where this generalization about inability of publicly funded and highly political social programs to survive opposition may not apply. Federally funded legal aid programs have provided legal counsel for the poor since the 1960s and have resulted not only in the relief of personal legal difficulties but also in federal court decisions that have shaped crucial social policy at national and state levels. For example, legal aid attorneys halted the attempt of Reagan administration appointees to systematically disentitle the chronically mentally ill to Social Security disability insurance benefits. Legal aid attorneys also routinely draw political fire because they represent the poor in landlord-tenant disputes. Even so, federal funding, although reduced, still supports legal aid; only congressional action and the energetic efforts of the American Bar Association (ABA) have ensured its continuance.

Legal aid operations have survived despite the need of their staff to take strong and unpopular stands in representing poor people in court, because legal aid also serves an important and current agenda of the ABA. Strict U.S. Supreme Court decisions require that all citizens charged with serious offenses be represented by legal counsel, which would *not* be forthcoming without legal aid services in local communities unless local lawyers gave substantial services free of charge. Even with legal aid in place the need is sufficient (given the yearly reductions in the legal aid budget) such that some state legislatures have imposed a mandatory fee (fine?) on those attorneys who do not volunteer legal representation for indigent clients. The success of legal aid indicates the general principle that public agencies that politicize their mission and operations cannot long survive, *except* where a controversial program can capture the financial self-interest of a powerful political constituency like the ABA—an example of "the exception that proves the rule."

Many current civil rights efforts designed to secure basic rights for women, for the disabled, and for gays and lesbians are financed with voluntary contributions. Some current welfare services that are privately financed are rape counseling centers, black adoption programs, shelters for battered women, and the growing numbers of privately financed emergency food storehouses and soup kitchens.

Voluntary financing has *at least three kinds of sources*: (1) individuals, (2) foundations and trusts, and (3) corporations. Differences in their tax status shape the quantity, locality, target, and duration of their contributions. Individuals target much of their social welfare contribution dollars toward highly visible and locally represented efforts like the American Red Cross, the United Way, and health-related programs like the American Cancer Society or the American Diabetes Association. Although corporate social welfare dollars are vital to these efforts, corporate giving in large volume is also directed toward educational research and medical institutions. Where corporations are closely held (a few people own most of the stock), their social welfare contributions may be channeled through their own trusts and foundations (for example the Ford Foundation).

Any discussion of the source of voluntary giving would be incomplete if the voluntary giving of family members (primarily women) were overlooked. Still the major source of help for people in need, family volunteer efforts have some important implications. On the one hand, these efforts go unrecognized by public policymakers because women do not receive Social Security credits or other benefits in return for providing major portions of the care needed for the nation's young, elderly, and disabled. This oversight can mean that these care givers have no disability or survivors' benefits and will face old age with inadequate retirement benefits. On the other hand, policymakers are often meticulous in their efforts to ensure that public financing not be used in such a way that family care giving would be reduced. Indeed, the increased emphasis on keeping people at home and in the community who were once cared for in public institutions, might be a way of shifting even more of the cost of care giving back on women. Certainly this will be the result if adequate public financing of home-based and community-based services does not accompany the closing of state institutions and the push to keep people in their home community.

Judgment of *adequacy of voluntary funding* depends on what functions our society calls on the voluntary sector to support. Conservative politicians can be counted on to call for a return to the traditions of "volunteerism" and voluntary contributions as a way to fill the gap caused by social welfare retrenchment. The reality these days is that many of the voluntary agencies depend heavily on publicly funded contracts. For example, Lutheran and Catholic social services, as well as many other religious-affiliated service agencies, receive Medicaid funds to provide residential services to mentally retarded people. When public funding is cut back, many voluntary agencies lose funding. Therefore, they are hardly in a position to fill a gap and in fact may have to lay off workers and discontinue services.

If government funding is curtailed, the corporate sector will be asked to provide more needed revenues for services. Indeed, corporate giving currently accounts for about 22 percent of the contributions to United Way nationwide.[14] Also, corporations fund a variety of model programs, efforts designed to help inner-city youth stay in school, provide for children of cocaine-addicted mothers, and reduce teen pregnancy. However, corporations make donations from discretionary funds, and as the economy improves, discretionary funds increase. As Karger has pointed out, when there is a recession, corporate executives are not in a position to commit to social services funds that the corporation may need later to weather the economic downturn.[15] Yet, it is during times of economic downturn that significant increases in need for social services can be expected.

When considering *year-to-year continuity of private voluntary contributions*, the goodwill, altruism, and tax benefits generated are important factors.

Dependence on the goodwill and altruism of private financial benefactors has resulted in interesting variability in the kinds of programs that have received continuing support. On the one hand (as mentioned earlier), many privately financed programs are rather conservative—the American Red Cross, the Girl Scouts, and the YWCA are examples that come immediately to mind. In contrast, radical social programs and social policies were pursued by Saul Alinsky's back-of-the-yards community organization, which was privately funded. History also bears out this variation. For example, the Tolstoy-inspired communities and the Robert Owens New Harmony, Indiana, experiments in radical utopias were privately financed in the 1800s. They stand in contrast to more conservative private efforts of the same era that were intended to solve social problems—such as the charity societies that attempted to alleviate unemployment and poverty with a combination of advice and moral exhortation.

Another factor that influences voluntary giving is the tax benefit available to donors—the result being that the benefits and services supported by these private donations are being indirectly funded in part by uncollected tax dollars. Congress regulates who can receive these tax benefits and under what conditions. For example, requirements for tax-exempt status for charitable foundations or trusts were tightened by the Tax Reform Act of 1969, which included the following requirements for charitable trusts and foundations: (1) They must expend at least 5 percent of their total assets each year. (2) Foundations must pay a 4 percent excise tax on their assets. (3) Their activities and assets must be made public. The logic of this law is that the tax exemption of a charitable foundation or trust is based on whether that foundation serves the public interest. Therefore, its operations and assets should be a matter of public record. A number of trusts and foundations have been motivated to expend money when their tax exemption was threatened by noncompliance with this law.

The Tax Reform Act of 1986 required that individuals itemize their income tax return if they wanted to claim contributions to charitable causes as deductions. Because middle-class contributors provide much of the revenue for the voluntary sector and because middle-class workers are less likely than upper-income groups to itemize their returns, this also reduces incentives for voluntary giving. The *distributional effects of private voluntary financing* are insignificant here because the money goes to such a large and diverse number of beneficiaries.

The costs accrued (profit made?) *between the point of collection of contributions and the point of provision of services* merits consideration. There is recurring controversy about the cost of collecting voluntary contributions and returning them to service recipients when the exorbitant administrative costs of fund-raising of some voluntary agencies come to light. It is incumbent on human service professionals to look carefully at these costs, to judge their appropriateness, and to expose them if they are excessive.

Because many people turn first to the voluntary sector—especially their churches—in time of need, *the impact of voluntary financing* on the person in need may be enormous. Many times the restrictions on receiving help are much less stringent than legally mandated and often free of stigmatizing eligibility rules that may be attached to publicly funded programs. These voluntarily financed services may be accessed at a time when individuals have not already depleted most of their personal resources. Volunteer services like home repair services, shopping, and transportation for the elderly may make it possible for the individual to maintain independence. They are not offered as a last resort but rather form part of the ongoing community support that undergirds us all and helps us to maintain what we mistakenly term "independent" lives.

GENERAL REVENUE APPROPRIATIONS

In terms of *funding sources*, many social welfare benefits and services are funded by general welfare appropriations made from the public treasury. That is, money from taxes, property, sales, and income are put in the public treasury, which Congress or state legislatures use for the purpose of administering social welfare programs. Local jurisdictions (counties and cities) may also levy taxes and provide services. General revenue appropriations fund a wide range of social programs at various levels of government: AFDC, Medicaid, food stamps, U.S. Public Health Service programs to control disease, home care programs for the elderly, and education and school nutrition programs.

The Supplemental Security Income (SSI) program is an example of a program financed entirely with federal general revenue appropriations. SSI is a means-tested program intended to provide a minimum safety-net cash benefit for aged, blind, and disabled persons and to supplement the benefits of other public programs for low-income persons. Each year Congress must decide how much benefit to pay and what services to give, calculate the cost, and then appropriate sufficient funds from the general treasury.

The Social Security Act was amended in 1972 to include the (SSI). Besides SSI and the social insurance programs previously discussed—UI and OASDHI including Medicare—the Social Security Act as amended now includes federal and state public assistance to poor families with dependent children under AFDC, and federal and state assistance in paying medical costs (Medicaid) for some categories of the poor. Clearly, various methods of financing have been devised for funding different components of the Social Security Act. Both AFDC and Medicaid require "matching funds," which are contributed from federal, state, and in some cases local general revenue.

Matching fund programs specify the percentage of contribution for the services for each level of government involved as a condition of receiving such financing. The immediate source of funds for these programs comes from both federal and state general revenue appropriations, which in turn come in large part from taxes paid by individuals. Sometimes county and city public funds are also part of the funding mix. AFDC is a good example of a matching fund program that relies on both federal and state general revenue appropriations for its immediate source of funds. The federal government is obligated to match the dollars each state appropriates for AFDC, subject to certain limitations, with additional federal dollars appropriated from the general treasury. The percentage of the costs covered by the federal match is based on the state's per-capita income and varies from state to state.[17] AFDC was established as part of the Social Security Act in 1935. However, in contrast to OASDHI (discussed earlier in the chapter), AFDC is a means-tested program paid for out of general revenue appropriations.

Adequacy of AFDC also varies from state to state. States are allowed to determine their own need level. In 1991 only five states provided AFDC benefits for a one-parent family of three persons equal to even 75 percent of the poverty threshold; thirty-four states provided benefits at less than 50 percent of the poverty threshold. Even when the food stamp benefit and AFDC benefit are combined, less than one-half of the states provide benefits equal to 75 percent of the poverty threshold.[18] AFDC, which primarily benefits poor children, is much less adequately funded than SSI, the means-tested federal program for aged, blind, and disabled recipients. SSI payments for an individual are at 74 percent of the poverty line for an elderly individual. In contrast, the median state AFDC benefit amounts to approximately 42 percent of the poverty level for a family of three. Because cost-of-living increases are not given often—in fact some states have reduced benefit levels—the value of the benefit is actually decreasing in many states.

The federal government took most of the responsibility from the states for financing the major means-tested income maintenance program that serves "worthy" poor people—the aged, blind, and disabled. However, AFDC continues to depend in part on state funds (about 25 percent in general), and this means there will be wide variation from state to state in willingness to care for families and in financial resources available to do so. When considering *issues of continuity and funding stability,* reliance on state funding means that when a state is in the midst of a deep recession and families are even more desperate, AFDC benefit levels may be cut because of declining state revenues. New state and federal appropriations are made annually for AFDC.

The *distributional effect of AFDC* results in increased income for poor families. However, the general public seems to believe that this distributional effect is far greater than it actually is. The bulk of spending on social welfare is often thought to be going to support of AFDC families. This is certainly not the case. In fact, AFDC and child support enforcement efforts together account for only 1 percent of federal spending.[19] The *impact of AFDC funding* on the client has already been discussed in relation to issues of equity and adequacy given the variation in benefit level from state to state and the overall inadequacy of the benefit.

It is also important to know other ways in which the tax system can be used to finance benefits and services. For example, earmarked taxes (mentioned earlier) are a special kind of tax that states and local jurisdictions may use to finance some types of social welfare programs. Local county/city mill levies on either property or sales to support local services for mental health or the developmentally disabled are good examples of earmarked tax. These levies can be locally mandated and controlled. Although typically the levy is small, it can still allocate important portions of the budget for local personal social service programs.

Some of the earliest earmarked taxes for social welfare programs were included in public health mill levies that most communities have had for years. Some public health programs, mental health services, and services for the developmentally disabled or the aged may be funded in this way.

Some benefits are financed out of taxes purposely not collected, or taxes refunded. For example, the Earned Income Tax Credit (EITC), enacted in 1975, provides tax credits for low-income families with children.[20] The EITC is remarkable in that this type of financing is typically reserved for benefits for the *non*poor. Use of the tax system to create incentives for businesses and home ownership has long been an accepted means of providing benefits to the middle class and the wealthy. Use of tax expenditures—that is, uncollected taxes, allows provision of benefits without stigma or marked expansion of bureaucracy. Although the maximum amount currently available under the EITC is not substantial, the concept on which it is based holds considerable promise for helping the working poor with children.

Block Grants

The federal government also allocates money to the states for social welfare services by providing *block grants*. These grants come with varying restrictions on how, when, and for what purposes they can be spent. The immediate *source of funds for block grants* are taxes collected at the federal level and transferred from the general treasury to the states and thus to the local taxpayers from which they originally came.

Federal grants to states requiring the expenditure of public monies on particular problems or in regard to particular groups of citizens have a long heritage in this country. The Morrill Act used monies generated by the sale of lands in the West during the westward expansion of the past century to establish all of what are called land-grant colleges and universities, schools generally devoted to agriculture and engineering. Kansas State University, Iowa State University, and Texas A&M University were all established as colleges of agriculture and mechanics.

Of special interest to social workers and others in the human service professions is the social services block grant, the intent of which is to finance personal social services. The enabling legislation for the social services block grant is Title XX of the Social Security Act, as amended in 1981. It is important to understand that Title XX is one of a long series of aid-to-states programs by which the federal government provided incentives to states to expand their personal social service systems. Through the 1930s and for many years afterward, responsibility for the personal social services belonged to states, local government, and private charitable agencies. In 1956 the federal government began providing a 50–50 matching fund to states that wanted more elaborate social services. In 1962, the federal share of the match was increased to 75 percent, and rehabilitation was added as a basic goal for social services.

Rehabilitation was a legitimate social service program objective. However, there was considerable confusion about what was meant by "rehabilitation."

Federal expenditures for social services rose in large increments during the next decade. By 1967 it was apparent that "rehabilitation" using case-centered or family-centered approaches to ameliorate poverty was not having the desired effect. Congress was disenchanted with the whole approach and began emphasizing on-the-job training programs for welfare clients, various work incentive schemes, and work-support programs like day care for working mothers. Results after the change in emphasis were similarly disappointing. In 1975 Congress enacted Title XX of the Social Security Act. Under original Title XX legislation, the general revenue funds of the federal government were provided to the states, on a 75–25 matching basis, for the purpose of providing programs of personal social services. A $2.5 billion cap on federal social service expenditures was already in place, and that ceiling was continued for Title XX.[21]

When Reagan assumed the presidency in 1981, he was determined to reverse the trend toward increased federal responsibility for social welfare by shifting these responsibilities back to state government and the private sector. Increased use of the block grant concept was part of the New Federalism strategy. Block grants now provide federal funds to state or local governments for general functions such as welfare, health, mental health, education, law enforcement, and community development. The money must be spent for the general function specified, but beyond that states and communities decide how to use the funds. The Reagan administration preferred block grants to *categorical grants,* which require federal review and approval of specific applications for defined activities by state and local government.

In 1981, the Reagan administration convinced Congress to radically amend Title XX. State matching requirements were eliminated, but federal contributions to social services decreased. Examination of Title XX funding from 1980 to 1990 provides dramatic evidence of the decline in funding. During that period Title XX funding declined in real terms by 38 percent.[22] Total federal government expenditures are currently capped at $2.8 billion, with states being free to use the money as they wish. The services most frequently provided are day care for children of welfare mothers and in-home services for the frail elderly.[23] Persons mentally ill or mentally retarded, drug and alcohol abusers, and abused children are examples of other groups who, depending on state decisions, may receive services provided in part with funds from the social service block grant. States choose what social services they will offer, to whom they will be offered, and the method of service delivery. Federal Title XX funds are allocated on the basis of state population.[24]

Reagan also collapsed funding for mental health services, drug abuse, and alcohol abuse into the Alcohol, Drug Abuse and Mental Health block grants, details of which will be discussed in Chapter 10. The amount of money available to states to provide these services was also reduced. As a result, *adequacy of funding* for such services became severely diminished, especially in states with few resources with which to augment the federal funds. *Year-to-year continuity for* these block grants depends on annual reappropriations from Congress. Professionals who have strong altruistic and economic interests in more social service programs and employment lobby hard for these appropriations.

Distributional effects of these income transfers are not significant because funds are so small relative to the number of persons receiving direct benefits.

When considering the *impact on clients* of this method of financing, an additional factor not previously covered in the discussion of impact of other financing methods merits attention. Citizens who are concerned with the aged, with the developmentally disabled, with the poor, and with particular ethnic groups compete heavily for Title XX funds, as well as for other block grant funds. The principle with which this book began was that *where resources are finite, a dollar spent on one group will be a dollar withheld from other groups.* Of course it is possible that state public competition may be more "democratic," for at least public opinion will be invoked, and public debate will occur about the relative seriousness of social problems as well as the relative merits of specific programs. It is true that final decisions about *which* social problems are of primary importance must be value oriented, and it may be that such values can best be gauged by local public opinion and debate. However, attempts to depart from traditional program approaches to social problems may receive more opposition on a local level. The social welfare effort could lose some of its (scarce) ability to be creative and innovative, and groups that fail to attract powerful advocates or constituencies, or whose client/consumers are considered "unworthy," may not receive anything approaching a fair share of the available resources.

We do know that policies and programs became more innovative in the years when responsibility for planning and administration was moving away from the local to the federal level than had previously been the case. For years, state-level service advocates had struggled to create "mothers' pensions" (an early AFDC-type program) and unemployment insurance programs. One reason that these social problems were taken up by the federal government is that the states absolutely failed in their efforts. That bit of history seems to be either forgotten or ignored by those currently charmed with the push to return administrative and financial responsibility for human services to the states. Despite many years of effort by hard-headed, reform-minded citizens, only New York State ever developed an unemployment insurance system on its own initiative. The various state income maintenance schemes, such as they were, did not remain solvent for long during the Great Depression of the 1930s. Prior to the 1930s, only five states were operating old age assistance programs, and although half the states had mothers' pensions, the benefits were totally inadequate.[25]

Reimbursement Mechanisms

In addition to assuming increased responsibility for resource allocation, state welfare administrators and workers are now being asked to assume new responsibilities for the purchase of service from private providers. In the past twenty years, there has been a dramatic shift from public provision of needed service to increased reliance on the private sector for service provision. These services are purchased with public monies and states must construct provider reimbursement or payment methodologies to determine the rates to be paid.

Method of reimbursement has profound effect on how services are provided. For example, there was unprecedented growth in child foster care when the federal government began reimbursing states for foster care costs at a rate of 100 percent of total costs.[26] Simultaneously, there was no fiscal incentive to states to keep and support children in their own parental homes. This reimbursement pattern drove services inevitably toward foster care placement.

The importance of careful reimbursement design is magnified by changes taking place in the public sector. Direct service provision in public facilities such as large state institutions is decreasing for a variety of client groups including those with mental illness and developmental disability. As these large state facilities downsize or close, private for-profit and nonprofit providers have increasingly been called on to provide community services. With the growth of privatization, human service professionals in the public sector who are attempting to design effective community service strategies increasingly find these programs are dependent on contracts with private providers. At the same time, human service professionals in the private sector may find themselves frustrated by reimbursement system restrictions that do not provide payment for those services they feel would be most effective. The challenge is to design reimbursement systems that support the policy and program goals of a service system.

However, professionals often see the results of poorly designed reimbursement systems. For example, case managers working to place a severely disabled and mentally retarded person in the community may find that no provider will accept this client because the provider is not reimbursed more for the additional services required for this client compared to more independent clients. Clients' lives are affected by these reimbursement design decisions.

Although it is tempting for human service professionals—especially those with number phobia—to think that reimbursement issues are beyond their scope, this is simply not the case. First of all, human service professionals are the "listening posts"; they must make sure that information on client impact gets back to those who design the reimbursement systems. Thus, practitioners can help to empower clients and their families to tell their stories firsthand by guiding them to the policymakers. Practitioners can also advocate in behalf of their clients.

Second, human service professionals must understand the incentives erected by reimbursement systems so that they can attempt to reduce client harm when such incentives are destructive and have confidence in them when they are not. For example, when provider reimbursement for treatment of child abuse is contingent on the child remaining in foster care, the human service professional may have to work harder to facilitate timely return of the child to the parental home. On the other hand, if a portion of the reimbursement is linked to return of the child to the parental home, it will be an incentive for timely return. Note that if the incentive is very strong, the practitioner will need to take care that children are not returned prematurely.

Third, human service professionals are often designed into the reimbursement system as gatekeepers. Public policymakers need reimbursement system designs that allow them to predict future costs of service provision and thus exert some control on these costs so that services can be paid for with available tax dollars. In order to do this, service access must be limited, and amounts of reimbursement must be controlled. By exercising professional judgment in individual cases, the case manager is in a key position to make such decisions. Case managers may be called on to determine who is eligible for a given program, what services may be reimbursed for a specific client, and even what amount will be reimbursed. Even though case managers have written rules or criteria to be followed in making their decisions, typically there is room for professional discretion. When human service professionals find themselves in a pivotal role in a reimbursement system they do not understand, it is difficult to make decisions that both safeguard consumers' rights and make most effective use of scarce tax dollars.

Two concepts basic to understanding reimbursement systems are unit of service to be paid for and amount to be paid. *Units of service* to be paid for include per day (or per diem), per treatment episode, per head (capitation), total budget, or per outcome. Table 9–1 illustrates some examples of positive and negative incentives created for providers based on choice of units of service to be reimbursed.

If unit of service paid is per diem as long as the condition persists, the provider may be rewarded for the client's lack of improvement. Also, because a variety of services are "bundled" into the per-diem payment, clients may be getting services they do not need. For example, a developmentally disabled client who simply needs a place to stay and some minimal supervision may be receiving unwanted additional hours of community skills training in the evening because it is part of the service package bought by the per diem paid to the group home. On the other hand, a per diem is a simple and unambiguous unit of service.

Payment on a per-service basis requires first that some method of determining eligibility and price for each and every reimbursable service be determined. Here there is an obvious incentive for the provider to provide the most profitable service as well as a large number of services, even if they are ineffective.

Payment for outcomes can promote achievement of desired outcomes, but to achieve this effect outcomes must be priced and someone must decide how much to pay for what outcome given a specific client's base level. If client's base level of functioning is not considered, there is a strong incentive for the provider to concentrate efforts on clients who show the most potential for achieving the desired outcomes, and to not admit or to abandon those clients who have the least potential for achieving the desired outcome. These examples are intended to help point out how unit-of-service decisions influence clients. Although space does not allow for elaboration of incentives for each possible unit of service, it is important that human service workers consider these issues in relation to the service they provide. Workers need to think through very carefully the incentives being created by unit-of-service options so they can help protect their own practice and, most important, their clients from perverse incentives.

The method used to arrive at service cost also has powerful implications for clients. Methods may include negotiation, bidding, grants, reimbursement based on last year's allowable costs plus inflation (prospective payment system), or payment for costs incurred (retrospective payment system). Negotiation involves the provider and the funding agency mutually agreeing on rates to be paid for service, a system that provides flexibility but also may result in widely differing rates for different providers serving similar clients. Bidding usually involves submission of a proposal that includes specifications of service(s) to be provided and cost of service. Competition between providers may be increased by this method. However, awards may hinge more on the providers' proposal writing skills than on the quality of service provided or the needs of the clients in their catchment (service) area.

Table 9–1   Examples of Reimbursement Incentives.

Unit to be reimbursed	Valence of the incentive (from point of view of the provider)*	Description of the incentive
1. Reimbursement on a per-day basis as long as condition persists	+ Incentive	Provider is not pressured to discharge prematurely
	− Incentive	Late or no discharge is rewarded; client improvement may result in lost revenue for provider
2. Reimbursement for a specific service	+ Incentive	Provider is rewarded for giving most profit-generating services irrespective of effectiveness
	− Incentive	Public funding agency may mandate use of cheaper or less-profitable services irrespective of effectiveness
3. Reimbursement on the basis of outcome	+ Incentive	Promotes achievement of desired outcomes rather than limiting focus to structure and process
	− Incentive	Where treatment process is crucial, this type of reimbursement may be negative because it stresses (pays for) outcomes, not process; thus, it may reward provider for shortcutting the care process essential to client well-being
4. Reimbursement on basis of diagnosis	+ Incentive	More reimbursement is provided for conditions requiring costly services
	− Incentive	Providers may overdiagnose in order to maximize reimbursement
5. Reimbursement on a "per capita" basis	+ Incentive	Predictability of reimbursement
	− Incentive	Underutilization of service is rewarded

* The valence of an incentive has everything to do with some particular ideological point of view—what is preferred as outcome and process.

After initial certification as an authorized provider, service vendors may also be reimbursed on a retrospective basis. That is, the providers submit allowable costs and are reimbursed by the public agency. If designated providers are assured they will be reimbursed retrospectively based on submission of reasonable costs incurred in providing service, they can provide services they feel the client needs without fear of not being reimbursed for their costs, which may include a certain amount of profit. On the other hand, this method may result in uncontrolled, unpredictable (even spiraling) costs for the public funding agency. Therefore, public agencies may adopt prospective systems whereby providers are reimbursed based on last year's costs plus inflation. This results in more predictable costs, but it also makes it difficult for providers to take clients with more severe needs because reimbursement will be based on what they spent last year on clients with less intense needs.

Human service professionals need to question how their services are reimbursed. They need to understand the incentives and disincentives created by the unit of service and the method of payment used for reimbursing their agency. Additionally, if their agency must submit an annual cost report to a public agency as part of the reimbursement process, this document is usually public information from which a great deal can be learned. Examination of the annual cost report can show what percentage of payment goes to direct care of clients, to administration, to property costs, and, sometimes, the percentage of profit.

Having a basic grasp of the reimbursement system may help practitioners understand the decisions of their supervisors. Additionally, without a rudimentary grasp of the reimbursement system, human service professionals cannot make the necessary decisions required to help their clients most effectively. Finally, the human service professional must consider the overall adequacy of the rate being paid for service. When it is obvious that the amount being reimbursed is inadequate, they must lobby their public officials and the private sector for adequate funds.

DIRECT OUT-OF-POCKET PAYMENT BY CONSUMER

Most citizens are familiar with admission or user fees requiring direct, out-of-pocket payment by the consumer. Such fees are charged by public facilities such as state and national parks and municipal swimming pools. Direct out-of-pocket payments are also used to partially finance some social welfare programs. Charges are paid individually by the client and are related to some unit of service delivered. Examples include fees for placing a child in adoption, day care fees, and fees for counseling services offered by public and private social agencies.

State medical hospitals and institutions for the mentally ill or developmentally disabled extract consumer payment for services in ways that other public programs ordinarily cannot. For large bills for clients who may be indigent at the time of service, most states file a lien on the client's estate or property. Payment is then collected upon client's death or upon client's receipt of an inheritance.

State or county welfare departments may offer a variety of services to families who are not poor and charge them based on a sliding scale keyed to family income. For example, disabled elderly people may receive services designed to help them maintain independence even though their incomes exceed poverty thresholds. The use of such a strategy makes it possible for states to offer services to economically vulnerable families and to those who may be endangered by social problems but not yet economically overwhelmed by them.

Obviously, the *source of financing* for *direct-pay programs* is the consumer. The mechanism that provides *continuity of funding* here is the demand for service. If consumer demand is insufficient, funding disappears and the program may be jeopardized or discontinued. Out-of-pocket payments for some services may be deductible from income tax obligations—day care for example. *Mechanisms for holding and transferring funds* are unnecessary in that direct payment is made by the person receiving services. Because out-of-pocket payment for social welfare services typically is small, *distributional effects* are negligible here, except where we consider very expensive services like medical care. It must be noted that the medical care industry receives income transfers from the private-pay patient to the extent that its profitability (which is very high) is disproportional to the actual benefit received by that patient. Patients whose bills are paid by third-party payers may also benefit at the expense of the private payer. Often, public and private third-party payers, such as Medicaid and large insurance companies, limit what they will pay for hospital and long-term care services. However, hospitals and nursing homes typically are free to charge the private-pay patient more to make up for limits imposed by more powerful third-party payers.

Requiring direct payment for service clearly has *impact* on clients. When direct out-of-pocket payment for social services is required, persons who have social problems but little money may not apply for or continue to receive important services. However, policies can be developed that ameliorate this problem. For example, fees can be assessed using professional or administrative discretion so that the amount a client is expected to pay can be based on income. However, if the agency is to continue providing service, some other means of financing must make up the difference between what a client can pay and what it costs to provide the service.

Finally, service overutilization, especially in relation to public medical care, is a widely discussed problem. Belief is widespread that even a small charge operates to deter overutilization of nonaddictive prescription drugs and public dental services. Common wisdom among some psychotherapists is that direct out-of-pocket payment is an important test of motivation so that clients use the therapists' time more efficiently. The logic behind this stance is that most people are not inclined to waste their own money. (I am not aware of firm evidence for this popular hypothesis.) It is obvious that such hypotheses cannot be tested in relation to a population of poor people who do not have enough money to exercise a choice about whether to pay a fee.

CORPORATE/EMPLOYMENT-BASED FUNDING OF BENEFITS

The business community in the United States provides benefit packages for a large segment of workers. Public sector employees also receive employment-based benefit packages. These fringe benefits, which may include health care, day care, and employee assistance programs as well as retirement benefits, are often available for employees' dependents as well. Benefits and services made available through the workplace have assumed increased importance in this country. Early in the twentieth century, most employees received only direct wages for time worked.[27] Needs related to old age, poor health, and death were to be met by the employee or through the family. During the 1940s and 1950s, the use of employee benefits to compensate workers in addition to wages gained acceptance. The growth of employee-related benefits continues today as both private and public sector employers experiment with new types of benefits and expand existing ones.

Employers use a variety of benefit funding mechanisms. The traditional method is the group insurance contract where the employer pays premiums to the insurance company in advance. Employees also must contribute for many benefits. The insurance company then has responsibility for administrative expenses related to claims if and when they occur, and for bearing the risk of claims being larger than anticipated. At the other extreme is the self-funded benefit package where the employer assumes responsibility for administering the program, paying all claims, and bearing the risk that claims will exceed expectations. Of course, the company also keeps and earns interest on premiums paid in advance. Very few companies have turned to total self-funding. In fact, many companies use a combination of the two approaches.

When considering the *source of funding* for employment-related benefits, note that there is considerable interplay of function between the public and private sector. Public programs (such as OASDHI) discussed earlier in this chapter with regard to the insurance principle are work-related and financed through payroll taxes collected from employers and employees. Programs such as Workers Compensation are legally mandated but financed by employers that typically purchase Workers Compensation coverage from private profit-making insurance companies. Other benefits such as private health, life, and dental insurance also make use of the insurance principle. These insurance programs, pension plans, and other benefits such as day care centers and wellness programs, can be financed directly by the employers or by both the employee and employers. However, in many instances, certain tax incentives provide these benefits; thus, tax dollars (in the form of tax expenditures, which are taxes deliberately uncollected) can be seen as an indirect source of financing for at least a portion of these benefits.

As Rein and Rainwater point out, this public/private interplay in the financing of social protection results in often-overlooked blurring of responsibility and function.[28] Although this blurring makes it difficult for social service workers to understand how programs are financed, it is crucial that they recognize these variations for the following reasons. First, they must help their clients make sense of their own package of social protection. Often a client in crisis is trying to piece together the resources needed to survive by using work-related and non–work-related benefits that are financed publicly and privately. Unless practitioners are aware of variation in requirements and rights guaranteed under these different systems, they cannot help clients effectively. For example, the beleaguered parents of a severely disabled child may be trying desperately to sort out what is covered under employment health insurance, what publicly financed programs their child may be eligible for, and whether there are private charities that may help. All this must be contended with while they continue working, nurture their children, and find solace for themselves. Human service professionals who understand that help must be accessed through a variety of sources are sorely needed to help such families.

A second important reason for focusing on this blurring of sources of social protection is to help human service workers grasp the variety of possible financing arrangements in extending a social protection, such as health care, to the entire population. For example, employers with a staff that exceeds a certain number could be mandated to provide health care insurance for all employees (just such a law was considered by Congress in 1991). Private insurance companies could be mandated to provide insurance coverage for uninsured people, and public funds could be used to pay portions of the premium on a sliding scale based on individual ability to pay. Of course, in deciding whether to funnel public funds through the insurance companies, the question of *how funds move from point of collection to point of service provision, and at what cost*, becomes crucial. On the other hand, all costs for health care could be shifted from the employer to the public sector. Policymakers must consider costs and benefits of different approaches. However, as mentioned, before choices can be made it is important to grasp the variety of existing financing options.

Adequacy of employment-related benefits is a difficult issue to analyze because benefits vary from company to company based on the status of the worker and whether the worker is full-time or part-time. *Adequacy* of pension plans is an especially troublesome issue. Private pension reserves are currently worth more than $1 trillion.[29] However, plan beneficiaries may lose benefits if they switch jobs or if their companies go bankrupt. Also, pension plans are attractive targets for corporate raiders, and benefits may be terminated and pension plans mismanaged. Obviously, some pension programs are more adequate than others; however, few private pensions provide automatic cost-of-living adjustments (COLAs)—without which the adequacy of a pension can quickly deteriorate. Additionally, private pension plans cover only about one-third of all workers and one-fourth of current workers.[30] Coverage under private pension plans appears to be decreasing despite substantial federal subsidies.

Stability of private pension plans is also of concern. Social workers are all too familiar with the plight of the older worker whose company has shut down or has gone bankrupt and left the worker without the pension expected. A company can elect to develop a "qualified" retirement plan that receives special federal tax benefits in return for being designed in accordance with federal regulations. Tax law and labor law govern pensions. The Employment Retirement Income

Security Act of 1974 (ERISA) established the Pension Benefit Guaranty Corporation (PBGC), which provides termination insurance for qualified defined benefits plans. This insurance, which helps protect participants from losing pension benefits if a plan terminates or an employer goes bankrupt, ensures *continuity of pension benefits*.[31] However, some employers insist that new laws and regulations are so costly that they may have to terminate their plans. As Winifred Bell has pointed out, the problems that beset private pension plans "make the social security system seem like the Rock of Ages." [32]

Additionally, it is important to examine how reimbursement strategies used by private insurance companies paid to provide employee benefits *influence both social worker and clients (impact)*. Examination of the effect of health insurance reimbursement on client diagnosis can yield some insights into these influences. As Kirk and Kutchins point out, reimbursement systems are a major factor in encouraging overdiagnosis.[33] For example, more serious psychiatric diagnoses may be made simply because insurance companies pay for therapy for those conditions whereas they may deny coverage for family problems. This practice may positively affect the social worker's economic well-being and also may provide a way to pay for needed client services. However, the negative consequences can be serious for the client, who may be stigmatized and later mistreated as a result of the misdiagnosis. Additionally, the social worker has behaved unethically. Social workers who are alert to incentives created by reimbursement systems can work to mitigate negative consequences for clients by reducing these incentives when possible and monitoring for misdiagnosis if such incentives cannot be reduced. As the number of social workers in private practice increases, pressure for such misdiagnosis may grow stronger. As pointed out earlier in this chapter, reimbursement based on diagnosis creates strong incentives that merit continuous scrutiny to safeguard clients.

It is also important to note that small-business employees and part-time workers may have minimal benefits packages or none at all (unemployed people obviously do not receive benefits). When this type of financing is used to provide for basic needs such as health care, people who lose their jobs also lose coverage when they are least able to pay for services out of pocket. Although it may *appear* that employee benefits result in redistribution of resources from employer to employee, benefits often are given in place of wage increases because of the attendant tax advantages.

Fringe benefit packages meet many of the health and welfare needs of large numbers of workers and their families. With the advent of employee assistance plans that provide a broad range of personal social services as part of the worker's fringe benefit packages, a greater variety of services are being offered, and human service professionals are becoming increasingly involved in service provision in the corporate sector. Coordinated public and private efforts that build on established private financing approaches may yield strategies that extend basic benefits to all citizens. One example is the inner-city day care center that is funded through a combination of corporate day care subsidies for workers, public day care subsidies for participants in AFDC-related work programs, and corporate-funded day care scholarships for working families who do not fit into either of the aforementioned categories but are unable to pay for day care. Such corporate investments, designed to meet the health and welfare needs of employees and their families as well as those of the community's children, help to produce a competent future workforce.

PUBLIC AND PRIVATE FUNDING: DISTINCTIONS

When attempting to use the tools for analysis presented in this chapter to understand how a specific service is financed, and to consider other possible sources of funds, students often confuse how a service is financed with how it is provided. Figure 9–1 illustrates four basic combinations of public and private financing and service provision.[34]

Examples of case 1, where services are both publicly funded and provided, include county welfare services, juvenile probation services, and services for the indigent in public residential facilities. Although much less common in the social services, an example of case 2, where services are privately financed and publicly provided, might be a financially able parent who pays the full cost for an adult child with mental retardation to live in a public group home and to attend the county-run day activity center. If we step beyond social services and look at the public university, examples of private funds being used to provide public educational services are plentiful.

Examples of case 3, where services are publicly financed and privately provided, are becoming much more commonplace. As pointed out in the discussion of reimbursement methods, public health and welfare agencies increasingly contract with private for-profit and nonprofit agencies to provide residential and therapeutic services. An example of case 4 is a service provided by a private religious organizations and paid for with private contributions, or services of a for-profit agency to private-pay customers.

An additional element that must be remembered when sorting out public and private roles is that private financing of a service can be publicly mandated.

Figure 9-1 Service Finance and Provision.

Provision	Source of funds	
	Public	Private
Public	Case 1 Service publicly financed and provided	Case 2 Service privately financed/publicly provided
Private	Case 3 Service publicly financed/privately provided	Case 4 Service privately financed and provided

Workers Compensation is an excellent example of a program that in some states is privately financed and privately provided; yet its provision is publicly mandated.[35] *Voluntary* and *private* are obviously not synonymous terms.

Once these distinctions are grasped, it is easier to understand how a private or public agency may provide services financed with public and private dollars. As Glennerster pointed out, in reality many agencies are not totally financed by either public or private funds, but rather draw on both sources.[36] Hopefully, heightened awareness of how sources of funds and public and private service provision blend will be the precursor to more creative thinking about integration of forms of financing and service provision to develop comprehensive social protection packages. However, as pointed out at the beginning of this chapter, the way in which a service is financed has a powerful impact on service provision. Different forms of financing are not simply interchangeable ways of funding the same service. The nature of the service will be shaped by the rules, regulations, or payer preferences that accompany the money to finance the service.

SUMMARY

To provide effective service to clients, human service workers need to understand how social welfare benefits and services are financed and how providers are reimbursed. This chapter has provided a framework for understanding basic elements of social welfare financing. Five major types of financing were discussed:

1. Prepayments and other variations on the insurance principle
2. Voluntary contributions
3. General revenue appropriations
4. Direct out-of-pocket payment by consumer
5. Corporate/employment-based funding of benefits

So that the human service worker can judge the merit of a particular type of financing for a specific policy or program, eight basic questions should be considered:

1. What is the immediate source of funds?
2. Are funds adequate to pay for the cost of providing needed service?
3. How is fund security and year-to-year funding continuity ensured?
4. What mechanisms are used to ensure funding stability in the wake of economic and demographic changes?
5. What is the distributional effect of this method of financing?
6. How are funds transferred from point of collection to point of service or benefit provision, and at what cost?
7. What methodology is used to reimburse the service provider?
8. What is the impact of this method of funding and provider reimbursement on the client?

Basic elements of reimbursement were highlighted to heighten awareness of how reimbursement methods shape service provision of current and emerging structures. Practitioners need to understand how choice of unit of service and method of determining amount to be paid create incentives and disincentives for effective service delivery.

Distinctions between public and private funding and service provision were illustrated, along with possibilities for blending public and private financing. Throughout the chapter, the interplay of public mandates, public tax dollars, and other forms of funding were explored.

EXERCISES

1. Determine how services are funded in an agency where you might like to work. Specifically, what are the sources of funds? What reimbursement methodologies are used? Use the eight questions suggested at the beginning of the chapter to consider the advantages and drawbacks of this type of financing for both worker and client.

2. Compare and contrast the ways in which basic services and benefits are financed for the poor and the nonpoor in our society. How does the way we finance our schools and health care contribute to perpetuating poverty?

3. Determine what alternative results you can anticipate when the federal government mandates states to provide a service but does not increase federal funding sufficiently to pay for it. What are the implications for other services the state may already provide?

NOTES

1. B. T. Beam and J. J. McFadden, *Employee Benefits* (Homewood, IL: Irwin, 1988).
2. D. A. Hardcastle and D. E. Chambers, "O.A.S.I.: A Critical Review," *Journal of Social Welfare* (1974) 2(3), pp. 19–26.
3. E. R. Kingson, "Misconceptions Distort Social Security Policy Discussions," *Social Work*, (July 1989), pp. 357–62.
4. A. Munnell, *The Future of Social Security* (Washington, DC: The Brookings Institution, 1977), pp. 130–32.
5. J. Brittain, *The Payroll Tax for Social Security* (Washington, DC: The Brookings Institution, 1972), pp. 60–81.
6. The Villers Foundation, *On the Other Side of Easy Street* (Washington, DC, 1987).
7. Op. cit.
8. Robert Wood Johnson Foundation, *Challenges in Health Care* (Princeton, NJ, 1991).
9. Ibid., Kingson.
10. Op. cit.
11. Ibid., Bean and McFadden.
12. Op. cit.

13. F. Horowitz and L. Paden, The Effectiveness of Environmental Intervention Programs. In B. Caldwell and H. Riciutti, editors, *Child Development and Social Policy* (Chicago: University of Chicago Press, 1973), p. 365.

14. United Way of America, *United Way of America Research Services Campaign Summary Survey* (Alexandria, VA, 1991).

15. H. J. Karger and D. Stoesz, *America Social Welfare Policy: A Structural Approach* (White Plains, NY: Longman, 1990).

16. Social Security Administration, *SSI for the Aged, Blind and Disabled* (Washington, DC, 1982), publication no. 05–11111.

17. U. S. Department of Health and Human Services, Family Support Administration, Office of Family Assistance, (1989). *Characteristics of State Plans for Aid to Families and Dependent Children under Title IV-A of the Social Security Act* (Washington, DC, 1989).

18. Committee on Ways and Means, *Green Book (Overview of Entitlement Programs)* (Washington, DC: U.S. House of Representatives, 1991).

19. Children's Defense Fund, *A Children's Defense Budget, F.Y. 1989* (New York, 1989).

20. R. D. Plotnick, "Directions for Reducing Child Poverty," *Social Work* (1989), pp. 523–30.

21. Ibid., Committee on Ways and Means.

22. Op. cit.

23. U. S. Department of Health and Human Services, Administration for Children and Families, Office of Policy, Planning, and Legislation, *Social Services Block Grants, Summary of Pre-expenditure Reports, Fiscal Year 1990* (Washington, DC, 1991).

24. Ibid., Committee on Ways and Means.

25. R. Nathan, A. D. Manvel, and S. E. Calkins, *Monitoring Revenue Sharing* (Washington, DC: The Brookings Institute, 1977).

26. A. Kadushin, *Child Welfare Services*, 4th ed. (New York: Collier Macmillan, 1988).

27. Ibid., Beam and McFadden.

28. M. Rein and L. Rainwater, editors, *Public/Private Interplay in Social Protection* (New York: M. E. Sharpe, 1986).

29. Ibid., Karger and Stoesz.

30. Op. cit.

31. Ibid., Beam and McFadden.

32. W. Bell, *Contemporary Social Welfare*, 2nd ed. (New York: Macmillan, 1987), p. 187.

33. S. Kirk and H. Kutchins, "Deliberate Misdiagnosis in Mental Health Practice," *Social Service Review* (June 1988), p. 235.

34. For a fuller discussion of these and other contributions of public and private finance and provision, see Glennerster, cited in note 36.

35. Ibid., Beam and McFadden.

36. H. Glennerster, *Paying for Welfare* (New York: Basil Blackwell, 1985).

CHAPTER 10

Analysis of Interactions among Policy Elements

INTRODUCTION

Policy elements, operating characteristics like entitlement rules and financing methods, are not singular and isolated; they are almost always interactive. So far we've looked at operating characteristics one at a time and now we need to consider how they interact in live situations. They interact in sometimes surprising and unforeseen ways: intended or by accident; complex or simple; to others' advantage or to their serious disadvantage. Sometimes the interaction is within a specific program, other times it is within closely related policies and programs. In order to have a convenient way to speak of these interactions, following is a simple classification of five interaction types:

1. Coentitlement: The use of one form of benefit automatically entitles a beneficiary to another.

2. Disentitlement: The use of one benefit automatically makes a beneficiary ineligible for another.

3. Contrary effects: The operation of one policy or program feature cancels out the effect of another feature.

4. Duplication: An intended or unintended receipt of the same benefit form arises from more than one source for the same purpose.

5. Government-level interaction: Benefits or services administered or financed at one level of government affect those at another level of government (federal and state levels, for example).

These classifications are neither mutually exclusive nor exhaustive, but they are believed to account for the main types. A discussion of each, along with a clarifying example, follows.

COENTITLEMENT

In most child welfare programs that offer foster home care services, a child is also eligible to use the sponsoring agencies' resources for medical care or therapy. As a rule, foster care services come as a package even though there might be a separate price, a separate billing, and even a separate staff who administer them. Some social agencies that offer congregate meals for the elderly (nutritious main meals free or at low cost) also offer transportation services that are free or subsidized. Both are examples of coentitlement as an *intentional* policy. Simultaneous availability of two types of benefits is advantageous in that the benefit is more accessible or used more consistently by more people, or it increases the effectiveness of one benefit because of the simultaneous use of the other. Some coentitled benefit packages are very extensive. (Though it is now less extensive, the AFDC program is a good example of that.) Whereas full elaboration cannot be given because, as you may recall, AFDC is state administered and state designed and therefore varies widely state by state, here is a partial list of the benefit types for which AFDC children and their caretakers are most often eligible.

1. The cash benefit based on the number and age of children (in October 1980, that averaged $141–$422 in terms of differences among states).
2. Medical care (under Medicaid) is paid in full upon presentation of a medical card. Coverage includes prescription drugs, appliances, and immunizations.
3. Food stamps are benefits for which AFDC families are automatically entitled in most states (because the income and asset rules for AFDC are so much more stringent than for food stamps).
4. WIC benefits (Women, Infants and Children nutrition program), which supply extra food stamps for food believed especially appropriate for children under age three and for pregnant women. The intention is to ensure proper nutrition for families at the poverty level.
5. Vocational training through the Work Incentive Program (WIN). Note that all mothers of children over age five must either enroll in WIN or register for employment with the state employment service.
6. Supportive services (through Title XX) provided by vendor payments to personal counselors for fragile families, special education, or health services.
7. Family planning services: advice, medical care, birth-control appliances, or birth-control drugs by prescription. Abortion on demand is included in some states.

So that the full impact and complexity of social welfare benefit interactions can be appreciated, Figure 10–1 is presented. It was prepared by Lewis and Morrison in their attempt to understand interactions of the AFDC program with the most obvious of common coentitled benefits: dependent care tax credit, day care expenses, earned income tax credit, Social Security contribution, federal income tax, food stamps, Medicaid, and excess shelter cost allowance (a part of benefit calculations for AFDC). Excepting the cash benefit, these benefits are given sometimes by administrative rules and regulations and sometimes at the administrative or professional discretion of the operating agency. Although coentitlement is automatic from a policy perspective, clients are not always informed of such coentitlement; to obtain the benefit or service they sometimes must ask for it. One way practitioners can serve their clients is to have current and accurate information about these kinds of coentitlements. Other examples of coentitlement abound simply because most social problems require a number of services simultaneously. Most child abuse programs maintain temporary shelter care facilities, and most shelters for battered women maintain counseling and medical services. Traditionally, Workers Compensation has not just a single goal but a whole set: income replacement, medical care, workplace safety, and rehabilitation. It must therefore have a diverse set of coentitlements: cash benefits, medical payments, rehabilitation counseling, prosthetics (artificial limbs and braces for example). A set of multiple goals will almost always imply the presence of coentitlements. Attention should also be called to instances where entitlement to multiple benefits is unintentional. That type of interaction will be referred to here as a "duplication" and will be discussed at some length below.

To illustrate the complexity of the interactions among social welfare program benefits, here is an example of how a relatively "simple" coentitlement works for an AFDC family living in Pennsylvania and consisting of one adult and one child, where the child does not require day care for the parent to work.[1] With less earnings from work this family would have received $3,612 from AFDC, $1,782 from food stamps, and $1,531 from Medicaid for a total disposable income of $6,925 annually.

DISENTITLEMENT

When legislators, program designers, or administrators wish to avoid the added expense of one person receiving duplicate benefits for the same social problem, they will install an entitlement rule that specifically rules out receipt of one benefit while simultaneously receiving another. A disentitlement policy that probably affects more people than any other is the one Congress installed in the DI program. Any person receiving Social Security Disability benefits must report whether he or she also receives Workers Compensation; if so, then the dollar amount of the Workers Compensation benefit must be deducted from the disability benefit. Imagine how a worker totally disabled in a work-related accident could also be covered under DI. Although it may seem unfair to disentitle a worker from a part of the DI benefits on the basis that the injury was work related and the person receives Workers Compensation, a reasonable case can be made for it under the present circumstances of both systems. First, workers do not pay for the full cost of Social Security benefits, and they pay nothing at all for Workers Compensation insurance. Second, the Social Security system is in good shape now but may be under some strain after 2010 due to demographic change (more retirees, less workforce). (Given even a modest or slow economic recovery, Social Security trust funds might be *very well off* by that year!) Third, Social Security DI benefits are not extravagant but they are generally more adequate than Workers Compensation and they continue beyond the eight- to ten-year limitation on Workers Compensation. Those facts suggest that there is a case for prohibiting two such simultaneous payments as long as the worker is getting back in disability payments at least what was paid in, plus interest.

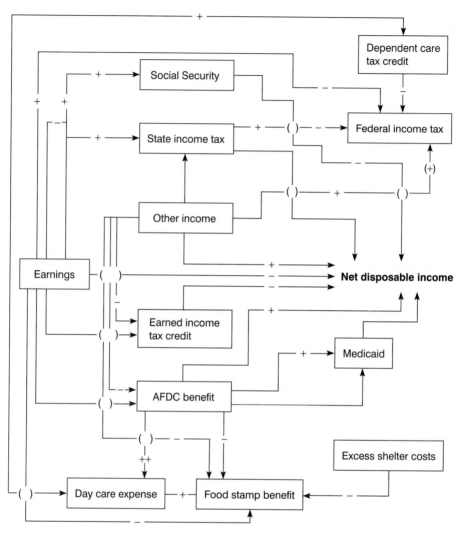

Figure 10–1   Relationships among Social Welfare Tax and Transfer Programs.
Lewis, G., and Morrison, R. *Interactions among Social Welfare Programs*. Discussion paper no. 866–88. Madison, WI: University of Wisconsin, Institute for Research on Poverty, 1988, p. 2. Reprinted by permission.

Furthermore, until the Social Security financing picture becomes clear, permitting the drawing of two payments could result in further system deficits and it is conceivable that some beneficiaries could wind up receiving even less-than-adequate benefits. As it stands now, the dollar amounts saved by this disentitlement rule simply reduce the Social Security withholding tax present workers must pay. If the disentitlement rule were abandoned and Social Security deficits continue, then withholding taxes would have to be raised.

A different disentitlement is embedded in most Workers Compensation legislation. As mentioned, benefits are restricted to eight or ten years. The intent of

Workers Compensation laws is to compensate workers for workplace injuries, thus placing the cost burden for that injury on industry, which is expected to pass it on to the consumer by incorporating the cost into the price of products or services. But, if Workers Compensation benefits cease in eight to ten years and the worker continues to be disabled, he or she will almost certainly apply for and receive Social Security Disability benefits. Consequently, the Social Security system is certain to be saddled with a cost the industry and its consumers should pay but avoid unfairly—an effect that no doubt contradicts the basic historical rationale behind Workers Compensation legislation. It is odd that no research has been done to estimate the overtime fiscal effects of this policy interaction on Social Security trust funds.

Another classic instance of interaction among policy elements, in this case between an entitlement rule and a program goal, produced very negative effects for people in need. Called the *relatives-responsibility* rule, this entitlement criterion required parents and children to exhaust their own resources on behalf of each other before any one could be eligible for public assistance benefits. This historical example (no longer in effect but still discussed as a possible solution to some problems) was nearly universal in the United States up to the mid-1950s. Relatives-responsibility policies, whatever merit they may have had, led to all kinds of mischief, chief among which was that they often disentitled those the program was most directly intended to benefit. Requirements were so strict in many places that unless both parents and their adult children could pass a means test for public assistance, neither family member was eligible. Some elderly parents simply went without, knowing than an application for assistance would be denied because their children were marginally able to give them money; but then their children (and perhaps their grandchildren) would be deprived. Such heroic efforts are no longer heroic when, in fact, the richest society in the world does not need such martyrdom. The relatives-responsibility policy was eliminated as increasingly large proportions of the population were covered by OASI and thus had retirement and old age resources other than their children.

The basic problem with the relatives-responsibility policy as a type of public assistance eligibility rule for programs like Old Age Assistance (OAA; its successor is SSI) was that it made achievement of the program goal (a minimum subsistence standard of living for the elderly) nearly impossible for a large number of people. The reason for this had little or nothing to do with their need for assistance. Instead, it had to do with pride, arrogance, interpersonal conflict, and such, on the part of some elderly parents. For example, the relationship between parents and adult children can become painfully complicated when one is newly dependent on the other for regular money support. These and other reasons inhibit needy elderly people from applying for aid in a relatives-responsibility atmosphere. None of this is to argue social (even moral) financial responsibility between parents and adult children but to point up the irony that financial need in such cases often remains unmet precisely because parents and children care very much for each others' well-being. Another real problem with relatives-responsibility policies vis-à-vis eligibility is linked to the rise of the nuclear rather than the extended family as the economic and social unit of choice in modern Western society. The relatives-responsibility policy arose in the context of multigenerational households that had fewer elderly when the economic and social norm was the extended, not the nuclear, family. Such a norm probably made functional sense in the context of a more rural and agrarian economy. Western economies, now centered on high-tech industry and large-scale social and geographic mobility, make use of the nuclear, not the extended, family as the basic social unit.

One obvious way disentitlement occurs in means-tested social welfare programs is through the effect of earnings. For the one-adult, one-child Pennsylvania family mentioned earlier, annual earnings up to $3,455 are more than offset by reductions in AFDC. *But* these reductions in turn *increase* the amount of food stamps and earned income tax credits (EITC) for which the family is eligible; thus the total disposable income for earnings up to $3,455 would then have risen by only a few dollars—a "wash" for all practical purposes.[2]

CONTRARY EFFECTS

Contrary effects produce both a negative and positive condition in which the effectiveness of at least one benefit characteristic is canceled out or seriously diminished. Recall that the ideal social welfare service-delivery system is characterized by integration, continuity, accessibility, and accountability. This section will consider two kinds of contrary effects. One is concerned with the unforeseen problem that an improvement in one of these ideal characteristics is likely to decrease performance in another ideal characteristic. Think about what happens when an administrator increases organizational integration. As discussed in Chapter 8, the common way to do that is to centralize authority over various program operations, for example, placing a single person in charge of many separate services to young mothers (health, family planning, nutrition) so that all clients are told about all services, and services are scheduled with attention to the need for simultaneous benefits. With one person "running the show," problems would be more easily resolved. Yet, however appealing such integration might be, it can create other problems; using the example above, integration redistributes (centralizes) authority by adding another layer of administration, which can mean a reduction in organizational accountability to consumers. That is, when (not if) the organization makes a mistake, there is one more layer of decision making through which the aggrieved consumer must pass before ultimately reaching a decision maker who might be the only person who can right the wrong. Note that the problem is made serious only if an organization fails to take accountability seriously. The point is that an organizational change like centralization always creates other problems, but those problems are serious or disabling only if the organization is unaware of the paradoxical nature of the enterprise it is tinkering with.

Is it possible for the opposite problem to occur—*for an increase in accountability to decrease accessibility?* Yes. Imagine the reaction of organizational employees to increased public criticism or a recent scandal. The most human reaction, most would agree, is to move more slowly, move with greater certainty, and reduce the occasion for taking risks in decision making and in the conduct of ordinary organizational affairs. That certainly slows the work of the organization and on that account decreases accessibility of benefits and services to those who need them.

A second contrary effect is an increase in the tendency toward organizational "paper trails," that is, copying all decisions made and referring constantly to written policy so that in the event of a demand to account for actions and decisions, the "evidence" of history and policy consistency are ready at hand. Does that mean that public criticism of organizations is unjustified? Not at all. Increased organizational attention to policy clarity and consistency generally has positive effect for client/consumers. Do paper trails signify bad outcomes? Again, no. Paper trails can protect an ethical professional who is legitimately opposing organizational leaders on behalf of needful clients. Life in an organization is not always simple; the best-intended changes can create unforeseen and sometimes negative effects. The prudent practitioner will want to anticipate these effects in order to circumvent (or minimize) them. Aside from these examples of interacting policies that produce contrary effects, there is the more straightforward type where one operating characteristic interferes seriously with another. For example, a particular entitlement rule might create difficulties for achieving a policy goal, or a particular service-delivery feature might create serious problems by inflating the demand for service and thus overwhelming the customary financing method. An easy example of the former (obstacles to goal attainment) are the Medicare entitlement rules for achieving the program goal—best available medical care for the aged. No one seriously disputes the idea that, in general, the frail elderly get the best care in their own home with family. But until 1982 (despite the fact that the cost of nursing-home care was averaging more than $1,600 per month nationally), there was no entitlement rule that could pay even a part of that cost for families to care for their elderly at home. Finally, Congress created an experimental program (called the Medicaid Waiver program) allowing states to use a small part of their Medicaid funds (with a limit on the total amount) for such a purpose.

The view of congress was that the entitlement rule restricting payments to licensed nursing homes was designed to ensure high-quality medical care for the aged; but in some unknown number of instances, it was producing poor care in miserable institutional surroundings even though some relatives would have provided home care if they could have afforded to give up working so they could stay home and care for their elderly loved ones. The waiver program has expanded greatly in most states. States have to show that each person who uses it would have occupied a nursing-home bed were it not for care received by relatives at home. The rub is that now some states have used the program so much that they run into another policy feature that prohibits its expansion. States are allotted Medicaid waiver money on the basis of a proportion of existing nursing-home beds. Some states have used it to the maximum, and because they have (wisely) discouraged the provision of new nursing-home beds there is no way to expand the waiver program to further progress toward a superior form of home care for the aged. This allocation policy of the Medicaid waiver program, once quite reasonable, is now dysfunctional precisely because the program is success-ful in a number of ways.

Other examples of the interaction of entitlement rules and goals comes easily to mind. The well-known problem of "institutionalization" of the mentally ill is just such an example. When mental institutions were humanized there arose what was called an *open-door* policy; it simply meant that the resources and facilities of the hospital were available to former patients on request, always ready to serve them. The intention was laudable and probably served some patients well, but others became addicted to the sheltering arms of a hospitable staff and never learned to withstand the rigors of an unaccustomed and harsh real world. Such institutional dependence is created by the "on-demand" feature of the entitlement rule because a long history of institutionalization and expo-sure to overprotective attitudes of staff members are a requisite accompanying factor. Nonetheless, under those conditions, as long as the entitlement rule is framed that way, it will substantially interfere with the achievement of the pro-gram's goal of personal independence for patients.

One of the recent controversies about the Social Security system centered on the need to resolve an instance of a contrary effect. In this case it concerned the payment of a minimum benefit for the Old Age and Survivors Insurance (OASI) program. The original Social Security Act conceived of the minimum benefit as a temporary measure to provide benefits to retirees, but through no fault of their own, they had not yet worked long enough to build up an adequate benefit. That is always a problem when starting a new public retirement system, but it was not a major problem in the program's early years.[3] Currently, the majority of those receiving minimum benefits are not the workers for whom it was intended but those who have worked for very low wages, albeit over a long peri-od of time! The original framers of the Social Security Act intended to cover only those working full time in the primary workforce. This minimum benefit coverage puts Social Security in the position of making up for the low-wage fea-tures of the labor market. The reason it is a problem now is because the already-beleaguered Social Security trust fund can hardly pay its regular obligations, and continuing the minimum benefit policy will create more obligations not paid for by contributions. This creates a fiscal threat to the trust fund. The example is one of how a particular operating characteristic (like this minimum benefit enti-tlement rule), a good thing in and of itself, creates substantial problems for another operating characteristic—the trust fund's prior contribution method of financing. The contrary effects were resolved in some measure by Congress in the 1983, first session, when a policy was passed prohibiting approval of new minimum benefits (old minimum benefits will still be paid). No doubt, financing minimum benefits out of current contributions was always an idea full of poten-tial mischief; far better to have financed relief of the problem of low wages out of general revenue from which the trust fund could have been reimbursed. Inadequate or low-wage income is a problem of the whole society, not just Social Security contributors. Notice, however, that elimination of minimum ben-

efits in Social Security will take away an important source of income maintenance funds for the young, long-term disabled who presently use it extensively.

In the above example of disentitlement in the AFDC program, there is a serious contrary effect. To grasp the full meaning of program interactions, the welfare transfer elements of the federal tax system must be taken into account. Part
of the intent of the AFDC program is to encourage work and earnings on the
part of recipients, but the disentitlement that occurs via the administrative rule
that decreases the AFDC grant proportional to earnings is a serious work disin-
centive. However, there is a strange spin to the operation of this policy: after
earnings of this AFDC family exceed $3,455 ". . . disposable income rises more
rapidly until at earnings of $6,150 reaching a peak at $8,820, *falling thereafter*
until earnings rise to $7,911 where they resume a rise until food stamp eligibility
is lost at earnings above $8,754".[4]

DUPLICATION

The next interactive effect we will consider is duplication, specifically the *unintended* duplicate receipt of social welfare benefits or services as described in the
earlier discussion on coentitlement. Coentitlement is in fact a form of duplication, but is distinguished by the fact that it is intentional. One of the most widely
publicized instances of duplication is what the popular press has called *double
dipping*, the simultaneous receipt of Social Security retirement benefits *and* federal civil service or armed service retirement benefits. That particular duplication was clearly unintended by Congress in the construction of any of the three
federal retirement systems. Few, if any, anticipated early retirements from the
civil or armed services such that a person could work for the ten years required
to be entitled to Social Security. The result, of course, is a windfall for armed
forces and civil service retirees and one with which the financing methods were
not prepared to cope. In 1982 Congress passed legislation that prevents this
kind of duplication by deducting a large part of the civil service or military pension from the Social Security benefit. In the mid-1980s Congress folded these
retirement benefit systems into the Social Security system, a more general policy
solution to the whole problem.

Notice that the most immediate reason why unintended duplication occurred
in the above example is because the entitlement rules overlap in ways that were
not anticipated—most unintended duplication occurs in that way. Such duplication occurs not only among programs that deliver material benefits but actually
more frequently among programs that deliver social services. One of the most
striking studies of social services delivery in the 1960s was reported as what was
generally known as the "St. Paul Study." Among its many findings was the fact
that 10 percent of the midwestern metropolitan area study population received
95 percent of the social services. Of relevance here are the conclusions about the
extensive duplication of services, even within this relatively small proportion of
the population. Not only were the services strongly concentrated, they were
unintentionally double-dosed. That situation was not unique to the 1960s or to

that particular location. A brief glance at the usual organization of services in most metropolitan areas today would produce striking examples.

How many "counselors" does a child have who is adjudicated by almost any local juvenile court? First, there is the juvenile officer who nearly without exception is officially charged with advising and supervising the child. Then there is very likely to be the school counselor who also has official responsibility for counseling activities, albeit in relation to the child's life at school. Note, however, the few school counselors who would tell you that they only counsel about school problems. It is entirely likely that the same child will have a counselor at a local mental health clinic, and if the child's family receives welfare benefits (AFDC perhaps), there will be a social worker from the welfare department who has counseling duties. Nor is this necessarily the end of the list. Think of the family minister and the group leader of the local boy scouts or girl scouts who may (rightly enough) feel called on to serve this child in a counseling function. This catalogue of horrible examples is not intended to imply that none of the counselors has a legitimate role, only that such duplication is uncoordinated, unnecessarily expensive (at the least) or destructive for the child (at the worst). Any of the well-formed entitlement rules that brought counseling services to this child potentially can be replicated by its interaction with others.

GOVERNMENT-LEVEL INTERACTION

Finally, Lewis and Morrison note "informal evidence" that by raising benefits less than the rate of inflation, states could shift some of the burden of their AFDC costs to the federal government. The reason for that is that AFDC benefit increases at exactly the cost of inflation would result in reduced food stamp benefits. In that the federal government pays all food stamp costs but only part of AFDC costs, letting AFDC benefits rise less than the rate of inflation shifts some of the burden from the state onto the federal Food Stamp program.[5]

SUMMARY

Chapter 10 presented several important types of intended and unintended interactions among policy operating characteristics and between closely related but separately administered policies and programs. The practical analyst should be alert to the presence of the consequences of at least five types of policy interactions:

1. Coentitlement
2. Disentitlement
3. Contrary effects
4. Unintentional duplication
5. Government-level interaction

Interactions between operating characteristics of social policy and programs can only be evaluated against their contribution or their detraction from the ability of the program or policy to contribute to the solution of the social problem of concern. In contrast to other operating characteristics, note that there is no inherently negative policy interaction; interactions are "good" or "bad" only insofar as they prevent some other operating characteristic from reaching its own ideal state.

NOTES

1. G. Lewis and R. Morrison, Interactions among Social Welfare Programs (Madison, WI: University of Wisconsin, Institute for Research on Poverty, 1988). Discussion Paper DP #866–88, p. 5.
2. Op. cit.
3. E. Burns, *The American Social Security System* (Boston: Houghton-Mifflin, 1949), p. 95.
4. Ibid., Lewis and Morrison.
5. Op. cit., p. 7.

PART THREE

Analysis of Social Policies and Social Programs Using the Basic Concepts and Evaluation Criteria: An Example

That's not a regular rule, you invented it just now," said Alice. "Yes, and that is the oldest rule in the book," said the King.

Lewis Carroll, *Alice in Wonderland*

INTRODUCTION

This final section of the book presents a series of demonstrations on how the concepts discussed in Parts one and two can be used in analyzing social policies and social programs. Note that this same style of analysis and way of proceeding can also be used to design a new social policy or program. That will not be done here because, for most social workers or human service practitioners, the main problem is to understand the imperfect, day-to-day world of existing policies and programs. Included in the example will be some suggestions for policy or program (or legislative) changes that are implied by the analysis. Adventurous practical analysts may want to try their hand at using the results of a policy analysis to redesign a social policy or create a new program. Free rein can be given to the most utopian impulse; sometimes it is just those idealistic conceptions that generate the best new ideas.

To demonstrate that this method has widespread usefulness, the example in this chapter will deal with a social problem (and its associated policies and programs) that is familiar to social work and human service practitioners: CMI—chronic mental illness, those referred to as the chronically mentally ill when reference is made to sufferers.

Remember that in Chapter 1 we concluded that the analysis of a social policy system cannot intelligently proceed without a clear understanding of the social problem that policies and program operations are intended to solve. Therefore, the demonstration analysis will begin with a serious study of the social problem

257

viewpoints that were important in shaping the final legislation and program designs. These viewpoints are outlined below.

1. Analyzing Policy and Program Context of Chronic Mental Illness
   a. The Social Problem Context
      —Identifying the point of view of the program or policy with respect to the social problem with which it intends to deal (problem definition, ideology, causation, etc.)
   b. The Historical Context of U.S. Public Policy
      —Searching out the relevant program and policy history, including relevant aspects of the social history of the time (key actors, key events, etc.)
   c. The Judicial Context
      —Searching out the case law which frames the social problem issues and constrains or frees program operations (judicial decisions of U.S. Supreme Court, federal appeals courts, etc.)
2. Analyzing Social Policy and Social Program Systems for the Chronically Mentally Ill
   a. Applying Basic Concepts and Recommended Typologies
      —Discovering the six basic operating characteristics (the descriptive analysis revealing goals and objectives, entitlement rules, etc.) as a basis for understanding the policy or program under consideration
   b. Applying Evaluation Criteria
      —Relating fundamental value perspectives on adequacy, equity, efficiency and value perspectives prescribed by the analytic method (unique to the operating characteristic and unique to the analyst) to program implementation of each of the six operating characteristics and drawing conclusions from those value perspectives
3. Making Final Judgments and Conclusions about Program or Policy Merit

CHAPTER 11

An Analysis of the Social Policy and Social Program Features Embedded in the Community Mental Health Centers Acts of 1975 and 1980 and Related Subsequent Legislation

THE SOCIAL PROBLEM CONTEXT

The first step in a social policy analysis is to analyze the underlying social problem. The public documents we will use to establish the social problem context are various reports of the Joint Commission on Mental Health issued by the National Institute on Mental Health,[1] the four-volume report of President Carter's Commission on Mental Health,[2] and various documents concerning the Omnibus Budget Reconciliation Act (OBRA) of 1980. We will also use selected research studies such as Paul Lerman's *Deinstitutionalization*,[3] and Goldberg and Huxley,[4] among others. These are authoritative sources from which we can (1) see how the problem is defined and quantified and (2) understand ideological and causal explanations of major importance to the community mental health view of the social problem of chronic mental illness (CMI). There are other sources and other views of CMI, of course. For example, if we chose to analyze the social problem view underlying the policies of the privately financed and endowed Menninger Psychiatric Foundation, we would need to choose an entirely different set of documents and would surely find a different viewpoint.

The location of documentary sources is not an altogether straightforward matter, so we need to pause here to review briefly how documents can be located. First, the legislative hearings that preceded the Community Mental Health Centers (CMHC) Acts were attempts by Congress to become informed about CMI; thus, a careful reading of this process is mandatory because few other single sources set out the understandings and ideology of the legislators. A second source is academic, human service, and social work journals used by legislative committees as reference points. A quick review of their annual indexes will locate relevant articles, along with source notes. Some journals of particular use for this purpose are *Hospital and Community Psychiatry*, *The International Journal of Social Psychiatry*, *Social Service Review*, *The American Journal of Community Psychiatry*, *Public Welfare*, *Social Work*, *Social Policy*, *Journal of Social Policy*, *Policy Studies Review*, *Policy Studies Journal* and *The Community Mental Health Journal*. The practical policy analyst should be alert to the several resources that abstract articles from these and many other professional and academic journals. In regard to social welfare problems and social welfare policy issues, some that are generally helpful are *Social Work Research and Abstracts*, *Sociological Abstracts,* and *Index Medicus.* Some excellent material can be found in the academic social science journals, but few are routinely good for our purpose here. Note that the *Journal of Social Policy, Policy Studies Review* and *Social Policy* (and others) are not mainline social science journals but are interdisciplinary in nature and purpose. Some are British journals whose articles are of immense interest to the North American reader.

Finally, it is often useful to check into the more reliable journalistic sources because carefully selected news reports can be an excellent source of social problem data and policy history. Here are some of the better candidates: the *Washington Post*, the *New York Times*, the *Wall Street Journal*, the *Economist*, and the *London Times* (even on U.S. issues, sometimes the latter two British papers have better coverage). Sometimes it can be worthwhile searching the publication lists and newsletters of prestigious research institutes for data, policy, and program history. Here are some examples: The Brookings Institution and the Urban Institute (both in Washington, D.C.); the Institute for Research on Poverty (University of Wisconsin), and the Center for the Study of Democratic Institutions (Princeton University). These publications often list good sources in their footnoted articles. However, their findings are not necessarily unbiased, for the Urban Institute and the Brookings often reach opposing conclusions.

Definition of the Social Problem

The first step in the social problem analysis is to identify how the problem is defined and to locate estimates of the magnitude and descriptions of qualitative variation (subtypes) based on that definition. Although all social problems present definition problems, few are so replete with definitional controversy as is CMI. For example, there is controversy about whether mental illness is a disease in the medical sense or whether it is simply a socially defined behavioral deviance. There is even controversy about *whether* there is such a thing as mental illness. Lucy Ozarin concludes that the original community mental health legislation of the 1960s and 1970s was mainly directed toward CMI.[5, 6]

Review of the *Congressional Record* clearly and repeatedly shows the intent of Congress to try to change the pattern of care away from custodial mental hospitals. Senator Hill said, "Centers will be used for the treatment of the majority of patients afflicted with mental illness." The CMHC Act of 1963 says that "services are for the mentally ill person."[7] With this in mind it is logical for us to turn to the third edition of *The Diagnostic and Statistical Manual of Mental Disorders (DSM-III)* of the American Psychiatric Association (APA) for further definitions and qualitative descriptions of types and varieties of conditions included within the general social problem of mental illness. DSM-III refers to three major types of psychiatric conditions:

1. Clinical syndromes and conditions that are not mental disorders but are a focus of treatment
2. Personality and developmental disorders
3. Physical disorders and conditions (*Diagnostic and Statistical Manual*, 1980, pp. 8, 23)

We are mainly concerned with conditions 1 and 2. These mental disorders—thought to occur in about sixteen subtypes—are not (it should be noted) always easily distinguished, even by experts. Of these subtypes, we are primarily concerned with schizophrenic disorders, paranoid disorders, organic mental disorders, psychotic disorders, and affective disorders. There are a number of types of psychotic disorders and a number of types of schizophrenic disorders. This diagnostic scheme notes affective, paranoid, and schizophrenic reactions as the main subtypes of psychosis. Affective disorders entail extreme depression or mania (bipolar states), for example, the primary characteristic of paranoid states is the idea of being persecuted; and schizophrenia entails bizarre behavior (perceptual distortions such as making strange sounds, or speaking words and phrases out of context) (*Diagnostic and Statistical Manual*, 1980, pp. 181–84, 199–203, 206–15).

Having made qualitative distinctions that enrich our understanding of the different forms in which this social problem can be expressed, we can now turn to the quantitative aspects of the problem of CMI. The President's Commission on Mental Health suggested some striking figures on the extent to which the U.S. population is subject to this social problem. Note that the precision of our quantitative estimates depends on the clarity of our definitions; because the definitions of the various types of CMI are gross and depend entirely on such notoriously hazy terms as *bizarre behavior or speech* and *persecutory ideas*, our estimates of "how many" will be crude indeed. The Commission's study presents the following statistics:

■ Two million Americans could be diagnosed as schizophrenic and 600,000 receive treatment in any one year. This amounts to 3 percent of the population.

■ About 1 percent of the population suffers from profound disabling depressive disorders and 0.3 percent from manic depressive psychosis.

■ More than 1 million U.S. citizens have organic psychoses of toxic or neurologic origin or permanently disabling mental conditions of varying causes.[8]

The Ideological Perspective

The next step in social problem analysis is to identify the ideology underlying the community mental health (CMH) movement. The document chosen to provide relevant statements in that regard is written by Jack Zusman, M.D. Zusman's concern is to present "a system of underlying beliefs," and it is precisely those beliefs with which ideology is concerned.

In setting out what he believes to be the basic principles of this system Zusman describes a set of four important ethical beliefs that we will use as close approximations to the ideological position for which we are searching.[9]

1. Good mental health services should be available to all those who need them regardless of other personal characteristics.

2. Each person should control his or her own destiny to the greatest extent possible.

3. Close, long-term relationships, particularly those within small groups, are valuable and to be fostered.

4. The strength that comes from humans banding together in social groups is to be prized and utilized.

Note that these are value statements. There is an *egalitarian* value bias in the first statement. That is, public services (mental health services) should be available to all citizens as a matter of right, regardless of social or economic circumstances. There is a clear commitment to *self-determination* in the second statement: The freedom implied in most concepts of self-determination is nothing if not concerned with the control of persons over their own destiny. Note also the indication of a commitment to individualism in the choice of the term *person* in the statement. It is not families, kin groups, neighborhoods, or ethnics who should control their own destiny but individual *persons*.

However, in the next two statements there are commitments not to individuals but to the value of the human groupings to which the individual is allied. Is there a conflict between these two ideological commitments? It is certain to occur for practitioners who work in this social problem context. Suppose a CMI patient insists (acts to control his or her own destiny) on behaving in ways that set one member of the family against others. The practitioner can ally with the patient who acts to control his or her destiny and get the family to help toward that end or ally with the family to preserve the close family relationship for all concerned. But the practitioner cannot always do both at the same time. It is common for ideological sets underlying a social problem view to contain such basic conflicts. Few if any are tight-knit, rationally consistent systems. We can summarize our conclusions about the ideological system underlying the CMH movement's view of the social problem of mental health in the following three statements:

1. All people should be considered equal, and the personal difficulties created by the CMI of one citizen should not be considered necessarily more important than other kinds of economic or social circumstances.

2. All persons have a right to be self-determining to the maximum extent possible.

3. Human relationships arise in small groups, such as communities and families.

These ideological commitments are not empty abstractions; in fact, they have a marked impact on how programs and practitioners within them behave. For example, Zusman believes that the commitment to egalitarianism also leads to the feeling that "professionals all should do more or less the same tasks, regardless of level of training, pay scale or responsibility."[10] Thus, the ideological commitment to egalitarianism leads to the frequent use of nonmedical staff in many community mental health centers (CMHCs) and, in some cases, less reliance on the authority of physicians in the operation of the program and in the direction of its treatment personnel, a marked departure from tradition.

Causal Analysis

The next step in analyzing the social problem of CMI is to identify the causal explanations used to understand this problem and to guide programs and policies in the CMH movement. Earlier we identified two types of chronic mental illness: (1) impairment of the brain tissue and/or physiology (organic conditions) and (2) psychosis. Both produce an unrelenting condition. With respect to these chronic conditions there is no explanatory theory of sufficient power to produce interventions that will alter the fundamental condition. No one knows how to restore damaged brain tissue or normal neural physiology; many believe that genetics is strongly implicated. Some practitioners believe that schizophrenia is a product of social interactions but, as interesting as those ideas are, there is no hard evidence that they can be used to reverse the course of the disease or restore normal development.

It is fair to characterize the explanatory and causal notions common to community mental health policy and practice as "adjustive" or "habilitative"—causal notions that seek to explain not the origin or etiology of CMI but the conditions for achieving some kind of socially satisfactory adjustment to it. Three explanations and their sources are cited below:

1. *Deviance theory and the labeling perspective.* These ideas explain mental illness as a deviance from prevailing social norms. The focus of the social problem in this view is on those who create the definitions rather than those judged to be deviant.[11, 12, 13]

2. *The environmental perspective and social stress theories.* These ideas take the general view that mental illness is determined by the character of the environment rather than the emotional or developmental features of the patient's intrapsychic life. Note that deviance theory is simply a special case of the environmental perspective.[14, 15]

3.   *Learned helplessness as an institutional consequence.* This idea views hospitalization as the key factor in inducing chronicity by isolating the patient from the family, likely the most significant social and emotional asset available.[16]

All three of these theories generate social policy and program designs and a range of interventions to be performed by social practitioners working with or on behalf of CMI sufferers. For example, the deviance and labeling perspective focuses the program and practitioner on social norms. Therefore, the practitioner can work toward one of these objectives: (1) changing the perspective of the significant community person who defines the patient as deviant or (2) working with the patient so as to change the behaviors that transgress or threaten the norms or (3) working with the patient to increase his or her tolerance for the negative consequences of labeling. Of course the most common case is for a practitioner to work on all three simultaneously in an attempt to find a mutual accommodation. The learned helplessness concept generates program elements such as day hospitals and emergency psychiatric clinics to replace long-term hospitalization and to keep "patients" in a more "normal" social environment. These programs are intended to provide the technology for coping—mediation, respite care, daily support systems, and technical and practice advice about the problems of everyday living—while focusing on the patient as the locus of responsibility for the conduct of his or her life. Simultaneously the focus will be on maintaining continuous contact with family and community members who provide routine human support. Institutions are viewed as places where helplessness is learned—where helplessness is in fact rewarded. A return to an institution is believed to teach a pattern that is fundamentally destructive to patients' ability to direct their own lives.

Gainers and Losers

The last step in social problem analysis is to identify who gains and who loses by virtue of the existence of the social problem of CMI in the view of those allied with the CMH movement. A brief look at the major recommendations in the *Final Report of the Joint Commission on Mental Health* will give us a source from which we can readily draw inferences. This report is generally credited with having been the impetus for the first CMHC Act of 1963. The act provided for the first extensive federal participation in the delivery of mental health services at the community level—the concrete and programmatic expression of the ideology of the CMH movement.[17] In Jack Ewalt's summary of the recommendations of the 1960 report, there is a clear picture of who, in the CMH movement viewpoint, bears the major cost of the social problem of CMI. The report recommends "reduction in the size of state hospitals and provision of care nearer home."[18] Plainly the report views CMI patients who remain isolated in state hospitals as major losers; their loss is the support and care of kin who are believed to be able to make a major difference in whether such person can adjust outside a hospital.

Ewalt also notes that the report emphasizes the "expansion of the use of semi- and non-professional persons as mental health workers. . . ."[19] One infer-ence is that the report views the CMI sufferer among ethnic, racial, and cultural subgroups as bearing especially heavy costs of the social problem because the traditional mental health professions have had difficulty in delivering expert services to those groups. Those whose cultural experience leads to a fundamental mistrust of white officialdom transfer it to white professionals who dominate the mental health professions (psychiatry, psychology, social work, and nursing). Ewalt's summary of the report notes its recommendation for "creation of more effective treatment, rehabilitative services for long term or chronic patients. . . ."[20] Thus there is little doubt that the report views the CMI group, among all those afflicted with mental problems, as those who bear especially heavy costs.

THE JUDICIAL CONTEXT

The judiciary has rendered important decisions that have created special effects on entitlement rules for CMHCs. Examples are the rulings of both state courts and the U.S. Supreme Court that have established certain (limited) rights of mental patients: the right to treatment, the right to refuse treatment, and the right to treatment in the least-restrictive environment. One landmark case in Alabama, *Wyatt v. Stickney* (1976), took care to describe what constitutes minimum standards of patient care and ordered that a patient could not be involuntarily held for treatment unless such minimum treatment were in fact offered.[21] In an interesting twist to the issue of entitlement as established by judicial discretion, the ruling declares that if citizens are to be deprived of their freedom and civil status, then not only are they entitled to treatment but to some measure of "adequate" treatment. Of course the application of this decision is restricted to committed patients and to CMHCs that admit patients. But it is clear that the practice of commitment for outpatient treatment is becoming more widespread and that although there is no court ruling on this point, there seems little doubt that courts would view such commitment as entailing some loss of civil freedoms. If this is the case, then the logic of the U.S. Supreme Court's judicial entitlement rule of "adequate" treatment for the committed holds in this case as well.

THE HISTORICAL CONTEXT

The Community Mental Health Centers Acts of 1963, 1975, 1980 and Other Relevant Legislation

We are now ready to analyze a major instrument of national policy intended to relieve the social problem of CMI as analyzed. Note that there were major legislative developments after the 1975 act, the Mental Health Systems Act of 1980 and certain key provisions of the 1980 act contained within 1980 OBRA. As we shall see, the OBRA provisions derailed much of the central guidance for community mental health centers contained in the 1975 and 1981 acts, but we shall still view them as the crucial legislation and public policy on this matter because they stand as guiding ideals for many if not most practitioners and administrators implementing its provisions. Of that, more later.

It is to history that the CMHC Act is responding. One lesson from the past, recalling what has already been said in the social problem analysis, is that CMI care in state mental hospitals creates overwhelming costs, ambiguous results (at best), and proceeds on unacceptable ideological presumptions. Another important piece of programmatic history is that the treatment (rather, the control) of the CMI has not required much treatment in closed institutions since the emergence of psychotropic drugs in the 1950s. The effect of these pharmaceuticals can be seen in the very dramatic change in the number of persons admitted as residents and released from state mental institutions since 1950. Figure 11-1 shows that change graphically. It is clear that whereas total admissions have gone *up*, the number of patients who are residents in state hospitals has gone *down* by nearly one-third from its peak in the mid-1950s. Most of that change has been brought about by the use of drugs that enable the management of chronic mental patients outside large congregate institutions and the use of nursing-home facilities for elderly senile patients. In regard to the latter, note that within a relatively short period, 1969–1974, the proportion of patients over sixty-five with a mental illness who were in state hospitals decreased by 50 percent, whereas the proportion in nursing homes increased by more than 50 percent.[22] A major shift in the locus of care for the aged mentally ill has occurred.

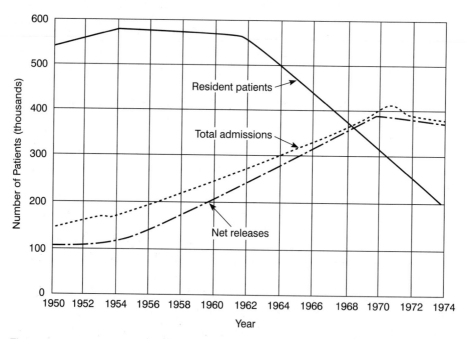

Figure 11–1   Number of resident patients, total admissions, net releases and deaths, state and county mental hospitals, United States: 1950–1974.
(*Source: The President's Commission on Mental Health,* Volume II Appendix, Figure 3, p. 57.)

The CMHC Act of 1975 is another in a series of acts (the first was the CMHC Act of 1963). Written as a response to the *Final Report of the Joint Commission on Mental Health,* the 1975 act established sanction for the first federal fiscal support of mental treatment facilities this country had ever known and is a landmark on that account. The history of U.S. public policy concerning mental illness is unique because although federal financing was first passed by Congress in the mid-1860s, it took a hundred years to recover from President Franklin Pierce's veto. Thus, although federal funding for mental health programs was proposed earlier than for almost any other social problem, it was one of the last to be effected. It was fought by opponents from all sides at various times—by the American Medical Association (AMA), many state legislatures, the American Psychiatric Association (APA), and a Congress concerned about further erosion of states' rights and responsibilities.

Henry Foley and others have reported several major factors leading to the construction of a commission to study the provision of treatment of mental illness in this country: (1) concern over the "large" proportion of draftees rejected for military service on account of psychiatric disablement, (2) the political acumen of several young and eager psychiatrists who held administrative posts for the army and navy psychiatric facilities during World War II, and (3) the strong adherence by those professionals to the public health concept of the prevention of disease.[23]

Some of the controversy about this CMHC act revolved around who would be in charge. The APA prevailed, and as a result physician control over mental health centers funded from CMHC funds is sure and uncontested in the basic structure of the act. Many in Congress who were concerned about the prevention objectives of the act were unconvinced that was a "cure" for CMI and feared the act could develop uncontrollable expenditures by trying to prevent a condition that was basically incurable by known technology. Innovations in the CMHC Act of 1963 lay in basing treatment for mental illness in communities, not institutions, and in requiring a continuum of service—inpatient, outpatient and emergency treatment, and partial hospitalization, for example.

It is one of those splendid ironies found so often in social history that the mental institution—the chosen policy instrument that pioneer mental health advocate Dorothea Dix worked so hard to establish to solve a social problem of the 1800s—is itself a major aspect of the social problem the CMHC Act of 1963 was intended to solve. It is important to understand that the congregate mental institution, of which the state mental hospital is the archetype, was a singular, humane improvement over the chains and vicious imprisonment that were standard features of the fate of the mentally ill while Dix was an active reformer. With the advent of psychotropic drugs for managing chronic mental illnesses, Dix's solution involving large congregate, state-run mental institutions became obsolete. Caring for the psychotic and severely mentally disabled outside locked doors and within a "normal" community environment became plausible.[24]

The 1975 Mental Health Centers Act was preceded by much controversy about both the mission, past performance, and future of community mental health centers. In fact, President Nixon's attitude was that the CMHCs were a demonstrated success and therefore should be phased out on the view that their continuation and expansion should be funded privately and/or by local government. So determined was he that in 1972 when Congress funded them anyhow, he impounded the budgeted money, refusing to implement the act until civil suits pried it loose. The confrontation between the chief executive and the Congress on this issue continued into succeeding years. Congress passed the 1975 Mental Health Centers Act and its budgetary authorization over President Ford's veto, and there were even significant (failed) attempts to fold the CMHCs under various categorical programs including Medicare and Medicaid. Even against the will of the chief executive, Congress and the CMHC advocates were determined to move treatment of the mentally ill fully into the mainstream of medicine and ". . . build a one-class system of care with guaranteed continuity."[25]

The 1963 Community Mental Health Centers Act mandated five essential services—inpatient care, emergency services, partial hospitalization, outpatient care, and consultation/education, all intended to build a strong alternative to state hospitalization. Even so—*mirabile dictu!*—the vital links between state hospital care and local community care were *not* mandated, for example, preadmission and postdischarge services for state hospital patients. Given neither fiscal incentive nor regulatory mandate, mental health money did not, indeed could not, follow patients from the state hospitals to local communities for community care of the chronically mentally ill. The absence of these mandates were political and legislative compromises and they turned out to be very costly in the long run; its consequence, in Foley and Scharfstein's view, ". . . was the failure of most local CMHCs to develop even minimal rehabilitation and after care services for the CMIs discharged or diverted from state mental hospitals."[26] From a social service planner's point of view, perhaps it was plausible that it could have worked: centers were in place, psychiatric beds in community hospitals had increased fourfold in the previous twenty years,[27] earlier Medicaid legislation could now provide for payment for nursing-home care of elderly and senile patients formerly consigned to state hospital care, and new and even more effective psychotropic medications were available.

The 1975 Community Mental Health Centers Act added seven other mandated services to the five already specified by the 1963 act. One of those was, not coincidentally, the follow-up care and transitional services for the CMI. In addition the 1975 act reflected its contemporary history in requiring drug and alcohol services—societal concern about those social problems was rising rapidly. The requirement of client/consumer representation on CMHC boards of directors was a similar reflection. The argument among professions as to who was to be in charge of CMHCs continued but psychiatry was losing ground rapidly: only 26 percent of center directors were psychiatrists by 1977 and social workers and psychologists increasingly assumed those positions (perhaps mainly in the small and/or rural centers).[28] Increasingly, the professional associations of social work, nursing, and psychology were advocating for CMHC legislation in the halls of Congress.

But if there were many gains in these early years, as Foley and Scharfstein note, there was also a debilitating disillusionment with the centers, for they had failed to cope with the problems of successfully relocating the state hospital population of the chronically mentally ill back in their own communities.[29] They reappeared on the streets and in the alleys of every U.S. inner city. By 1991 the homeless were a recognizable phenomenon, and reasonably good studies were beginning to report that as much as one-third of them were the chronically mentally ill.[30]

In this context, President Carter assumed office, and one of his first actions was to establish the President's Commission on Mental Health. By this time, constituencies concerned about mental health as a national problem were clear that mental health care in the United States was overly complicated, inflexible, disorganized, fragmented, and hardly a system at all. Even the Commission report noted the scarcity and inadequacy of insurance coverage for mental health, the inflexibility of centers in initiating new programs, and the pressing needs of groups (some new, some old) still underserved: the chronically mentally ill, children, minorities, and the elderly. Even so the report was notable and effective for its evenhandedness and the fact that it never fell captive to any single interest group. Although its proposals were few, it did have strong suggestions for giving national priority to a national plan for services to the chronically mentally ill: coordinated planning for their medical care (via Medicare/Medicaid); for housing (via HUD); and for providing them with long-term, dependable income benefits (via the Supplemental Security Income (SSI) program. One of the key actors was First Lady Rosalyn Carter who, as the first Presidential wife to appear before Congress since Eleanor Roosevelt, introduced the 1980 Mental Health Systems Act. She was a key player in the subsequent complicated negotiations over the next eighteen months.[31] The Mental Health Systems Act of 1980 (passed in Congress as P.L. 96-938) was, to an important degree, based on the conclusions of the Commission report. The 1980 act mandated many policies linking information, personnel, and patients. Those policies operationalized the idea of continuum of care (from state hospital to local CMHC). They provided new funding for the underserved and the vulnerable using a "seed money" concept as well as systems for close tracking of patients via case management strategies, emphasized the states' responsibilities to protect the chronically mentally ill, and included a strong patients' bill of rights.

But a month after the act was passed, President Reagan was elected and brought with him the idea of devolving significant governmental functions down to states and local government. To some extent Reagan was elected on an anti–big government platform and as a former governor of California it was a platform he took seriously. Many of his political agendas were pursued in OBRA 1980, in whose legislation nearly all federal mental health services program money was funneled into a large block grant to states. The block grant had few restrictions, certainly nothing like mandated services. That feature—part of and wholly consistent with the Reagan administration's focus on the desirability of local funding and initiative—made it possible for each state to choose its own priorities in CMHC funding, irrespective of the earlier Community Mental

Health Centers Acts or the Mental Health Systems Act of 1980. Twenty years of federal policy was overturned in a few days of budget activity in 1981 in the OBRA enactment. "[T]he federal government was entirely removed from the direction of the program and became a mere conduit of funds." Not only that, the amount of funding was very short of what had been expected to fund the 1980 act, so that even funding existing services was doubtful.[32]

With this historical context in mind, we can proceed to analyzing the documentary evidence for signs of the social policy designs inherent in the CMHC acts and the associated legislation.

THE SOCIAL PROGRAM AND POLICY SYSTEM ANALYSIS

Goals and Objectives

Community mental health practitioners must be concerned with program goals and objectives, aspects of social policy that affect them significantly. Not only are goals and objectives the standard against which practitioners' performance is judged, they are the source for standards of judgment that determine how extensively money, time, and other resources will be allotted. Other material resources include office space, autos, clerical support, and the like.

Ozarin makes clear from her review of a wide variety of authoritative sources that the stated target group specified in the CMHC Act of 1975 were those who suffered from CMI. The intent of the act was to create local mental health clinics in order to change the focus of treatment from large congregate state institutions to local clinics in the patient's own community.[33] Thus the major goal of the act was to effect treatment of chronic mental illness, but other problems were targeted as well. For example, services were also mandated to the developmentally disabled, to children, the elderly, and alcohol and drug abusers. (For purposes of simplicity, we will restrict our concern to chronic mental illness.) Several issues emerge in accounting for the multiplicity of target groups. One is to recognize that the United States was beginning to be deeply concerned about substance abuse, an issue that forcefully came to public attention in the 1960s and 1970s. Another is to recognize that, from its earliest days, the National Institute of Mental Health (NIMH) had very broad basic concepts that were public health oriented. Thus, there was an urgency about prevention in the broadest sense (perhaps oversimplified) that if programs were developed to keep people well and healthy, then the treatment of illness would be accomplished in the most cost-effective way imaginable. And, of course, the successful public health campaigns against communicable disease via the control of disease carriers gave proponents much hope that mental illness might yield to the same approach. That broad focus on prevention suggested inclusion of many social problem conditions with "mental" or "emotional" consequences and thus it was easy to think about the mental health aspects of the elderly, children, or drug and alcohol abusers.

Again, the goal of the CMHC Act was rather concrete: Change the locus of CMI treatment from large congregate state institutions to local clinics in the patient's own home community. Although as a goal the treatment of CMI is an important characterization of the general purpose of the act, we will need to be more specific—that is, we will need to identify concrete objectives. Remember that for any given goal there is likely to be a number of more specific/concrete objectives that, taken together, reinforce the goal statement. Almost all standard sources in the community mental health literature note six to eight specific objectives in the CMHC Act. We will use the version of those eight objectives found in The President's Commission on Mental Health and the 1975 Community Mental Health Centers Act. (Report of the Task Panel . . .," 1978; P.L. 94–63, Sec. 101(b)(1), 84 stat. 1567).

1. Increasing the range and quantity of mental health services
2. Making services equally available and accessible
3. Providing services in relation to existing needs in the community
4. Maximizing citizen participation in community programs
5. Decreasing the number of state hospital admissions and residents
6. Preventing the development of mental disorders
7. Coordinating mental health–related services in catchment areas
8. Providing for the continuity of care between the state hospital system and local mental health resources and services

Whatever may be the case with respect to federal initiatives, the historical fact is that responsibility for basic policy and program direction for mental health was effectively handed to the states by the Reagan administration (and Congress) via the funding provisions of OBRA 1980. (Recall the earlier discussion about the mental health block grants in the discussion of historical context in the above social problem analysis.) That decentralization of authority allows states wide latitude in defining program and policy system goals and objectives, consistent with the block grant rationale the presupposition for which is that states know better than the federal government what unique social policy and social program directions should be taken given their individual social problems. On that account (and because we cannot deal here with all the local variety in how that was worked out), let us take as an example the mental health reforms in one state. Kansas is an interesting example because reform efforts that began in the early 1980s provided the occasion for a close look at many policy issues, including goals and objectives, all of which creates an opportunity to see how they came out at the state level. We will use a document that subsequent history shows to have been influential in producing some major mental health initiatives in this state,[34] and two state legislative documents that are useful to our analysis here.[35,36] Rapp and Hanson assert that ". . . the chronically mentally ill are the priority target for public mental health policy,"[37] and it is clear from this that the goal of Kansas's mental health system is to integrate the CMI citizen into the community.

Objectives and their behavioral measures relating to this goal for programs for the CMI include the following:

- Increasing the tenure in the community, as measured by reductions in incidence and patients' length of stay in institutional care
- Increasing independent living status, as measured by clients moving to the highest expectable level of independent living arrangements
- Increasing social supports and social activities with emphasis on forms utilized by ordinary citizens

Resolutions of the Kansas legislature also speak to the issue of goals and objectives in directing local CMHCs to establish community support programs to provide mental health care in local communities, which is the least restrictive environment.[38,39] It is clear that these goals and objectives are quite compatible with federal government goals, to provide large proportions of the funding for local CMHCs. Further, such goals meet our evaluation criteria for clarity and measurability at a level even higher than those that characterize the federal goals and objectives. Now we need to draw some conclusions about these goals and objectives: Do they have merit as goals and objectives? The way to answer that question is to use the evaluation criteria for goals and objectives discussed in Chapter 5.

First, it is clear that these goals are satisfactory as to the criterion that they are indeed set at a general level and that there are concrete stated objectives that express their specific operational meaning. It is also clear that these goals are satisfactory in the sense that they include target group specifications (i.e., refer to the chronically mentally ill, drug and alcohol abusers, children and the elderly). But there is a problem in the sense that these target groups are very large and none of the official documents takes notice of whether there is sufficient funding for the *total* subpopulation within these groups. That will create problems later when Congress and opponents of the CMHCs ask why the many people included in those target groups weren't served. It seems plausible to say that no one, but no one in the mental health alliance, actually expected the centers to have such financing. Standing alone, the Kansas statements of objectives are clearly superior; but remember, even though the objectives are superior by itself does nothing about state underfunding of its mental health system.[40] It cost the state very little to be clear in what it *hoped* to do.

The evaluation criteria also call for *clarity* of goals and objectives. We should not expect to find close definitions of those groups in the legislation itself, of course (legislation rarely is that specific, being the political creature it is), but knowing that the act was based on the 1978 President's Commission report, we can turn there for definitions. Were we to do so we would find somewhat clear definitions, certainly those of the various subtypes of chronic mental illness (our focus here) based on the diagnostic categories found in the APA's *Diagnostic and Statistical Manual* for example.

How clear are the definitions of mental disorders found there? Not very, actually, and one important piece of evidence is their well-known unreliability—

there is significant disagreement among professionals when they are applied to specific cases for the purposes of psychiatric diagnosis. Space does not permit discussion of the research or the technicalities on that issue, so let us say (as the British might) that these definitions are only "rough and ready"—meaning that they are serviceable, handy to use—and not much else is available; but neither are they very accurate or precise. That will naturally lead us to expect certain problems in implementing the policy following from this act. If this classification of chronic mental illness is itself difficult to apply reliably, then it will be difficult to say whether CMHCs in different communities really serve the same groups of people, for example. That presents difficulties in both estimating populations at risk and in identifying which CMHC programs are the most effective. Differences might be due to undiscovered and undiscoverable differences in groups of patients, rather than in program merit.

Our evaluation criteria also call for judging whether the goals and objectives are *measurable and manipulable.* For the most part, their main operating terms are quite measurable when one thinks of goals such as accessibility of services, citizen participation, hospital admissions, and the like. Is the phenomenon referred to by the term "hospital admissions" manipulable? It is. Admissions can easily be decreased. The method envisioned by the CMHC Act is to ensure that treatment facilities are available and accessible to citizens in their own communities so that they will not appear for admission to the local state hospital. Of course some methods of decreasing admissions are not necessarily good treatment: summarily closing down state institutions or transferring the chronically mental patients to nursing homes where their care might be either substandard or lacking altogether, for example.

Note also that by all counts, chronic mental illnesses are not conditions that are well understood in any important sense; thus, any objective that speaks of "preventing mental disorders" cannot (logically) be expected to be achieved because it is not basically manipulable: it is a simple matter, one cannot produce an effect unless one clearly understands and knows its cause; few would say that the cause of mental disorders, especially chronic mental illness, is clearly understood. Note that the goals and objectives for CMHCs expressed at the state level as discussed above do not foster this same mistake since they do not speak of prevention at all. In fact the document titled *Towards an Agenda for Mental Health Reform* is quite clear in focusing the goals of program efforts on *remedial treatment* for the chronically mentally ill, for example, medication management, defusing emergency crisis and development, and acquisition of those reasonably concrete resources needed for everyday survival in the community.[41]

We must also judge whether these objectives contain *performance standards* to which the program or policy system must be held accountable. The 1978 President's Commission report made a strong case for "performance contracts" between the federal government and states concerning the gradual elimination of large congregate state hospital systems. The performance standards suggested that agreements should be made in advance on activities and outcomes to which states would commit themselves, and that performance in that regard be a condition for future federal mental health funding to the relevant state.[42] The reader should note that performance standards are distinct from the idea of mandated services. To mandate a service is not the same as setting out performance standards for *how well* that service achieves its objectives and upon which continued funding might depend. It is not a trivial matter for what we have argued is that, absent performance standards built into statements of objectives, the service-delivery system cannot be held accountable. So long as it provides services of *whatever level* of outcome, performance is satisfactory. Funding is too scarce to tolerate that, for the most certain generalization in the social policy world is that dollars spent in one place almost always deprive someone in need in some other place.

Whereas the goals and objectives in the report meet our evaluative standard in some minimal way and is a hopeful sign, if the objectives of this policy system are to qualify as totally satisfactory, of course one would need documentary evidence that those performance contracts were in fact "up and running." Given the sources we are working with here, there isn't much evidence of that. Note that in the goals and objectives statements for the state level (Kansas) program referred to above, measures were included for judging their attainment. The great utility of specifying measurability within those statements is clear here because they instantly provide a good basis for the kinds of performance standards that we are looking for here. For example, once a statement is made that suggests that increases in community tenure for the chronically mentally ill is to be measured by reductions in the incidences and lengths of stay of patients in institutional care, all that remains is to specify a performance standard that answers the question *How much reduction counts as satisfactory performance during a given time period*? That is not an easy question to answer, but the ability to pose it is the first step toward an answer.

An important concept used to analyze goals and objectives is the means-ends distinction; that is, the concept is that goals and objectives must *refer to ends, not means,* and *refer to outcomes, not inputs, processes or methods of intervention.* This is an important point here because some goals in the CMHC Act fail this test. Four of the six goals/objectives listed (numbers 1,2,3, and 7) are in fact means of achieving outcomes, not outcomes that could stand as acceptable and worthwhile in their own right. The clue to that failure is signaled by the use of the terms "services." SERVICES ARE, WITHOUT EXCEPTION, MEANS TO ENDS, NOT ENDS IN THEMSELVES. For example, think of whether it would be acceptable to "increase the range and quality of mental health services" just for the sake of doing so. Would that be an acceptable use of funds, time, and talent—all of which are at a premium? Unquestionably not.

Note that at the state rather than federal level of operations the goals and objectives expressed do not repeat the same errors for *any* of the goals and objectives expressed in the Rapp and Hanson report; nor do they refer to services at all, only outcomes. It is worthwhile noting that the state legislative documents do, however, refer almost exclusively to directions to CMHCs to provide certain kinds of services. One of the important reasons why so many policies and programs go wrong is that no one bothered to develop clear goals; it was simply assumed that implementing a particular program was sufficient to achieve some goal that was itself vague.

This analysis can be more clear about what CMHC objectives really are because they can be "boiled down" to the two essentials: (1) maximizing consumer participation and (2) decreasing state hospital admissions and residencies. Note that consumer participation can stand alone, so to speak, as a legitimate objective in that it serves values relating to client/consumer empowerment (or autonomy), a value position that stands outside a particular social problem ideology. Because these two objectives are so complex they drive nearly the whole program and policy effort. It is fortunate that their meaning and concrete references are fairly clear and relatively unambiguous.

It should be clear to the reader that the mental health programs and policy of concern to CMHC legislation are hybrids—they concern the provision of *both* personal social services and public social utilities. For example, state hospital care is clearly a public social utility: In part it provides tangible benefits like food, clothing, and medication; it is also a personal social service in that it provides counseling of various kinds, some types of educational programs, close emotional support, even active "supervision" of a kind. Because the policy system with which we are concerned contains personal social service features, the practical public policy analyst must be aware of the need for an additional set of objectives that are unique to *each client*—no mystery here because it is obvious that what is required for a chronically mentally ill individual to maintain himself or herself in the community is to some extent unique to that person and that community. Clearly what is needed for a positive community adjustment depends on the characteristics of the person and the resources and response of the particular community to his or her presence.

Note that we will not find those kinds of objectives in the act or even in organizational regulations; rather, we will find them expressed in local programs, probably in the records of street-level local practitioners, or in the minds of the practitioner and their client/consumers. Thus, we need to evaluate here whether the policy system makes it a point to require such objectives for individual program consumers. And, although the primary sources we are looking at here provide no hard evidence for that, there is clear evidence in the historical accounts of the development of federal policy for the chronically mentally ill. Note that the NIMH has emphasized case-management demonstration projects in the allocation of federal research monies.[43] Case management (in its several varieties) is one of the main technologies of choice for personal social services with respect to the chronically mentally ill.[44,45] Case management is very clear in its insistence on behavioral objectives of exactly the kind we are speaking here. State-level documents concerned with CMHCs (referred to earlier in this chapter) placed heavy emphasis on case management, and from that we can infer that the basic policy direction in this local example is toward importance of goals and objectives, including those at the client/consumer level.

This set of goals and objectives is clearly linked to a social problem analysis whose ideology represents a bias in favor of a person-environment viewpoint. The whole thrust of the CMHC Act expresses that in its critique of the state hospital as an isolating, alienating *environment* despite its potential for helping the chronically mentally ill. Furthermore, its solution is to replace that environment with another that is both benign and enabling toward the client/consumers with whom we are concerned—local communities with all the supportive relationships and sociological familiarity they can provide. The CMHC ideology is also quite committed to an emphasis on *client-consumer empowerment*, another value commitment embedded in the analytic perspective of this method. Recall that Zusman had found that one explicit and underlying ideological belief characteristic of the whole CMHC is that ". . . each person should control his or her own destiny. . . ." [46] At the state level of implementation, the documents referred to above are clear in their emphasis on empowerment. For example, one document speaks of the goals of the continuum of service (from hospital to community) being ". . . reintegration of a person with chronic mental illness in to the community *at an independent or semi-independent level of functioning*"(emphasis added).[47]

Likewise, the CMHC legislation is clear in its commitment to social justice—expressed here in several forms. One example is establishment of a priority for mental health services for the chronically mentally ill over other target groups, on the view that they have been most neglected in the past and are most in need in terms of the severity of their problems. Another example is in establishment of special groups judged to be underserved and thus due priority in the future allocation of services: the elderly, children, and others mentioned expressly in the CMHC Act of 1975. Thus we can give high marks in our value-critical analysis of the CMHC legislation at both the federal and state levels in its commitment to expressing the person-environment bias, the empowerment value, and the bias toward justice for underserved populations to which this author as policy analyst is committed.

Certainly the CMHC Act has a good fit with its social problem analysis with respect to its goals and objectives. Note that in the above paragraph we concluded that the CMHC Act(s) expressed a commitment to social justice in establishing priorities for those groups judged to be underserved by the mental health establishment. In drawing that conclusion we were also making explicit a conclusion about commitment of the CMHC Act(s) to equity—here a proportional equity, that concerned with serving justice by allocating resources according to need. In addition, after having sorted out the CMHC objectives as we did earlier, it is clear that they are quite direct in their focus on the deinstitutionalization of the chronically mentally ill and single-minded in directing efforts to abolish the state hospital in favor of community care for these client/consumers. Recall from Chapter 1 that the rule with respect to judging the fit of the goals and objectives with the social problem analysis calls for showing the relationship between the terms in which the objectives are defined (outcomes) and the independent variables in the causal sequences in the social problem analysis. The independent variables there spoke of environmental factors in the hospital institution (e.g., learned helplessness), which present barriers to the chronically mentally ill with respect to their leaving and factors in the community (e.g., labeling, lack of support, and social and economic resources), which both project them out of the community and prevent their reentrance. The outcomes expressed in the objectives and in their rationale relate directly to those factors.

One of the issues for community mental health, this hybrid of personal social services and tangible welfare benefits, is that it may always work close to the edge of serving simply for the social control of deviance. The reader should recollect the special problems social control poses for social programs and social policy systems. This analysis can never take social control as a first-priority goal or objective, for to do so would contradict the aforementioned basic value commitments to client empowerment. It is fortunate from this point of view that the basic ideology of the CMHC movement and the legislation it generated say almost nothing about social control as an objective. But the practical policy analyst must remember that we also spoke of goals and objectives in two forms— *manifest* and *latent*. The social control issue raises the possibility that social control is a logical candidate for a latent (unarticulated but viable) objective of the CMHC act(s). A look at the congressional hearings on the Mental Health Systems Act of 1980 will easily verify that this issue was on the minds of some. How will local communities cope with deviant people in their midst? Can local communities cope without the state hospital as a resource for containment of not only the seriously disturbed but the potentially dangerous as well? And certainly it is, in part, to those concerns that reference to provisions for psychiatric treatment in local general hospitals is made in the various CMHC acts.

The state-level documents referred to above do make explicit reference to the social control agenda in discussing the whole mental health system arrangement. In that regard it makes clear that the state hospital, private psychiatric hospitals, and intermediate care facilities ". . . share a common purpose: to . . . protect the patient, the community or both from harm."[48] Nor is such a concern unwarranted. Although only a negligible proportion of the chronically mentally ill are dangerous, it takes only a few instances to raise danger as a popular issue, given the seriousness of the risk they can represent. Serious social control, specifically in this regard, represents an entirely legitimate objective that does not intrude on the value placed here on client/consumer empowerment. Indeed, this issue represents the limiting case of same, and it is entirely arguable that at some (extreme) level of CMI violence and danger, social control is in the service of both the community and the client/consumer. The matter is reasonably simple— no client/consumer is served by having to deal with the consequences of a violent episode on their part, one that presents a danger to others or to self. It seems plausible to argue that the CMHC Act, its associated legislation, regulatory implementation, and program-level policy would be best served by making this latent objective manifest *but* being clear about when, where, and to whom it applies.

Entitlement Rules

The main objective of our analysis in this section is to discover whether any rules—implied or explicit—restrict or rationalize the distribution of benefits and services to recipient/citizens. Legislation is not always explicit about these matters. Sometimes legislative documents simply enact permissive legislation, appropriate funds, and specify the general purpose for which they can be spent, leaving such details as we are interested in here to the discretion of administrative officials. That is not entirely the case here, although it is plain that much mental health policy must be made by administrative discretion if a program is to operate at all. Here we will go only so far as the federal legislation will take us, and turn to Kansas as an example of local implementation. A complete understanding of our national social policy with respect to mental illness can be obtained only by an analysis of both local and federal policy and program operations in that our government operates on both levels.

With respect to national policy, the CMHC Acts make it clear that community mental health centers are to serve entire populations within the geographic (catchment) area they serve. Thus, a primary characteristic of the eligibility rule for this national social policy is that, even though it intends to provide benefits *universally*, there is an entitlement condition of geographic residence. Because not every geographic area has a mental health center, universal entitlement is only an intent, not a reality. Note also that the language of the act *permits no means test:* ". . . services are to be provided . . . to any individual residing or employed in such an area regardless of ability to pay. . . ."[49] (89 Stat. 309, Title II, Pt. A, Sec. 201(a). 1A-B). Furthermore, the act disallows any rule or policy that would bar a resident from receiving services on account of "current or past health conditions . . ." (89 Stat. 309. Sec. 201(a) 1,B). Thus, no mental health center funded under this act would appear to be able to use *administrative or professional discretion* to limit its services—for example, to those who are the least or the most affected. As if to avoid any remaining ambiguity, this section of the act adds a final phrase noting that the *administrative rule* will be that services are to be provided to all persons regardless of "any other factor."

Evaluating the Merit of the Entitlement Rules Embedded in CMHC Acts and Related Documents

Although legislation does not allow restriction of eligibility by administrative rule, clearly it does accept allocative priorities, that is, appropriations to finance the program are not unlimited, certainly, and they are not intended to cover the cost of providing universal mental health benefits. The act clearly states that providing services is mandatory only "within the limits of . . . capacity." (89 Stat. 309 Sec. 201(a) 1, B). Where choices must be made about who is to be served, the subpopulations specified in the act are to be served: The act clearly mandates services for "the mental health of children . . . the mental health of the elderly . . . for persons being considered for admission to a state mental health facility for inpatient treatment . . . for persons discharged from a state facility . . . alcoholic and drug addiction and abuse. . . ." (89 Stat. 309 Sec. 201(b)(1)A-C and E-H). Thus, the act seeks to allocate services so that a priority is given not to persons with particular individual characteristics, but to certain population subgroups believed to be especially needful.

Finally, with respect to the types of entitlement entailed in the CMHC Act, it is clear that the major form of entitlement is at *professional discretion*. All treatment benefits and services are given on the basis of professional judgment, usually that of a physician. However, that professional judgment is curbed in some unique ways. In specific phrases the CMHC Act of 1975 bars professional judgment from excluding citizens on the basis of "past health conditions;" no doubt that phrase is there because CMHCs have been known to choose for treatment the "easiest" of the mentally disturbed and to resist the idea of treating the CMI.

What conclusions can be drawn with respect to the merit of these entitlement rules? Using the evaluation criteria for entitlement rules discussed earlier, it seems plain that *off-targeting, underutilization, and stigmatization* are the main problems and they are created by reliance on professional discretion. As noted earlier, the CMHC Acts placed increasing restrictions on professional discretion with respect to the freedom of a professional staff to choose its own clientele. The 1975 Act's prohibition against selecting consumers on the basis of past history or seriousness of illness is interpreted here as a policy response to professionals' avoidance of the most demanding and least professionally rewarding patient. Where that occurs, it is clear that significant off-targeting is taking place; that is, the resources of the act are not being spent on the population group that is the primary intended target, the CMI. There is no reason why CMHCs cannot serve others under their mandated goal to "prevent" mental disorders, but that goal cannot take precedence over the primary goal to serve the CMI. If it does, not only does it create off-targeting but it also creates an underserved population (and thus underutilization), often a consequence of off-targeting.

The increasing practice of state courts to rule on the constitutional right to treatment can discharge large numbers of the seriously mentally ill into the community where the expectation is that they will be the responsibility of the local CMHC.[50] Although the intent of the Alabama supreme court was to force the improvement of treatment services (as discussed earlier in Chapter 3), the state legislature did not increase appropriations to accomplish that end; it chose instead to see to it that involuntary patients were not kept for treatment but were returned to local communities. The functional capacity of many CMHCs is often so limited it cannot handle that kind of demand.

The adequacy of the treatment that can be offered by CMHCs for the chronically mentally ill is also affected by the entitlement rules embedded in the *private contracts* we have come to call private insurance coverage. Obviously, the ability of some client/consumers of CMHCs to pay for their service through their private insurance payments makes it possible for (nonprofit) CMHCs to use such funds to deliver services to those who have no insurance. For many years, private insurance carriers have been shy of covering mental treatments and hospitalization. At present, even the most liberal policies routinely limit mental health coverage to 30 days of inpatient care and $1000 of outpatient treatment. Many carriers will not cover treatment except by a licensed M.D. and will not cover treatment by psychologists, nurse practitioners, or social workers—clearly an issue for CMHCs where psychologists, nurse practitioners, and social workers far outnumber staff physicians. There is little doubt among those experienced in the field that professional credentialing is no guarantee of the adequate treatment for nonorganically based mental and emotional problems; much less is it a guarantee of "best" treatment—that is, that state-of-the-art treatment is available from practitioners in every basic mental health profession. The problem shows some marginal signs of diminishment. Some states, Illinois for example, have legalized psychologists for the prescribing of psychotropic medications, in recognition of that competence for some nonmedically trained practitioners. Also, a 1991 Medicare ruling allowed payment to social workers for the first time, and that ruling will now include services to the chronically mentally ill.

The problem created by these limitations on coverage is that it leads to *underutilization* of needed mental health services and because mental health treatment of the chronically mentally ill is expensive, it is definitely a barrier for the mentally ill for all but the wealthy. But, whereas this stance of insurance companies is to be regretted and surely imposes a hardship for people in need, there is a case to be made that the health insurance industry's systematic discrimination against covering mental treatment may be impossible to avoid. Insurance payments provide an incentive to keep patient/consumers in hospitals and in long-term treatment for as long as the insurance will pay for it. Hospital staff are given bonuses for keeping hospital beds in psychiatric care facilities full—clearly an incentive to fudge on judgments of when a patient is ready to leave or on whether a person needs treatment at all.[51] (*New York Times,* Nov. 12, 1991).

If there is good reason to suspect that some hospitals and practitioners conduct treatment in a way that is beyond what is useful, it is little wonder that insurance companies are cautious about mental health coverage. The mental health field itself has work to do here in order to find a means of limiting these abuses of professional discretion. It is, of course, an ethical problem of great magnitude, though we won't dwell on that here. The whole idea of insurance, any insurance, is based on ability to make predictions about the occurrence of an (usually undesirable) event. The same thing is true for health coverage, including coverage for mental treatment. The as-yet-unresolved problem for an insurance company covering mental conditions is the great difficulty in predicting exactly how many among a population will seek treatment—of what kind and for how long (for those factors also will affect benefit costs). Thus, if those in the mental health field believe that private insurance has any merit as a financing mechanism, they must solve that problem. Once valid consensus has been achieved on those issues, it will serve as a basis for administrative rules that can shape the presently unencumbered professional discretion that is creating all this policy and financing mischief.

There is another *interaction* between financing methods and entitlement rules that is problematic in this policy system. One consequence of the 1980 change from federal grants, which left states relatively unencumbered with respect to the use of federal mental health funds, is that it is possible for each state (or localities within states) to be (nearly) free to construct their own priority populations and other policy features out of which entitlement rules are generated. Indeed, that is exactly what the change in federal policy hoped to achieve— rationalized on the basis that localities and regions know best about such things (and of course that position can have merit). There is a *trade-off* here because the cost of that state-to-state variability is the potential for *inequity* at the client/consumer level. A consequence is that the probability for the same client/consumer being entitled to mental health services (or the same quality and intensity of services) varies from one state or locality to another. Given the mobility of our society, an *equity* problem is created in that the same citizen with the same problem can get mental health service in one place but not in another. Whereas *administrative discretion* always has a certain value in allowing for maximum individualization in policy applications, it can provide the occasion for expressing all the negative social prejudices of which individual administrators, policy designers, and practitioners are capable. Nor is there strong reason to believe that, somehow, professionals and ordinarily committed and competent administrators are immune from such prejudice.

Entitlement mechanisms based on professional discretion also leave opportunity for *political interference* in the entitlement decisions, an experience every mental health administrator has probably had. For example, when a politically influential person asks for services in any public agency, especially a person known to have direct access to public officials who can determine its budget and personnel policy, the application assumes an importance that others do not. Nor are private operations immune from political incursions, although their external politics may revolve around other issues (keeping referrals coming or hospital beds full, for example). Although administrative rules are not a guarantee against such political interference, they are a certain protection to administrators who then must justify exceptions if they expect to protect their accountability as administrators.

Examples of political interference in mental health service allocation and entitlement policy are not restricted to decisions about individuals. Many CMHCs (as well as other agencies) serve local courts for the purpose of doing alcohol and substance abuse evaluations, which are frequently court-ordered and used as a part of the sentencing information.[52] Whereas it is an important service, note that a good bit of money is involved, for an evaluation can cost $250 and in many if not most states, the DUI defendant is required to pay. Because many cities can count on 1,000 or more first-offense DUI court appearances, simple arithmetic shows that the cost of alcohol evaluations for DUI charges alone can run to $250,000 in such a community. Even these modest estimates can be an enticing budget feature for most CMHCs, wherever they are. Political interference in the systematic "awarding" of these evaluations to some centers rather than others can probably be inferred from the many casual reports of substantial kickbacks to the judiciary and court service personnel for evaluation referrals. The judiciary sometimes strongly resists political pressure or financially unscrupulous behavior; some judges have begun to refuse to refer DUI defendants to evaluation agencies that operate *both* an evaluation service and a residential or part-time hospitalization or day treatment center (where convicted or "diverted" alcoholics or other substance abusers are court-ordered to treatment). Thus, it is tempting for clinicians to suggest in their reports to the judge that entering a treatment center should be a sentencing or diversion condition, whether or not that is really indicated.

Finally, the fact that CMHC entitlement rules are associated with a psychiatric diagnosis—private insurance coverage requires it, in fact, and is commonly given the strong medical orientation of many CMHCs—*stigmatization* can be a common consequence of being judged entitled to CMHC services. A sizable body of opinion holds that psychiatric diagnosis confers negative social labeling and that, where the labeling is part of a person's public identity, it creates a set of negative expectations for the CMI person. Although research on the subject does not appear to support the hypothesis fully, many remain convinced of its truth.[53,54] At the least, it is said, psychiatric labels affect the coping strategies of diagnosed patients. Patients incorporate labels into their own expectations of themselves and thus destructive behavioral symptoms are perpetuated. To the extent that is true, the entitlement rules built into the CMHC Act create social stigma, and where that occurs alienation is likely to result.

Forms of Benefits and Services

The CMHC Act is more detailed than other legislation about the particular form the program should take. What is to be delivered are *expert services*—personal, social, and medical—as well as cash or tangible material benefits but only in inpatient and day hospital care where the food and shelter aspects are purely accidental means to the end of delivering the aforementioned personal social services. On those grounds the CMHC Act envisions what Chapters 4 and 5 called a hybrid social service, personal social services some of which are delivered in the context of tangible material benefits. A brief look at the act shows that a CMHC is required to offer comprehensive services; the act specifically defines the program elements that are meant by the term *comprehensive*:

- Inpatient services, outpatient services, day care and other partial hospitalization services, emergency services
- Consultation and educational services for . . . schools, courts, law enforcement personnel, clergy, public welfare personnel. . .
- Assistance to courts in screening residents considered for referral to a state mental health facility
- A continuum of care (follow-up in the community) for persons discharged from mental health facilities
- A program of transitional halfway house services
- Coordination of services with provision of services by other health and social service agencies

Evaluating the Merit of the Benefit and Service Form in the CMHC Acts and Related Documents

In general, among the benefits to be provided in carrying out the goals of this social policy are direct services to individuals, consultation and educational services to others serving those with mental problems, subprograms of halfway houses, partial hospitalization facilities, and coordinative efforts. This is a very large and varied package. In evaluating these benefit forms (see Chapter 6) it was clear that these expert CMHCs services are often troubled with the type of target inefficiency and stigmatization that result from the unconstrained use of professional discretion as an entitlement method. Recall that *stigmatization* is a problem resulting from the interaction between entitlement via professional judgment and the labeling inherent in psychiatric diagnosis. *Target inefficiency* results from the reluctance of many professionals to serve patients with CMI—currently a seriously demanding and nonstatus-rewarding group. Note that the *cost effectiveness* of outpatient expert services is more rewarding than with inpatient state hospital care. It has not proven to be less costly where CMHCs offer inpatient care; in the community it can be considerably more costly, in fact, even though it is often better-quality care. Nor is it necessarily the case that partial hospital care (care during the day or only at night) is less costly than state hospital care. Where the CMI can maintain some degree of independence by caring for their own daily needs, there is no doubt a cost saving.

The expert service of physicians prescribing psychotropic medications is a crucial feature of any benefit form that addresses the problem of the CMI. Note, however, that pharmaceuticals only make possible a life outside an institution. Drugs modify behavior to a level of social tolerance, but they do not necessarily create the capacity for independence so that a patient can attend to basic needs: to develop work skills so as to be financially self-sufficient, to judge the limits of ordinary social tolerance for deviance so as to avoid police attention. The kind of expert and supportive services that aim to increase those capacities are not the kind the medically trained expert usually provides. More cost effective would be greater reliance on indigenous workers or nonmedical experts—recovered mentally ill, social workers, public health nurses and other human service professionals.

According to some views, lack of ability to earn income for basic survival or to rely on family support degrades the value of further contributes to expert services in the CMHC operation. At present, the basic public income support programs available to indigent CMI are the SSI and the Food Stamp programs. In 1992, SSI (cash) benefits could be estimated at around $485 per month plus a state SSI payment of (on average) $65 per month plus food stamps that could be worth about $140 per month—a total monthly spendable income of $690.[56] Even with Medicaid (which in many states does not pay for medication), it is unlikely that a marginally functional person can live in more than substandard housing or a shelter for the homeless, thus open to physical violence and constant crises. This amount is just at the 1991 U.S. official poverty level. No expert service can substitute for common food and shelter, it simply cannot succeed absent such basic provisions.

Consumer sovereignty is often at risk where expert services are involved; for example, involuntary patients cannot refuse radical treatments like electric shock. The problem is that the professional discretion involved in expert services cannot ordinarily be curbed, especially in closed institutions. Where expert services are given on an outpatient basis, patients have the opportunity to exercise their own will—they come and go at their own behest.

Administrative and Service-Delivery System

As a rule, service-delivery systems that implement social policies of the kind discussed here are held to three types of standards for managing an administrative and service-delivery system: (1) integrated and continuous service, (2) accessibility and (3) accountability for its actions and decisions. In a number of ways, the central thrust of the CMHC Act is to construct a new and different kind of system to deliver mental health services. It avoids the fractured and inaccessible aspects of the traditional state mental hospital system with its staff and facilities geographically isolated and estranged from the local communities of the patients it was intended to serve. The CMHC Act does not provide funding for any unique and specific program element, it simply provides a financial incentive to provide "good" services universally and comprehensively in local communities— to provide *ALL* those services to ALL of its residents. Let us now look briefly at this attempt at service-delivery innovation.

Evaluating the Merit of the Administrative and Service-Delivery System for Implementation of the CMHC Acts

The CMHC Act of 1975 chose a particular administrative strategy by explicit design. That basic strategy is decentralization and localization. Congress could have chosen state instead of federal authority to administer the act but did not; no doubt a persuasive factor in this choice was the fact that state government had failed to reform state mental institutions. The act chose to grant financial support to local (city, county, and area) community mental health centers. It does make some concession to state planning by requiring a state plan to be submitted as a condition for a local clinic grant application (89 Stat. 309, Title II, Part A, Sec. 20(a), 1A).[57] The act appears to strain toward a number of provisions to achieve integration and continuity, one of which is found in its objective directed toward coordination of services. Another provision is that all vital mental health services should be available within the confines of a single clinic. Such centralization of services is one way of achieving integration and continuity. Another provision comes close to mandating that CMHC contracts provide services with health maintenance organizations (HMOs) wherever they are operating (Ibid., Sec.(c)1c). Providing mental health services in the context of an all-purpose HMO is one important method of achieving integration and continuity with other health-related services.

The act also has provisions that appear to be aimed at providing for increased *accessibility* to mental health services. Of course, situating clinics in local communities as a remedy to regional and widely scattered state hospitals is intended to achieve that purpose. The act goes beyond that, however, in its concern for access of ethnic and racial groups to mental health services, groups traditionally underserved when it comes to the distribution of mental health services and facilities. Using strong language the act says:

> . . . in the case of a CMHC serving a population including a substantial proportion of individuals of limited English-speaking ability, the center (must) develop a plan . . . responsive to the needs for service within the language and cultural context most appropriate to such individuals and identify . . . (a staff member) who is fluent in both that language and English . . . to provide guidance to . . . staff . . . with respect to cultural sensitivities and bridging linguistic and cultural barriers (89 Stat. 312 Sec. 206(c)G).

There is also a provision for special funds to be applied to those CMHCs that serve geographic areas with predominantly poverty-level income groups (Ibid., Sec 206(c)G). It concerns the identification of those groups and the special provisions for their eligibility for basic mental health services.

Finally, the act also has explicit provisions concerned with accountability of this administrative and service-delivery system. The responsibility for making basic policy resides with a governing board which shall be composed of residents of (the geographic area) "who shall . . . establish all general policies including hours of service . . . approve budgets . . . hire the director. . . ." (89 Stat. 310 Sec 201(c), (1)A,B). Those residents also represent all of the potential consumer group to whom this administrative system is accountable, a fact borne out by the requirement that the board members must reflect the demographics of the area. Yet another level of accountability built into the CMHC Act is that owed by professional practitioners to their peers—evidenced by the mandate that CMHCs institute peer-review systems as a condition for receiving federal funds (89 Stat. 311, Sec. 20(d)). It also requires centers to convene official advisory boards made up of the peers of the various professions who practice on the staff of the center to act as consultants to review policy and program changes (Ibid).

The reader will recollect that the Mental Health Systems Act (MHSA) of 1980 was effectively neutralized when Congress and the Reagan administration invoked the block grant strategy which redirected mental health funding to states rather than to cities and local CMHCs and without federal constraints on use. This 180-degree turn devolved policy and administration to the states. Now, few if any federal constraints bear on the expenditure of mental health block grant funds. And without recourse to withholding federal funds, there is no effective way for the federal government to hold states to the previously described objectives and mechanisms of the CMHC and Mental Health Systems acts.

But even had the block grant system not come into effect, the CMHC Act had some serious shortcomings, as revealed by our analysis. Could the provisions of the act have provided integrated and continuous services? Unfortunately, it does little to integrate the services of CMHCs with the state hospital system. It does try to work in this direction by mandating that CMHCs must accept referrals from state hospitals but it cannot, of course, control state-operated and state-financed institutions, so hospitals do not always refer, or if they do, CMHCs do not always follow through with continuous services. Nor can the act control judicial commitments to state hospitals. In the literature there is little disagreement with the conclusion that the continuity of service between the state hospital systems and CMHCs is seriously lacking.[58] With respect to the other criteria for service-delivery systems, the CMHC design seems sound. Accessibility is designed into the provisions for centering service on specific local geographic regions and on acknowledging requirements for ethnic and racial diversity among staff and in programming. There is an accountability system defined by the act based on peer-review systems.

It is true that the MHSA of 1980 added some important features to the administrative and service-delivery system design of community mental health centers. For example, in a section titled "Bill of (patient) Rights" it specifies a great many such rights, including the right to treatment as well as the right to refuse treatment under certain conditions (94 Stat. 1599, Title V, Sec. 501(D)).[59] However, no real mechanism is provided by which such rights can be exercised. As stated in Chapter 8, accountability is a major criterion on which the merit of service-delivery systems should be judged. Accountability to consumers is as important as accountability to the general public (and its legislative arms) and cannot be achieved without formal mechanisms. Remember we are speaking here of consumers whose social problem concerns their ability to function in their own self-interest, so they, more than most, need mechanisms that are clear and simple to use. In that nothing is specified by way of administrative mechanisms (such as appeal procedures for consumer grievances), we must give the MHSA of 1980 bad marks on that account.

The 1980 MHSA, like the CMHC Acts it succeeded, has a built-in implicit program design often referred to in terms of "comprehensive mental health services." The act specifies a number of services and speaks of them in a mandatory fashion: inpatient services (for example day care and halfway houses), emergency services, and outpatient services that include evaluations of mental health status (screening) for courts and other public agencies, follow-up care, consultation to schools and courts, law enforcement, and prevention and treatment of alcohol and drug abuse. (94 Stat. 1567 Sec. 101(b)1 A-B). The act refers specifically to the issue of continuity of care in the shift away from state hospital to community care (94 Stat. 1567 Sec. 2). But, of course, the way this is implemented is always at the initiative of the state. The most common program design to serve that end is *case management*. Space does not allow here for illustration of such a program design. (For an example of a personal social service program design, see the Figure 8–2). However, we can discuss one version of a local CMHC case-management program design, selected for its clarity. We must look to local implementation because, as mentioned before, we cannot expect an act of legislation to contain such specifics.

One locality envisions a program that features the idea of implementing a "continuum of care" so that services follow the client/consumer into the community, either subsequent to mental hospital discharge or in prevention of an admission in the first place. The continuum system is bounded by hospitalization at one end and by simple supportive services (monitoring or assisting with medication) at the other—in between are case management, certain residential services (group homes, adult family homes, board and care homes, supervised apartments), partial hospitalization programs featuring daily structured environments (day or night) and some psychosocial programs that feature outreach activities, social clubs of ex-patients, and volunteers matched with patients (Compeer, for example).[60] Each of these has a specific program design.

Case management comes in a variety of types, but the design in Figure 8–2 focuses on personalized help by a mental health professional who collaborates with clients to put an individual plan of treatment into operation so that community integration will be maximized. The hallmarks of that plan are achieving a certain self-dependence in living arrangements, a job, stability in a community, and a more or less normal supportive social group. The practitioner/helper supplies constant monitoring and assessment, some kind of counseling (emotional support certainly), teaching and modeling and advocacy, when needed.[61] This program design features assertive outreach so that contact with the service consumer occurs in the community, not in a local mental health center's formal offices. It involves intensive work with collaterals of the chronically mentally ill—landlords, families, employers, social service and income maintenance agencies, and the like. This particular design expresses a preference toward client empowerment in focusing on client strengths rather than deficits and constructing and implementing objectives based on consumer aspirations and wishes. Finally, case management here works without time boundaries—it is always available and varies only in intensity as befits any chronic illness.

Financing and Other Fiscal Issues

The financing of CMHCs in the 1975 CMHC Act and the 1980 MHS Act is reasonably straightforward. Local centers apply directly to the federal government for funds, in this case to the Department of Health, Education and Human Services. The source of these funds is tax dollars appropriated by Congress from general revenues. Financing is available for planning, operations, consultation, education, buildings, and for new and operating centers. A requirement is that no center may receive funding until there is an overall state plan for centers, as discussed earlier. The fiscal strategy in the act was to provide funds to establish the centers with the expectation that local communities and state governments will take on funding responsibility after eight years. The act specified that no center can receive more than eight years of funding in total; that has been extended because the preceding expectations have not materialized.

What is described here is the funding pattern contained in the CMHC Act of 1975. There have been a number of important amendments to the act, so that actual dollar amounts are not specified here because they have changed with succeeding amendments. A complete analysis would follow those changes carefully, for they are prime evidence in regard to whether the policy can in fact be successfully implemented.

Even though it has turned out that the CMHCs have been funded mainly by grants from federal general revenue, that was not the original intention. The assumptions built into the CMHC Act of 1975 were that federal revenues were seed money and that the centers would become self-supporting from three sources: fees from consumers for service, third-party payments for service (from insurance carriers), and subsidies from local government. All three expectations have suffered deep disappointments.[62–64] First, the consumers of CMHCs services are poor, in the main, and the CMI are seriously disabled. It should not be surprising that such a clientele does not pay fees; most are not members of the workforce at all and, if they are, they are likely to be in the secondary labor pool earning minimum wage. Second, insurance coverage is so often a consequence of employment in the primary labor force that it is an unlikely accompaniment to the casual employment of the CMI. Even where there is health insurance for mental illnesses it is routinely very limited. Third, there has been little significant real dollar increase in state or local community support for CMHCs.

Evaluating the Merit of the Financing Provisions in the CMHC Acts

On these counts the financing provisions of the CMHC Act are a failure. Year-to-year continuity has been a constant problem: operations frequently go on hold awaiting congressional decisions about funding levels and guidance for dealing with the fact that state and local fiscal support has not lived up to expectations—the seed money concept has not "germinated," shall we say. Some of the reasons for these failures are not very subtle. There are "hidden rewards" for states and local communities *not* to come forth with financing—after all Congress always has. Furthermore, at this point in time, decreases in mental hospital census are not likely to take place as a result of CMHC operations.

Of course the most important financing issue for CMHCs since the 1980 MHSA is the change delivering all federal monies directly to state mental health authorities through mental health block grants. In order to generalize about how this has affected local mental health centers, let us use one local experience with it as a case study. In the state of Kansas, the federal block grant strategy has indeed resulted in greater authority and freedom of the state to determine its own mental health services, *but the cost was a devastating reduction in federal program funding*—somewhere between 10 and 38 percent of the former total expenditures. The state has had to make up that difference. Further, between 1981 and 1990 mental health expenditures have risen in Kansas by 51 percent. Nearly 80 percent has been borne by the state.[65] The block grant funding mechanism has been a failure in this case. The state cannot exercise its main virtue—newly won freedom to apply its efforts to unique local problems—because of the severe scarcity of funds for any purpose whatsoever. Community services that would fund the bedrock continuum of care idea are simply not being appropriated by the state legislature (here or almost anywhere else, apparently). *Most state funds are still being spent on state hospital costs: only 7 percent of Kansas state mental health funds are spent on community-based services*. Of course Kansas is not a leading state in that regard either, because the national average is around 30 percent of total mental health expenditures for that purpose. And it ranks 35th among states in its per capita total mental health expenditures, though 13th in per capita income.[66] But if the block grant strategy was intended to somehow stimulate low state legislative appropriations, Kansas is surely an excellent test case and, just as surely, a complete failure on that score.

Interactions with Other Services and Benefits

Interactions among the policy elements of the CMHC Act are of some importance although they are quite intentional for the most part. Of most interest are a number of the coentitlements—that is, a patient who is entitled to one comprehensive package of services may be co-entitled to other services offered by a CMHC, given the exercise of professional discretion. For example, a patient is entitled to both counseling services and emergency hospitalization where the latter is offered by a CMHC. There are also coentitlements across programs—for example, where the psychiatric diagnosis is of sufficient severity and longevity, entitlement to the psychiatric services of a CMHC also has implications for entitlement to Social Security Disability. Where the consumer is entitled to CMHC psychiatric diagnostic services (and is also over sixty-five years of age), he or she is also entitled to payment for prescription drugs paid for through Medicare. None of those coentitlements is peculiar to CMHCs but are part of any program that offers medical diagnoses as condition of entitlement to its own services. Those are, of course, intended coentitlements to a "package" of benefits and services in almost every case.

There are also some significant *disentitlements* that occur as a result of interactions between CMHC policy and the policy of other related social programs. They are deliberate disentitlements despite their negative effects from the point of view of the need of the CMIs. First, there is the nearly universal and serious time limitation on coverage for inpatient treatment of mental illness set by insurance policies in the United States. That same restriction applies to very few other medical conditions. The second *disentitlement* of note is the Medicaid restriction on payment for treatment of the indigent at facilities exclusively devoted to the treatment of mental illness. Medicaid will pay for treatment at general hospitals and even for nonmedical maintenance at nursing homes. It is responsible for nursing homes becoming the principal alternative to state hospital care. These DISENTITLEMENTS are the result of the interaction between the CMHC policy, which actually entitles the person for CMHC services, and the policy of another program that disentitles another service or benefit. From the legislative point of view these Medicare policies are intended to protect the financial structure of the Medicare and private insurance arrangements, but it is accomplished at the cost of good care to those in need.

There was also an interaction between CMHC policy and the policy of SSI— a significant disentitlement because SSI benefits (small in any case but significant to this group) cannot be paid as long as a person lives in a psychiatric facility. It was a serious interaction because it meant that the CMI could not receive this safety net income program benefit if he or she lived in some alternative to the state hospital: a halfway house or a CMHC-sponsored apartment shared with other patients. That interaction has now been partially eliminated from the latest legislation. When it was in effect it produced important contrary effects. Although the entitlement rules for CMHC services are in some measure intended to contribute to the goal of keeping the CMI out of state hospitals and living independent lives in communities, the person who took advantage of certain kinds of CMHC services (for example, a community-based halfway house) can lose an SSI monthly income benefit and thus the financial means by which one form of independent living was made possible. As Bassuk and Gerson note:[67]

> The combined effect of the Federal programs has been to limit the development and use of community-based facilities. Their eligibility requirements have channeled many patients into nursing homes and substandard housing with minimal opportunities for psychiatric services and have undermined the development of a full range of outpatient services and residential treatment programs.

SUMMARY OF THE EVALUATIVE CRITIQUE

Several conclusions seem justified here. First, the terms in which the goals and objectives of the CMHCs are expressed suitably fit the definitions of the social problem of concern found in the legislative history and relevant documents. Second, operating characteristics of the service-delivery system provided by CMHCs show strong relevance to the ideology and value stance underlying the CMHC Act and the documents describing its legislative history. Egalitarianism is strongly pursued in program and policy features that provide mandatory services to all people within particular geographic areas, non–English-speaking capability among staff, and special funding for poverty areas. On those equity standards, the CMHC policy and program operations should be highly rated.

Third, however, there is substantial idiocy in this policy response to the social problem because it lacks a serious funding penalty mechanism for failure to perform mandatory contacts between the CMHC program system and the state hospital system it hopes to affect. It is significant because a federal initiative cannot hope to force requirements on a system that is controlled at the state level; nor can a federal initiative force constraints on a state judiciary that, for other reasons, is required to maintain independence from the executive and legislative branches of government.

Fourth, there is a serious contradiction between CMHCs' clear objective to "prevent" mental disorders and their causal analysis, which is so committed to rehabilitation and adjustment objectives (not cures). There are two issues here: This contradiction is a serious problem because it commits CMHCs to goals that are not achievable and must, therefore, be a cost from scarce resources. Nowhere is there an adequate causal theory to serve as a basis for "primary prevention" in regard to the social problems of this group. Also, it creates further mischief because it can off-target the efforts of CMHC programs in providing a rationalization for services of various sorts to vaguely defined "at-risk" groups. Sometimes this simply means middle-class families who have what might be called painful but expectable garden-variety adjustment reactions to crisis and life transitions. They do not constitute the chronically mentally ill group, a group that is ordinarily well motivated, with good potential for recovery, with or without help. And happily, they are also those whose involvement as service consumers can generate considerable support from the local community for the continued operation of the CMHC.

Finally, CMHC service-delivery design is based on physician control of the organization and centers strongly around expert services of a medical nature—features that are not entirely consistent with a causal analysis that defines problems of habilitation and community adjustment as the core problem for the CMI. The medical contribution is a necessary part of helping the chronically mentally disabled get along in society, but the emphasis here appears to be more than a little out of balance.

NOTES

1. *Action for Mental Health: Final Report of the Joint Commission on Mental Health* (New York: Basic Books, 1961).
2. *The President's Commission on Mental Health* (Vols. I–IV, plus appendixes) (Washington, DC: U.S. Government Printing Office, 1978).
3. P. Lerman, *Deinstitutionalization, a Cross Problem Analysis* (Rockville, MD: Drug Abuse and Mental Health Administration, National Institute on Drug Abuse and Mental Health Administration, National Institute on Alcohol Abuse and Alcoholism, 1981).
4. D. Goldberg and P. Huxley, *Mental Illness in the Community* (London: Tavistock Publications, 1980).
5. D. Mechanic, *Mental Health and Social Policy* (Englewood Cliffs, NJ: Prentice-Hall, 1969), p. 14.
6. L. Ozarin, Community Mental Health: Does it work?—Review of the Literature. In W. E. Barton and C. J. Sanborn, editors, *An Assessment of the Community Mental Health Movement* (Toronto: Lexington Books, 1977), pp. 121–22.
7. Op. cit.
8. *President's Commission*, vol. II, p. 16.
9. J. Zusman, The Philosophic Bases for a Community and Social Psychiatry. In W. E. Barton and C. J. Sanborn, editors, *An Assessment of the Community Mental Health Movement* (Toronto: Lexington Books, 1977), pp. 25–26.
10. Op. cit.
11. Op. cit.
12. Ibid., Mechanic, pp. 22–26.
13. Ibid., Ozarin, pp. 142–44.
14. Ibid., Mechanic, pp. 22–26.
15. R. Lamb, Treating Long-Term Schizophrenic Patients in the Community. In *Progress in Community Mental Health* (Vol. 3) (New York: Brunner/Mazel, 1975), pp. 122–25.

16. D. Langsley, Community Mental Health, a Review of the Literature. In W. E. Barton and C. J. Sanborn, editors, *An Assessment of the Community Mental Health Movement* (Toronto: Lexington Books, 1977), pp. 36–49.
17. D. Musto, The Community Mental Health Center in Historical Perspective. In W. E. Barton and C. J. Sanborn, editors, *An Assessment of the Community Mental Health Movement* (Toronto: Lexington Books, 1977), p. 9.
18. J. Ewalt, The Birth of the Community Mental Health Movement. In W. E. Barton and C. J. Sanborn, editors, *An Assessment of the Community Mental Health Movement* (Toronto: Lexington Books, 1977), p. 17.
19. Op. cit.
20. Op. cit.
21. M. Levine, "The Role of Special Master in Institutional Reform Litigation," *Law and Public Policy* (1986) 8, pp. 275–321.
22. *President's Commission*, vol. II, p. 16.
23. H. A. Foley and S. S. Scharfstein, *Madness and Government* (Washington, DC: American Psychiatric Association, 1983), p. 86.
24. E. Bassuk and S. Gerson, "Deinstitutionalization and Mental Health Services," *Scientific American* (February 1978) 238(2), pp. 46–53.
25. Ibid., Foley and Scharfstein, p. 84.
26. Op. cit., p. 85.
27. Z. J. Lipowski, "Holistic-Medical Foundations of American Psychiatry: A Bicentennial," *American Journal of Psychiatry* (1981) 138, pp. 888–95.
28. Ibid., Foley and Scharfstein, pp. 92–93.
29. Op. cit., pp. 94–95.
30. "New Survey of the Homeless," *New York Times*, November 6, 1991, p. A1.
31. Ibid., Foley and Scharfstein, p. 126.
32. Op. cit., p. 135.
33. Ibid., Ozarin, p. 120.
34. C. Rapp and J. Hanson, *Towards an Agenda for Mental Health in Kansas*. The Committee on Mental Health, Kansas State Legislature, December 1987.
35. Kansas State Senate Resolution No. 1889, March 12, 1986. Hereafter referred to as *Resolution 1889*.
36. Kansas House of Representatives Resolution No. 6216, March 12, 1986. Hereafter referred to as *Resolution 6216*.
37. Ibid., Rapp and Hanson, p. 4.
38. *Resolution 6216*.
39. *Resolution 1889*.
40. Ibid., Rapp and Hanson.
41. Op. cit., pp. 10–11.
42. Ibid., Foley and Scharfstein, pp. 115–16.
43. Op. cit.
44. C. Petr and R. Spano, "Evolution of Social Services for Children," *Social Work* (1990) 1(35), pp. 228–34.
45. C. Rapp and R. Chamberlain, "Case Management Services to the Chronically Mentally Ill," *Social Work* (September 1986) 30(5), pp. 417–22.
46. Ibid., Zusman.
47. Ibid., Rapp and Chamberlain, p. 4.
48. Op. cit., p. 7.
49. The parenthetical statutory references throughout this and the following sections are from the CMHC Act of 1963, 89 Stat., Part A or B (where applicable), Title II. Section numbers, of course, vary as noted.

50. Ibid., Bassuk and Gerson, p. 52.
51. "The Insurance Industry versus the Therapists" (Part 1), *New York Times*, November 12, 1991, p. A1. (Part 2), November 13, 1991, p. C1.
52. I am indebted to Thomas Gregoire, Ph.D., for this example.
53. D. F. Caetano, "Labeling Theory and the Presumption of Mental Illness in Diagnosis, an Experimental Design," *Journal of Health and Social Behavior* (June 1974) 15, pp. 160–70.
54. J. M. Townsend, "Cultural Conceptions, Mental Disorders and Social Roles," *American Sociological Review* (December 1975) 40, pp. 742–49.
55. K. Moore and M. Burt, *Teenage Childbearing and Welfare* (Washington, DC: The Urban Institute, 1981), p. 82.
56. "Income Maintenance Programs in the U.S. Social Welfare System," *Social Security Bulletin*, January 1991.
57. See Note 49.
58. M. Levine and D. Perkins, *Principles of Community Psychology*. New York: Oxford University Press.
59. Parenthetical statutory citations in this section are from the Mental Health Systems Act of 1980, 94 Stat., Title V. Section numbers, of course, vary as noted.
60. Ibid., Rapp and Topp, pp. 7–9.
61. Op. cit., p. 11.
62. T. G. McGuire, *Financing Psychotherapy*. Cambridge, MA: Ballinger Press, 1981.
63. R. J. Weiner, J. Woy, S. Scharfstein, and R. Bass, "Community Mental Health Centers and the Seed Money Concept," *Community Mental Health Journal*, 15:2 (Spring 1979), pp. 129–36.
64. G. Landsburg and R. Hammer, "Possible Consequences of CMHC Funding Patterns, *Community Mental Health Journal*, 13:2 (Spring 1977), pp. 63–67.
65. C. Rapp and D. Topp, *From Mortgaging to Investing: Changing the Direction of Social Service Functioning in Kansas*. Paper delivered at the University of Kansas, Social Welfare Policy Conference, November 1991, p. 7.
66. Ibid., Rapp and Hanson, p. 19.
67. Ibid., Bassuk and Gerson, p. 51.

Bibliography

Aaron, H. (1982). *Economic effects of social security*. Washington, DC: The Brookings Institution.

The American Bar Association. (1982). *Joint AMA-ABA guidelines: Present status of serologic testing in problems of disputed parentage*. Washington, DC: Author.

Arnhoff, F. (1975). Social consequences of policy toward mental illness. *Science, 188,* 1277–1281.

Baker, J. (1978). *The neighborhood advice project in Camden*. London: Routledge and Kegan Paul.

Baumheier, E. C. (1971). *Intergenerational dependency, a study of public assistance in successive generations*. Unpublished doctoral dissertation, Brandeis University, Waltham, MA.

Beam, B. T., & McFadden, J. J. (1988). *Employee benefits*. Homewood, IL: Irwin Co.

Bebbington, A., & Davies, B. (1983). Equity and efficiency in allocating personal social services. *Journal of Social Policy, 3,* 309–330.

Bell, W. (1987). *Contemporary social welfare* (2nd ed.). New York: Macmillan.

Bellak L., & Barton, H. (1975). *Progress in community mental health*. New York: Brunner/Mazel Co.

Bernstein, B., & Meezan, W. (1975). *The impact of welfare on family stability*. New York: Center for New York City Affairs.

Best, F. (1981). *Work-sharing, issues, options and prospects*. Grand Rapids, MI: W. E. Upjohn Institute on Employment Research.

Bickman, L. (1987). The functions of program theory. In L. Bickman (Ed.), *Using program theory in evaluation* (pp. 5–18). New Directions For Program Evaluation Series. San Francisco: Jossey-Bass Co.

Biestek, F. (1977). *Client self determination in social work*. Chicago: Loyola University Press.

Boulding, K. (1962). Social justice in social dynamics. In R. B. Brandt (Ed.), *Social justice*. New York: Prentice-Hall.

Brager, G. (1965). The indigenous worker: A new approach to the social work technician. *Social Work, 10,* 33–40.

Brenner, R. (1956). *From the depths*. New York: New York University Press.

Brittain, J. (1972). *The payroll tax for Social Security*. Washington, DC: The Brookings Institution.

Brown, M. (1981). *Working the street: Police discretion and dilemmas of reform*. New York: Basic Books, Inc.

Brown v. Topeka Board of Education, 347 U.S. 483 (1954).

Burke, V., & Townsend, A. (1974). Public welfare and work incentives: Theory and practice. In *Studies in public welfare*, Paper #14, Subcommittee on Fiscal Policy, Joint Economic Committee, United States Congress, April 15, 1974.

Burns, E. (1949). *The American social security system*. New York: Houghton-Mifflin.

Burns, E. (1968). Childhood poverty and the children's allowance. In E. Burns, (Ed.), *Children's allowances and the economic welfare of children* (pp. 1–9). New York: Citizens Committee of New York.

Burt, M., & Blair, L. (1974). *Options for improving the care of neglected and dependent children*. Washington, DC: The Urban Institute.

Canon, B. C. (1982). A framework for the analysis of judicial activism. In S. C. Halpern & C. M. Lamb (Eds.), *Supreme court activism and restraint* (pp. 86–99). Lexington, MA: Lexington Books.

Cassetty, J. (1978). *Child support and public policy*. Toronto: Lexington Books.

Chambers, D. E. (1971). Residence requirements for welfare benefits. *Social Work, 14,* 29–36.

Chambers, D. E. (1985). The Reagan administration's welfare retrenchment policy: Terminating social security benefits for the disabled. *Policy Studies Review, 5,* 207–215.

Chambers, D. E. (1987). Policy weaknesses and political opportunities. *Social Service Review, 42,* 87–99.

Chambers, D. E., & Rodwell, M. K. (1989). Promises, promises: Predicting child abuse. *Policy Studies Review, 4,* 66–77.

Chapin, R., & Chambers, D. E. (1991). *Targeting payment in community residential services providing social skills development*. Mimeographed manuscript, University of Kansas.

Children's Defense Fund. (1988). *A children's defense budget, F.Y. 1989*. New York: Author.

Committee on Ways and Means. (1991). *Green book: An overview of entitlement programs*. Washington, DC: U.S. House of Representatives. Congressional Research Service.

Connecticut General Statutes §17-34a(b)1.

Conrad, K., & Miller, T. (1987). Measuring and testing program philosophy. In L. Bickman (Ed.), *Using program theory in evaluation* (pp. 19–42). New Directions For Program Evaluation Series. San Francisco: Jossey-Bass Co.

Costin, L., & Rapp, C. (1984). *Child welfare policies and practices*. New York: McGraw-Hill Book Company.

Damer, S., & Hague, C. (1971). Public participation in planning: A review. *Town Planning Review, 42,* 224–228.

Danziger, S., & Portney, K. (1988). *The distributional impacts of public policies*. New York: St. Martin's Press.

Deitchman, W. (1980). How many case managers does it take to screw in a light bulb? *Hospital and Community Psychiatry, 31,* 788–789.

Department of Health and Social Security (U.K.). (1971). *Child benefit* (Leaflet #CH1). London: Her Majesty's Stationery Office.

Department of Health and Social Security (U.K.). (1977). *Social security benefit rates* (Leaflet #NI 196). London: Her Majesty's Stationery Office.

DeNitto, D. M. (1991). *Social welfare: Politics and public policy*. Englewood Cliffs, NJ: Prentice-Hall.

Derthick, M. (1979). *Policy making for social security*. Washington, DC: The Brookings Institution.

DeSchweinitz, K. (1939). *England's road to social security*. New York: A. S. Barnes Co.

Doern, G. B., & Phidd, R. W. (1983). *Canadian public policy: Ideas, structure, process*. Toronto: Metheun Co.

Donison, D. (1979). *Power to the poor*. London: Basil Blackwell & Sons.

Ehrmann, H. W. (1976). *Comparative legal cultures*. Englewood Cliffs, NJ: Prentice-Hall.

Feagin, J. (1975). *Subordinating the poor*. Englewood Cliffs, NJ: Prentice-Hall.

Federal Register, Vol. 40, #125, June 27, 1975, p. 27355. Concerning Section 228—Social Services Programs for Individuals and Families, Title XX of the Social Security Act.

Feldman, R., Wodarski, J., & Flax, N. (1973). Pro-social and anti-social boys together. *Social Work, 19*, 26–36.

Festinger, T. (1976). The impact of the New York court review of children in foster care; A follow-up report. *Child Welfare, 8*, 515–544.

Geron, S. (1991). Regulating the behavior of nursing homes through positive incentives: An analysis of the Illinois Quality Incentive Program (QUIP). *The Gerontologist, 31*, 299–301.

Gilbert, N., & Specht, H. (1974). *Dimensions of social welfare policy*. Englewood Cliffs, NJ: Prentice-Hall.

Ginzberg, E. (1975). What next in health policy? *Science, 188*, 1182–1186.

Glennerster, H. (1985). *Paying for welfare*. New York: Basil Blackwell.

Goering, J., & Coe, R. (1970). Cultural versus situational explanations for the medical behavior of the poor. *Social Science Quarterly, 51*, 309–319.

Goldsborough, et al. (1963). *The Social Security Administration: An interdisciplinary study of disability evaluation*. Mimeographed manuscript, George Washington University Law Center, Washington, DC.

Goodwin, L. (1972). *Do the poor want to work?* Washington, DC: The Brookings Institution.

Gordon, K. (1975). Introduction. In J. Pechman & P. Timpane (Eds.), *Work incentives and work guarantees*. Washington, DC: The Brookings Institution.

Handler, J. (1979). *Protecting the social services client*. New York: Academic Press.

Hannan, M., Tuma, N., & Groeneveld, L. (1977). Income and marital evidence from the income maintenance experiment. *American Journal of Sociology, 82*, 345–367.

Hansen, W. L., & Byers, J. G. (Eds.). (1990). *Unemployment insurance*. Madison, WI: University of Wisconsin Press.

Hardcastle, D. (1971). The indigenous nonprofessional in the social service bureaucracy: A critical examination. *Social Work 16*, 56–64.

Hardcastle, D. A., & Chambers, D. E. (1974). O.A.S.I.: A critical review. *Journal of Social Welfare, 2*, 19–26.

Horowitz, D. (1977). *The courts and social policy*. Washington, DC: The Brookings Institution.

Horowitz, F., & Paden, L. (1973). The effectiveness of environmental intervention programs. In B. Caldwell & H. Riciutti (Eds.), *Child development and social policy* (pp. 362–368). Chicago: University of Chicago Press.

Hoshino, G. (1965). Simplifying the means test. *Social Work, 39,* 98–103.

Howlett, M. (1991). Policy instruments, policy styles and policy implementation: National approaches to theories of instrument choice. *Policy Studies Journal, 19,* 1–21.

Hunter, R. (1965). *Poverty.* New York: Harper and Row Co.

In re Shannon S., No. 562 A.2d 79 (Conn. Super. 1989).

In the Matter of the Adoption of Schoffstall, No. 368 S.E.2nd 720 (W. Va. 1988).

Jackson, D. (1990). A conceptual framework for the comparative analysis of judicial review. *Policy Studies review, 19,* 161–71.

Janson, B. S. (1990). *Social welfare policy: From theory to practice.* Belmont, CA: Wadsworth Publishing Co.

Jones, M. A. (1988). *The history of the Australian welfare state.* Sydney: George Allen and Unwin.

Jones, K., Brown, J., & Bradshaw, J. (1979). *Issues and social policy.* London: Routledge and Kegan Paul.

Kadushin, A. (1986). *Child welfare.* New York: Macmillan.

Kahn, A. J. (1963). *Investments in people: A social work perspective.* New Brunswick, NJ: Urban Studies Center, Rutgers University.

Kahn, A. J., & Kammerman, S. (1980). *Social services in international perspective.* New Brunswick, NJ: Transaction Books.

Kammerman S. B., & Kahn, A. J. (1976). *Social services in the United States.* Philadelphia: Temple University Press.

Kansas Statutes Annotated, §59-2101(a)(1).

Karger, H. J., & Stoesz, D. (1990). *American social welfare policy: A structural approach.* White Plains, NY: Longman.

Katz, S., & Gallagher, U. (1976). Subsidized Adoption in America. *Family Law Quarterly, 10,* 3–54.

Keith-Lucas, A. (1975). A critique of the principle of client self-determination. In F. E. McDermott (Ed.), *Self determination in social work* (pp. 43–53). London: Routledge and Kegan Paul.

Kingson, E. R. (1989, July). Misconceptions distort Social Security policy discussions. *Social Work,* 357–362.

Kirk, S., & Kutchins, H. (1988). Deliberate misdiagnosis in mental health practice. *Social Service Review, 43,* 230–235.

Kolata, G. (1991, September 30). Parents of tiny infants find care choices are not theirs. *New York Times,* pp. A1, A11.

Kopolow, L. E. (1976). A review of major implications of the O'Connor v. Donaldson decision. *American Journal of Psychiatry, 133,* 379–383.

Kotz, N. (1979). *Hunger in America.* New York: The Field Foundation.

Krammer, R. (1970). *Community development in Israel and the Netherlands.* Berkeley: University of California Press.

Krause, H. D. (1981). *Child support in America.* Charlottesville, VA: The Mitchie Company.

Legal analysis: Infrequent contacts with the child, grounds to terminate parental rights in abandonment cases. (1989, December). *ABA Juvenile and Child Welfare Reporter, 8,* 157–158.

Lewis, O. (1975). The culture of poverty. *Science, 188,* 865–880.

Lewis, G., & Morrison, R. J. (1988, September). *Interactions among social welfare programs.* Discussion Paper No. 866-88. Madison, WI: University of Wisconsin, Institute for Research on Poverty.

Lewis, G., & Morrison, R. (1988). *Interactions among social welfare programs.* Discussion Paper DP #866-88. Madison, WI: University of Wisconsin, Institute For Research on Poverty.

Linder, S. H., & Peters, B. G. (1989). Instruments of government: Perception and contexts. *Journal of Public Policy, 9*, 35–38.

Lipsky, M. (1980). *Street level bureaucracy: Dilemmas of the individual in public services.* New York: Russell Sage Foundation.

MacDonald, M. (1975). *Food stamps and income maintenance.* New York: Academic Press.

Marmor, T. R. (1970). Public medical programs and cash assistance. In I. Lurie, (Ed.), *Interpreting income maintenance programs* (pp. 271–278). New York: Academic Press.

Marshall, J. D. (1968). *The old poor law* (pp. 14–15). London: Macmillan and Co., Ltd.

Mashaw, J., (1983). *Bureaucratic justice.* New Haven, CT: Yale University Press.

Matter of Adoption of B.C.S., 777 P.2d 776 (Kan.1989).

McDermott, W., Deuschle, K., & Barnett, C. (1972). Health care experiment at many farms. *Science, 175*, 23–30.

Menefee, J., Edwards, B., & Scheiber, S. (1981). Analysis of non-participation in the SSI program. *Social Security Bulletin, 44*, 3–21.

Mental Health Association of Minnesota v. Schweiker, 5543 Fed. Suppl., 157 (D.C. Minn., 1983).

Merton, R. (1957). *Social theory and social structure.* Glencoe, IL: The Free Press of Glencoe.

Miller, W. (1962). The impact of a "total community" delinquency control project. *Social Problems, 10*, 168–191.

Morgan, J., et al. (1974). *Five thousand american families: Patterns of economic progress* (Vol. 1). Ann Arbor, Michigan: Institute for Social Research.

Mott, P. (1976). *Meeting human needs, a social and political History of Title XX.* Columbus, OH: National Conference on Social Welfare.

Munnell, A. (1977). *The future of Social Security.* Washington, DC: The Brookings Institution.

Murdrick, N. The use of AFDC by previously high and low income households. *Social Service Review, 52*, 107–115.

Musgrave, R. (1961). *The theory of public finance.* New York: McGraw-Hill Co.

Myrdal, Alva (1968). *Nation and family.* Cambridge, MA: MIT Press.

Nathan, R., Manvel, A. D., & Calkins, S. E. (1976). *Monitoring revenue sharing.* Washington, DC: The Brookings Institution. National Underwriters. (1990).

Newton, K. (1976). *Second city politics.* London: Oxford University Press.

Notes, J. (1989). The least dangerous branch. *Revue de Droit de McGill, 4*, 1025–1028.

Orwell, G. (1937). *The road to Wigan Pier.* London: Golancz and Song.

Pechman, J. A., & Timpane, P. M. (Eds.). (1975). *Work incentives and income guarantees.* Washington, DC: The Brookings Institution.

Perlman, H. H. (1975). Self-determination: Reality or illusion. In F. E. McDermott (Ed.), *Self determination in social work* (pp. 65–80). London: Routledge and Kegan Paul.

Pettigrew, T. (1980). Social psychology's contribution to an understanding of poverty. In Vincent T. Covello (Ed.), *Poverty and public policy* (pp. 198–224). Cambridge, MA: Shenkman Publishing Co.

Phillips, D. (1974). Community health councils. In K. Jones (Ed.), *The yearbook of social policy in Britain* (pp. 62–76). London: Routledge and Kegan Paul.

Piore, M. (1979). Qualitative research in economics. *Administrative Science Quarterly, 24*, 560–569.

Piven, F. F., & Cloward, R. (1971). *Regulating the poor.* New York: Pantheon Books.

Plotnick, R. D. (1989). Directions for reducing child poverty. *Social Work, 32*, 523–530.

Podell, L. (1968) *Families on welfare in New York City.* New York: The Center for Study of Urban Problems.

Polyani, K. (1944). *The great transformation*. New York: Holt, Rinehart and Winston.

Rapp, C., & Chamberlain, R. (1985). Case management Services to the chronically mentally ill. *Social Work, 28,* 16–22.

Rein, M. (1983a). *From policy to practice*. Armonk, NY: M. E. Sharpe.

Rein, M. (1983b). Value-critical policy analysis. In D. Callahan & B. Jennings (Eds.), *Ethics, the social sciences and policy analysis* (pp. 83–112). New York: Plenum Press.

Rein, M., & Rainwater, L. (1978). Patterns of welfare use. *Social Service Review, 52,* 511–534.

Rein, M., & Rainwater, L. (Eds.). (1986). *Public/private interplay in social protection*. Armonk, NY: M. E. Sharpe.

Reynolds, B. C. (1942). *Learning and teaching in the practice of social work*. New York: Farrar and Rinehart.

Rossi, P. (1979). *Evaluation, a systematic approach*. Beverly Hills, CA: Sage Publishing Co.

Sawhill, I. (1975). *Income transfers and family structure*. Washington, DC: The Urban Institute.

In re Schoffstall, No. 368 S. E. 2nd 720 (W. Va.) 1988).

Schorr, A. (1965). Income maintenance and the birth rate. *Social Security Bulletin, 28,* 2–3.

Schultz, T. (1962). Reflections on investment in man. *Journal of political economy, LXX* (Supplement), 2.

In re Shannon S., No. 562 A. 2d 79 (Conn. Super. 1989).

Sharon, D. (1972). Eduardo the healer. *Natural History,* [1972], 32–49.

Sheehan, S. (1976). *A welfare mother*. New York: Signet Books.

Shyne, A., & Schroeder, A. (1978). *National study of social services for children*. Rockville, MD: Westat Co.

Social Security Administration. (1982a). *Social security handbook* (Social Security Regulations No. 83-15,16,17). Washington, DC: U.S. Government Printing Office.

Social Security Administration. (1982b). *SSI for the aged, blind, and disabled* (Publication No. 05-11111). Washington, DC: U.S. Government Printing Office.

Spargo, J. (1968). *The bitter cry of the children*. New York: Quadrangle Books.

Stanford Research Institute and Mathematics Policy Research, (1978). *The Seattle-Denver Income Maintenance Experiment, midexperiment results and a generalization to the national population*. Menlo Park, CA: Author.

Steiner, G. (1976). *The children's cause*. Washington, DC: The Brookings Institution.

Tarasoff vs. The Regents of University of California. Supreme Court of California (July 1, 1976).

Tate, C. N. (1990). Introductory notes. *Policy Studies Review, 19,* 76–80.

Tax Reform Act of 1969, P.L. 91-972, H.R. 13270

Titmuss, R. (1968). Welfare state and welfare society. In *Commitment to welfare* (pp. 130–134). London: George Allen and Unwin, Ltd.

Tucker, D. (1980). Coordination and citizen participation. *Social Service Review, 54,* 17–18.

United Nations, Food and Agricultural Organization. (1977). *The fourth world food survey,* Statistics Series No. 11. Rome, Italy: Author.

U.S. Congress, House of Representatives (1988). *Medicaid source book. Background data and analysis*. Washington, DC: U.S. Government Printing Office.

U.S. Congress, Senate Subcommittee on Oversight of Government Management of the Senate Committee on Governmental Affairs. (June 8, 1983). *SSDI reviews: The role of the administrative law judge,* Hearing Report (and Appendix), 98th Congress, 1st Session. Washington, DC: U.S. Government Printing Office.

U.S. Department of Health, Education and Welfare Office of the Secretary. (1980). *Annual report to the Congress on Title XX of the Social Security Act, Fiscal Year 1979*. Washington, DC: U.S. Government Printing Office.

U.S. Department of Health and Human Services, Administration for Children and Families, Office of Policy, Planning, and Legislation. (1991). *Social services block grants, summary of pre-expenditure reports, fiscal year 1990*. Washington, DC: U.S. Government Printing Office.

U.S. Department of Health and Human Services, Family Support Administration, Office of Family Assistance. (1989). *Characteristics of state plans for aid to families and dependent children under Title IV-A of the Social Security Act*. Washington, DC: U.S. Government Printing Office.

U.S. Department of Health and Human Services, Social Security Administration, Office of Family Assistance. *Characteristics of state plans for aid to families with dependent children-1984*. Washington, DC: U.S. Government Printing Office.

United Way of America. (1991). *United Way of America research services campaign summary survey*. Alexandria, VA: Author.

The Villers Foundation. (1987). *On the other side of Easy Street*. Washington, DC: Author.

Walker, H., & Cohen, B. (1985). Scope statements: Imperatives for evaluating theory. *American Sociological review, 50*, 288–301.

Webster, C. D. (1984). On gaining acceptance: Why the courts accept only reluctantly findings from experimental and social psychology. *International Journal of Law and Psychiatry, 7*, 407–414.

Wedel, K. (1991). Designing and implementing performance contracting. In R. L. Edwards & J. A. Yankee (Eds.), *Skills for effective service management* (pp. 106–118). Silver Springs, MD: NASW Press.

Wedel, K., & Colston, S. (1988). Performance contracting for human services: Issues and suggestions. *Administration in Social Work, 12*, 73–87.

Weick, A. (1987). Reconceptualizing the philosophical base of social work. *Social Service Review, 42*, 218–230.

Weick, A., & Pope, L. (1975). *Knowing what's best: A new look at self-determination*. Mimeographed manuscript, Lawrence, KS: The University of Kansas.

Weissman, H. (1970). *Community councils and community control*. Pittsburgh: University of Pittsburgh Press.

Wootton, B. (1959). *Social science and social pathology*. London: George Allen and Unwin.

Index

ISBN 0-02-320582-2

90000>